A JOURNEY THROUGH *the* CATECHISM

"Fr. Daniel J. Mahan unpacks the good news of Jesus Christ with a marvelous depth and accessibility honed through decades of experience as a pastor and evangelizer. This text provides a comprehensive catechesis that carefully demonstrates how the timeless truths of our Catholic faith inform and give meaning to our day-to-day lives. *A Journey through the Catechism* will compel and edify both the beginner and the lifelong Catholic. The timing here could not be better: the field of adult faith formation will greatly benefit from this practical and winsome exposition of the Catholic faith—aimed at the salvation of souls and the glory of God—which can be put directly into the hands of adults to stir conversation and uplift minds and hearts."

Scott R. Sollom
Associate Chair of Theology and Director of the Catechetical Institute
Franciscan University

"Fr. Mahan is an expert on the *Catechism of the Catholic Church* and in 1998 led an eye-opening, informative three-year walk through it. His love for God, knowledge of the scriptures, and familiarity with the Holy Land puts him in the unique position to make the *Catechism* accessible to everyone. *A Journey through the Catechism* builds upon years of his labor, is clearly written, and takes the reader through the four pillars of the *Catechism*. With the help of Fr. Mahan's thought-provoking reflections, those who are inquiring to the forever faithful will discover God's love for man and what his or her response to that love should be. The question-and-answer format creatively demystifies the *Catechism* to allow the reader to see the wisdom of the faith derived from scripture and tradition. My journey to the diaconate is due in part to Fr. Mahan and his three-year walk through the *Catechism*. *A Journey through the Catechism*, when studied with an open mind and heart, will leave you thirsting for more and can change your life."

Mark Henry
Deacon
Archdiocese of Indianapolis

"This is an impressive achievement. Fr. Mahan has zoned in on the essentials and presented them accessibly. For those interested in a shorter presentation of the faith, this book could be self-sufficient. But the book's larger intention is to introduce readers to the *Catechism of the Catholic Church* in a way that will make them want to read it more completely and, over time, to acquire its riches more fully. This is truly a great service. Highly recommended."

John C. Cavadini
Director
McGrath Institute for Church Life, the University of Notre Dame

"Fr. Mahan's book opens the treasures of the Catholic faith in a trusted companion to the *Catechism of the Catholic Church* written for a wide audience. On every page, the reader is led by Fr. Mahan's pastoral voice to discover the gift of an evangelizing catechesis that invites a life-transforming encounter with Jesus Christ in the power of the Holy Spirit. Written in a user-friendly question-and-answer format with theological depth and pastoral sensitivity, Fr. Mahan's journey with the *Catechism* offers concise chapter summaries, in-depth reflections, and engaging visuals to nourish the minds and hearts of all seekers of truth, beauty, and goodness."

Jem Sullivan
Associate Professor of Practice and Catechetics
School of Theology and Religious Studies, the Catholic University of America

"In *A Journey through the Catechism*, Fr. Mahan provides his readers a rich and comprehensive summary of the Church's faith from an exciting, rediscovered perspective. Mindful of the many challenges we face in our contemporary culture, Fr. Mahan returns us to the primordial message of the Gospel—the offer of salvation in Jesus Christ. He invites catechumens and all believers to rejoice in Christ's salvific message as lived through the rich teachings of the Church. I found *A Journey through the Catechism* intellectually refreshing, spiritually invigorating and a compelling invitation to understand our Catholic faith as truly good news for our modern times."

Most Rev. Frank Caggiano
Bishop
Diocese of Bridgeport

A JOURNEY THROUGH *the* CATECHISM

Unveiling the Truth, Beauty, and Goodness of the Catholic Faith

Fr. Daniel J. Mahan

AVE MARIA PRESS AVE Notre Dame, Indiana

Scripture texts in this work are taken from the *New American Bible, revised edition* © 2010, 1991, 1986, 1970 Confraternity of Christian Doctrine, Washington, DC, and are used by permission of the copyright owner. All Rights Reserved. No part of the *New American Bible* may be reproduced in any form without permission in writing from the copyright owner.

Excerpts from the English translation of the *Catechism of the Catholic Church* for use in the United States of America Copyright © 1994, United States Catholic Conference, Inc.—Libreria Editrice Vaticana. Used with Permission. English translation of the *Catechism of the Catholic Church*: Modifications from the Editio Typica copyright © 1997, United States Conference of Catholic Bishops—Libreria Editrice Vaticana.

Nihil Obstat: Reverend Monsignor Michael Heintz, PhD
                    Censor Librorum

Imprimatur: Most Reverend Kevin C. Rhoades
                    Bishop of Fort Wayne–South Bend
                    Given at Fort Wayne, Indiana, on 23 January 2024

The *Nihil Obstat* and *Imprimatur* are official declarations that a book or pamphlet is free of doctrinal or moral error. No implication is contained therein that those who have granted the *Nihil Obstat* or *Imprimatur* agree with its contents, opinions, or statements expressed.

Founded in 1865, Ave Maria Press is a ministry of the United States Province of Holy Cross.

www.avemariapress.com

Paperback: ISBN-13 978-1-64680-241-8

E-book: ISBN-13 978-1-64680-242-5

Cover images © Getty and Photos.nd.edu.

Cover and text design by Andy Wagoner.

Printed and bound in the United States of America.

Library of Congress Cataloging-in-Publication Data is available.

To my parents, who first taught me
the Catholic faith
William E. Mahan
and
Betty C. Mahan

Did not our hearts burn within us while he talked to us on the road, while he opened to us the scriptures?

—Luke 24:32
(RSV)

Contents

Preface

Come to me, all you who labor and are burdened, and I will give you rest. Take my yoke upon you and learn from me, for I am meek and humble of heart; and you will find rest for yourselves. For my yoke is easy, and my burden light. (Mt 11:28–30)

You will never get a better invitation than the one that comes from Jesus, for to follow him is to find the meaning of life, and to live life to the full. The choice to follow Jesus makes all the difference in the world, and all the difference unto everlasting life.

A Journey through the Catechism: Unveiling the Truth, Beauty, and Goodness of the Catholic Faith will help you to know and learn about Jesus from two main sources: the Bible and the *Catechism of the Catholic Church*. The *Catechism* itself describes the primacy of Sacred Scripture as the place where "God speaks only one single Word" (CCC, 102) and that Word is Jesus Christ. We learn about Jesus through the four individual biographies written by his disciples Matthew, Mark, Luke, and John. The writers of the Gospels open the door for us to know about Jesus and to grow to love him in a personal way. *A Journey through the Catechism* draws from the Gospels and all of Sacred Scripture in a significant way.

A Journey through the Catechism is also organized around the structure of the *Catechism of the Catholic Church*, a text Pope John Paul II called a "sure norm for teaching the faith" in *Fidei Depositum*, 3, and a source for knowing Jesus more deeply:

> In reading the *Catechism of the Catholic Church*, we can perceive the wonderful unity of the mystery of God, his saving will, as well as the central place of Jesus Christ, the only-begotten Son of God, sent by the Father, made man in the womb of the Blessed Virgin Mary by the power of the Holy Spirit, to be our Savior. (*Fidei Depositum*, 2)

This book, like the *Catechism*, has four parts intended to teach how Catholics:

- profess their faith

- worship

- live their lives in society

- pray

While organized like the *Catechism*, *A Journey through the Catechism* explains the teachings of the *Catechism* with personal reflection, sound reasoning, and practical examples to help make Church teaching more accessible to Catholics who want to be better informed about their faith, catechumens who are preparing to be received into the Church, and any seeker who would like a comprehensive resource about what it means to be a Catholic and a disciple of Jesus Christ.

Originally published in 1992, the *Catechism* has been a key part of my life as a priest. In fact, I became familiar with the *Catechism* seven years *before* its publication. In October 1985 I had the privilege of studying in Rome when bishops from around the world gathered with Pope John Paul II to commemorate the twentieth anniversary of the close of the Second Vatican Council. During this extraordinary synod, a recommendation was made to develop a new universal catechism so that the teachings of the faith could be summarized in one complete source and made available primarily as an aid to bishops and priests, teachers, and other Church leaders to help them pass on the faith to others.

My connection with the *Catechism* was only beginning at the 1985 extraordinary synod. Since then, I have used it as a reference in my homilies. I have taught the *Catechism* from front to back in parishes throughout the Archdiocese of Indianapolis. I am presently the director of the Institute on the Catechism, an initiative of the Secretariat for Evangelization and Catechesis of the United States Conference of Catholic Bishops, which, in part, reviews catechetical materials used in schools and parishes for their conformity and complete presentation of the *Catechism*.

Interestingly, when the *Catechism* came out, it drew interest from well beyond the intended audience and was sold in droves to everyday Catholics and others seeking clear answers from the Church. But the material, intended originally to be a reference source for those who would decipher and teach the faith, can sometimes be dense. This is one of the reasons I offer this summary of the teachings of the Catholic Church as a companion, of sorts, to the *Catechism*. Written in a conversational style, this book offers the reader the opportunity to dig deeper into both the *Catechism* and Sacred Scripture so as to penetrate more deeply "the unfathomable riches of salvation" (*Fidei Depositum*, 3).

As we set out together on this journey through the richness of Church teaching, I offer this prayer from an earlier American catechism, known as the *Baltimore Catechism*, that Catholics from previous generations learned and memorized by heart:

> May the Lord open for you the door that will help you "to know Him, to love Him, and to serve Him in this world, and to be happy with Him for ever in heaven."

To watch videos where I highlight the themes covered in this book, visit https://www.avemariapress.com/journey-through-the-catechism.

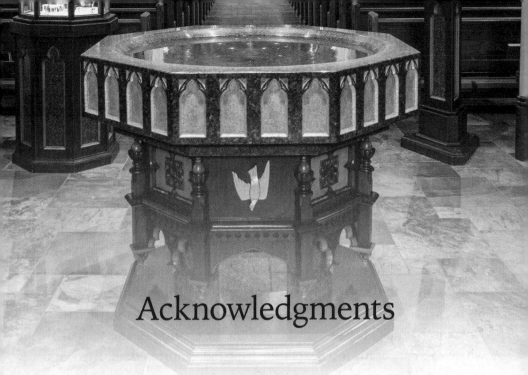

Acknowledgments

I am grateful to Jean Zander for reading this text and offering very helpful suggestions and much-needed encouragement.

Likewise, I am indebted to Dr. Anthony Montanaro for his careful reading of the manuscript and his insightful thoughts and suggestions.

Dr. Lawrence J. Welch is a loyal friend and trusted adviser on matters theological, for which I am most grateful.

I could not have asked for a better editor than Michael Amodei of Ave Maria Press.

I continue to be amazed by the creativity and enthusiasm of Fr. Jonathan Meyer in exploring and teaching the treasures of the Catholic faith.

Bishop Louis LaRavoire Morrow, SDB (1892–1987), wrote a popular book titled *My Catholic Faith*. His succinct explanations, compelling illustrations, and innovative typography helped me to understand the Catholic faith at a very young age.

I was privileged to be formed at seminary and serve as a priest under the Most Reverend Daniel M. Buechlein, OSB (d. 2018). Archbishop Buechlein led the efforts of the United States Conference of Catholic Bishops to ensure that textbooks and catechetical materials were in conformity with the *Catechism* through their authenticity and completeness. I admire the leadership of Bishop Frank J. Caggiano in carrying on and expanding the efforts of Archbishop Buechlein, and I am thankful for the wisdom and guidance of Archbishop Alfred C. Hughes, the successor to Archbishop Buechlein as chairman of the Ad Hoc Committee to Oversee the Use of the Catechism and who serves so graciously as archbishop emeritus of New Orleans.

I am grateful to the countless members of the parishes of the Archdiocese of Indianapolis who have encouraged me to teach the *Catechism of the Catholic Church*, especially those from St. Mary, Rushville; St. Rose of Lima, Franklin; St. Luke the Evangelist, Indianapolis; St. Louis, Batesville; St. Jude the Apostle, Spencer; St. John the Apostle, Bloomington; St. Barnabas, Indianapolis; All Saints, Dearborn County; St. Lawrence, Lawrenceburg; St. Teresa Benedicta of the Cross, Bright; and the parish where so many of my forebears were baptized, confirmed, married, and buried, St. Mary of the Immaculate Conception, Aurora.

The Friars of the Immaculate from the Mother of the Redeemer Retreat Center took great care in recording my presentations on the *Catechism*, making them available free of charge on the internet. In particular I appreciate the efforts of Br. Didacus Cortes, FI, and Br. Roderick Burke, FI.

The way in which they consistently emphasized the importance of examining primary sources makes me proud to have been formed by the monks of St. Meinrad Archabbey. I am indebted to the Dominican friars at the Angelicum who taught me the wisdom of St. Thomas Aquinas and the Benedictine monks at Sant' Anselmo who showed me the depth and beauty of the sacramental life of the Church.

My faith is deepened with every pilgrimage to the Holy Land. I am so grateful to Jack Halis and the many Palestinian Christians who have taught me to appreciate and love their Holy Land, the spiritual home of all who follow the Lord Jesus.

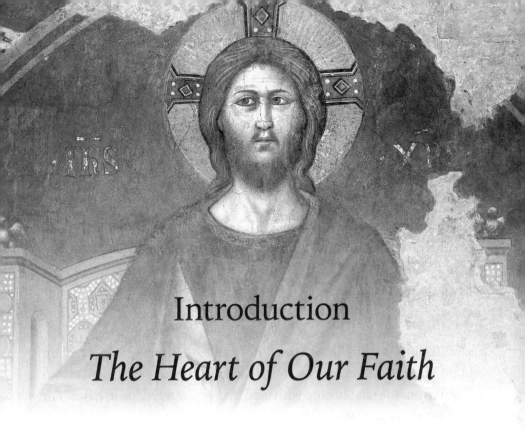

Introduction

The Heart of Our Faith

The subject of this book can be summarized by the Greek word *kerygma*, which translates as "a basic message, the very heart of something great and eventful." In the ancient world, *kerygma* was associated with the actions of a person—the *kerux*, who was a messenger who ran from village to village bringing the most important news from the ruler. Sometimes the subject of the news was the outcome of an important battle or the succession of power from a king to his successor. The *kerux* announced the "headline," which was known as the *kerygma*. While there was always more news that followed the *kerux's* initial visit, it was this herald of important news that had the potential to change everyday life for those who heard it. The Christian *kerygma* has this same effect, but in a much more profound way.

The *kerygma*, or basic message of our Catholic faith, was first announced by the Apostles and other evangelizers who stood in the public square to proclaim the Gospel, the Good News of Jesus Christ. While the Apostles preached in different places to people of different ethnic and religious backgrounds and sometimes adapted the Gospel message as such, they were sure to express very clearly four constant truths of the *kerygma* that have stood the test of time ever since. In fact, they are as relevant for you and me today as to those who first heard the core of the message. The subject of the *kerygma* is a message that stands in perpetuity of the human experience. It is summarized as follows:

◖ Creation

You were created to be in union with God. God has a loving plan for humanity that includes a plan for your life. You were made to be in relationship with God. "See what love the Father has bestowed on us that we may be called the children of God" (1 Jn 3:1).

◔ Fall

Sadly, this union is broken by sin. Sin separated our first parents (Adam and Eve) from God, and our own sins can have eternal consequences. Sin keeps us from the relationship with God that we are intended to have. "For the wages of sin is death" (Rom 6:23).

✚ Redemption

Fortunately, God has the answer. "God so loved the world that he gave his only Son, so that everyone who believes in him might not perish, but might have eternal life" (Jn 3:16). Jesus Christ, true God and true man, allows himself to be sacrificed on the Cross so that our relationship with God might be healed. From the Cross, Jesus gives us the Church and her sacraments so that we might have eternal life.

◓ Restoration

Furthermore, God invites you to live in the way you were created to live, and to lead others to Jesus by your words and actions. "Repent and be baptized, every one of you, in the name of Jesus Christ for the forgiveness of your sins; and you will receive the gift of the holy Spirit" (Acts 2:38).

This four-part message of *kerygma* is the very kernel of our Catholic faith.

How the *Kerygma* Is Shared

Whereas the *kerygma* expresses the very basis of our faith in Jesus Christ and our life in his Church, the *Catechism of the Catholic Church* articulates and provides depth to the teachings of the Church. We can refer to the teachings of the *Catechism* as *echoes of the kerygma*. In fact, the root of the word *catechism* is the word *echo*. If you look closely, you can see most of the word "**ech**o" contained in the word "cat**ech**ism."

By following the outline of the *Catechism of the Catholic Church*, and by faithfully relating its teachings, this book will show how the inspiring, basic-message *kerygma* of ⊖ Creation, ◐ Fall, ✜ Redemption, and ◕ Restoration has grown into an impressive body of teaching of Catholic beliefs, practices, morality, and prayer. As you proceed through this book, these four aspects of the *kerygma* will be noted at the end of each chapter to relate specific teachings of the Church that you have learned about to one or more aspects of the *kerygma*. In this way, you will be able to imagine our Catholic faith growing like a small acorn into a mighty oak.

We will call these symbols *kerygmatic echoes*, for they will show how the original message of Christian *kerygma* echoes throughout the entire body of Catholic thought and life today. Everything that we believe, practice, live, and pray can be traced back to the fundamental message of the *kerygma*:

⊖ You are created for a purpose by a loving God. God has a plan for you.

◐ The tragedy of sin, the tragedy of "missing the mark" in your relationship with God, can have deadly, eternal consequences.

✜ God has the answer. God sent his Son into the world to pay the price for your sins. The ransom is paid and your freedom is secured through the Blood of Jesus shed from the Cross and the sacramental life of the Church that flows from his wounded side. By his love, you are redeemed.

◕ God will never stop calling you to repentance and conversion. But God does not give you all the time in the world. There is great urgency to

God's invitation to make a commitment to follow him. If today you hear his voice, harden not your heart (cf. Ps 95:8, Heb 3:15).

Think about this: When you yell "Hello" into a canyon or tunnel, the word softens in volume with each successive echo. Echoes in nature diminish in volume and intensity, like ripples from a stone thrown on a pond. Not so with kerygmatic echoes and the proclamation of the Catholic faith. With each successive proclamation of the *kerygma* in word and deed, our words grow louder and our faith grows stronger. Though tyrants may rage and put to death good and faithful Christians, the echo of the *kerygma* resounds with otherworldly intensity. In every age, God raises up great witnesses to the faith—women and men, girls and boys who would give their lives before compromising their belief in Jesus Christ. God's grace is made manifest in the witness to the *kerygma* given by the holy martyrs of every age. As you learn more about the Catholic faith through this book and through your study of the *Catechism*, always remember that our faith is a living faith, a faith that grows stronger every time it is expressed in word or deed. The kerygmatic echoes grow only louder as our Catholic faith is proclaimed anew.

Using This Book

Because you are reading this book, you are interested in learning more about the Catholic faith. Perhaps you are curious about what Catholics believe, or you are thinking about becoming a Catholic, or you are already Catholic and want to learn more about your faith. Whatever the reason, I am glad that you have opened this book, and I encourage you to read it from cover to cover and encourage others to do the same.

A Journey through the Catechism is organized in four parts that follow the same four-part structure of the *Catechism of the Catholic Church*. Each part has chapters that begin with a short introduction and then proceed with related questions and answers around the particular topic. You may read the book straight through, or you may choose chapters to read based on topics of personal interest or as part of a group study, for example in a catechumenal process like the Order of Christian Initiation. If you are using this book as part of your Christian initiation, you will also find helpful a chart listing the Sunday readings, reflection questions on the Sunday readings, and collations with questions in this book at www.avemariapress.com/journey-through-the-catechism. You may also use the index of questions to locate topics about the faith in which you are interested.

How to Navigate the Bible

References to the Holy Bible are given not by page numbers, but by book, chapter, and verse. These references are usually abbreviated. A list of the abbreviations used in this book for each book of the Holy Bible is found on page 399. For example, Dt 5:6–21 means the Book of Deuteronomy, chapter 5, verses 6 through 21. Every Bible has a table of contents for those who are as yet unfamiliar with the name, classification, and order of the books of the Bible.

Footnotes, glossaries, maps, and introductions to each book of the Holy Bible are included in most any edition and presented as helps to the reader. They are not considered to be the *inspired* Word of God. More information on inspiration will follow as well.

You will find in this book plentiful references to Sacred Scripture and the *Catechism of the Catholic Church*. I encourage you to have at hand both a Bible and a *Catechism* as you study the Catholic faith. Both are available to read free of charge online, or to purchase secondhand for less than a couple of visits to a coffee shop.

What kind of Bible should you have? Billy Graham once answered this very question with "One that you will read." My answer is the same, with a recommendation that you have a *Catholic* Bible, one that does not omit seven important books of the Old Testament as is the case in many *Protestant* Bibles. Perhaps you didn't even know there were different types of Bibles. This issue will be addressed as you read through this book.

To be more specific, most of the Scripture citations in *A Journey through the Catechism* come from the *New American Bible, revised edition* (*NABRE*), while a few come from the Catholic edition of the *Revised Standard Version* (*RSV*) or its later edition, the *New Revised Standard Version* (*NRSV*). I endorse each of these translations of the Sacred Scriptures to accompany your reading of this book. They are all printed in various trim sizes and designs, with different weights of paper, and in hard or soft cover. In choosing the format of your Bible, I endorse the words of Reverend Graham: Pick one that you will read, carry with you, and cherish. The Bible is God's Word speaking to you, and you should read from your Bible every day.

Besides having a copy of the Bible, you should also read this book accompanied by the *Catechism of the Catholic Church*, second edition, revised in accordance with the official Latin text promulgated by Pope John Paul II. This edition also includes a revision of paragraph 2267 on the subject of the death penalty that was promulgated by Pope Francis. The *Catechism of the Catholic Church* is a treasury of information, combining many verses from the Bible, the teachings of great saints from every age and place, and citations from the Fathers of the Church, including several who were taught by St. John the Apostle, the beloved disciple who was close to our Lord and who took care of the Blessed Virgin Mary.

How to Navigate the Catechism of the Catholic Church

The *Catechism of the Catholic Church* is abbreviated *CCC*. References to the *Catechism* are given not by page numbers but by paragraph numbers. The numbers in the outer margin near each paragraph are cross-references to other *Catechism* paragraphs related to the same topic.

For example, *CCC*, 1428 teaches about ongoing conversion in the context of the Sacrament of Penance and Reconciliation. The paragraph numbers in the outer margin tell us that the topic of conversion is also taught in *CCC*, 1036 (the call to conversion), *CCC*, 853 (the way of penance and renewal), and *CCC*, 1996 (the teaching that God's grace prompts us to conversion). The threads of Church teaching on particular topics wind through all four parts of the *Catechism*, creating a beautiful fabric of consistency, a symphony of faith in four movements.

The *Catechism* thoroughly quotes other writings of the saints and popes and several Church documents. These quotations are footnoted and abbreviated at the bottom of each page. A key to the abbreviations used in the footnotes is included in the *Catechism*, usually in the appendix, between the glossary and the index.

The *Catechism* paragraphs are introduced by lead paragraphs for particular sections. Don't be intimidated by the denseness of the lead paragraphs! Everything that is squeezed into the lead paragraph is unpacked in the text that follows and is summarized in the *In Brief* notes at the end of each section.

Although the *Catechism of the Catholic Church* comes in several free online versions, I recommend that you have your own printed edition of the *Catechism*, if possible. If you want to go deeper into any subject that I have taught in this book, you can find a reference to it in the *Catechism*. A printed edition will allow you to keep handwritten questions or notes that come up in the reading of this book and that you cross-reference in the *Catechism*.

Let's Get Started!

As we get ready to proceed with learning about the teachings of the Catholic faith, I am reminded of the words of Herb Brooks, the coach of the famous "Miracle on Ice" United States hockey team that upset the powerful Soviet Union in the 1980 Olympics. In a pregame speech before the gold-medal game, Brooks said to his team: "You were born to be a player. You were meant to be here. This moment is yours."[1] For the young, inexperienced players, it was a moment that permanently changed them, a moment that would forever impact the trajectory of their lives.

You too were born for much more than you can imagine. You are meant for God. You are meant to share a life with the Almighty God here on earth and in eternity. You are meant to live with God and enjoy great happiness that will last longer than the sun and the moon and the stars. By picking up this book, you have taken the first step to discover or deepen your connection to God and to delve more deeply into the great mystery of your relationship with Jesus Christ and the Catholic Church. This book is intended to guide you along this journey. Be assured as you read this book that you are loved by God, and God has a plan for you.

In one of his Father Brown short stories, the late G. K. Chesterton (d. 1936) used the figurative image of "an unseen hook and an invisible line which is long enough to let [someone] wander to the ends of the world, and still to bring him back with a twitch upon the thread."[2] This image helps illustrate how we are always connected to God. He so desires you to be on the right path in life that he stays connected to you in ways you cannot possibly imagine. Yet God's plan for you and for every human being is made known through the teachings of Jesus Christ as contained (or revealed) in Sacred Scripture (or the Holy Bible) and the Sacred Tradition (or the Tradition of the Catholic Church), particularly as they are articulated in the *Catechism of the Catholic Church*.

The book you are holding in your hands will guide you through the *Catechism* with a special view to helping you understand and appreciate more fully God's great plan for you and God's powerful action in your life. No matter your age or situation, you are connected to the God who gives a "twitch upon the thread" at exactly the right moment. That twitch, however and whenever it is given, calls you to repentance and conversion, a change of mind and heart, and challenges you to get things right with God. This "twitch upon the thread" is a metaphor for the essence of the Gospel and is the kernel of everything we believe about the power of Jesus Christ to rescue us from that which can bring eternal harm to our immortal souls. This is the fundamental message of our Catholic faith, the *kerygma*.

Part I

WHAT CATHOLICS BELIEVE

To one who has faith, no explanation is necessary.
To one without faith, no explanation is possible.

—St. Thomas Aquinas

CHAPTER 1

Faith: We Are Made for God

(CCC, 26–141)

Scientists tell us that the universe is ninety-six billion light years in size. That huge number is how long it would take to get from one end of the universe to the other traveling at the speed of light, some 186,000 miles per second. Like the Hubble Telescope before it, the James Webb Space Telescope of today brings us stunning and previously unimaginable views of distant planets and galaxies that give us insight into the question posed to God by the psalmist:

> When I see your heavens, the work of your fingers,
> the moon and stars that you set in place—
> What is man that you are mindful of him,
> and a son of man that you care for him?
> O LORD, our LORD,
> how awesome is your name through all the earth!
> Psalm 8:4–5, 10

We begin our search buoyed by the fact that in spite of God's immensity, he "reveals and gives himself to man, at the same time bringing man

a superabundant light as he searches for the ultimate meaning of his life"
(*CCC*, 26).

1.   We cannot see God. How can we come to know that he exists?

We can know from our human nature that God exists. God has made
human beings to be different from all other animals. We can certainly
take great delight in the magnificence of the world of nature and in the
capacity of animals to make for themselves what is needed for their existence: the spider's web, the beaver's dam, the robin's nest. While each of
these creations shows fascinating and intricate design, only human beings
make works of art, monuments to fallen heroes, and feats of design that
show their capacity to go beyond what is necessary and to give expression
to the desire to be creative.

Ars gratia artis is the motto surrounding the famous lion at the beginning of every MGM movie: "Art for art's sake." Among the creatures
on this earth, human beings alone possess the ability to transcend the
merely practical and to seek the meaning and purpose of their lives. We
alone long with all of our being for truth, beauty, and goodness. We seek
beyond the limited to what is infinite. We cannot help but ask questions
about the origin of the vast universe, and whether there is a God who is
its source and origin (cf. *CCC*, 33).

2.   Do we have proof that there is a God?

We can use our intellect, that is, our rational mind, to know with certainty
that everything we see around us has a cause. The oak tree came from
the acorn, the baby came from his or her parents. And every cause has a
cause of its own. We can trace our own existence through the generations
of our forebears. We can go back and back into the origins of our planet
and our universe, but we cannot go back infinitely. There had to be a *first
cause*, some uncreated thing or person to set everything in motion.

That "first cause" is what we call God. This is one of five proofs offered
by St. Thomas Aquinas of God's existence. There are other proofs as well

that demonstrate how we human beings can come to know that there is a God by using our rational abilities. The Church expresses this succinctly by teaching, "God, the first principle and last end of all things, can be known with certainty from the created world, by the natural light of human reason" (*Dei Verbum*, 6).

3. If there is proof for God's existence, why doesn't everyone believe?

Our rational mind gives us the amazing ability to discover, to analyze, and to create. Sadly, our mind can be deceived. The tragedy of war, injustice, and senseless violence are sufficient to demonstrate that we are prone to sin and error. One of those errors is that many fail to acknowledge through human reason the existence of God.

St. Paul speaks about those in his day who did not believe in God and whose minds had become darkened in spite of all the evidence for God's existence:

> For what can be known about God is evident to them, because God made it evident to them. Ever since the creation of the world, his invisible attributes of eternal power and divinity have been able to be understood and perceived in what he has made. As a result, they have no excuse; for although they knew God they did not accord him glory as God or give him thanks. Instead, they became vain in their reasoning, and their sense-less minds were darkened. While claiming to be wise, they became fools. (Rom 1:20–22)

Perhaps St. Paul's words grate against contemporary sensibilities. Sadly, in the quest for truth about the origin of all things, some who presently deny the existence of God have been given poor directions along the way or have been taught deliberate falsehoods. It is not polite to call someone a fool, yet the opposite of foolishness is wisdom.

The wise person seeks the truth about the nature of all things. The wise person seeks justice when deceived by the false promises of a con artist. The wise person seeks the way to everlasting life. Thankfully, one is never too old to grow in wisdom, and the desire for transcendence that lies deep within the human heart can never be fully extinguished. There is hope even for the most hardened atheist (cf. *CCC*, 37).

4.   Can we know everything about God through our human reason?

We are religious creatures. Human beings are created with a capacity for transcendence, a capacity for God. The "desire for God is written in the human heart" (*CCC*, 27). Furthermore, there is a bond between God and the people God has created, such that there is something missing at the very core of our being when we exclude God.

By our reason we can know that there is a God, yet there are limits to what we can know about God through reason alone. Even with what we can discover through human reason, it is impossible for our words to describe God perfectly. St. Thomas Aquinas teaches that "we cannot grasp what he is, but only what he is not, and how other beings stand in relation to him" (cited in *CCC*, 43). For example, we can say that "God is good," but he is so far beyond our limited conception of goodness that the statement, though true, does not fully comprehend God's goodness.

Although God is our Creator, we simply cannot know through our own reason or intellect many things about God. Nor can we fully appreciate what we do discover about him through reason. Fortunately, what mere human reason cannot provide on its own is assisted by God's self-Revelation to humanity.

God comes to meet us, to teach us about himself and his plan for us. We speak of this process of God's self-Revelation as *Divine Revelation*, the gradual unveiling of God's plan for humanity. We all have known teachers who were experts at pedagogy, the method and practice of teaching. God is a teacher *par excellence*. God has a "divine pedagogy" by which we will come to know not simply that there is a God, but that God is deeply in love with human beings, the creatures who bear his image and likeness (*CCC*, 50).

5.   How does divine pedagogy work? How does God teach us about himself?

God is the master teacher, and so he teaches gradually and patiently. A mathematics teacher does not teach calculus until the student has first studied algebra. In the same way, God did not teach our forebears in the faith everything about himself all at once. Only gradually did God reveal himself to the world through his words and mighty deeds. God's early self-Revelation to the people of Israel was to prepare them and the world for the fullness of Revelation in Jesus Christ (cf. *CCC*, 51–53).

God's self-Revelation was accomplished over the course of many centuries, all according to his plan and through many stages. The initial stages were recorded in the first five books of the Bible, the Jewish Torah, or *Pentateuch* ("five books" in Greek):

- God revealed himself to our first parents, giving them the experience of profound closeness to him, walking and talking with God "in the cool of the day" (Gn 3:8, cf. *CCC*, 54).

- Even after their fall from grace, God would give the first human beings the "hope of salvation and the promise of redemption" (*CCC*, 55). In a glimpse of the great things to come, and in what is called the *protoevangelium* or "the first proclamation of the Gospel," God warned the tempter and predicted the ultimate victory of good over evil: "I will put enmity between you and the woman, and between your offspring and hers; he will strike at your head, while you strike his heel" (Gn 3:15, NRSV).

- Through his covenant with Noah, God gave expression to the principle that all people and nations would be saved. God gave hope to those who would live according to the covenant of Noah, thus giving hope for those who would await the Savior, Jesus Christ, who would "gather into one the dispersed children of God" (Jn 11:52, cf. *CCC*, 56–58).

- God called Abraham to be the father of a multitude of nations, telling him that his descendants would be "as countless as the stars of the sky and the sands of the seashore" (Gn 22:17, cf. *CCC*, 59–61). The descendants of Abraham, the Chosen People who were heirs to this promise, would "prepare for that day when God would gather all his children into the unity of the Church. They would be the root onto which the Gentiles would be grafted, once they came to believe" (*CCC*, 60).

- Abraham's descendants would make their way to Egypt, where they would become enslaved by Pharaoh. God delivered his people from slavery through his mighty deeds recorded in the Book of Exodus and the Book of Deuteronomy. Through their forty-year passage through the desert, God formed his people Israel, teaching them his commandments through Moses and revealing himself as the one, true God. This people, the first to hear God's Word, would soon be taught by the prophets to look for the Savior who was to come (cf. *CCC*, 62–63).

6.   Who were the prophets?

The word *prophet* means "one who speaks for God." While the prophets often foretold the future, sometimes in stunning detail, their primary role was to call the people of Israel to conversion of heart and fidelity to God's covenant, so that they might be ready for the coming of the Savior.

The major prophets are Isaiah, Jeremiah, Ezekiel, and Daniel. The minor prophets are Hosea, Joel, Amos, Obadiah, Jonah, Micah, Nahum, Habakkuk, Zephaniah, Haggai, Zechariah, and Malachi. The prophets are labeled major and minor based on the length of their writings. The writings of the major and minor prophets are in their eponymous books found in the Old Testament. "Through the prophets, God forms his people in the hope of salvation, in the expectation of a new and everlasting covenant intended for all, to be written on their hearts" (*CCC*, 64).

7.   When were the words of the prophets fulfilled?

In Jesus Christ, God reveals himself in a definitive way. "In times past, God spoke in partial and various ways to our ancestors through the prophets; in these last days, he spoke to us through a Son, whom he made heir of all things and through whom he created the universe" (Heb 1:1–2). God has nothing more to say than what he says in his "one, perfect, and unsurpassable Word" (*CCC*, 65).

8. Will God have any further Revelation for us?

We expect no further public revelation from God until the Second Coming of his Son at the end of time. God has said all that he needs to say, and his divine Word can be found in Scripture and apostolic Tradition. Both Scripture and apostolic Tradition are handed on by the Church and aid us in deciphering the full significance of God's public revelation.

Through the centuries, some have experienced private revelations, and some of these have been recognized by the Church as authentic. Examples include the visions of the Sacred Heart of Jesus experienced by the seventeenth-century mystic St. Margaret Mary Alacoque and the nineteenth-century apparitions of the Blessed Virgin Mary to St. Bernadette in the village of Lourdes, France. These and other approved private revelations do not add to God's definitive Revelation in Jesus Christ, but they help those of a particular moment in history to live out more fully their faith in Jesus.

On the other hand, we cannot accept "'revelations' that claim to surpass or correct the Revelation of which Christ is the fulfillment, as is the case in certain non-Christian religions and also in certain recent sects which base themselves on such 'revelations'" (*CCC*, 67). The Church of Latter-Day Saints, the Jehovah's Witnesses, and the Seventh-Day Adventists are examples of recent sects that have incorrectly claimed further disclosures to God's Revelation.

9. What is God's plan for communicating his Revelation in our day and age?

Since the coming into the world of God's only begotten Son, Jesus Christ, this has been God's plan for communicating his Revelation:

Professions of Faith

The Apostles' Creed

I believe in God,
the Father almighty,
Creator of heaven and earth,
and in Jesus Christ, his only Son,
    our Lord,
who was conceived by the Holy
    Spirit,
born of the Virgin Mary,
suffered under Pontius Pilate,
was crucified, died, and was
    buried;
he descended into hell;
on the third day he rose again
    from the dead;
he ascended into heaven,
and is seated at the right hand of
    God the Father almighty;
from there he will come to judge
    the living and the dead.

I believe in the Holy Spirit,
the holy catholic Church,
the communion of saints,
the forgiveness of sins,
the resurrection of the body,
and life everlasting.
Amen.

The Nicene Creed

I believe in one God,
the Father the almighty,
maker of heaven and earth, of
    all things visible and
    invisible.
I believe in one Lord Jesus
    Christ,
the Only Begotten Son of God,
    born of the Father before
    all ages.

God from God, Light from Light, true God from true God, begotten, not made, consubstantial with the Father; through him all things were made.

For us men and for our salvation he came down from heaven, and by the Holy Spirit was incarnate of the Virgin Mary, and became man.

For our sake he was crucified under Pontius Pilate, he suffered death and was buried, and rose again on the third day in accordance with the Scriptures.

He ascended into heaven and is seated at the right hand of the Father.

He will come again in glory to judge the living and the dead and his kingdom will have no end.

I believe in the Holy Spirit, the Lord, the giver of life, who proceeds from the Father and the Son, who with the Father and the Son is adored and glorified, who has spoken through the prophets.

I believe in one, holy, catholic, and apostolic Church.

I confess one Baptism for the forgiveness of sins and I look forward to the resurrection of the dead and the life of the world to come.

Amen.

- First, God's full Revelation, accomplished in the Divine Person of Jesus Christ, was communicated through the preaching of the twelve Apostles. Jesus sends forth his Apostles with the words, "Go, therefore, and make disciples of all nations, baptizing them in the name of the Father, and of the Son, and of the holy Spirit, teaching them to observe all that I have commanded you. And behold, I am with you always, until the end of the age" (Mt 28:19–20). Filled with the Holy Spirit on the day of Pentecost, the Apostles traveled far and wide, passing on to others what they had received personally from Jesus Christ.

- Under the inspiration of the Holy Spirit, the twelve Apostles and those who knew them "committed the message of salvation to writing" (*Dei Verbum*, 7, cited in *CCC*, 76). These writings are found in the New Testament.

- God's Revelation comes to us not through the Bible alone, but also through the living Tradition of the Church, the very Church that gave birth to the Bible (cf. *CCC*, 78). Sacred Tradition includes all the teachings handed on by the Apostles from Jesus Christ. These teachings are witnessed in the Church's practice, including her worship, her prayers, and her celebration of the sacraments. St. Paul speaks of this living Tradition when he calls the Church the "pillar and the foundation of truth" (1 Tm 3:15).

God intends to reveal himself to all people in every age. Indeed, God "wills everyone to be saved and to come to knowledge of the truth" (1 Tm 2:4).

10.   What is the relationship between Sacred Scripture and Sacred Tradition?

Sacred Scripture and Sacred Tradition both flow from the same font of Divine Revelation. They are closely bound to each other. Each one makes present and fruitful the mystery of Christ in the Church. Christ promised to remain with the Church until the end of time (cf. *CCC*, 80).

Though they flow from the same font, Sacred Scripture and Tradition are distinct modes of transmission:

- Sacred Scripture is God's speech, "put down in writing under the breath of the Holy Spirit" (*CCC*, 81).

- Sacred Tradition transmits the Word of God in its entirety, that Word that has been communicated through Jesus Christ and the Holy Spirit. That Word is transmitted to the successors of the Apostles, so that they may preserve and spread the Word through their teaching and preaching (cf. *CCC*, 82).

We are to honor Scripture and Tradition with equal sentiment and devotion (cf. *CCC*, 82). The Scriptures were born from the Church in that the New Testament books were written by the Apostles and their coworkers and that it was their successors, the bishops, who discerned what books belonged in the Bible. However, the Church does not teach by Scripture alone. St. Paul, who contributes more words to the New Testament than any other author, praises those who "hold fast to the traditions, just as I handed them on to you" (1 Cor 11:2). There is great beauty in the interplay between Sacred Scripture, which is fully accessible to us through the Holy Bible, and Sacred Tradition, which is fully available to us through the teachings, prayers, sacraments, structure, and fellowship of our Catholic Church that is vibrant and alive.

While it is wonderful to learn about these matters of Sacred Scripture and Sacred Tradition, there is nothing that compares with entering more deeply into them through the Church, which keeps each alive. It is like comparing the reading of the rules of baseball with the thrill of attending a major league game. More aptly, it is like comparing sitting in the stands with playing on the field. We are all to be participants in knowing about and sharing Sacred Scripture and Sacred Tradition.

In fact, the heritage of the faith is entrusted by the Apostles to the whole Church. Every member of the Church is responsible for preserving and passing on the Deposit of Faith contained in Scripture and Tradition (cf. *CCC*, 84). We do this depending on our particular vocations:

- The bishops, in communion with the pope and under the direction of the Holy Spirit, exercise the teaching office or *Magisterium* of the Church. Theirs is the task of interpreting authentically Scripture and Tradition amidst the circumstances of our times (cf. *CCC*, 85).

- The faithful, who live out the faith in their daily lives, have the responsibility and duty to pass on to others the truth that has been revealed by God through Scripture and Tradition (cf. *CCC*, 91).

The Church teaches, "The whole body of the faithful . . . cannot err in matters of belief. This characteristic is shown in the supernatural appreciation of faith (*sensus fidei*) on the part of the whole people, when, from the bishops to the last of the faithful, they manifest a universal consent in matters of faith and morals" (*Lumen Gentium*, 12). This mysterious, God-given *sense of the faithful* plays an important role both in preserving the integrity of the faith and in applying the faith to the circumstances of our day and age (cf. *CCC*, 92–93).

We must also distinguish between Tradition, sometimes called "tradition with a capital T," and the various traditions by which the Church in various times and places has expressed the greater Tradition. These traditions are subject to modification or even suppression should they no longer serve their purpose. An example would be the past tradition in some Catholic parishes in which men and women sat on opposite sides of the main aisle, a tradition that largely disappeared in the early twentieth century (cf. *CCC*, 83).

By God's wise arrangement and the guidance of the Holy Spirit, Scripture, Tradition, and the Magisterium support one another like a three-legged stool. Each in its own way, and all three working together, contribute to the salvation of souls (cf. *CCC*, 95).

11.   My Protestant friends bring their Bibles to church. My Catholic friends do not. What exactly does the Church teach about the Bible?

While most Catholics do not bring their Bibles to church, the prayers and readings of the Mass are profoundly Scriptural. In many ways, participating in Holy Mass is a way of experiencing the Scripture coming alive. Nevertheless, here are the key teachings of the Church on the Holy Bible:

- **The Church has a close bond with the Scriptures, a bond that comes both from producing and being nourished by them.** "The Church has always venerated the divine Scriptures as she venerated the Body of the Lord" (*Dei Verbum*, 21).

- **The Scriptures bring us into an encounter with the living God.** In the words of St. Jerome, the fourth-century translator of the texts of the Scriptures into Latin, the vernacular language of the day, "Ignorance of the Scriptures is ignorance of Christ."

- **"God is the author of Sacred Scripture"** (*CCC*, 105). God made use of human authors, who, under the inspiration of the Holy Spirit, used their God-given talents and abilities to write whatever God wanted, and no more (cf. *CCC*, 106).

- **The Scriptures are inerrant.** The Scriptures teach without error the truth that God wants us to know for our salvation (cf. *CCC*, 107).

- **Christianity is a religion of the Word of God, not a religion of a book.** The Eternal Word, through the Holy Spirit, makes the Scriptures come alive and opens our minds to their meaning (cf. *CCC*, 108).

- **The Scriptures are to be read literally and are to be understood according to standard rules of literary interpretation** (cf. *CCC*, 116). This means that texts must be read according to their respective genres; for example, some passages are historical, some are poetic, and some are parables.

- **The Scriptures are also to be read spiritually.** They have deep spiritual meaning in three particular ways:
  1. The *allegorical sense*, for the Scripture relates events that have deeper significance in Jesus Christ;
  2. The *moral sense*, for the Scriptures teach us how to live according to God's will; and
  3. The *anagogical sense*, from a Greek word that means "to lead," for the Scriptures contain deeper meaning related to the eternal destiny of the soul, the Church, and the world (cf. *CCC*, 117).

- **There is a unity between the Old Testament and the New Testament.** The Old Testament is indispensable (cf. *CCC*, 121), for the Old Testament books "bear witness to the whole divine pedagogy of God's saving love" (*CCC*, 122). From the earliest days, the Church has believed that "the New Testament lies hidden in the Old, and the Old Testament is unveiled in the New" (*CCC*, 129).

The Holy Bible is very important to Catholics. If you attend daily Mass each day for three successive years, you will hear proclaimed aloud vast swaths of the Bible, including nearly 90 percent of the Gospels. Also, notice how many Scripture citations are listed in the footnotes of the *Catechism of the Catholic Church*.

12.   Why is the Catholic Bible different from the Protestant Bible?

In fact, Catholics and Protestants agree upon the list of the twenty-seven books of the New Testament. Martin Luther moved all or parts of seven Old Testament books (Baruch, Judith, 1 and 2 Maccabees, Sirach, Tobit, and Wisdom) to the appendix of what became the "Protestant Bible," considering them not to be part of the Sacred Scriptures but still worthy of the attention of Christians. The *King James Bible* and many subsequent Protestant Bibles have been printed without that appendix, considering them *not* to be part of the Sacred Scriptures, even though they have been accepted by the Church since ancient times. The complete list of books in the Catholic Bible can be found in the *Catechism of the Catholic Church*, paragraph 120.

Chapter Summary and Reflection

You were born for much more than this world. You are meant for God.
You are connected to a God who loves you more than you can imagine.
To you belongs the life-changing call to discover your connection to God,
or to delve more deeply into the great mystery of your relationship with
God through Jesus Christ and the Catholic Church.

Guided by the Magisterium, both Sacred Scripture and Sacred Tradition will accompany you along your journey of faith where you will
discover the incredible richness of what God has done for you, and of
all that God intends for you. Your faith in Jesus Christ is your entry into
eternal life. You are meant to live with God and enjoy great happiness that
will last longer than the sun and the moon and the stars. You are loved
by God. God has a plan for you.

⬤ *Creation*

Every person has his or her own set of gifts, talents, interests, aptitudes,
and strengths. What part of you reveals God's plan for your life?

◑ *Fall*

Time is the great equalizer. No matter how rich or poor, everyone has
the same twenty-four hours of opportunities and challenges each day.
What are the bad habits that have crept into your life that keep you from

responding to God's call to love him with all your heart, mind, soul, and strength?

Redemption

God exercises his divine pedagogy in revealing himself to human beings, culminating in his definitive self-Revelation through Jesus Christ. How have you experienced God's divine pedagogy in your life? How have witnesses to the *kerygma* helped you to grow in your relationship with the Lord over the course of the years?

Restoration

Regular Bible reading is vital in the Christian life. What is your plan for reading and study? Do you think you could ever read the entire Bible in a year? How might you devote fifteen minutes per day to Bible reading?

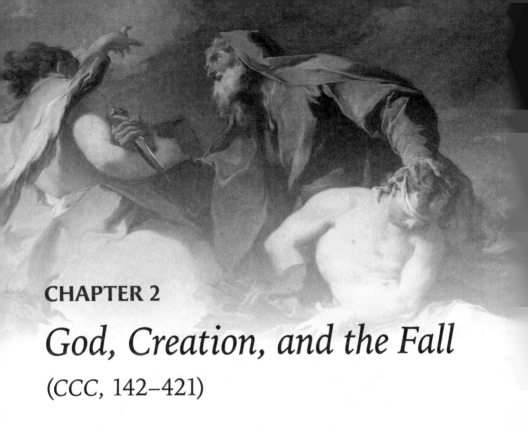

CHAPTER 2

God, Creation, and the Fall
(*CCC*, 142–421)

God reveals himself to human beings and invites us to trust in him. Faith is our proper response to that invitation (cf. *CCC*, 142–143). We believe that there is a God, and we believe God. We listen to his direction for our lives and we obey him. In fact, the words *obey* and *listen* are closely related in the Latin language. To obey God is to follow in the example set for us by the saints.

The Bible defines faith as "the realization of what is hoped for and evidence of things not seen" (Heb 11:1). While faith certainly evokes a supernatural experience, it also speaks to everyday occurrences. We have faith that our loved ones will be there for us. We have faith that the signals at intersections will function properly and not be the cause of traffic accidents. This kind of everyday faith in little things boosts our confidence that we can trust in God in the big things. He promises that there is more to this life than meets the eye and that our greatest hopes will be fulfilled if we embrace his will for our lives and walk steadfastly in his ways.

13.   What does it mean to have faith?

Abraham was the model of obedient faith. He picked up his family and moved across the desert to a new land after God spoke to him. Later, he showed willingness to sacrifice his son because he had faith that it was God's will. God rewarded him by sparing his son and making him the father of the Chosen People. The exemplar of faith is the Blessed Virgin Mary (cf. *CCC*, 148–149). Of her is said, "Blessed are you who believed that what was spoken to you by the Lord would be fulfilled" (Lk 1:45). Faith begins with the statement "I believe." Additional cornerstones of personal faith are these:

- Faith is believing in Jesus Christ, whom God sent by sharing in his Spirit (cf. *CCC*, 151, 152).

- Faith is a gift from God, a virtue that gives us the ability to believe in him (cf. *CCC*, 153).

- Faith is "contrary neither to human freedom nor to human reason" (*CCC*, 154). Faith is above reason, but does not contradict it (*CCC*, 159).

- Faith is certain because God is believable (cf. *CCC*, 156, 157).

- Faith is aided by God, who helps us to believe, especially through the miracles of Jesus, the fulfillment of Old Testament prophecy, the stability of the Church, and the lives of the saints (cf. *CCC*, 156).

- Faith is not coerced. God calls us to believe in him and to have faith, but God does not force us to embrace faith (cf. *CCC*, 160).

- Faith (in Jesus Christ) is necessary for salvation (cf. *CCC*, 161).

- Faith is a gift from God, but we can lose this precious gift. We must be dedicated to persevering in faith until the end. Faith is nourished by the study of God's Word, prayer, and the practice of charity (cf. *CCC*, 162).

Today, "we walk by faith, and not by sight" (2 Cor 5:7). But if we persevere, faith will give way to sight, when we see God face-to-face and join the company of the saints in heaven, from whose example and intercession we can draw great strength along the way (cf. 1 Cor 13:12, *CCC*, 163–165).

14. Where is a summary of what Catholics believe?

The teachings of the Church are summarized in a *creed*. The word *creed* comes from the Latin word *credere*, which means "to believe." An early creed during the persecution of early Christians was the phrase "Jesus Christ, Son of God, Savior." In Greek, this phrase is an anagram that spells out the word *ΙΧΘΥΣ*, meaning "fish." Early Christians who lived under the dangerous rule of the Romans used the anagram fish as a way to stay under cover from the Roman leaders and soldiers.

A more complete creed is taught to converts and recited in prayer. It is structured by the persons of the Trinity: God the Father, God the Son, and God the Holy Spirit. Examples include the Apostles' Creed and the Niceno-Constantinopolitan Creed, both of which were introduced in Chapter 1 (see page 8) and are recited at Sunday Mass.

The synopsis of the content of the faith contained in a creed allows us to proclaim our faith in union with the whole Church and to pass the faith on to others. Meditating upon the words of the creed helps us to delve deeper into the mystery of our faith in the Three Divine Persons of the Blessed Trinity: the God who creates, redeems, and sacrifices (God the Father, God the Son, and God the Holy Spirit).

15. What does God reveal about himself?

We can know that God exists through our natural reason (cf. *CCC*, 37). But to know what God is like, we rely upon the details that God himself provides through the gift of Revelation:

- **God reveals he is one.** Polytheism, the belief that there are many gods, was prevalent in the ancient world. Contrary to their neighbors, the people of Israel believed that there was only one God. They believed this because God had taught this through the prophets, especially Moses: "Hear, O Israel! The LORD is our God, the LORD alone! Therefore, you shall love the LORD, your God, with your whole heart, and with your whole being, and with your whole strength" (Dt 6:4–5, cf. *CCC*, 201). This revelation of God's uniqueness would be made complete in the person of Jesus Christ. To say "Jesus is Lord" is to profess his divinity, without in any way compromising our belief in one God (cf. *CCC*, 202).

- **God reveals his name.** Throughout the four hundred years between Abraham and Moses, the people of Israel worshipped "the God of Abraham, and Isaac, and Jacob," for God had not yet revealed his name (cf. Gn 50:24, also Ex 3:15). Only during God's appearance to Moses at the burning bush did God reveal his name. God commanded Moses to go to Pharaoh to demand that he release the Israelite slaves. Moses responded that

  if I go to the Israelites and say to them, "The God of your ancestors has sent me to you," and they ask me, "What is his name?" what do I tell them? God replied to Moses: "I am who I am." Then he added: "This is what you will tell the Israelites: I AM has sent me to you. . . . This is my name forever; this is my title for all generations" (Ex 3:13–15, cf. *CCC*, 203–204).

  God choosing to reveal his name is a defining moment in divine pedagogy. God reveals himself as the one who has been faithful to the people of Israel for centuries and whose mercies have not been exhausted. God reveals himself as the one who is faithful to his promises and who will rescue from slavery his people in bondage.

  The name "I AM WHO I AM" is both mysterious and near. His name is mysterious because God himself is shrouded in mystery. His name is near because God intervenes in human history, bringing freedom to the enslaved, hope to the hopeless. God makes himself close to his people. "God, who reveals his name as "I AM," reveals himself as the God who is always there, present to his people in order to save them" (*CCC*, 207).

- **God reveals that he is faithful and merciful.** In promising to be forever present to his people, God anticipates the inevitable infidelity of his people to his commandments. God, who creates the human person, knows well how the tragedy of sin continues to play out. Nevertheless, God is full of mercy and compassion. Of himself, God says, "The LORD, the LORD, a God gracious and merciful, slow to anger and abounding in love and fidelity" (Ex 34:6, cf. *CCC*, 210–211).

- **God reveals that he *is*.** The Glory Be is a traditional and popular Catholic prayer that praises God who is Father, Son, and Holy Spirit with the acclamation, "As it was in the beginning, is now, and ever shall be, world without end. Amen!" God has always been, for God is the creator of everything in the universe. God *is*, for he is ever present in our lives. God will forever be, for he is eternal, and he invites us to be with him in heaven for all eternity (cf. *CCC*, 212–213).

- **God reveals he is truth.** God does not deceive. God is trustworthy. God is truth itself, the fixed point by which we can align the moral compass that we follow through life. God keeps his promises. God's words are spoken with true and lasting wisdom. God sends his only begotten Son into the world "to testify to the truth" (Jn 18:37). Jesus is "the way and the truth and the life" (Jn 14:6). In him we can place all our confidence; through him we find our way to everlasting life (cf. *CCC*, 214–216).

- **God reveals he is love.** Throughout their relationship with God, the people of Israel would come to know that the single motivation for God's choosing them from among all other nations was his magnanimous and faithful love. Like a father for his children, God never gave up on his people, no matter how heinous their sinfulness. In the fullness of time, God's only begotten Son would become flesh to dwell with us as the living embodiment of his infinite love. "For God so loved the world that he gave his only Son, so that everyone who believes in him might not perish but might have eternal life" (Jn 3:16). Furthermore, God *is* love, for love is of his essence, his very being.

"God is love, and whoever remains in love remains in God and God in him" (1 Jn 4:16, cf. *CCC*, 218–221).

16.   What does all this mean for you to believe in God?

Being able to say that you believe in God, and that you love him with all your heart, makes for a tremendous difference in your life (cf. *CCC*, 222). Specifically, it means:

- knowing that you are serving the God who is the creator of all things, the Lord of the universe (cf. *CCC*, 223)

- being a grateful person, for you know that God is the giver of every good thing in your life (cf. *CCC*, 224)

- being in solidarity with all others, for we are each made in God's image and likeness (cf. *CCC*, 225)

- being a good steward of God's many gifts, choosing to bring into your life only those created things that bring us closer to God, and choosing to remain detached from those things that lead us away from him (cf. *CCC*, 226)

- finding in God the peace that this world cannot bring

Believing in God means that you can trust that God will see you through every difficulty, every problem, every circumstance in life. Sixteenth-century mystic St. Teresa of Avila says this beautifully:

> Let nothing trouble you / Let nothing frighten you
> Everything passes / God never changes
> Patience / Obtains all
> Whoever has God / Wants for nothing
> God alone is enough. (cited in *CCC*, 227)

In summary, believing in God makes all the difference in the world.

17. What does making the Sign of the Cross communicate about what Catholics believe?

The Sign of the Cross is a simple yet profound prayer. Catholics trace the cross of our Lord, beginning with the forehead, moving down the torso, and then across both shoulders from left to right while saying, "In the name of the Father, and of the Son, and of the Holy Spirit. Amen." The Sign of the Cross is a statement of belief that begins or ends simple prayers such as the blessing before meals as well as great prayers such as the Holy Mass.

The Sign of the Cross recalls Christian Baptism, through which a person enters into the life of the one true God, Father, Son, and Holy Spirit. It acknowledges the central mystery of the Christian faith: God's self-Revelation as one God in Three Divine Persons, also known as the mystery of the Holy Trinity. Note that we speak of the *name*, not the *names* of the Father, Son, and Holy Spirit. The most fundamental truth of the faith is that there is only one God, and he reveals himself as Father, Son, and Holy Spirit to bring salvation to all people (cf. *CCC*, 232–234).

18. How does God reveal the mystery of the Holy Trinity?

We can use our human reason to discern that there is a God. But the mystery of the Holy Trinity can only be known because it has been revealed to us by God himself (cf. *CCC*, 237). The mystery is multifaceted. Among its main elements are these:

- **God is Father.** To call God "Father" is to speak of God as both the one who creates all things and the one who lovingly and tenderly cares for his children. Sadly, there are earthly fathers who do not live up to the ideals and standards set by our heavenly Father and who thus disfigure in tragic ways the image of fatherhood. Nevertheless, we call God Father because he exemplifies fatherhood in a perfect way, for "no one is father as God is Father" (CCC, 239, cf. CCC, 238–239).

  We learn about the Father from the Son. It is the Son who reveals the Father. Jesus teaches not only that God is our loving and merciful

Father, but that in a manner not previously heard of, God is the Father of the Son from all eternity, and that he (Jesus) is the Son "only in relationship to the Father" (*CCC*, 240). "No one knows the Son except the Father, and no one knows the Father except the Son and anyone to whom the Son wishes to reveal him" (Mt 11:27).

- **The Son is God.** The Scriptures are clear that Jesus is God, the eternal Word of God through whom all things were created. The Gospel of John opens with the same words as Genesis, Chapter 1:

> In the beginning was the Word, and the Word was with God, and the Word was God. He was in the beginning with God. All things came to be through him, and without him nothing came to be. What came to be through him was life, and this life was the light of the human race; the light shines in the darkness, and the darkness has not overcome it. (Jn 1:1–5)

The Church speaks of the Father and the Son as being consubstantial, or "of the same substance" (cf. *CCC*, 241–242). There is no other relationship between father and son like that between the First and Second Persons of the Blessed Trinity.

We learn about the relationship between the Father and the Son from the Holy Spirit. The fullness of the mystery of the Trinity is revealed through the coming of the Holy Spirit on the day of Pentecost. At the Last Supper, Jesus says, "The Advocate, the holy Spirit that the Father will send in my name—he will teach you everything and remind you of all that [I] told you" (Jn 14:26, cf. *CCC*, 243–244).

- **The Holy Spirit is God.** In the Nicene Creed, the Church proclaims the eternal divinity of the Holy Spirit: "I believe in the Holy Spirit, the Lord, the giver of life, who proceeds from the Father and the Son. With the Father and the Son he is worshipped and glorified. He has spoken through the Prophets" (cf. *CCC*, 245).

The Three Persons of the Holy Trinity are distinct, yet God is one. The Divine Persons are neither modalities nor ways of acting, as a human person can be at the same time a wife, a mother, a sister, a scholar, an athlete, and a humanitarian. "The divine persons do not share the one divinity among themselves but each of them is God whole and entire" (*CCC*, 253). Their distinctiveness "resides solely in the relationships which relate them to one another" (*CCC*, 255). This can be illustrated as shown here:

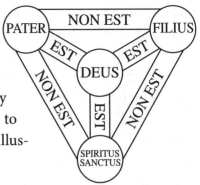

The Father (Pater) is (est) God (Deus); the Son (Fillus) is God and the Holy Spirit (Spiritus Sanctus) is God. Thus, God's unity is professed. Equality among the persons is symbolized by the equilateral triangle.

19. Why is it important to understand the mystery of the Blessed Trinity?

Catholics must understand and share the mystery of the Blessed Trinity with others because belief in the Trinity is at the heart of the Christian faith. Jesus sent forth his Apostles saying, "Go, therefore, and make disciples of all nations, baptizing them in the name of the Father, and of the Son, and of the holy Spirit" (Mt 28:19). In his letters, St. Paul uses Trinitarian greetings such as, "The grace of the Lord Jesus Christ and the love of God and the fellowship of the holy Spirit be with all of you" (2 Cor 13:13, cf. *CCC*, 249).

The early Church sought to clarify its teaching on the Trinity. Early church councils, the writings of the Fathers of the Church, and the faith of God's People defended the mystery of the Trinity from errors and distortions (cf. *CCC*, 250). The Church used wisdom and terms from Greek philosophy while at the same time giving "a new and unprecedented meaning to these terms, which from then on would be used to signify an ineffable mystery, 'infinitely beyond all that we can humanly understand'" (*CCC*, 251, quoting Pope Paul VI).

However, the mystery of the Holy Trinity is not a problem to be solved but an experience of divine, perfect love into which we are drawn. God reveals himself as a Trinity of Persons so that you might be drawn into his life. Mystery in this sense is used in a way analogous to how we speak of the closeness of family relationships; for example, the relationship between husband and wife, or between parent and child. Try as we might to explain them, the dynamics of family relationships remain ultimately mysterious. Similarly, the mysterious love between the community of Persons of Father, Son, and Holy Spirit is so powerful that it is able to extend to every human person. You are called to be a dwelling place for God, a temple of the Holy Spirit: "Whoever loves me will keep my word, and my Father will love him, and we will come to him and make our dwelling with him" (Jn 14:23, cf. *CCC*, 257–260).

God is Father, Son, and Holy Spirit, a Holy Trinity to be adored and worshipped, but not from afar. God makes his dwelling within you and invites you to a close and personal relationship with him. He invites you to accept him into your life through the sacraments, to commit to following him in his Church, and to persevere along the journey of faith so that you might for all eternity abide in him and he in you (cf. 1 Jn 4:13). Nothing is more important than that. Nor are you meant to take this journey alone. You are accompanied by the Communion of Saints, and to you is given the noble task of reaching out to others, bringing them along with you.

20.   If God is all-powerful, why is there evil in the world?

This question is incredibly painful for many of us to consider. How we wish that the number of God's miraculous cures would be greater, or that even one precious child in the oncology ward would be spared from the ravages of cancer. Surely it wouldn't be too much trouble for an all-powerful God to do just a little bit more to make lighter the burdens of those who suffer? We wonder how an all-powerful (cf. *CCC*, 268–269) and merciful God (cf. *CCC*, 270) permits the innocent to suffer.

This question has vexed the minds of many saints through the ages. Many faithful Christians have trouble with this question and feel powerless when challenged by nonbelievers on God's apparent dereliction of duty. What does the Church teach about this? Several points apply:

- **Suffering can test our faith.** "Faith in God the Father Almighty can be put to the test by the experience of evil and suffering. God can sometimes seem to be absent and incapable of stopping evil. But in the most mysterious way God the Father has revealed his almighty power in the voluntary humiliation and Resurrection of his Son, by which he conquered evil" (*CCC*, 272).

- **God is present in our suffering, not absent.** Our loving Father did not spare his only begotten Son but permitted him to be crucified and to die so that the evil of sin and death might be conquered. Through the Resurrection of Jesus from the dead, and by giving us entrance into eternal life through that same Resurrection, God proves his immeasurable greatness, his mercy, and his incredible love (cf. 273–274). He did not abandon his Son. He was with him at every step of his Passion and Death. So, too, is God with you in your darkest moments, mysteriously but surely leading you through the cross and into the hope of new life.

- **God permits but does not cause evil.** God could have created a world in which all things were ordered properly and where there was no suffering, pain, or death. In fact, he did! (Remember the story of creation in the Book of Genesis and what the world was like before our first parents sinned.) Yet God created human beings with free will, which means that he created a world in which sin and death could enter. Without willing evil to exist, God permits moral evil within his creation, but only so that an even greater good might emerge from it (cf. *CCC*, 311).

We cannot fully grasp the ways of God, "for the foolishness of God is wiser than human wisdom, and the weakness of God is stronger than human strength" (1 Cor 1:25). Yet, in the midst of incredible trials, Christians find great hope in the Cross of Jesus Christ, through which evil seems to triumph, only to be rendered powerless by the goodness, mercy, and love of God (cf. *CCC*, 312–313).

Never forget that God has a perfect plan and you are part of it. "From the greatest moral evil ever committed—the rejection and murder of

The Tree of Life

The Archabbey Church of Our Lady of Einsiedeln is at the center of the grounds of St. Meinrad Archabbey in southern Indiana. The first stone for this church was laid in 1899; construction went on for eight years as local citizens hauled in large sandstone blocks using horses and mules from the abbey's quarry a mile away.

Among the stained-glass windows that were produced both in St. Louis and in Germany is the one shown here, which depicts the story of salvation. In the lower panel, Adam and Eve are ejected from paradise by God for their disobedience in eating fruit from the tree of knowledge of good and evil. Yet, the tree that once gave us death now gives life as it is transformed into the Cross of Christ. From the Cross, Christ overcomes sin and death and is raised from the dead. St. Irenaeus said, "as by means of a tree we were made debtors to God, [so also] by means of a tree we may obtain the remission of our debt."[2]

St. Paul calls Jesus the New Adam (cf. Rom 5:12). Just as sin entered into the world through one person (Adam), so through one person (Jesus) does the grace of God overflow. Death reigns through Adam; grace and justification reign through Christ (cf. Rom 5:17). One transgression by Adam brings condemnation for all, whereas one righteous action through Jesus brings acquittal and life (cf. Rom 5:21).

God's only Son, caused by the sins of all men—God, by his grace that 'abounded all the more,' brought the greatest of goods: the glorification of Christ and our redemption. But for all that, evil never becomes a good" (*CCC*, 312, quoting Rom 5:20).

There are no pat answers to the problem of evil. We must always remember that God's ways are not our ways (cf. Is 55:8). As St. Paul writes, "Oh, the depth of the riches and wisdom and knowledge of God! How inscrutable are his judgments and how unsearchable his ways! For who has known the mind of the Lord or who has been his counselor?" (Rom 11:33–34). Though the reason why God permits evil will never be completely made known to us in this life, the ways and wisdom of God *will* be made known to us when we see him face-to-face (cf. *CCC*, 314).

21. What does the Church teach about creation and the origins of the universe?

The very first words of the Bible are about God creating the universe and all that is contained within it. The word *genesis* literally means "the beginning" (Gn 1:1, Jn 1:1, cf. *CCC*, 280). The Scriptures offer insights into the questions of the origin of the universe that can shape our views on the very meaning and purpose of our lives (cf. *CCC*, 282). In fact, many later scientific discoveries support the insights of the Book of Genesis and lead us to an even greater admiration of the Creator and his marvelous ways (cf. *CCC*, 283).

When we think about it, our questions about how the universe began do not just involve what, when, or how, but *why*. That is, our questions about the origin of the universe are inevitably intertwined with questions of a higher order, questions about the meaning of our place in creation. Is the world around us simply the product of the random collision of atoms? Or can we find meaning and purpose within the universe? Human reason tells us that there is a God and that God is the creator of all things. Faith tells us that there is a reason behind his creation (cf. *CCC*, 286).

God does not provide the answer to every question posed by geologists and paleontologists, but Scripture and Tradition do provide answers to questions that fall beyond the domain of the natural sciences, answers that are essential to our salvation. God wants us to know everything about his creation that is necessary for our salvation (cf. *CCC*, 287). From the Book of Genesis we learn the following important lessons about creation:

- **Creation is part of God's covenant.** God reveals his work as Creator to the people of Israel, teaching them that he is "the One to whom belong all the peoples of the earth, and the whole earth itself; he is the One who alone 'made heaven and earth'" (*CCC*, 287). God's creation is "the first and universal witness to God's all-powerful love" (*CCC*, 288).

- **Creation is the work of the Holy Trinity.** "In the beginning, when God created the heavens and the earth—and the earth was without form or shape, with darkness over the abyss and a mighty wind sweeping over the waters—Then God said: Let there be light, and there was light" (Gn 1:1–3). God the Father creates through his spoken Word, his Eternal Word, the Word who becomes flesh and dwells among us (cf. Jn 1:14). Furthermore, the spoken Word is inseparable from its breath. The Church speaks of the action of the Holy Spirit from the very beginning of creation. St. Irenaeus, the second-century bishop and martyr, says, "There exists but one God . . . he is the Father, God, the Creator, the author, the giver of order. He made all things by himself, that is, by his Word and by his Wisdom," "by the Son and the Spirit," who, so to speak, are "his hands" (cf. *CCC*, 290–292).

- **The world was created for the glory of God** (cf. *CCC*, 293). God creates to show forth the glory of his wisdom and power, and also his goodness and love. Furthermore, according to St. Irenaeus, human beings—God's greatest creature—reveal God's greatest glory: "The glory of God is man fully alive; moreover man's life is the vision of God: if God's revelation through creation has already obtained life for all the beings that dwell on earth, how much more will the Word's manifestation of the Father obtain life for those who see God." From his love and wisdom God creates the world for you, so that through his creation, you might be led further toward the Creator and the salvation he has in store for you (cf. *CCC*, 293–295).

- **God creates out of nothing.** Before the material universe existed, God was. God not only created the universe; he made the material out of which the universe is fashioned. The God who created *ex nihilo* (out of nothing) is more than capable of rescuing poor sinners, creating within us a new heart and raising us up to eternal life (cf. *CCC*, 296–298).

The Church does not require us to believe that God created the universe in six days, each twenty-four hours in length, though God is capable of anything! Nevertheless, we can see in the brief words of the Book of Genesis an indication of God's plan and order in creation. In the first three "days," God gives the world its form by separating his creation into various realms. In the next three "days," God fills each realm with occupants according to the day on which it was defined:

	God gives the world its form.		**God gives occupants to each realm.**
Day 1	God separates day from night (Gn 1:3–5).	**Day 4**	God creates the sun, moon, and stars (Gn 1:14–18).
Day 2	God separates the waters below (ocean) from the waters above (sky) (Gn 1:6–8).	**Day 5**	God creates fish for the ocean and birds for the sky (Gn 1:20–22).
Day 3	God separates the waters from the land (Gn 1:9–12).	**Day 6**	God creates animals and human beings for the land (Gn 1:24–27).

And when he was finished creating the lights, the land, and the animals, God said, "it is good." The essence of the account of creation in the Book of Genesis is that God creates with great order, and that everything he makes is good. God does not create evil (cf. *CCC*, 299).

God is separate from his creation yet also the one who upholds and sustains his creation. In other words, God transcends creation. Through his providence, God carries out his plan. God cares for all his creatures, including you. He knows you intimately and personally. We are called to childlike trust in God's providence, even when things in life do not seem to make sense (cf. *CCC*, 300–305).

22.   Who are the angels?

Angels are spiritual beings without bodies. God creates angels to be his messengers and servants. Their existence is spoken of throughout the Bible, as is their responsibility to help us get to heaven. Angels are "ministering spirits sent to serve, for the sake of those who are to inherit salvation" (Heb 1:14).

23.   Do we have a guardian angel?

To each of us is assigned a *guardian angel* to protect and guide us along the right path, all the while respecting fully our free will. Guardian angels help us to overcome temptation and to choose what is helpful for our eternal salvation (cf. *CCC*, 328–336). St. John Vianney (1786–1859) teaches us that we should never hesitate to ask our guardian angel for help: "Our guardian angels are our most faithful friends, because they are with us day and night, always and everywhere. We ought often to invoke them."

24.   What does it mean to say that human beings are created in the image and likeness of God?

One cannot read the first chapters of the Book of Genesis without concluding that human beings are profoundly different from God's other creatures. Though human beings live interdependently with other animals, the Scriptures are clear that the summit of God's creation is the human person.

Apart from the angels, no other creature can "share, by knowledge and love, in God's own life" (*CCC*, 356). Like the angels, we have received the gift of free will so that we might respond to God, offering him our faith and love (cf. *CCC*, 357). This again sets us apart from other earthly creatures. We are created by God "to know him, to love him, and to serve him in this world, and to be happy with him forever in heaven" (*Baltimore Catechism*).

Because *all* human persons are created in God's image and likeness, there is to be a solidarity and unity among the peoples of the earth, embracing people of every land and culture (cf. *CCC*, 360–361).

25. What is the soul?

Within the human person is the breath of God, animating the body so that we might enter into the life of God himself, Father, Son, and Holy Spirit. Genesis describes God breathing life into the human person, thereby bringing into the world a creature both material and spiritual (cf. Gn 2:7). Whereas the body is our material principle, the soul is our spiritual principle. The soul is created instantaneously by God and is not produced by our parents.

Body and soul are so closely united in the human person that the soul can be called the *form* of the body (cf. *CCC*, 362–365). The soul is immortal and lives on when separated from the body at death. The soul will be reunited with the body in the resurrection (cf. *CCC*, 366). More will be discussed about this in Chapter 8.

26. What does God intend for males and females in his plan?

Men and women are created for each other. Man and woman are made for communion with one another, with their masculine and feminine complementarity making possible the transmission of life and the building up of the human family: "Be fertile and multiply," God tells our first parents, and in so doing they cooperate with God's work of creation (Gn 1:28, cf. *CCC*, 372).

Human beings are given by God both dominion and stewardship over the earth and all creatures upon it. Human beings are to be responsible in the use of earthly resources and to love the created world in a godly way, for they are created in the image and likeness of God (cf. *CCC*, 373).

The Scriptures are also clear that God reveals insights into his plan for the human race by the very way in which he creates men and women in perfect equality. At the same time, the differentiation between the sexes is also part of the goodness of God's plan (cf. *CCC*, 369–370).

God creates woman to be a partner for the man in a way that no other creature can be. Woman is fashioned from the rib of the man, which brings forth from him a sense of great wonder: "This one, at last, is bone of my bones and flesh of my flesh"(Gn 2:23). The man and the woman are created in a state of *original justice*, enjoying harmony with one another, peace with God's other creatures, and a deep friendship with God himself (cf. *CCC*, 372). Adam and Eve would walk and talk with God "in the cool of the day" (cf. Gn 3:8). Our first parents were also free from *concupiscence*, which is to say that that they were not subjugated "to the pleasures of the senses, covetousness for earthly goods, and self-assertion, contrary to the dictates of reason" (*CCC*, 377).

Life in the Garden of Eden was very good for our first parents as they shared in God's life in a state of original holiness and original justice (cf. *CCC*, 375). Sadly, much was about to change. The harmony planned by God for the human race would be lost in the great tragedy of sin, an event known as the Fall. Yet what was lost in the Fall would pale in comparison with the glory to be revealed in the new creation in Jesus Christ (cf. *CCC*, 374).

27. How does the Fall impact us today?

Evil and suffering can be seen all around us. Crime in the streets, nations at war, innocent people mistreated and abused, and countless other examples face us daily. Marxists would say that these things are the result of economic injustice and unfair social structures. Some philosophers inspired by Darwin's theories would say that human beings have yet to evolve into a higher level in which these terrible things would not take place. Freudians would say that the evil of crime is the result of something amiss in the basic human development of the criminal.

The Scriptures say otherwise. From their origins, human beings have abused freedom, leading to their downfall (cf. *CCC*, 387). The abuse of human freedom is better known as *sin*. Yet what went wrong in the Garden of Eden would also be the beginning of the Good News of our redemption through the Death and Resurrection of Jesus Christ. This means that we cannot understand our salvation without first understanding sin (cf. *CCC*, 388).

The Scriptures and the Church have been very clear that God is not the origin of evil in our world. God is good, and everything that God creates is good. Evil arises not from God, but from human beings expressing opposition to God. The rejection of God that first took place among humans in the Fall has brought untold pain, suffering, and discord into the world. This is the clear teaching of the early chapters of the Book of Genesis. Only by the light of God's Revelation can we make sense of the reality of evil (cf. *CCC*, 386).

28. Was the first sin really the eating of the wrong apple?

There is no mention of an apple tree in the account of the Fall. "The account of the fall in Genesis 3 uses figurative language, but affirms a primeval event, a deed that took place at the beginning of the history of man. Revelation gives us the certainty of faith that the whole of human history is marked by the original fault freely committed by our first parents" (*CCC*, 390).

More literally, our first parents heard a seductive voice bidding them to disobey the limits God placed upon their freedom. Scripture and Tradition identify the tempter as the devil named Satan, a fallen angel from the ranks of those beings who chose to reject God. Assenting to the temptation presented to them, our first parents not only disobeyed God but scorned him, choosing themselves over him. In their sin, the first human beings chose against their relationship with God and against their own good. This is the first sin, the Original Sin (cf. *CCC*, 397–398).

The consequences of this choice to disobey God were drastic for our first parents and for all of humanity. Original justice and original holiness were lost. Friendship with God was compromised because of the distorted way in which the first human beings regarded the limits placed upon their freedom. Tensions arose between man and woman—tensions that would eventually manifest themselves in domination and lust. Creation became hostile toward human beings. Death entered the world, and the corruptible bodies of men and women would return to the dust from which they were created (cf. *CCC*, 400). Brother would murder brother (cf. Gn 4:1–16). The covenant God made with our first parents was transgressed, and sin became universal from that day forward (cf. *CCC*, 401).

29.   What do the Fall and Original Sin have to do with me?

Every human being is affected by Adam's sin (cf. *CCC*, 402). "Therefore, just as through one person sin entered the world, and through sin, death, and thus death came to all . . . just as through one transgression condemnation came upon all, so through one righteous act acquittal and life came to all" (Rom 5:12, 19).

Original Sin is at the root of all the maladies, tragedies, and sorrows that have plagued the human race (cf. *CCC*, 403). The fact is that we have contracted from our first parents the effects of a sin that we did not commit. "It is a sin which will be transmitted by propagation to all mankind, that is, by the transmission of a human nature deprived of original holiness and justice. And that is why original sin is called 'sin' only in an analogical sense: it is a sin 'contracted' and not 'committed'—a state and not an act" (*CCC*, 404).

Though we are all wounded by Original Sin, we are not totally despoiled by it. Original Sin "is a deprivation of original holiness and justice, but human nature has not been totally corrupted: it is wounded in the natural powers proper to it, subject to ignorance, suffering and the dominion of death, and inclined to sin—an inclination to evil that is called concupiscence" (*CCC*, 405).

The antidote for Original Sin is Baptism, through which the grace of life in Christ is imparted. Baptism into Christ Jesus takes away Original Sin and turns the one who is baptized back to God. Sadly, the consequences of Original Sin remain in our lives for now, making us susceptible to moral weakness. This means that throughout our time on earth we are engaged in a spiritual battle, and we must remain vigilant against the wiles of the enemy, the devil, who "prowls about the world seeking the ruin of souls" (cf. *CCC*, 405; St. Michael the Archangel prayer).

30.   What is the hope for humanity?

The tragic legacy of Original Sin in our lives and in our world is not difficult to see. "Ignorance of the fact that man has a wounded nature inclined to evil gives rise to serious errors in the areas of education, politics, social action and morals" (*CCC*, 407, citing John Paul II).

Although Original Sin deprived our first parents of their original, privileged relationship with God and life in the Garden of Eden, God did not abandon human beings. Immediately following our first parents' act of disobedience, God made a striking promise that is known as the *protoevangelium*, the first proclamation of the Gospel: "I will put enmity between you and the woman, and between your offspring and hers; he will strike at your head, and you will strike his heel" (Gn 3:15 NRSV). In this passage, God foretells the coming of the Messiah, a descendant of the woman who will be victorious in battle with the ancient serpent and who will not only restore the human race but make all things new (cf. *CCC*, 410, Rv 21:5).

There will be a "New Adam" to confront the evil brought about by the first Adam's disobedience: "For since death came through a human being, the resurrection of the dead came also through a human being. For just as in Adam all die, so too in Christ shall all be brought to life"

(1 Cor 15:21–22). Jesus Christ is the New Adam, who is "obedient to death, even death on a cross" (Phil 2:8).

Likewise, many wise and learned Christians in the early centuries of the Church identified the Blessed Virgin Mary as the "New Eve," for through her obedience to the will of God, her Son, the Savior, would enter the world. "And thus also it was that the knot of Eve's disobedience was loosed by the obedience of Mary. For what the virgin Eve had bound fast through unbelief, the virgin Mary set free through faith."[1]

Summary and Reflection

Our creeds contain a summary of Catholic beliefs. The creeds consist of statements of belief concerning God the Father, our Creator; Jesus Christ, the Son; and the Holy Spirit, the Third Divine Person of the Blessed Trinity. However, it is God's gift of faith that allows us to recite these statements of belief in confidence and helps each of us to find answers to what and why we believe.

Delving into the mysteries and wonders of creation leads us to discover that sin and evil befell the world through a choice made by our first parents. Further reflection through the insight of faith allows us to consider how the spread of evil in the world is an effect of that Original Sin we did not personally commit. However, God did not withhold as a secret his plan to rectify sin and evil. Through his promise of a Savior, the New Adam birthed by the New Eve, he made it possible for all of us to experience abundant life in him.

● *Creation*

The Book of Genesis teaches that God takes the initiative in his relationship with the human person. He takes the initiative with you in a personal manner. How have you experienced God reaching out to you? How did you experience the initial stirrings of his calling you to a deep, personal relationship?

☉ *Fall*

Sin puts us at a distance from God, sometimes in small ways, sometimes in significant and serious ways. How do you deal with things in your life that distract you from God and that tempt you to let other things get in the way of your relationship with God?

✝ *Redemption*

Even though our first parents sinned, God did not abandon them. Rather, God promised redemption, and delivered on that promise by sending into the world his only begotten Son, our Lord and Savior, Jesus Christ. In what way have you been thrown a lifeline by the Lord? How have you experienced Jesus as the Good Shepherd who brings you back to where you need to be?

☉ *Restoration*

Who are the great witnesses of faith in your life? What are some of their habits of discipleship that you would like to imitate more closely? What resolution will you make to embrace a habit that will keep you close to the Lord every day of your life?

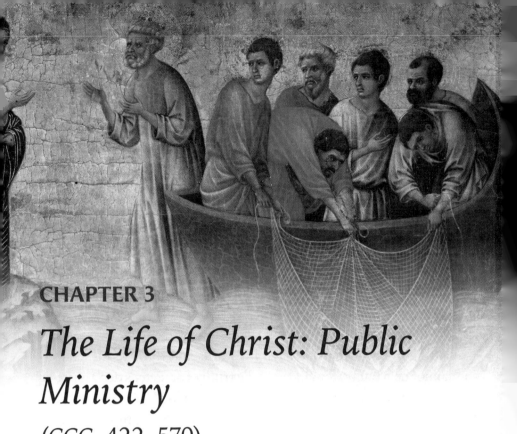

CHAPTER 3

The Life of Christ: Public Ministry

(CCC, 422–570)

A young man who had been raised in the Catholic faith and who had been very active in his parish growing up returned home for Christmas after his first semester in college. His mother asked him how he liked going to the Catholic student parish on campus. Much to his mother's dismay, the young man said that he hadn't attended Mass since starting college. He explained that one of his professors had taught that "the Christian faith and religion itself is a human invention, and that those who are truly intelligent can easily dismiss Christianity as a pious myth, a moralistic story, or a delusional fantasy." At first, the young man's mother was at a loss for words. As she pondered her son's unexpected pronouncement, she knew instinctively how she would respond.

"What about Jesus?" she asked her son.

Christianity is not a philosophy, nor is it a program. Christianity is not a set of rules or doctrines. Christianity is not worship and ritual. The very heart of the Christian faith is the *person of Jesus Christ*, born in a particular time and place in fulfillment of promises and prophecies. Jesus Christ is the Eternal Word of God. He is God who became incarnate as a human being to dwell among us, to teach us how to live, to die for our sins, and to rise again to give us the hope of everlasting life.

Jesus Christ is the eternal Son of God, the Second Person of the Holy Trinity. He treats us as friends, not subjects or slaves. Through this one man, we find answers to our deepest questions, consolation in times of sorrow, and fulfillment of our most profound desires. No program or philosophy can make such promises. Jesus Christ is hardly a pious myth or purveyor of a moralistic story or delusional fantasy—even his enemies testified to his presence, life-giving words, and miraculous works.

Getting to know Jesus through his words and through his Church, one cannot help but be convinced of the truth of St. Peter's declaration of faith: "You are the Messiah, the Son of the living God" (Mt 16:16, cf. *CCC*, 422–429). The key question for any person who seeks meaning, purpose, and direction in life is the one posed by the mother of the young man: "What about Jesus?"

31.   What is the meaning of the name "Jesus"?

"Jesus" was a common first name among Jews in the first century, and the name quite literally means "God saves." The Scriptures are clear that the name "Jesus" was chosen by God and made known through the archangel Gabriel at the Annunciation (cf. Lk 1:31). "Jesus" is etymologically similar to "Joshua," the name of the famous figure in the Bible closely connected to the Exodus. God saved his people from slavery in the Exodus and led them through the desert to the Promised Land. God also gave his people his law, the Ten Commandments, to guide them away from sin and onto the path of holiness. As Joshua was a key figure in the Exodus, so would Jesus be the one who would establish a new and everlasting covenant with his people, to save us from the power of sin and to lead us to heaven.

Because "Jesus" is the name of the one who saves us, it is the most powerful name in the world when spoken in prayer: "Because of this,

God greatly exalted him and bestowed on him the name that is above every name, that at the name of Jesus every knee should bend, of those in heaven and on earth and under the earth, and every tongue confess that Jesus Christ is Lord, to the glory of God the Father" (Phil 2:9–11, cf. *CCC*, 430–435).

32.   Why is Jesus called "Christ"?

"Christ" is not the family name of Jesus. In his day, Jesus would have been known as "Jesus, son of Joseph" or "Jesus of Nazareth." "Christ" is from the Greek word *christos*, which means "the anointed one." In Hebrew, "Christ" is translated as "Messiah."

While in Jesus's day one would be ceremonially anointed as a prophet, a priest of the Temple, or as king of Israel, the name "Christ" is fitting for Jesus because he fulfills perfectly his mission as Messiah, being the prophet who would announce the Good News, the priest who would offer the perfect sacrifice of his Body and Blood upon the Cross, and the king (cf. Rv 19:16) who would exercise dominion over all creation.

Unlike others who were anointed ceremonially by human hands, Jesus was consecrated in the Holy Spirit from all ages by the Father who sent him into the world. At his birth, the angels announced to the shepherds his messianic nature and mission: "Do not be afraid; for behold, I proclaim to you good news of great joy that will be for all the people. For today in the city of David a savior has been born for you who is Messiah and Lord" (Lk 2:10–11).

Some in Jesus's day expected the Messiah to be a political leader who would reestablish Israel as an independent nation, but Jesus would reveal himself as a Messiah whose kingdom is not of this world (cf. Jn 18:36). Instead, Jesus's throne would be a cross, and his crown would be made of thorns. The Christ, the Messiah, would be the Suffering Servant who would give his life as a ransom for many (cf. Mt 20:28, *CCC*, 436–440).

33.   How can we say that Jesus is the Only Son of God?

The term *Son of God* is used in the Old Testament to refer to a godly person, without carrying any connotation of divinity. For example, the kings in the line of David are called sons of God (cf. 2 Sm 7:14). Perhaps some people in Jesus's day called him Son of God because of his wise discourse and mighty deeds. As he continued to reveal himself to those of his day, however, the uniqueness of Jesus's Sonship became quite clear. When Simon Peter declared, "You are the Messiah, the Son of the living God," Jesus responded, "flesh and blood has not revealed this to you, but my heavenly Father" (Mt 16:16–17). Convinced that it was no mere man who had died upon the Cross, the centurion and others proclaimed, "Truly, this was the Son of God!" (Mt 27:54). On the occasions of Jesus's Baptism and Transfiguration, the Scriptures testify that the Father's voice came from the heavens, speaking of him as "my beloved Son" (cf. Mt 3:17, cf. Mt 17:5). Jesus is revealed as Son of God in an unprecedented manner. When Christians speak of Jesus as the Son of God, we do so in testimony to his unique relationship to the Father and to his eternal divinity (cf. *CCC*, 441–445).

34.   What does it mean to say, "Jesus is Lord"?

In the United Kingdom and Commonwealth nations, the title *Lord* is bestowed out of deep respect for a gentleman's accomplishments or status in society. In Jesus's day the title carried the same significance. Those who addressed Jesus as "Lord" did so to show respect for his wise teaching and admiration for his wondrous miracles. Yet there was a deeper significance to the word *Lord* than was understood by faithful Jews.

The divine name YHWH, translated as "I Am Who I Am," was considered an ineffable name. Although the divine name is written in the Hebrew Bible, it was never spoken aloud by those who read the Scriptures in the synagogue. The divine name was spoken aloud only once a year, and then only by the high priest within the Temple's Holy of Holies.

Events in the Life of Jesus

Jesus is truly human and truly divine. Jesus comes to reveal the face of God, something he does through the wisdom of his teachings and the compassion of his miracles. He bears witness to his divinity by calming storms and quieting waves, and, in a practice that will get him in great trouble with the authorities, he publicly forgives the sins of others. Jesus resolutely makes his way to Jerusalem, where he knows he will be arrested, put to death, and then rise again on the third day.

Note these key events in the life of Jesus, their significance, and when they are celebrated by the Church today.

Event	Significance	Celebration
God prepares his people for the coming of the Messiah (cf. *CCC*, 522)	Everything in the Old Testament finds its fulfillment in Christ.	Season of Advent (four weeks before Christmas)
John the Baptist as the forerunner of Christ (cf. *CCC*, 523)	The immediate preparation of God's People for the coming of the Messiah.	Feast of the Baptism of the Lord (a few weeks after Christmas)

Event	Significance	Celebration
The Annunciation (cf. CCC, 494)	The archangel Gabriel announces to the Virgin Mary that she is to be the mother of the Messiah.	Solemnity of the Annunciation, March 25
The birth of Christ	Jesus is born into a poor family amidst adverse circumstances. "In this poverty, heaven's glory was made manifest" (CCC, 525).	Solemnity of Christmas, December 25
The Circumcision	The first shedding of the Savior's blood; Jesus is incorporated into God's covenant with Abraham (cf. CCC, 527).	Traditionally observed on January 1
The Epiphany	The Magi find the Christ child, a sign that the Gentiles will find salvation through Christ (cf. CCC, 529).	Traditionally January 6, or two Sundays after Christmas
The presentation in the Temple	Jesus is shown to be the firstborn Son who belongs to the Father (cf. CCC, 529).	February 2
The flight into Egypt and the massacre of the Holy Innocents	Jesus is marked for persecution his entire life (cf. CCC, 530).	Feast of the Holy Innocents, December 28
The finding in the Temple	Jesus shows his profound connection to his heavenly Father from the earliest years (cf. CCC, 534).	Often recalled on the Feast of the Holy Family, the Sunday after Christmas

Event	Significance	Celebration
Jesus is baptized by St. John the Baptist	The Sacrament of Baptism is prefigured, through which Christians are reborn in water and the Holy Spirit and walk in newness of life (cf. *CCC*, 535–537).	The Feast of the Baptism of the Lord, usually on the Sunday after Epiphany
Jesus's temptations in the desert	Jesus's forty days in the desert recall the forty years spent in the desert by the people of Israel (cf. *CCC*, 538–540).	The season of Lent, especially the first Sunday of Lent
Jesus proclaims the Kingdom	Jesus draws others into the mystery of the Kingdom of God through the preaching of parables and the working of signs and wonders (cf. *CCC*, 541–550).	The Church meditates on these events throughout the whole of the year, especially during the Sundays of Ordinary Time
The Transfiguration	Jesus confirms St. Peter's confession of faith (cf. Mt 16:18ff) and prepares his Apostles for the scandal of the Crucifixion (cf. *CCC*, 554–556).	The Feast of the Transfiguration (August 6) and also the second Sunday of Lent
Jesus's messianic entrance into Jerusalem	Residents of Jerusalem, the city of King David, welcome Jesus with palm branches, acclaiming him as Messiah and King (cf. *CCC*, 558–560).	Palm Sunday (the Sunday before Easter)

Event	Significance	Celebration
The Last Supper, and the betrayal of Jesus	Jesus institutes the Sacrament of the Eucharist and the Sacrament of Holy Orders as he gathers his Apostles for a Passover meal, "the memorial of his voluntary offering to the Father for the salvation of men" (CCC, 610).	Holy Thursday
The Death of the Lord	Our Lord offers himself on the Cross as the perfect sacrifice for the forgiveness of sins (cf. CCC, 613–618).	Good Friday
The Lord's burial and descent into hell	Christ enters into the realm of the dead to free the just souls who lived and died before him (cf. CCC, 631–635).	Holy Saturday
The Resurrection	Jesus rises from the dead on the third day, in fulfillment of the Scriptures (cf. CCC, 638–655).	Easter Sunday
The Ascension	Jesus with his human nature ascends into heaven, taking his place at the right hand of the Father (cf. CCC, 659–664).	The Solemnity of the Ascension, celebrated either on the fortieth day of the Easter Season or in place of the seventh Sunday of Easter

Event	Significance	Celebration
The descent of the Holy Spirit	The Holy Spirit descends upon the Apostles gathered at prayer with the Blessed Mother, giving them the strength to proclaim the Good News to the nations (cf. *CCC*, 731–732).	Pentecost Sunday, fifty days after Easter

Instead, on other occasions, the word *Adonai* was substituted. *Adonai* is Hebrew for the word *Lord*. In fact, in your Bible, it is highly likely that throughout the Old Testament you will find the name LORD written in capital letters. Out of deep respect, LORD is substituted for every use of the divine name YHWH.

After Jesus's Resurrection, the term *Lord* is no longer used as a mere sign of respect, but as a profession of belief in his divinity. The Apostle Thomas sees the Risen Lord and falls to his knees in adoration saying, "My Lord and my God!" (Jn 20:28). There is an even deeper significance to speaking of Jesus as Lord. The Romans who persecuted Christians in the first three centuries regarded their emperor as divine. Romans would often exclaim, "Caesar is Lord!" Christians of that time risked a death sentence by contradicting their Roman neighbors and exclaiming instead, "Jesus is Lord!" (cf. *CCC*, 446–451).

35. What does it mean to say that the "Word became flesh"?

God created the world by means of his all-powerful Word: "Then God said: Let there be light, and there was light" (Gn 1:3). St. John begins his Gospel by echoing the first words of the Book of Genesis, the words that recall the creative activity of God's Word: "In the beginning was the Word, and the Word was with God, and the Word was God. He was in the beginning with God. All things came to be through him, and without him nothing came to be" (Jn 1:1–3). St. John goes on to say, "And the Word became flesh and made his dwelling among us" (Jn 1:14).

The Word becoming flesh is known as the *Incarnation*. The root of this term is the Latin word *carne*, which means "flesh." God takes flesh in the person of Jesus Christ, the eternal Word. This is at the heart of what it means to profess the Christian faith:

> Have among yourselves the same attitude that is also yours in Christ Jesus, Who, though he was in the form of God, did not regard equality with God something to be grasped. Rather, he emptied himself, taking the form of a slave, coming in human likeness; and found human in appearance, he humbled himself, becoming obedient to death, even death on a cross. (Phil 2:5–8)

God became flesh so that we might be saved. He takes up our flesh, our human nature, body and soul, so that we might enter into relationship with him and become like him. This is summed up in the prayer the priest offers at Mass when adding a drop of water to the wine: "By the mystery of this water and wine may we come to share in the divinity of Christ who humbled himself to share in our humanity" (*Roman Missal*, cf. *CCC*, 456–463).

36.   How did the Church respond to heresies about Jesus's divinity?

Early Christians found themselves persecuted mercilessly by authorities of the Roman Empire. The first three centuries of the Church were marked by the heroic witness of women and men, girls and boys, who bravely died for Christ rather than renouncing their faith. During those years of persecution, there was little opportunity to organize church teachings or write them down in a systematic way. As a result, errors crept in from place to place about the humanity and divinity of Jesus Christ.

When Christianity was legalized by the emperor Constantine in AD 313, the Church was finally in a position to dispute errors and to clarify that Jesus Christ is truly God and truly man, without confusion and without mixture. Jesus—the Word who became flesh—was truly man while at the same time being truly God. The Church responded to several specific heresies:

- Against the heresy of Gnostic Docetism, which denied the humanity of Jesus Christ and taught that Jesus was God simply taking the guise of a human being, the Church responded that Jesus is God incarnate, God "come in the flesh" (*CCC*, 465).

- Against Paul of Samosata and others who denied the divinity of Christ, the Church affirmed in a third-century council in Antioch that "Jesus Christ is Son of God by nature and not by adoption" (*CCC*, 465). Jesus was not simply a human being whom God chose or "adopted" for a particular role.

- Against the heresy of Arianism that claimed "the Son of God 'came to be from things that were not,' and that he was 'from another substance' than that of the Father," the Council of Nicaea in 325 responded with the Nicene Creed that the Son of God is "begotten not made, of the same substance [consubstantial] with the Father" (Council of Nicaea, cited in *CCC*, 465).

- Against the heresy of Nestorianism, which regarded "Christ as a human person joined to the divine person of God's Son," the Third Council of Ephesus in 451 responded that "the Word, uniting to himself in his person the flesh animated by a rational soul, became man." Because of this, the Council of Ephesus also showed that "Mary truly became the Mother of God by the human conception of the Son of God in her womb: 'Mother of God, not that the nature of the Word or his divinity received the beginning of its existence from the holy Virgin, but that, since the holy body, animated by a rational soul, which the Word of God united to himself according to the hypostasis, was born from her, the Word is said to be born according to the flesh'" (Council of Ephesus, cited in *CCC*, 466).

- Against the heresy of Monophysitism, which taught that the human nature of Jesus ceased to exist when it was assumed by the Divine Person of God the Son, the Council of Chalcedon in 451 responded: "Following the holy Fathers, we unanimously teach and confess one and the same Son, our Lord Jesus Christ: the same perfect in divinity and perfect in humanity, the same truly God and truly man, composed of rational soul and body; consubstantial with the Father as to his divinity and consubstantial with us as to his humanity; 'like us in all things but sin.' He was begotten from the Father before all ages as to his divinity and in these last days, for us and for our salvation, was born as to his humanity of the virgin Mary, the Mother of God" (Council of Chalcedon, cited in *CCC*, 467).

- Against those who "made of Christ's human nature a kind of personal subject," the Council of Constantinople in 553 said that there is only one person in Jesus Christ, a Divine Person who has two natures, human and divine. Everything that happens in the human nature of Jesus Christ is to be attributed to his Divine Person, his miracles as well as his death on the Cross: "He who was crucified in the flesh, our Lord Jesus Christ, is true God, Lord of glory, and one of the Holy Trinity" (Council of Constantinople, cited in *CCC*, 468).

- Against Apollinarism, which claimed that Christ's human soul was replaced by the divine Word, the Church taught that Christ had a human soul that was assumed by the Son of God. Our Lord's human soul, though assumed by the Son of God, was not unlimited in human knowledge, and so our Lord can properly be said to have "advanced [in] wisdom and age and favor before God and man" (Lk 2:52, cf. *CCC*, 472). At the same time, Christ's human knowledge "expressed the divine life of his person" (*CCC*, 473). Our Lord possessed keen insight into all that he was called to reveal in his earthly ministry and was able to read the hearts of those around him (cf. *CCC*, 474).

- Against Monothelitism, which said that Christ had only one will, and against Monoenergism, which held that Christ had only one energy (or operation), the Third Council of Constantinople in 681 taught that Christ had two wills, human and divine, and also had divine and human operations, and that his wills and operations are not opposed to one another but cooperate for our salvation. The human will of Christ "does not resist or oppose but rather submits to his divine and almighty will" (Council of Constantinople III, cited in *CCC*, 475).

- Against the iconoclasts, who believed that artistic representations of the face of Christ and the saints were graven images and were thereby forbidden by the First Commandment, the Second Council of Nicaea in 787 declared that because the Word of God became flesh and showed himself to humanity in a finite body, it is thereby legitimate that his body be represented in artwork. While approving the religious art that adorns nearly every Catholic church building, the Council of Nicaea also affirmed that when a believer shows great respect (veneration) for sacred art depicting our Lord, the one "who venerates the icon is venerating in it the person of the one depicted" (Council of Nicaea II, cited in *CCC*, 477).

Can you see where some of these heresies have crept into false beliefs today? For example, some continue to doubt that Mary is truly the Mother of God. Others claim that Catholics have made idols out of statues. Catholics treasure and display religious art because, like the picture of a loved one, religious art reminds us of and draws us closer to the God who loves us so much "that he gave his only Son, so that everyone who believes in him might not perish but might have eternal life" (Jn 3:16, cf. *CCC*, 476–477).

37. What can we learn about Jesus from the events of his life?

Every moment that Jesus spent upon this earth teaches us a profound lesson, so much so that the Church urges us to read about and meditate upon his life on a daily basis from Scripture. Every day at Mass, a selection from one of the four Gospels is presented, a moment from the life of Christ that gives us insight into his Person, his message, and his plan for our lives. Many Catholics find it helpful to read and study the Gospel of the day, which is referenced at the United States Conference of Catholic Bishops website under the heading "Daily Readings" (www.usccb.org).

Another way to reflect and pray on the life of Jesus is by reciting the Holy Rosary each day. The intention of the Rosary is to think about key events in the life of Jesus around his entrance into our world (joyful mysteries, prayed on Mondays and Saturdays), his public life (luminous mysteries, prayed on Thursdays), his suffering and Death (sorrowful mysteries, prayed on Tuesdays and Fridays), and his Resurrection (glorious mysteries, prayed on Wednesdays and Sundays).

Summary and Reflection

Having great familiarity with the content of the Gospels keeps one focused upon Jesus. Christianity is not a philosophy, nor is it a program of self-improvement. The Christian life is all about a person, namely Jesus Christ, and participation in his life through the Church he established and the sacraments he instituted. He is the Way, the Truth, and the Life (cf. Jn 14:6).

The Gospels do not contain a record of everything that Jesus did, nor were they written to satisfy our every curiosity. Rather, the Gospels were written "that you may [come to] believe that Jesus is the Messiah, the Son of God, and that through this belief you may have life in his name" (Jn 20:31).

The public ministry of Jesus Christ culminates in the unfolding of the Paschal Mystery, the events of his Death, Resurrection, and Ascension into heaven, the subject of Chapter 4.

◖ *Creation*

You were made for union with Christ. Which parable of Jesus is your favorite?

○ *Fall*

What do we learn from the misunderstandings about Jesus that led to so many heresies in the first millennium? When do you sense a misunderstanding about Jesus today among your peers and acquaintances?

✝ *Redemption*

Of the names "Jesus," "Christ," "Son of God," and "Lord," which one do you use most in your prayer? With which name were you most familiar in previous years, and how has that changed throughout your life, if it has changed at all?

◑ *Restoration*

In his miracles, Jesus restores wholeness and well-being to the blind, the deaf, the crippled, and even the dead. How have you experienced the restorative power of Jesus in your life or in the lives of others?

CHAPTER 4

The Life of Christ: The Paschal Mystery

(CCC, 571–682)

The Cross of Jesus is arguably the most prominent religious symbol in the world. Whether it be mounted atop a grand steeple or worn around the neck as jewelry, the Cross of Jesus can be found on every continent and represented in nearly every artistic style.

First used by the Persians and the Carthaginians, crucifixion on a cross was a torturous method of capital punishment, inflicting severe pain on every part of the human body, resulting in death by asphyxiation after far too many cruel hours. The Roman soldiers who crucified Jesus as well as those who witnessed his death would never have imagined the prominence of the Cross two thousand years later.

In spite of the horrific connotations of the Cross, St. Paul says, "we proclaim Christ crucified, a stumbling block to Jews and foolishness to Gentiles, but to those who are called, Jews and Greeks alike, Christ the power of God and the wisdom of God. For the foolishness of God is wiser than human wisdom, and the weakness of God is stronger than human strength" (1 Cor 1:23–25). For St. Paul, the agonizing death our Lord accepted upon the Cross would reveal a far greater love than the world has ever known and would open for us the gates of heaven. In the light of the Resurrection, the Cross of Jesus stands at the center of the Good News meant for the whole world (cf. *CCC*, 571).

These events that lead to our salvation are a great mystery. We speak of our Lord's saving Death and glorious Resurrection as the *Paschal Mystery*, from the Hebrew word *pesach*, which means "Passover," for these great events not only took place during the time of Passover but represent the definitive triumph of goodness over evil, life over death, and the freedom of God's children over slavery to sin.

38. Was Jesus in control of the events around his Passion, Death, and Resurrection?

Several times in the Gospels the crowds make moves to kill Jesus, only to have him vanish from their midst. These are not moments of cowardice on the part of Jesus but rather, indications that he is in complete control of the means by which he will manifest the glory of his Passion, Death, and Resurrection. He chooses to offer the perfect sacrifice of his Body and Blood not just anywhere, but in Jerusalem, and not just at any time, but during the annual commemoration of Passover. Jesus desires to teach us the full significance of the Paschal Mystery through each of the details of his Death and Resurrection (cf. *CCC*, 557).

39. What is the significance of Jesus's triumphant entry into Jerusalem?

Every year on Palm Sunday, in one of the most popular and colorful liturgies of the church year, the faithful hold blessed palms in their hands as the priest enters the church. In so doing, they recall how the people of Jerusalem greeted Jesus with palm branches and with shouts of "Hosanna," a word that means "give salvation!" Their greeting was one usually reserved for royalty and would serve on this occasion to acclaim the coming into their city of the Messiah, the King of Kings. In the yearly Palm Sunday liturgy at the beginning of Holy Week, the faithful acclaim Jesus Christ as the Lord of their lives and prepare to walk with him through the saving and redemptive events of Holy Week (cf. *CCC*, 559–560).

40. What is the significance of Jesus being betrayed by Judas for thirty pieces of silver?

At the most basic level, the betrayal of Jesus by Judas, and his denial by St. Peter, shows just how fragile the Apostles were prior to our Lord's Resurrection. Both turned their backs on the Lord in his hour of need. Judas would hang himself in despair over his sin, but in a moment of great grace after the Resurrection, St. Peter would experience three times the Lord's forgiveness for his threefold denial of knowing Jesus (cf. Jn 21:15–19).

The betrayal of Judas brings to mind another famous betrayal, that of the Old Testament patriarch Joseph by his brothers for twenty pieces of silver (cf. Gn 37). Joseph, left for dead by his brothers, would rise to a position of great importance in the court of the Pharaoh of Egypt and would be the means by which his brothers were saved from the ravages of a famine. The account of Joseph is one that prefigures the betrayal, Death, and Resurrection of the One who saves us from sin and death. Also significant is that the thirty pieces of silver is really a pittance, representing the insultingly low wages paid to shepherds of Israel (cf. Zec 11), though enough to buy a potter's field for burial or to pay restitution for the murder of a slave.

41.   Why was Jesus condemned to death?

The Gospels are very clear that Jesus's condemnation to death was the result of his repeated words and actions that caused others to think that he was claiming to be God. Jesus forgave sins and healed on the Sabbath. He settled disputes on his own authority, and he repeatedly used the phrase "I AM" to describe himself, thereby appropriating for himself the very name of God ("YHWH" or "I AM who I AM)." Jesus would even say with great solemnity, "The Father and I are one" (Jn 10:30). By all accounts, he was claiming to be God, which would be the capital sin of blasphemy if it were not true (cf. *CCC*, 574–591).

42.   Are the Jewish people responsible for the death of Jesus?

There is a long and tragic history of Christians mocking and persecuting Jewish people and calling them "Christ killers." Such an outlook is unacceptable for Catholics. While many Jewish authorities of his day had a role in his condemnation, such as Caiaphas, Annas, and the Sanhedrin, "neither all Jews indiscriminately at that time, nor Jews today, can be charged with the crimes committed during his Passion. . . . [T]he Jews should not be spoken of as rejected or accursed as if this followed from holy Scripture" (*Nostra Aetate*, cited in *CCC*, 597).

Many Jewish people of his time remained loyal to Jesus, such as Nicodemus and Joseph of Arimathea. In fact, it was the Roman procurator, Pontius Pilate, who ordered Jesus's Crucifixion, and it was Roman soldiers who put him to death.

Still, there is a broader tradition suggesting that guilt for Jesus's Crucifixion must not be imparted to the Jewish leaders and Roman rulers alone. In fact, Jesus died for all sinners—that is to say, for you and for me. "The Church does not hesitate to impute to Christians the gravest responsibility for the torments inflicted upon Jesus" (*CCC*, 598). St. Francis of Assisi reminds us, "nor did demons crucify him; it is you who have crucified him and crucify him still, when you delight in your vices and sins" (cited in *CCC*, 598). All sinners were the authors of Christ's Passion.

43. What was accomplished by the death of Jesus on the Cross?

St. Paul teaches clearly, "Christ died for our sins in accordance with the scriptures" (1 Cor 15:3). The death of Jesus upon the Cross fulfills the prophecy of Isaiah, uttered centuries before: "Yet it was our pain that he bore, our sufferings he endured. We thought of him as stricken, struck down by God and afflicted, But he was pierced for our sins, crushed for our iniquity. He bore the punishment that makes us whole, by his wounds we were healed" (Is 53:4–5, cf. *CCC*, 601).

Jesus is the Lamb of God, by whose blood we are saved for all eternity, just as the blood of the Passover lamb brought temporal salvation to the people of Israel. Also, whereas the flesh of the Passover lamb would be eaten every year in memory of the saving event of the Exodus, so too would Jesus leave us the means by which his perfect sacrifice would be re-presented in every offering of the Holy Sacrifice of the Mass. The night before he died, Jesus instituted the Sacrament of the Eucharist, and the Sacrament of Holy Orders by which the Holy Eucharist would be offered until his return in glory. The Death of Christ on the Cross is the culmination of his life of obedience to the Father. By this obedience, the disobedience of Adam is undone.

44. How is the Holy Eucharist a re-presentation of Jesus's sacrifice on the Cross?

The Church teaches with great clarity: "Jesus gave the supreme expression of his free offering of himself at the meal shared with the twelve apostles 'on the night he was betrayed'" (*CCC*, 610). Since that night, the Holy Eucharist has been offered as Jesus commanded: "Do this in memory of me" (Lk 22:19, cf. *CCC*, 610). At every Mass, we take our place at Calvary, at the foot of the Cross of Jesus, and participate in the offering

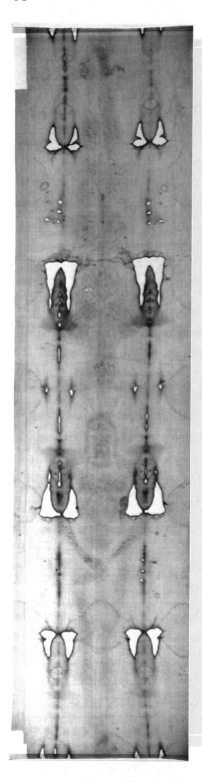

The Shroud of Turin

There may be one piece of historical evidence from the Crucifixion of Christ that remains; it is the linen, or shroud, that Christ was wrapped in after he was taken down from the Cross. Since the fourteenth century, a fourteen-foot linen cloth discovered in the city of Turin (Torino) in northern Italy has been thought to be the actual burial cloth of Christ. It is known as the Shroud of Turin. Pope Benedict XVI, on a visit to Turin in 2010, said that the shroud corresponds to everything the Gospels say about Jesus. For example:

- John 19:34 tells us that the body of the recently expired Jesus was pierced with a lance by a Roman soldier. The shroud has an impression of the torso of a man with a gash measuring six centimeters between his fifth and sixth ribs. Roman soldiers knew human anatomy well enough to deliver a death blow with a lance or spear, exactly through the fifth and sixth ribs, piercing the heart without breaking a bone. Furthermore, the blades of Roman spears in museums measure six centimeters in width.

- Luke 23:53 reports that Joseph of Arimathea wrapped the body of Jesus in a linen cloth before burying it in the tomb. Linen was an expensive material made from flax. The weave of the linen of the shroud is identical to linen cloths found in the Holy Land that date to the first century.

The human blood found on the shroud has been tested with the latest forensic tools, revealing that the blood was not from a living human being but from a dead one. The blood type is AB, the same blood type found in each of the many Eucharistic miracles documented beautifully by Blessed Carlo Acutis, a young man who lived early in the twenty-first century who was adept at computer programming and data collection.

Carbon 14 testing was done on a piece of the shroud in 1988. Scientists no longer trust that datum, for it is known that the testing was done not on the fabric of the shroud itself but on a patch sewn into the shroud after it was damaged in a fire in 1532. Pollen spores on the linen shroud itself can be shown scientifically to have come from within six miles of Jerusalem and from flowers that are indigenous only to the Holy Land.

Other doubts as to the shroud's authenticity have always been present. Many claim that the image was painted onto the cloth, yet no pigment has been found on the shroud, nor does the image correspond to the way in which our crucified Lord was depicted throughout the Middle Ages, with the nail marks passing through the palms of his hands. The man on the shroud has had the nails hammered through his wrists, a practice that has been acknowledged scientifically as the only way a human body could possibly be suspended upon a cross.

Furthermore, when a picture of the shroud was first taken in 1898, the photographer observed that the negative of the photo revealed a positive image. Photography was invented in 1827, making a photographic negative of an image well-known for centuries before nothing short of a miracle. Many believe that the image of the crucified man could only have been left on the shroud by a great burst of energy or light, completely consistent with our faith in the accounts of the Resurrection of Jesus.

The gory details of the man on the shroud reveal him to be a man who was brutally scourged and crowned with thorns, just as is recorded in the Gospels. The shroud reproduces exactly the marks from the scourging, accomplished by two men flogging the man on the shroud from two different directions, exactly as ancient accounts of scourging describe. Marks from the crown of thorns are clearly visible upon the shroud and show a crown that fit upon the head like a cap rather than a wreath.

Our faith in the Resurrection of Jesus is based upon the testimony of eyewitnesses recorded in the Sacred Scriptures, not upon any physical artifact, not even our Lord's empty tomb in Jerusalem. Our faith in the Paschal Mystery would be just as strong if the shroud did not exist. Nevertheless, how providential that God would leave behind an artifact whose true significance would be overlooked by those of earlier ages who did not possess twenty-first-century technology that would be able to date and locate pollen spores, unlock the 3D coding within the shroud, and discover things that we never before imagined about this remarkable piece of cloth.

of his Body and Blood, Soul and Divinity. The Mass is the same sacrifice as the one, perfect sacrifice that Jesus offered upon the Cross, albeit in an unbloody manner (cf. *CCC*, 1367). (More information on the Sacrament of the Eucharist will be shared in Chapter 10.)

45. What does it mean to say that Jesus descended into hell?

After being taken down from the Cross, Jesus was buried in a nearby tomb, thanks to the generosity of St. Joseph of Arimathea (cf. Mt 27:60). His body was wrapped in a linen cloth, with a separate cloth wrapping his head (cf. Jn 20:7). Formal preparation of his body with a mixture of myrrh and aloes would have to wait until the completion of the Sabbath.

Jesus truly died, entering into the realm of the dead, a place that ancient people called *sheol* (Hebrew), or *Hades* (Greek). Those who dwelt there were deprived of the vision of God, whether they be just or unjust. It is this realm to which the Apostles' Creed refers ("he descended into hell"). Jesus did not go to hell to endure further punishment, nor did he go there to destroy it: "Jesus did not descend into hell to deliver the damned, nor to destroy the hell of damnation, but to free the just who had gone before him" (*CCC*, 633). An ancient homily that is part of the Liturgy of the Hours on Holy Saturday morning speaks of Jesus descending into the realm of the dead in search of Adam and Eve, the first parents of the human race. Like the Good Shepherd in search of the lost sheep, Jesus cries out to Adam and Eve, "I am your God, who for your sake have become your son. . . . I order you, O sleeper, to awake. I did not create you to be a prisoner in hell. Rise from the dead, for I am the life of the dead" (cited in *CCC*, 635).

46. Did Jesus really rise from the dead?

All historical evidence points to an early, deep, and widespread belief that Jesus rose from the dead. In a New Testament passage dated to the mid-50s, St. Paul writes the following:

> For I handed on to you as of first importance what I also received:
> that Christ died for our sins in accordance with the scriptures;
> that he was buried; that he was raised on the third day in accor-
> dance with the scriptures; that he appeared to Cephas, then to
> the Twelve. After that, he appeared to more than five hundred
> brothers at once, most of whom are still living, though some
> have fallen asleep. (1 Cor 15:3–6, cf. *CCC*, 639)

St. Paul attested that well over five hundred people saw the Risen Lord and were able to offer testimony to the fact. Furthermore, early Christians were willing to risk persecution and endure martyrdom so as to bear witness to the Resurrection of Jesus. It is unlikely that anyone would risk his or her life for the sake of a fable, a fairy tale, a myth, or a legend. Only for the sake of the truth would a martyr shed blood, and there is no evidence that the early martyrs were gullible fools. In fact, the early martyrs included men and women known for being well-educated and upstanding members of the community. We rightly speak of the Resurrection of Jesus as a historical event (cf. *CCC*, 645–656).

47.   Was Jesus's body resuscitated like that of Lazarus?

Lazarus was raised from the dead by Jesus, but he would later die (cf. John 11:1–44). St. Paul says, "We know that Christ, raised from the dead, dies no more; death no longer has power over him" (Rom 6:9). So, no, Christ's resurrection from the dead was not like that of Lazarus.

The New Testament describes the appearances of the Risen Lord in such a way that we must conclude that the Resurrection is both a historic event and a transcendent event. For example, we can say that the Resurrection is a historic event because Jesus's followers were able to dine with him, touch him, and speak with him. They recognized his appearance when they saw him. Yet there was also something different about Jesus's body than there was before. He walked through locked doors. He was able to conceal and then reveal his identity to Mary Magdalene and also to the disciples on the road to Emmaus. He appeared and disappeared at will.

The Resurrection is also rightly called a transcendent event because Jesus's glorified body is not subject to decay but rather has ascended into heaven, where our Lord sits at the right hand of the Father, victorious over sin and death, fully divine and fully human in his glorified body (cf. *CCC*, 647–650).

48. What is the meaning of Jesus's Ascension into heaven?

At the Resurrection, Jesus's body is glorified. During the forty days after Easter, his glory remains veiled under the appearances of ordinary humanity. At the Ascension, Jesus's humanity irreversibly enters into divine glory. It is only by exception that Jesus will appear again prior to his coming in glory to judge the living and the dead at the end of the age (cf. *CCC*, 659–679).

Just before his Ascension into heaven, Jesus offered his farewell to his Apostles: "Go, therefore and make disciples of all nations, baptizing them in the name of the Father, and of the Son, and of the holy Spirit, teaching them to observe all that I have commanded you. And behold, I am with you always, until the end of the age" (Mt 28:19–20). With great solemnity does Jesus assure his Apostles that he will be with them always. Then he vanishes from their sight, never to be seen again! The irony is palpable, yet the Lord never makes a promise without keeping it. Indeed, though he reigns from heaven, the Lord is fully present to his disciples (including you and me) through his Word, the Sacred Scriptures, through his Church, and through the sacraments of the Church, especially the Sacrament of the Eucharist, through which he is really and truly present in a substantial manner.

Summary and Reflection

The Paschal Mystery is not a puzzle that belongs to a distant era, but the saving activity of Jesus Christ. His sorrowful Passion, his descent into hell, his glorious Resurrection, and his Ascension into heaven is a mystery into which each of us enters as we live out our Baptism and participate in the sacramental life of the Church. Participating in the Paschal Mystery brings us into closer union with the Lord, a life that bids us to put into practice on a daily basis the teachings of our Catholic faith, especially our obligation to look after the poor and less fortunate.

● *Creation*

The Resurrection of Jesus is at the very heart of our Catholic faith. St. Paul says that our faith would be in vain if it were not for the Resurrection (cf. 1 Cor 15:14). How can the Resurrection of Jesus be likened to a new creation, a new beginning, a new life for you?

⊙ *Fall*

Every year during Holy Week the Church recalls with great solemnity the events of our Lord's sorrowful Passion. These moments in the life of Jesus are painful to remember, especially because so much suffering was inflicted wrongfully upon our Savior, whom we love. Why is it important to remember the sufferings of Jesus?

✝ *Redemption*

How would you describe the Paschal Mystery to someone not familiar with that term? What is an example of someone living out the Paschal Mystery in his or her daily life? Who is a holy person in your life who is a clear example of how to live out the Paschal Mystery?

⊙ *Restoration*

How is the Resurrection of Jesus different from the resuscitation of someone whose heart has stopped beating?

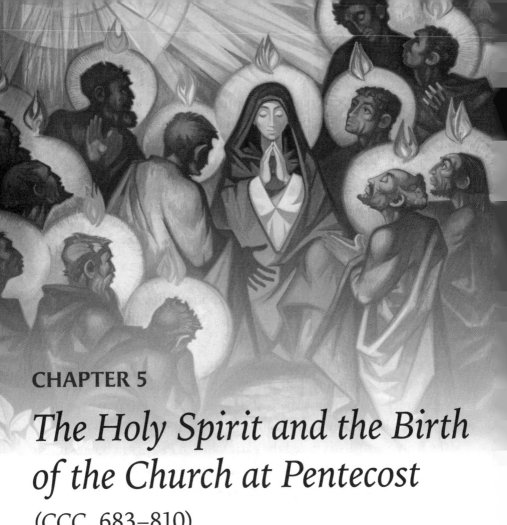

CHAPTER 5

The Holy Spirit and the Birth of the Church at Pentecost
(CCC, 683–810)

Following Jesus's Resurrection and return to the Father in heaven, God's tangible involvement in history did not end. On the day of Pentecost, for Jews a harvest feast fifty days after Passover, a new era of God's relationship with humanity began. The Holy Spirit was given to the Church from the Father and the Son so that the Church could continue the work of Christ in proclaiming and establishing the Kingdom of God.

This means that God remains incarnate in the world in the Church. The Church herself has become the Body of Christ on earth, and each member of the Church is a member of that body. Today it is primarily through the Church that God chooses to be made known, present, and tangible. It is primarily through the Church that God communicates truth and grace. The Church is the "sacrament of salvation," pointing people toward God and making God an accessible reality for them. The miracle of the Church is that despite all of humanity's failings and weaknesses, God loves us so much and places so much trust in us that he is willing to act and to be known through us to those who do not know him as well.

49.   How do we know about the Holy Spirit?

We know about the Holy Spirit through the Sacred Scriptures, where we can find the Holy Spirit in both the Old and New Testaments. The Holy Spirit inspired the writers of the sacred books of the Bible to communicate what God wants us to know for the sake of our salvation. We come to know the Holy Spirit through the life of the Church: in her sacraments, in her apostolic and missionary activity, in the charisms and ministries through which the Church grows, and through the witness of her saints, who offer us clear examples of holiness and virtue (cf. *CCC*, 688).

The Holy Spirit also guided the early Church Fathers in their witness to Sacred Tradition, through which we come to know so much about God's plan for his Church, especially her sacramental life and her moral teaching.

In the sacraments, the Holy Spirit is called down through a prayer known as an *epiclesis*, a Greek word that means "invocation." At Mass near the beginning of the Eucharistic Prayer, the priest extends his hands and prays to God to "send down his Spirit" on the gifts. All Catholics come to know the Holy Spirit in prayer, through which we can offer the powerful invocation, "Come, Holy Spirit!"

50.   What is the connection between the Holy Spirit and anointing?

In the Bible we find many references to the Holy Spirit and anointing. St. John tells us in reference to the Holy Spirit that "you have the anointing that comes from the holy one" (1 Jn 2:20). St. Paul encourages us with the image of the Holy Spirit as a seal on our hearts: "the one who gives us security with you in Christ and who anointed us is God; he has also put his seal upon us and given the Spirit in our hearts as a first installment" (2 Cor 2:21–22). In the life of the Church, an anointing with holy oil takes place within the sacraments, in particular the Sacraments of Baptism, Confirmation, Holy Orders, and the Anointing of the Sick (cf. *CCC*, 695).

Sacramental anointing signifies and makes present the power of both the Holy Spirit and the Spirit of Christ, whose very name means "anointed" ("Messiah" in Hebrew). This profound connection between the Son and the Holy Spirit in the sacramental life of the Church is described by fourth-century St. Gregory of Nyssa using the natural image of the skin being anointed with oil:

> The notion of anointing suggests . . . that there is no distance between the Son and the Spirit. Indeed, just as between the surface of the body and the anointing with oil neither reason nor sensation recognizes any intermediary, so the contact of the Son with the Spirit is immediate, so that anyone who would make contact with the Son by faith must first encounter the oil by contact. In fact there is no part that is not covered by the Holy Spirit. That is why the confession of the Son's Lordship is made in the Holy Spirit by those who receive him, the Spirit coming from all sides to those who approach the Son in faith (St. Gregory of Nyssa, quoted in *CCC*, 690)

Thus the Church speaks of the joint mission of the Son and the Holy Spirit, with both Divine Persons of the Blessed Trinity acting in our lives for the sake of our sanctification and our salvation.

51. Who is the Paraclete?

Paraclete is one of the titles for the Holy Spirit from the New Testament. Jesus says, "I will ask the Father, and he will give you another Advocate to be with you always, the Spirit of truth" (Jn 14:16–17). *Paraclete* is the Greek word that is translated in this verse as "Advocate," or "he who is called to one's side." The term also means "consoler" or "counselor." There are other titles for the Holy Spirit found in the New Testament:

- Spirit of Truth (Jn 16:30)

- Spirit of the Promise (Gal 3:14)

- Spirit of Adoption (Rom 8:15)

- Spirit of Christ (Rom 8:9)

- Spirit of the Lord (2 Cor 3:17)

- Spirit of God (Rom 8:9)

- Spirit of Glory (1 Pt 4:14, cf. *CCC*, 692–693)

52.   What are some other names and descriptions of the Holy Spirit?

The word *spirit* is the English translation of the Greek word *pneuma*, a word familiar to those who are mechanically inclined. We can think of a mechanic using a pneumatic drill, a powerful tool that works through the use of highly pressurized air. *Spirit* is also a translation of the Hebrew word *rûah*, a word whose second syllable has a distinctively breath-like sound. Jesus likens the Holy Spirit to the wind: "The wind blows where it wills, and you can hear the sound it makes, but you do not know where it comes from or where it goes; so it is with everyone who is born of the Spirit" (Jn 3:8).

On the day of Pentecost, the Apostles experienced the Holy Spirit as a "strong, driving wind" (Acts 2:2), akin to the "mighty wind sweeping over the waters" on the first day of creation (Gn 1:2). Although many people think of the creation of the heavens and the earth as a work of God the Father, we must remember that it is actually the work of all Three Persons of the Holy Trinity. Through the Son of God, God's Eternal Word, the world was created, for God said, "let there be light" (Gn 1:3). And through the Holy Spirit and the mighty wind hovering over the waters (cf. Gn 1:2) the world was created. Man himself was brought forth from the dust when God "blew into his nostrils the breath of life, and the man became a living being" (Gn 2:7). Thus "the Word of God and his Breath are at the origin of the being and life of every creature" (*CCC*, 703).

53. In the Creed we say that the Holy Spirit has "spoken through the prophets." What does this mean?

The Holy Spirit inspired the writings of the major and minor prophets of the Old Testament, including the writings that foretold the coming into the world of our Lord, Jesus Christ. The term *prophet* also refers to the central figures who carried out God's plan for his Chosen People. These figures include:

- Abraham, the one who is called the father of many nations (Gn 17:5), a prophecy fulfilled perfectly through his descendant, Jesus, who brings the many nations (the Gentiles) into the New Covenant (cf. *CCC*, 705–706).

- Moses, to whom God revealed himself and his holy name in the burning bush and who brought to God's People both freedom from slavery in Egypt and the Ten Commandments, God's law that would lead them to the fullness of Revelation in Christ (cf. *CCC*, 707–708).

- King David, to whom God promised a kingdom that would last forever, a prophecy fulfilled in the Kingdom of God that was established through the Life, Death, and Resurrection of Christ (cf. *CCC*, 709).

- Those whose sins and infidelity brought about the darkest moment in the history of God's People, the Babylonian exile. Yet in the midst of the exile, God promised through the prophets restoration and new life, a promise that is fulfilled in the life of Christ and his Church (cf. *CCC*, 710).

- The prophet Isaiah, who foretold the coming of the Suffering Servant of God, a prophecy that was fulfilled with haunting accuracy in the Passion and Death of Jesus (cf. *CCC*, 713).

- The prophets Jeremiah, Ezekiel, and Joel, who prophesied the outpouring of the Holy Spirit, a promise wonderfully fulfilled on the day of Pentecost (cf. *CCC*, 715).

- John the Baptist, who stood at the intersection of the Old and New Testaments, the prophet who had the privilege of personally introducing to the world the Lamb of God, who came to take away our sins (cf. *CCC*, 717–720, Jn 1:33–36).

The Holy Spirit has indeed spoken through the prophets, and we can marvel at the way in which those prophecies were fulfilled in the person of Jesus Christ. So too can we marvel at how those prophecies speak to our hearts, as God continues to call us out of the darkness of sin and into the wonderful light of the Lord. The Church encourages us to meditate upon the passages of the Old Testament, for they shed great light upon how the Lord continues to act in our lives in a very personal way.

54. How is the Holy Spirit present throughout the life of Christ?

From the beginning of Jesus's life on earth, his mission can be seen as a fulfillment of the work of the Holy Spirit. In fact, the Church speaks of the "joint mission of the Son and the Holy Spirit" (*CCC*, 727):

- Jesus is conceived in the womb of the Blessed Virgin Mary by the power of the Holy Spirit (cf. *CCC*, 723).

- The Holy Spirit prepared Mary for her role as the mother of the Messiah by his grace, keeping her free from sin from the moment of her conception (cf. *CCC*, 722). (Much more will be said about the Blessed Virgin Mary in Chapter 7.)

- In his baptism by John, Jesus is identified as the one upon whom the Holy Spirit will descend and remain, and that Jesus will baptize "with the Holy Spirit and with fire" (Jn 1:33–36, cf. *CCC*, 719).

- At the Last Supper, Jesus promises the coming of the Holy Spirit: "When the Advocate comes whom I will send you from the Father, the Spirit of truth that proceeds from the Father, he will testify to me" (Jn 15:26, cf. *CCC*, 729).

- The moment of Jesus's death upon the Cross is described by St. John as Jesus "handing over the spirit" (Jn 19:30).

In summary, "the entire mission of the Son and the Holy Spirit, in the fullness of time, is contained in this: that the Son is the one anointed by the Father's Spirit since his Incarnation—Jesus is the Christ, the Messiah" (*CCC*, 727).

55. How is the mission of the Holy Spirit continued in the Resurrection of Jesus?

St. Paul speaks of the Holy Spirit raising Jesus from the dead (cf. Rom 8:11). The Church explains the Resurrection of Jesus as the work of the whole Trinity, the Three Persons acting as one, with each making visible his own characteristics (cf. *CCC*, 648). We can see clearly in the events of the Resurrection and the appearances of Jesus leading to his Ascension the joint mission of the Son and the Holy Spirit:

- In his first appearance to the Apostles on the evening of the Resurrection, Jesus breathed upon them and said, "Receive the holy Spirit. Whose sins you forgive are forgiven them, and whose sins you retain are retained" (Jn 20:22–23). The power of the Holy Spirit is clearly manifest in the authority the Apostles receive to forgive sins, a power that is communicated to us through the Sacrament of Penance and Reconciliation. By giving the Holy Spirit to his Apostles immediately upon seeing them, Jesus shows that "the mission of Christ and the Spirit becomes the mission of the Church" (*CCC*, 730).

- Before his Ascension into heaven, Jesus promised his disciples that the Holy Spirit would soon be poured out upon them: "He presented himself alive to them by many proofs after he had suffered, appearing to them during forty days and speaking about the kingdom of God. While meeting with them, he enjoined them not to depart from Jerusalem, but to wait for 'the promise of the Father about which you have heard me speak; for John baptized with water, but in a few days you will be baptized with the holy Spirit'" (Acts 1:3–5).

"Veni Creator Spiritus"

Every community has its cherished songs and treasured
anthems. The Catholic Church has a robust repertoire of sacred
music, including one particular hymn that is sung on important
occasions, such as the ordination of priests and bishops, the
beginning of church councils and synods, and even the corona-
tion of kings and queens. That hymn is "Veni Creator Spiritus,"
or "Come, Holy Ghost." It is typically sung as Gregorian chant,
but composers have arranged the hymn in a variety of musical
styles. The lyrics date to the ninth century and not only tell of the
qualities of the Holy Spirit, the Third Person of the Holy Trinity,
but speak of the great love and respect that Christian people
have for the Holy Spirit.

Come, Holy Ghost, Creator, come
from thy bright heav'nly throne;
come, take possession of our souls,
and make them all thine own.
Thou who art called the Paraclete,
best gift of God above,
the living spring, the living fire,
sweet unction and true love.
Thou who art sevenfold in thy grace,
finger of God's right hand; his promise,
teaching little ones
to speak and understand.
O guide our minds with thy blest light,
with love our hearts inflame;
and with thy strength, which ne'er decays,
confirm our mortal frame.
Far from us drive our deadly foe;
true peace unto us bring;
and through all perils
lead us safe beneath thy sacred wing.
Through thee may we the Father know,
through thee th'eternal Son,
and thee the Spirit of them both,
thrice-blessed three in One. Amen.

56.   What happened in the upper room on Pentecost?

After Jesus's Ascension into heaven, the Apostles anticipated the fulfillment of his promise of the Holy Spirit, waiting in prayer in the upper room
in which the Last Supper had been celebrated and in which the Lord had
appeared to them on the first Easter night. The Blessed Mother joined the
Apostles in prayer (cf. Acts 1:14).

On the day of Pentecost, "suddenly there came from the sky a noise like a strong driving wind, and it filled the entire house in which they were. Then there appeared to them tongues as of fire, which parted and came to rest on each one of them. And they were all filled with the holy Spirit and began to speak in different tongues, as the Spirit enabled them to proclaim" (Acts 2:1–4, cf. *CCC*, 731–732). The Apostles witnessed their faith in the Resurrection to the Jewish people who had gathered in Jerusalem from many lands to celebrate the traditional harvest feast. Soon the Apostles would bring the message of the Gospel "even to the ends of the earth" (Acts 1:8, cf. *CCC*, 726).

57. Why is Pentecost called the "birthday of the Church"?

Because of all that happened through the power of the Holy Spirit on the first Pentecost, we can rightly call the Feast of Pentecost the birthday of the Church, and it is celebrated as such every year on the fiftieth day of the Easter season.

The annual celebration of Pentecost reminds us of the profound connection between the Holy Spirit and the Church. We can say that the Church shares the very same mission as Christ and the Holy Spirit. We can say this because the Church is a *sacrament* of Christ and the Holy Spirit, "a sign and instrument . . . of communion with God and of unity among all" and the means by which God draws all people to himself (*CCC*, 775).

To be in relationship with God, one must be in communion with the Church. The Church is the sacrament formed by God and the means by which God's plan for human beings is being accomplished. Of all the things that can occupy our attention, our energy, and our life, can we imagine investing ourselves in anything so important as God's plan for humanity?

58. How is the Church both human and divine?

Just as Jesus is both human and divine, so is the Church. Specifically, the Church has a human and visible structure to support her spiritual and divine dimension. It is commonplace to think of the Church as a multinational organization like those that exist in the world of banking, manufacturing, and commerce. Like those organizations, the Church has a hierarchical structure and common features that are easily recognized around the world. That the Church is also of divine origin, and is sustained by the power of the Holy Spirit, is proved by the fact that the Church is still standing after nearly two thousand years. In fact, in spite of the great sins of some of the members and leaders of the Church, the Holy Spirit continues to flourish in the Church (cf. *CCC*, 749).

The Church is where we find the authentic teaching of Jesus, handed down from the Apostles to their successors even to this very day. The Church is where we find the Lord himself in the sacraments that he instituted so as to keep his solemn promise, "I am with you always, until the end of the age" (Mt 28:20, cf. *CCC*, 739). The Church is the one institution on earth that steadfastly advocates for the dignity of the human person from conception until natural death and gives us clear guidance on the most difficult moral questions of our day (cf. *CCC*, 740). The Church is the place of encounter with God, for it is the Holy Spirit who teaches us to pray as we ought (cf. *CCC*, 741). The Church sends forth her sons and daughters in mission, to proclaim the living Lord Jesus and to be his eyes, ears, hands, and feet through the corporal and spiritual works of mercy (cf. *CCC*, 738). These reasons make it possible for us to proclaim, "I believe in the Holy Catholic Church."

Summary and Reflection

The *Catechism of the Catholic Church* teaches that the Church is instituted and structured by Christ to provide a means of grace through the
sacraments that guide us to our eternal destiny (*CCC*, 871–879). Catholics
are often asked to defend that statement by sharing where such teachings
about the Church are found in the Bible.

Perhaps the better question would be, "Where is the teaching about
the Church *not* found in the Bible?" Throughout the Old Testament, the
Church is prefigured by the special place God has for the people of Israel,
holding them as the apple of his eye (cf. *CCC*, 761–762, Zec 2:8). Our Lord
calls together his twelve Apostles from diverse backgrounds and talents

and forms them through his teachings and miracles to be the leaders of the nascent Church. After the day of Pentecost, the Apostles would travel to the ends of the earth, proclaiming the Good News and building up the Church through the sacraments. "Through the Church's sacraments, Christ communicates his Holy and sanctifying Spirit to the members of his body" (*CCC*, 739).

Jesus institutes his Church for you, so that you might be

- born anew through the Sacrament of Baptism

- strengthened in faith through the Sacrament of Confirmation

- nourished for service through the Sacrament of the Eucharist

- absolved of sin through the Sacrament of Penance

- consoled and healed in the Sacrament of the Anointing of the Sick

- at the service of communion in the Church through the Sacrament of Holy Orders or the Sacrament of Matrimony, or in a life of consecrated service to the Lord

Jesus institutes the Catholic Church and promises to guard her through thick and thin so that you might bear the fruit of the Spirit in abundance (cf. *CCC*, 737, Jn 15:8, 16). The Church is for you, and the Church is able to accomplish her mission because of you. Salvation is not a self-help project. We are saved through the Church as members of the Body of Christ (cf. *CCC*, 738).

● Creation

A creative person is often described as being *inspired*, with the artist's works referred to as *inspiring*. Both of these descriptors contain within them the root of the word *spirit*. How was the Holy Spirit active in the creation of the world (cf. Gn 1:2)? How was the Holy Spirit active in the birth of the Church at Pentecost (cf. Acts 2:1–13)?

◐ *Fall*

Sin gets in the way of our relationship with God. Sometimes even well-in-
tentioned words or actions quench or stifle the Holy Spirit (cf. 1 Thes 5:19).
How have you experienced the tragedy of sin interfering with God's plan
for your life?

✝ *Redemption*

Light shines through the darkness, hope overcomes despair, death is never
the last word. How have you recovered from sin and experienced new life
through Christ and the action of the Holy Spirit?

◑ *Restoration*

Reread the words of the "Veni Creator Spiritus" hymn on page 80. What
phrase or phrases will you bring to your personal prayer? Why?

CHAPTER 6

The Church: One, Holy, Catholic, and Apostolic

(CCC, 748–865)

St. Paul wrote about the unity of members of the Church because of their membership in the Body of Christ. A few years after, St. Ignatius of Antioch added that there could be only one Church and that Church was known by her unbroken connection with the Apostles. St. Irenaeus of Lyons (d. 202) maintained that the role of the Church is to unite people with Christ.

The teachings of St. Paul, St. Ignatius, and St. Irenaeus were formalized in the Nicene Creed in the early fourth century. In 381 at the First Council of Constantinople, the words "I believe in one holy, catholic and apostolic church" were officially added to the creed. These characteristics are known as the *four marks of the Church*. The Church does not possess them of herself but from Christ, who is their source. The four marks of the Church help demonstrate how the nature of the Church is an expression of Jesus Christ. Through the Holy Spirit, Christ makes the Church one, holy, catholic, and apostolic.

59.   What is the definition of "Church"?

The word *church* translates a Greek word that means an assembly of people, in this case the people called by God to worship as an assembly. The Church is the people that belongs to God (cf. *CCC*, 751–752). "Church," of course, can also refer to the physical building in which Christian worship takes place. But for our purposes, the *Church* (capitalized) is the people gathered by God to be his own, the community that is made real as a Eucharistic assembly.

60.   What are the origins of the Church?

The Church is born from the heart of Jesus Christ, for from the wounded side of Christ on the Cross there flowed out water and blood (cf. Jn 19:34)— the water of Baptism and the blood of the Holy Eucharist, the sacramental life of the Church. Just as from the side of the sleeping Adam did God bring forth Eve, so is the Church, the Bride of Christ, "born from the pierced heart of Christ hanging dead on the cross" (*CCC*, 766). Jesus gathers his little flock of Apostles and believers and sends them forth to the ends of the earth to proclaim the Good News (cf. Lk 12:32, *CCC*, 759–765).

61.   What are some images of the Church from Scripture?

The Scriptures offer several images that help us to understand the nature of the Church:

- *The Church is the sheepfold*, to which Christ alone grants access. Jesus is the good and faithful shepherd, the one who takes care of his sheep (cf. Ps 23), holding them close to his heart (cf. Is 40:11), searching out those that are lost (cf. Mt:18:12–14), and even going so far as to lay down his life for his flock (cf. Jn 10:11). As members of his sheepfold, we receive the blessings of Christ's wisdom, mercy, and pastoral care (cf. *CCC*, 754).

- *The Church is the cultivated field*, the vineyard planted by God, where Christ is the vine and we are the branches (cf. Jn 15:5). In the Church we put down spiritual roots into the fertile and tilled soil that the Lord himself prepares for us. We have true and eternal life when we remain connected to Christ, the true vine. We rely upon his mercy and compassion to bring us back to life when we have sinned, grafting us back to the vine, the only source of everlasting life (cf. Rom 11:17, *CCC*, 755).

- *The Church is the building of God*, with Christ himself as the foundation and as the very cornerstone once rejected by the builders (cf. Mt 21:42). The Apostles are the pillars (cf. Gal 2:9) of the building, with St. Peter as the solid rock on which Christ builds his Church (cf. Mt 16:18). The Church is not only a building (in a spiritual sense) but the holy temple, the dwelling place of God among human beings, the place where we encounter in Word and sacrament the living and true God, Father, Son, and Holy Spirit (cf. *CCC*, 756). You are a living stone in this building of God: "Like living stones, let yourselves be built into a spiritual house to be a holy priesthood to offer spiritual sacrifices acceptable to God through Jesus Christ" (1 Pt 2:5).

Guided by the Holy Spirit, the Church goes forth on its mission to make disciples of all the nations, thereby building up the Kingdom of God here on earth, a kingdom that will be brought to perfection through great trials, until all are gathered together in the presence of God in the new and eternal Jerusalem (cf. *CCC*, 767–769).

62. How is the Church a mystery?

The Church is the mysterious means by which Christ continues to communicate to human beings both truth and grace. In understanding the Church as a mystery, realize she is much more than a riddle to be solved, a cold case waiting to be cracked. Mystery in the sense of the Church suggests a profound sense of awe and wonder. Think of what it means to explore the mysteries of outer space, the ocean depths, or a single strand of DNA. We are fascinated to the core when we view the latest photos from the James Webb Space Telescope, or when we visit a world-class aquarium, or when we study the latest discoveries of all that is contained within every single cell of living organisms. Furthermore, when we reflect upon the closest and most intimate human relationships, do we not stand in awe and wonder of the mystery of love? These examples are closer to the way we should understand the Church as mystery.

St. Paul offers insight on how the Church is mystery in Ephesians 5 when he compares the relationship of a husband with his wife with the relationship of Christ to his Church:

> So [also] husbands should love their wives as their own bodies. He who loves his wife loves himself. For no one hates his own flesh but rather nourishes and cherishes it, even as Christ does the church, because we are members of his body. "For this reason a man shall leave [his] father and [his] mother and be joined to his wife, and the two shall become one flesh."
>
> This is a great mystery, but I speak in reference to Christ and the church. (Eph 5:28–32)

St. Paul speaks of the great *mystery* of the Church as the Bride of Christ. The Lord refers to himself as "the bridegroom" (Mk 2:19), for just as a faithful husband will lay down his life for the bride he loves, "Christ loved the church and handed himself over for her" (Eph 5:25, cf. *CCC*, 796). "It is in the Church that Christ fulfills and reveals the fullness of his own mystery as the purpose of God's plan: 'to unite all things in him'" (Eph 1:10, cited in *CCC*, 772). The great mystery of Christ's love for the Church, expressed in his perfect sacrifice upon the Cross, is perpetuated in the structure of Church, which is completely ordered toward the holiness of its members (cf. *CCC*, 773).

63.   How is the Church as mystery connected with the sacramental life of the Church?

The Greek word for *mystery* used by St. Paul in his epistles is rendered in Latin by either of two words: *mysterium* or *sacramentum*. This is very important, because the Fathers of the Church recognized the profound connection between the abstract noun *mysterium* and the concrete noun *sacramentum*. Abstract nouns describe realities that cannot be seen, such as freedom, justice, and harmony. Concrete nouns describe things that are visible to the senses. In ancient Rome, a *sacramentum* was a public oath taken before giving testimony in courts of law or when entering the military service of the empire. In the latter case, the soldier would be marked with an indelible tattoo, a sign of his enduring loyalty to his oath. The relationship between mystery and sacrament is essential in understanding not only the meaning of the Church itself but also the *sacramental life* of the Church:

- Jesus Christ is the *mystery* of God made flesh. St. Augustine says, "There is no other mystery of God, except Christ" (cited in *CCC*, 774).

- "The Church, in Christ, is like a sacrament—a sign and instrument, that is, of communion with God and of unity among all men" (*CCC*, 774). The Church is the visible sign and instrument of the inner union between God and human beings, the communion of the members of the Body of Christ, and the means of the greater unity and communion yet to come (cf. *CCC*, 775).

The Seven Sacraments of the Church (called *mysteries* in the Eastern Churches) are the signs and instruments of the Holy Spirit by which grace is bestowed upon the members of the Church at particular moments in their lives. Like the indelible marks of the Roman soldiers, the Sacraments of Baptism, Confirmation, and Holy Orders bestow an inalterable character upon the one who receives them. (The sacramental life of the Church is the subject of the second part of this book.)

Rebuild My Church

St. Francis of Assisi is perhaps the best-known of all the saints who lived after the time of the Apostles. St. Francis is honored and respected not only by Catholics but also by Orthodox, Anglican, and Lutheran Christians. Many who do not have an interest in God or organized religion regard St. Francis as a friend of "Mother Nature" and therefore a spiritual ally in the cause of ecology and conservation. Statues of St. Francis adorn the gardens and bird-baths of many who know very little about his legacy of prayer and service that builds up the Church even to this day.

In 1205, the young Francis was searching for his place in life. The son of a wealthy merchant, Francis took no solace in material possessions. A former soldier and prisoner of war, Francis had lost interest in a life of conquest and gain. Francis paid a visit to the dilapidated church of San Damiano, located outside the walls of the city of Assisi in which he had been raised. Inside the church building that had been ravaged in a time of war, Francis heard a voice from the crucifix that hung above the altar: "Go, Francis, and repair my house, which as you see is falling into ruin."

Francis took this spiritual message literally and gathered the funds for the necessary repairs of the little church. Soon there-after, Francis realized that the voice that spoke to him from the crucifix was looking not for the skills of a general contractor but for a life well lived in radical conformity to the Gospel. Francis would renounce (in dramatic fashion) the possessions he had received from his father and surrender all claims to his inheritance. He would live a life of extreme poverty, begging for his daily provisions. He would dedicate himself to the material and spiritual care of the destitute and the outcast. He would follow a disciplined rule of life that kept him united to Jesus through prayer, the sacraments, and a life of utter simplicity.

Francis found himself followed by many who sought to imitate the way in which he lived out the Gospel. Faithful Christians who could not live the rigorous way that Francis proposed became his allies and supporters, drawing closer to the Lord as they imitated Francis's devotion to Jesus and service to the poor.

In 1208, Pope Innocent III formally approved Francis's rule of life, thus opening the way for orders of Franciscans to fortify the Church spiritually by living out vows of poverty, chastity, and obedience. After more than eight hundred years, the legacy of St. Francis of Assisi lives on, and the Church continues to be repaired and rebuilt by men and women of faith who live in the Franciscan way.

64.　How else is the Church described?

Various names are used to refer to the Church, each with its own wisdom, and no single name exhausts the richness or the depth of our understanding of the Church. Here are a few:

- *People of God.* The Church is full of people, of course! Yet this grouping of people is unlike any other group in history. The Church is a people formed by God, with Jesus Christ as the Head. By Baptism does one become a member of the People of God, being born again by water and the Holy Spirit (cf. Jn 3:3–5). Members of the People of God have the status of being sons and daughters of God, with Christ as her Head, and the New Commandment as her law: "Love one another as I have loved you" (Jn 13:34). The mission of the People of God is to be the light of the world and the salt of the earth (cf. Mt 5:13–16) and to transform the world by our witness to things unseen and hope for things to come. The destiny of God's People "is the Kingdom of God which has been begun by God himself on earth and which must be further extended until it has been brought to perfection by him at the end of time" (*CCC*, 782).

- *Body of Christ.* The Church is intimately connected with Christ, the Head of the Body of Christ. The Lord never stopped inviting his followers to abide in him, to rest in him, to make their dwelling with him. Apart from Christ, a Christian becomes like a branch cut off from the vine (cf. Jn 15:4–5). In no other way is this connection with the Lord more apparent or more powerful than in the faithful sharing through the Holy Eucharist in his very Body and Blood, Soul and Divinity. The Lord says, "Whoever eats my flesh and drinks my blood remains in me and I in him" (Jn 6:56).

- *Temple of the Holy Spirit.* St. Augustine says, "What the soul is to the human body, the Holy Spirit is to the Body of Christ, which is the Church" (cited in *CCC*, 797). As we discovered in Chapter 5, the Church never ceases to pray, "Come, Holy Spirit!" The Church prays that she will be built up into the "dwelling place of God in the Spirit" (Eph 2:22). The Church prays for an outpouring of the gifts of the Holy Spirit, the charisms that build up the Church to the benefit of the whole human family (cf. *CCC*, 799).

65. What is the meaning of each mark of the Church?

The early Church, emerging from a time of intense persecution, expressed her steadfast faith at the Council of Nicaea that the Church of God was marked with four characteristics that were both realized in the present moment and also to be experienced with greater intensity in the years and centuries to come. Those four marks of the Church—one, holy, catholic, and apostolic—will reach their apex when the Church is gathered in heaven. We get a sense of their meaning now:

- *The Church is one.* "The Church is one because of her source" (*CCC*, 813). The source of the Church is the Holy Trinity: God the Father; God the Son, who died to bring all people to the Father; and God the Holy Spirit, who brings about the communion of God's People in the Body of Christ. The Church is one, yet the Church is not uniform. A great richness of diversity exists within the Church, especially in the life and sacred liturgy of the Eastern Churches. This diversity of expression of the faith is not contrary to the unity of the Church, for these particular churches maintain their bonds of communion with the Church through their adherence to the faith that comes from the Apostles, the celebration of the sacraments, and through the apostolic succession in the Sacrament of Holy Orders.

- The Church is one, yet there are wounds to the unity of the Church. Personal sin is always a threat to the Church's unity, for sin always brings about division among people. Throughout history, sin has caused ruptures in the Body of Christ, such as the Great Schism of the Orthodox Churches of AD 1054 and the so-called Protestant Reformation that began in 1517. Tragically, these ruptures have led to the emergence of innumerable Christian groups that have separated themselves from full communion with the Catholic Church. The Church longs for and is working diligently for unity among Christians, so that the Lord's prayer might be fulfilled, "that they may all be one" (Jn 17:21, cf. *CCC*, 813–822).

- *The Church is holy.* As the Bride of Christ, the Church is washed clean by Christ's Precious Blood. Sanctified (made holy) by Christ, the Church in turn sanctifies her members. Through the Church, we are made holy.

  The Church is holy, yet imperfectly so. We are called to repent of our sins, to avail ourselves of the forgiveness and grace that come through the Sacrament of Penance, to change our lives, and to grow in holiness. Holiness brings forth an outpouring of charity. "Charity is the soul of holiness to which all are called" (*CCC*, 826).

The Church sets before us examples of holiness for us to follow, holy men and women of every age and place whose lives have been marked with heroic virtue and fidelity to the Lord's will. The saints are acknowledged as having obtained the vision of God in heaven and are put before us as models and intercessors. First among the saints is the Blessed Virgin Mary, the first to follow the Lord. We can read about the lives of saints for edification, study their writings for inspiration and instruction, and pray to them, asking them to pray with and for us as we strive to follow the Lord's will (cf. *CCC*, 823–829).

- *The Church is catholic.* The word *catholic* is derived from Greek and Latin words that mean "universal." "The Church is catholic because Christ is present in her" (*CCC*, 830). The Church is also catholic because she is on mission to reach out and bring all people on earth to Christ. This was true on the first Pentecost, and it is just as true today, especially as more and more souls become trapped in a culture of atheism, hedonism, and materialism. Even within a culture that is seemingly godless, the human heart longs for what is good, true, and beautiful. The human person cannot be truly happy without God, without reaching to that which transcends the limits of the material world.

- The Church is *catholic* because always and everywhere she points to the Lord Jesus as the Way, the Truth, and the Life. The Church has an obligation and duty to proclaim the Good News in season and out of season, even in the face of ridicule and persecution, all so that others might be drawn into the communion of the Holy Trinity, God the Father, Son, and Holy Spirit (cf. 2 Tm 4:2, *CCC*, 830–831, 849–856).

- The Church is *apostolic*. The word *apostle* means "one who is sent." The Church is apostolic because she is founded upon the Apostles, the ones formed by the Lord and sent forth to bring the Gospel to the ends of the earth. She is apostolic because she passes on to others the faith that comes to us from the Apostles and because she continues to be taught, guided, and sanctified by the successors to the Apostles, the college of bishops assisted by the priests, all in union with the successor to the Apostle St. Peter, the supreme pastor, the pope. The Church is apostolic because she continues the mission of those who were chosen to be witnesses to the Resurrection and who appointed successors by the laying on of hands (cf. 2 Tm 1:6, *CCC*, 857–864).

66. Do Catholics pray to Mary?

Catholics *do* pray to Mary (and to the saints). "To pray" does not mean "to worship." In fact, in court documents the word *pray* appears frequently, always in the context of one party praying that the judge will grant a motion, such as a continuance or a change of venue. "To pray" means to ask in a formal manner, both in court and in our Catholic faith. We ask Our Lady and we ask the saints in a formal way to pray with us and for us as we ask God for his assistance.

Summary and Reflection

Baptism is what makes one a member of the Church. After you are baptized, you are to participate fully in the sacramental life of the Church and to do your part to build up the Church through a life of holiness and witness to the Gospel.

If you have not yet been baptized and are making your way toward Baptism through participation in a catechumenate process at a local parish, you are doing a very good and noble thing, for you are preparing to become a member of the Body of Christ, the Church. Your eventual participation in the life of the Church will be a means by which the Church is built up.

If you have been baptized in a Christian community that is not Catholic, you might be reading this book because you are preparing to enter into the full communion of the Catholic Church through the Sacrament of Penance, by a profession of faith, and then by receiving the Sacraments of Confirmation and Holy Eucharist. Please be sure to get your questions answered so you may have a sense of peace when you are received into the full communion of the Catholic Church.

If you are still discerning whether to take the steps toward the sacraments, please keep reading this book and continue learning more about the Catholic Church. Please become connected with your local Catholic parish and inquire there about how you can learn more about the Catholic faith and how you might grow deeper in love with Jesus and help to build up the Church by your participation in it. Above all else, it is important that you pray, asking God to lead you to the truth and to guide you along the path of eternal life. Only through Jesus Christ can one be saved; pray that you will find him, and then welcome him into your life with an open heart.

⬤ Creation

Just as from the side of the sleeping Adam did God bring forth Eve, so is the Church, the Bride of Christ, born from the blood and water that flow from the pierced side of our Lord who died on the Cross. How does the image of the Church as the Bride of Christ connect with your experience of the Church?

◑ Fall

We know all too well how sinful behavior can ruin careers, break up families, and wreak havoc in our world. The Church is not exempt from her members and even her leaders succumbing to temptation leading to sin that brings about great pain and suffering. How has the tragedy of the sins of prominent leaders within the Church affected your participation in the life of the Church?

✝ Redemption

How is the Church a mystery, akin to the love of husband and wife (cf. Eph 5:25–33)? Describe in your own words.

◔ Restoration

St. Francis heard the call to rebuild the Church. How might God be calling you to be an instrument of restoration and renewal in the Church?

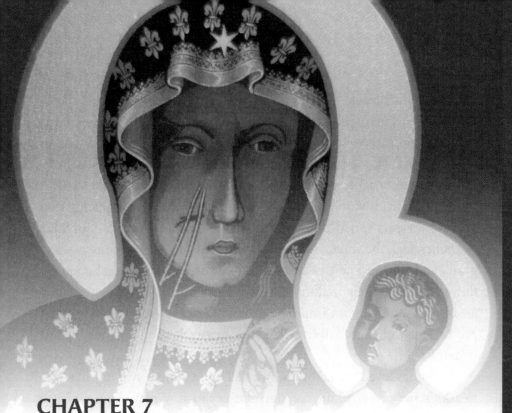

CHAPTER 7

The Blessed Mother
(CCC, 484–511, 721–726, 963–975)

Catholics have a special devotion to the Blessed Mother. Yet this devotion is often misunderstood by non-Catholics who think our reverence for Mary comes at the expense of our relationship with the Lord Jesus Christ. This is not true. "What the Catholic faith believes about Mary is based on what it believes about Christ, and what it teaches about Mary illumines in turn its faith in Christ" (*CCC*, 487).

Everything that Catholics believe about Mary is rooted in the Bible. In the Bible, Mary is present with Jesus at the most significant moments in his life. Mary is never mentioned in the Scriptures except in relation to Jesus. Mary is the one who always points to Jesus. She does so in the Scriptures, and she does so for you and me.

Just as the Blessed Mother was present with Jesus at the most significant moments in his life, so is the Blessed Mother present with the Church at pivotal moments. Mary was with the Apostles in the upper room on the day of Pentecost, the birthday of the Church (cf. Acts 1:14). The Church has consistently asked the intercession of the Blessed Mother at critical moments in her history: at church councils, at the beginning of missionary journeys, at the dedication of church buildings. So, too, do individual Catholics seek the intercession of the Blessed Mother at moments both grand and simple: a newly married couple offers a prayer and bouquet of flowers to her at their wedding Mass, a student prays a Hail Mary before an important exam, an imprisoned bishop facing torture requests her protection, and a football team asks for her to accompany them as they take the field.

Catholics love Our Lady, and we seek to include her in our lives and to ask for her powerful intercession at every turn. We can have no better friend as we embrace the challenge of being faithful disciples of Jesus amidst these turbulent times.

67.   Do Catholics worship Mary?

Catholics do not worship Mary. Worship is due to God alone, Father, Son, and Holy Spirit. Rather, Catholics show Mary the highest honor and respect, following the example of God the Father, who honored her with the privilege of being the mother of our Savior. We honor Mary as our mother according to the order of grace (cf. *CCC*, 969), and in so doing we keep the Fourth Commandment: "Honor your father and mother."

68.   How and why do we speak of the predestination of Mary as the mother of Jesus?

A familiar hymn sung in many Catholic parishes contains this verse in reference to Mary:

> Predestined for Christ by eternal decree,
> God willed you both virgin and mother to be.

Mary is a particular example of predestination in the same way that God chose each of us in Christ "before the foundation of the world, to be holy and without blemish before him. In love he destined us for adoption to himself through Jesus Christ, in accord with the favor of his will" (Eph 1:4–5).

Mary was chosen by God from all eternity to be the mother of his Son. There was no second choice. Through Mary, God keeps his promise made through the prophet Isaiah that "the virgin shall be with child and bear a son" (Is 7:14, Mt 1:24). Mary was predestined by God to say yes to the message of the archangel Gabriel (cf. Lk 1:26ff.), and through her own free will she did so (cf. *CCC*, 488–499). God chose and prepared Mary with special graces, and he foresaw her cooperation with these graces to give her fiat, her consent to be the mother of Jesus.

69.   What is the Immaculate Conception?

The doctrine of the Immaculate Conception teaches that Mary was preserved immune "from all stain of original sin" from the moment of her conception (*CCC*, 491). She was "full of grace" (Lk 1:28) and redeemed by the Blood of her Son from the first moment of her conception in her mother's womb. This was a singular grace and privilege, by virtue of the merits of Jesus Christ, Savior of the human race.

Note that the term *full of grace* spoken by the archangel Gabriel is unique in Sacred Scripture. In its original Greek it means "highly favored one." The only time these words appear in Sacred Scripture is in reference to the Blessed Mother. Mary was preserved from sin from the beginning of her life so that she might have the freedom to be obedient to God's will. Just as a single no of our first parents brought about the Fall, so a single yes on the part of the Blessed Mother brings into the world our Redeemer (cf. *CCC*, 490–494).

70.   How is Mary the "Mother of God"?

The doctrine on the divine motherhood of Mary is rooted in Scripture when her kinswoman Elizabeth asks Mary, "how does this happen to me, that the mother of my Lord should come to me?" (Lk 1:43).

Our Lady of Guadalupe

Franciscan friars arrived in Mexico in 1524 for the express purpose of sharing the Gospel with the indigenous people and baptizing them into the Church. For seven years, their efforts to spread the Gospel resulted in few conversions among the Aztec people. Then, suddenly, apathy turned to fervor. Nine million people would be baptized over the next seven years beginning in 1531, often in groups numbering up to ten thousand. What caused this dramatic change of heart?

In December 1531, an Aztec farmer named Juan Diego encountered a beautiful woman on the hills of Tepeyac near Mexico City. This was the first apparition of Mary in the New World. She asked Juan Diego to tell the local bishop to build a church on the site where they were. The bishop was skeptical of Juan Diego's claim and asked for proof. Juan Diego returned to the rocky hillside site of the apparition and gathered roses into his tilma (cloak) even though it was winter and the roses should have been out of bloom.

Unbeknownst to Juan Diego, his tilma carried a more impressive proof, a mysterious image of Our Lady, dressed in native garb and with features typical of a young Aztec woman. When he opened his tilma before the bishop, the roses fell to the floor and the bishop could see the image. This was all the proof he needed of the authenticity of the apparition, and it served as a means by which millions of indigenous people came to be baptized. To this day, the image of Our Lady of Guadalupe on the tilma is preserved in the church that was built where she requested in Mexico City. It is both a source of inspiration for the faithful and a great mystery for the scientific community. Several things about the image on the tilma remain inexplicable:

- Though the tilma was an inexpensive garment vulnerable to decay in the hot, humid Mexican climate, and though it was displayed for centuries in the open air, the tilma remains in pristine condition. The tilma remained undamaged after a nearby explosion and an accident involving nitric acid.

- The original image on the tilma does not appear to be painted. Examination of the image under ultraviolet light shows no brush marks, no corrections, and no sketch beneath the image. The origin of the image remains mysterious.

- The eyes of Our Lady tell an amazing story when they are placed under a high-power microscope. There appear in the eyes of Our Lady an image of the bishop and others who first witnessed the miracle of Juan Diego's tilma. Furthermore, the eyes reveal dynamics of ophthalmology unknown before the nineteenth century.

- The more the image has been studied using the latest scientific methods, the more mysterious (or miraculous) the origin of the image becomes.

The Our Lady of Guadalupe apparition was not only the first in the New World but the first officially approved Marian apparition anywhere. Our Lady of Guadalupe is the patroness of the Americas, and her feast day is in the month in which she first appeared to St. Juan Diego, on December 12.

The Church formally defined Mary's divine motherhood at the Council of Ephesus in AD 431 in response to a heresy being taught about the nature of Christ. The question had arisen in the Church whether Jesus Christ was a Divine Person or a human person. The council, affirming the teaching of the Church from the time of the Apostles, stated that Jesus is a Divine Person with a fully human nature and fully divine nature. Hence, because Jesus is a Divine Person (God), and since Mary is the mother of Jesus, Mary is the Mother of God. The teaching of the divine maternity of Mary is not directed at her but toward Jesus, affirming his divinity and humanity. As the Creed states, "true God and true man" (cf. CCC, 495).

Mary is called *Theotokos*, a term meaning "God bearer" or "Mother of God." In a secondary way, we remember that each of us is called to be one who bears Christ into the world in word and deed. Each of us is called to be a God-bearer, following in the example of the Blessed Mother: "While [Jesus] was speaking, a woman from the crowd called out and said to him, 'Blessed is the womb that carried you and the breasts at which you nursed.' He replied, 'Rather, blessed are those who hear the word of God and observe it'" (Lk 11:27–28).

71. What does the Church teach about Mary's perpetual virginity?

The virginal conception of Jesus is a teaching of the Scriptures (cf. Mt 1:18–25, Lk 1:26–38). The vast majority of Christians are united in this belief, for in Mary is the prophecy fulfilled, "the virgin shall conceive" (Is 7:14, Mt 1:24). Jesus's conception is a divine work that surpasses all human understanding and possibility, for nothing is impossible with God (cf. Lk 1:37, CCC, 502–507).

Catholics also believe in the perpetual virginity of Mary. Why was it necessary that Mary remain a virgin throughout her life? The perpetual virginity of Mary has been taught from the earliest days of the Church. The virginal conception of Jesus in the womb of the Blessed Mother was a tremendous gift to her and to the Church. "Christ's birth did not diminish Mary's virginity but sanctified it" (CCC, 499). Why would a woman of deep faith do anything to diminish the virginity that was preserved for her in the birth of Jesus? If God had honored the Blessed Mother with this gift, why would a man of faith like St. Joseph do anything to change Mary's virginal state?

Two objections are often made regarding the perpetual virginity of Mary. The first is a gospel verse referring to St. Joseph: "He had no relations with her until she bore a son" (Mt 1:25). It might seem that the word *until* suggests that marital relations between Joseph and Mary commenced after the birth of Jesus. However, the word *until* does not prove that point. Often, we use *until* in a way that refers to an ongoing state of affairs. For example, one can say, "We have flown the American flag designed by Betsy Ross until this very day." There is nothing in that sentence to suggest that we are going to fly a flag with a very different design today or tomorrow. The Gospel of Matthew has been read and studied by the Church since the first century. In all of that time, Matthew 1:25 has never been used to nullify the long and consistent teaching of the Church about the perpetual virginity of the Blessed Mother.

The second objection to the perpetual virginity of Mary has to do with the multiple Scriptural references to the brothers and sisters of Jesus. We must remember that in Jesus's culture, "brothers and sisters" meant not only siblings but also cousins. The "brothers and sisters" of Jesus mentioned in the Bible are not siblings but close relatives, sons and daughters of other parents. For example, there is a James who is called the brother of Jesus in Matthew 13:55. Yet James is identified as the son of Cleophas and a different Mary in Matthew 10:3 and Matthew 27:56. We know that Jesus had no brothers or sisters because from the Cross, our Lord entrusted the care of his mother to John, the beloved Apostle (cf. Jn 19:25–27). Why would Jesus have done this if he had siblings to care for their mother? Would this not have been a serious affront to them?

The Blessed Mother remained a virgin before, during, and after the birth of her Son, our Lord. Her perpetual virginity was more than a biological reality; it was at the core of her being, for she was fully consecrated to God. Mary's perpetual virginity points also to the Church, which can be considered a virgin mother by receiving the Word of God in faith. By preaching and teaching she brings forth children who are conceived by the Holy Spirit and born of God to a new, immortal life (cf. *CCC*, 507).

In this, Mary provides an example for each of us to follow, regardless of our state in life. Single or married, clergy or religious, each of us is called to strive to be consecrated to the Lord, living each and every day fully open to his will, ready to bear fruit in abundance through the works of mercy (cf. *CCC*, 496–507).

72. The Bible does not speak of the Assumption of Mary into heaven. Why do Catholics teach this doctrine?

Although a description of the Assumption of the Virgin Mary is not found in the Bible, from the earliest days Christians have taught that at the end of her life, Mary was assumed into heaven body and soul. This teaching corresponds with the fact that unlike other figures of the New Testament such as St. Peter and St. Paul, there has never been a claim to relics of the body of the Blessed Mother, nor of a tomb containing her body. Furthermore, the Church has recognized in the Book of Revelation a stunning image of the Blessed Mother in heaven: "A great sign appeared in the sky, a woman clothed with the sun, with the moon under her feet, and on her head a crown of twelve stars" (Rv 12:1).

Just as the Blessed Mother was kept free from the stain of sin from the moment of her conception by a singular participation in the grace won by Christ's death on the Cross, so too is she given a singular participation in his Resurrection by being rescued from the bodily decay and corruption of death. The doctrine of the Assumption of Mary is an anticipation of the resurrection of other Christians, when the mortal bodies of those who persevere in faith will be glorified (cf. *CCC*, 966, 989). In the Blessed Mother's Assumption into heaven we have a sign of the resurrection of our own body: what we are she once was; what she is we shall become.

73. What is the purpose of praying the Holy Rosary?

The Rosary is a journey through the life of Christ. Though we recite many Hail Marys while praying the Rosary, we are focused on Christ's entrance into the world, his Life, his suffering and Death, and his glorious

Resurrection. The Rosary consists of meditations around four sets of mysteries in the life of Christ. For each set of mysteries, we pray five decades consisting of an Our Father, ten Hail Marys, a Glory Be, and often the Fatima Prayer. The four sets of mysteries are all based in Scripture:

Joyful Mysteries	Luminous Mysteries	Sorrowful Mysteries	Glorious Mysteries
1. The Annunciation (Lk 1:26–38; Jn 1:14)	1. The Baptism of Christ in the Jordan (Mt 3:11–17; Mk 1:9–11; Lk 3:15–22; Jn 1:26–34)	1. The Agony in the Garden (Mt 26:36–46; Mk 14:32–42; Lk 22:39–46)	1. The Resurrection (Mt 28:1–10; Mk 16:1–18; Lk 24:1–49; Jn 20:1–29)
2. The Visitation (Lk 1:39–56)	2. The Wedding Feast at Cana (Jn 2:1–12)	2. The Scourging at the Pillar (Mt 27:26; Mk 15:15; Lk 23:16–22; Jn 19:1)	2. The Ascension (Mk 16:19–20; Lk 24:50–51; Acts 1:6–11)
3. The Nativity (Lk 2:6–20; Mt 1:18–25)	3. The Proclamation of the Kingdom (Mk 1:14–15; Mt 5:1–16; Mt 6:33; Mt 7:21)	3. The Crowning with Thorns (Mt 27:29–30; Mk 15:16–20; Jn 19:2–3)	3. The Descent of the Holy Spirit on Pentecost (Acts 2:1–41)
4. The Presentation (Lk 2:22–39)	4. The Transfiguration of Jesus (Mt 17:1–8; Mk 9:2–10; Lk 9:28–36)	4. The Carrying of the Cross (Lk 23:26–32; Mt 27:31–32; Mk 15:21; Lk 23:26–32)	4.The Assumption of the Blessed Virgin Mary (Rv 12:1)
5. The Finding in the Temple (Lk 2:41–51)	5. The Institution of the Holy Eucharist (Mt 26:26–28; Mk 22–25; Lk 22:14–20; Jn 6:33–59)	5. The Crucifixion (Lk 23:33–46; Mt 27:33–54; Mk 15:22–39; Lk 23:33–47; Jn 19:17–37)	5. The Coronation of Mary as Queen of Heaven and Earth (Rv 12:1)

We meditate on these mysteries of the Holy Rosary so that we might imitate what they contain and obtain what they promise. As St. Louis de Montfort stated in *The Secret of the Holy Rosary*, "Just as a painter who wants to do a life-like portrait places the model before his eyes and looks at it before making each stroke, so the Christian must always have before his eyes the life and virtues of Jesus Christ."

The Holy Rosary is a simple prayer to learn, yet it takes a lifetime to master. The many Hail Marys that we pray in a single Rosary are reminders that we do not walk alone on the journey of faith, that the Blessed Mother accompanies us every step along the way. The Blessed Mother loves you. You can always rely upon her powerful intercession to help you maintain your focus and persevere along the path of life.

Summary and Reflection

Five teachings about Mary are essential for Catholics to believe:

- Mary was predestined to be the mother of Jesus.

- Mary was conceived without sin in her mother's womb, a doctrine known as the Immaculate Conception.

- Mary is rightly called *Theotokos*, the Mother of God, according to Christ's human nature.

- Mary remained a virgin before, during, and after the birth of Jesus.

- At the end of her life, Mary was assumed body and soul into heaven, a dogma known as the Assumption of the Blessed Virgin Mary.

All of these beliefs about Mary point to her Son and have roots in Sacred Scripture. Understanding these beliefs helps us to correct some false notions non-Catholics may express about our relationship with the Blessed Mother.

⬤ *Creation*

You were created to be in union with God. What is Mary's role in bringing you closer to God and deeper in your relationship with her Son?

◐ *Fall*

Mary has been described as the "undoer of knots." This ancient description comes from St. Irenaeus, who says "the knot of Eve's disobedience was loosed by the obedience of Mary." How does the life of the

Blessed Mother give you hope in times of difficulty, perhaps even amidst the tumult and challenges of our present day?

✝ Redemption

Mary is an example of fidelity, standing at the Cross of Jesus, faithful to him to the very last. Many artists have depicted Mary at the foot of the Cross or holding her Son after he is taken down from the Cross. What insight or wisdom do you treasure when meditating upon the image of the Blessed Mother at the Cross of Jesus?

☉ Restoration

Every day the Holy Rosary is prayed by millions of people around the world who strive to meditate upon the mysteries of our Lord's birth, Life, Death, and Resurrection. Are you drawn to pray the Holy Rosary? If this is not a familiar prayer for you, what might help you to get started praying the Holy Rosary on a daily basis?

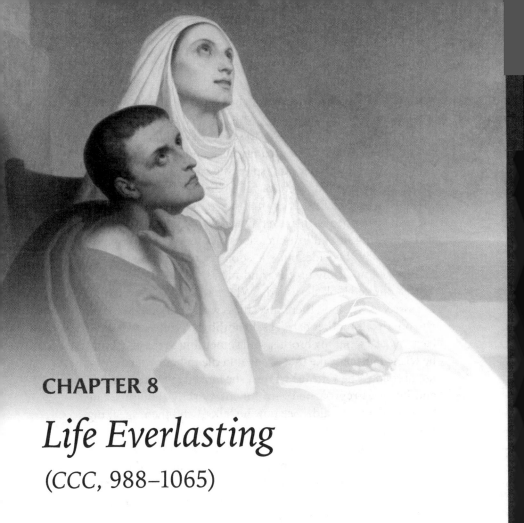

CHAPTER 8

Life Everlasting
(CCC, 988–1065)

While the man who would be known as St. Augustine searched for meaning and purpose in all the wrong places, his mother Monica prayed for his conversion. Eventually, her son did convert, was baptized, and became a bishop and great church theologian. With her work done, St. Monica fell ill and near death while she was a long way from her home in North Africa. Augustine and his brother were concerned that his mother would never make it back to her home alive or, at least, that they would not be able to bury her body there. Monica did not share those concerns. St. Augustine recalled these words of his mother and quoted them in his famous *Confessions*:

> My mother said, "My son, for my part I find no further pleasure in this life. What I am still to do or why I am here in the world, I

113

do not know, for I have no more to hope for on this earth. There was one reason, and one alone, why I wished to remain a little longer in this life, and that was to see you a Catholic Christian before I died. God has granted my wish and more besides, for I now see you as his servant, spurning such happiness as the world can give. What is left for me to do in this world?

. . . It was about five days after this, or not much more, that she took to her bed with a fever. One day during her illness she had a fainting fit and lost consciousness for a short time. We hurried to her bedside, but she soon regained consciousness and looked up at my brother and me as we stood beside her. With a puzzled look she asked, "Where was I?" Then watching us closely as we stood there speechless with grief, she said "You will bury your mother here." I said nothing, trying hard to hold back my tears, but my brother said something to the effect that he wished for her sake that she would die in her own country, not abroad. When she heard this, she looked at him anxiously and her eyes reproached him for his worldly thoughts. She turned to me and said, "See how he talks!" and then, speaking to both us, she went on, "It does not matter where you bury my body. Do not let that worry you! All I ask of you is that, wherever you may be, you should remember me at the altar of the Lord."

Although she hardly had the strength to speak, she managed to make us understand her wishes and then fell silent, for her illness was becoming worse and she was in great pain.[1]

On her deathbed, St. Monica witnessed to both the rock-solid faith of Christians in the resurrection of the body and the practice of ancient Christians burying their dead and remembering them in prayer at Holy Mass. While their pagan neighbors routinely practiced cremation of the dead, Christians buried their dead in places where they could gather to pray for their souls and even offer Mass on the anniversary of their death. The catacombs in Rome were carved out below the earth not as hiding places (as is commonly thought) but as places for the Christian dead to await the resurrection. St. Monica held the Christian faith in the resurrection of the body and asked her son to remember her at the altar, to pray for her soul, and to pray at Holy Mass that they would be reunited in the resurrection (cf. *CCC*, 988–991).

74. How can bodies rise from the dead, especially bodies that have long since disintegrated or those lost at sea?

With God, all things are possible. Jesus Christ, who most certainly died on the Cross, rose from the dead and was seen by his disciples many times in the weeks following the Resurrection. Those who saw him also ate with him, spoke with him, and touched him. The Resurrection of Jesus from the dead was experienced not as a dream or a hallucination, but as a genuine encounter.

St. Paul says that the manner of Christ's Resurrection from the dead is a preview of what will happen to us after our own deaths: "But now Christ has been raised from the dead, the first fruits of those who have fallen asleep" (1 Cor 15:20). God, who created the universe out of nothing and who raised up from the dead his own Son who was put to death by professional executioners, is more than capable of raising up our bodies in whatever condition they happen to be. And just as the body of Jesus after the Resurrection had different qualities than before his Death (such as the ability to pass through locked doors and to appear and disappear at will), so too will our risen bodies be like his glorified body (cf. Phil 3:21, *CCC*, 999).

75. Does everyone go to heaven?

Contemporary (and usually inaccurate) secular beliefs about death often outweigh what is truthfully taught about death in Sacred Scripture. It is not unusual to hear it said indiscriminately about someone who has recently died, "I'm sure he's in a better place." Often this is said without regard for how that person lived his life, how he treated others, and whether he even believed in God. Even when the person in question is known to be of high moral repute and a regular churchgoer, we must be humble enough to admit that whether that person is in heaven is a judgment not ours to make. Rather than offering empty platitudes to those who are mourning the loss of a loved one, it is better to say, "I am praying for the soul of your loved one and that God will comfort you in your loss."

Does everyone go to heaven? While the Church never makes a judgment about a particular person going to hell, the Church does teach that only in Jesus Christ will we be saved. Jesus Christ is the Way, the Truth, and the Life. Jesus is the Resurrection, whose death on the Cross opens the gates of heaven. Only in Jesus can we go to heaven (*CCC*, 992–996). We pray for the dead, including those who seldom manifested faith in the Lord, and even those who were not formally in the Catholic Church. We pray that they may not be lost for all eternity, but that they might be saved through the grace of Jesus, come to them through the Church in a mysterious way.

76. What does the Church believe about reincarnation?

Reincarnation is not taught by Jesus, nor is it mentioned anywhere in Sacred Scripture. We will not come back to life in another earthly body. "It is appointed for men to die once" (Heb 9:27, *CCC*, 1013).

77. How will our life be judged by God after we die?

Jesus teaches that we will be held accountable in the life to come for what we have done and what we have failed to do. The criterion of judgment is laid out clearly in Matthew 25:31–46. Jesus teaches that we will be judged on how we either cared for or neglected the least of our brothers and sisters, insisting that whatsoever we do for the least among us we do for the Lord. "'Lord, when did we see you hungry or thirsty or a stranger or naked or ill or in prison, and not minister to your needs?' He will answer them, 'Amen, I say to you, what you did not do for one of these least ones, you did not do for me.' And these will go off to eternal punishment, but the righteous to eternal life" (Mt 25:44–46, cf. *CCC*, 997–998).

78. What will heaven be like?

According to surveys conducted many times over past decades, what heaven will be like is a topic that churchgoers want to hear about more frequently. What we can state with confidence is that there *is* a heaven; it has been promised by the Lord: "Do not let your hearts be troubled. . . . I am going to prepare a place for you" (Jn 14:1–2). Just as Jesus drew people to himself here on earth, so will heaven be a profound experience of communion with him and with all the saints (cf. *CCC*, 954–958).

Heaven is essentially union with God: "Perfect life with the Most Holy Trinity . . . is called 'heaven.' Heaven is the ultimate end and fulfillment of the deepest human longings, the state of supreme, definitive happiness" (*CCC*, 1024). We will know our loved ones in heaven, but perhaps we will be slow to recognize them, for in heaven all is made new (cf. Rv 21:5), every stain of sin gone, every barrier removed that formerly kept love from being expressed authentically. "Heaven is the blessed community of all who are perfectly incorporated into Christ" (*CCC*, 1026).

We cannot know exactly what heaven will be like, but we do know that heaven will exceed our greatest expectations, which is every reason for us to keep our eyes fixed upon Jesus (cf. Heb 12:2) so that we might follow him where he leads us, always along the path of eternal life.

79. What does the Church teach about hell?

If heaven is eternal union with God, then hell is eternal separation from God. Jesus speaks of an "unquenchable fire . . . where 'their worm does not die, and the fire is not quenched'" (Mk 9:43, 48). Hell is the consequence of self-exclusion from communion with God and is the result of the free choice to live our lives without God. *Mortal sin* is the name of the self-imposed state by which one chooses freely to disobey God in a serious matter, with full knowledge of the wrongful nature of that action. Hell is the consequence of dying without having repented of mortal sin (cf. *CCC*, 1033). Those who are in hell are confined there by their own choice. As

Catholic Customs about Death and Funerals

The Church offers consolation to those who experience the death of a loved one, especially through prayers and sacred rites by which the dead are commended to the mercy and goodness of God.

When a Catholic is actively dying, it is important for a family member, friend, or acquaintance to alert the Church so that a priest can come to administer the Sacrament of the Anointing of the Sick, impart the apostolic pardon through which temporal punishment for sin is completely remitted, and offer a prayer called the Commendation of the Dying. The priest will come to the home or hospital for these prayers. It is also important for family members to offer their own prayers at the bedside of a dying person, especially familiar prayers such as the Lord's Prayer and the Hail Mary. Even if a dying person seems unable to respond to these prayers, we trust that prayer is always beneficial. Everyone should pray for the person after death as well. One prayer that is often prayed when a Catholic dies and when visiting the cemetery is as follows:

Eternal rest grant unto him/her, O Lord.
And let perpetual light shine upon him/her.
May he/she rest in peace.
Amen.
May his/her soul and the souls of the faithful departed,
    through the mercy of God, rest in peace.
Amen.

The funeral rites of the Church include prayers during visitation, the funeral Mass, and at the graveside. The funeral Mass is solemn yet marked with great hope in the Resurrection. The funeral Mass recalls that just as one dies with Christ in Baptism, so may one hope to rise with Christ in the Resurrection (cf. *CCC*, 1680–1690).

Many of the symbolic actions at a funeral Mass resemble the rites of Baptism: the sprinkling of holy water on the body, the clothing of the coffin with a white cloth, and the presence of the Paschal Candle near the body. Incense is often used at the funeral Mass, for this ancient practice is a symbol of prayers rising up to God. The burning of incense has a sacrificial dimension, recalling the sacrifice of Jesus Christ on the Cross for the forgiveness of our sins, the same sacrifice made present upon the altar in the Holy Sacrifice of the Mass. Eulogies are not typically given at the funeral Mass.

The funeral rites are already planned by the Church, and this is of great consolation in a time of grief. A relative does not need to plan a funeral service from scratch. Rather, the family may prepare for the Mass by choosing the Scriptures to be read. Be assured that your parish will help you in this time of grief. Also know that you may include in your final instructions a document that lists your wishes for your own funeral. This can be especially helpful if your survivors are not Catholic or have drifted away from regular practice of the faith. You may give a copy of your instructions to your parish to be kept on file.

The Church encourages the funeral Mass to take place in the presence of the body, and for the body to be buried in sacred ground. (This blessing can be done during the rites at the graveside.) Burial of the dead is a Christian custom that dates to the time of the Apostles and evokes the burial of our Lord after his saving death. Every person's life is so important that he or she should have a permanent resting place that others can visit and offer prayers. From the grave we await the resurrection of the body.

Cremation of the body is not encouraged but is permitted either before or after the funeral Mass. Sometimes practical circumstances can make cremation a prudent choice. Cremated remains are to be buried in sacred ground or placed in a columbarium at the cemetery. Cremated remains are not to be scattered, nor are they to be kept at home, though in 2023 the Vatican's doctrinal office amended this teaching to say that relatives may ask for "a minimal part of the ashes of their relative (to be stored) in a place of significance for the history of the deceased person."

C. S. Lewis famously said in *The Problem of Pain*, "The doors of hell are locked on the inside."

The sobering teaching on hell is a call to conversion of life. The Lord gives us the Ten Commandments so we might live by them. The Lord gives us the grace of the sacraments so we might be able to keep the commandments. The Lord gives his life on the Cross so that we might be inspired to keep the New Commandment: "Love one another, as I have loved you" (Jn 13:34). The Lord gives us today, but he does not promise us tomorrow. The time for conversion is now. There is great urgency in the call to conversion, for the actions of the present have eternal consequences. We know neither the day nor the hour, so we must be vigilant, lest we suffer the eternal punishment of the fires of hell (cf. Mt 25:13, CCC, 1036).

80. What is it like for the souls in purgatory, and how do our prayers help them?

The word *purgatory* is related to the verb "to purge." While *purging* refers to a cleansing action, it does not suggest a bubble bath! The Scriptures speak of a cleansing fire (cf. 1 Cor 3:15, 1 Pt 1:7), a treatment that will not be without pain. The pain of purgatory is like the pain experienced in the process of physical healing, accompanied by the pain of deep regret for not having followed the Lord more closely. Purgatory is a state in which the soul is cleansed of imperfections.

We can easily recognize the need for purgatory. Only those who are perfectly pure may enter heaven, yet many who die in the state of grace (without mortal sin) may still carry the impurity of venial (lesser) sin or have need to fulfill the burden of temporal punishment for venial sins committed. While not deserving of hell, these souls are not yet ready to enter heaven.

Fortunately, God is full of mercy and compassion. "All who die in God's grace and friendship, but still imperfectly purified, are indeed assured of their eternal salvation; but after death they undergo purification, so as to achieve the holiness necessary to enter the joy of heaven" (*CCC*, 1030–1031). The souls in purgatory are assured of their eventual entrance into heaven and are greatly assisted by our prayers, especially the Holy Sacrifice of the Mass offered for them (cf. *CCC*, 1032). May we pray for our loved ones who have died, and may others be inspired to pray for us when our time in this world comes to an end.

Summary and Reflection

We believe, as St. Paul so boldly proclaimed, that "Christ, raised from the dead, dies no more; death no longer has power over him" (Rom 6:9). Furthermore, those who believe in the Risen Lord and follow in his ways have reason to hope in their own bodily resurrection. St. Paul is emphatic about this point: "If Christ is preached as raised from the dead, how can some among you say there is no resurrection of the dead? If there is no resurrection of the dead, then neither has Christ been raised" (1 Cor 15:12–13).

From the very beginning, belief in the Resurrection has been central to the faith of Christians, and this belief continues to be expressed in the practice of praying for the dead. We pray that the souls of our loved ones will enter into eternal life with God in heaven, whether immediately after death or after cleansed of all venial sin in purgatory.

● Creation

You are made to be in union with God for all eternity. We often postpone thinking about death, and we can be reluctant to talk about death with loved ones. What struck you as new in this chapter on life after death?

○ Fall

How is the doctrine of purgatory an expression of the great mercy of God for poor sinners who die in a less than perfect state but who have no mortal sin upon their soul? How does the teaching on purgatory affect how you offer condolences to those who have recently lost loved ones?

✝ Redemption

Very frequently we see crosses in cemeteries near the graves of those who died. Why is the cross such a powerful and consoling symbol at the graveside of a loved one? What Christian symbol or symbols do you want upon your headstone?

○ Restoration

An old Christian adage says, "Remember death daily." Although this might seem morbid to some, how can this word of counsel be helpful to you as you strive to follow the Lord along the path of eternal life?

Part II

HOW CATHOLICS WORSHIP

How sweet, the presence of Jesus to the longing,
harassed soul! It is instant peace, and
calm to every wound.

—St. Elizabeth Ann Seton

CHAPTER 9

The Sacred Liturgy
(CCC, 1066–1209)

Thus far we have focused on Catholic beliefs. With this chapter we turn to the most sacred Catholic practices, namely, those associated with the way in which Catholics worship God and experience his presence through the sacraments.

If you have been to a Catholic church for Holy Mass, you have experienced a formal action involving many of your senses. There were sacred words and gestures, the proclamation of passages from Sacred Scripture, an array of sacred objects such as the tabernacle and the chalice, perhaps sacred music and the use of incense, all set in a worship space adorned with a crucifix, statues, icons, and sacred furniture such as an altar and pews. Maybe you have been to Mass many times throughout your life, or perhaps this was the first Mass you have ever attended. In either case, you might have enjoyed the experience, finding it prayerful and reverent,

127

or you might not understand the reasons for the formality of the prayers and the various postures in which worshippers engaged. The next few chapters will help you to understand better the great love that Catholics have for Holy Mass and the sacraments of the Church. Deeper knowledge of the sacraments will help you to enter more fully into the mysteries they present.

81. Where do all the symbols and rituals of the sacraments come from?

Directly or indirectly, all of the symbols and rituals of the sacraments come from God. This might seem to be a bold statement, especially since some customs at Holy Mass are of recent origin. Nevertheless, Scripture teaches us that God is very specific in giving his people instructions on how to worship.

In the Old Testament, for example, the Book of Leviticus is replete with God's instructions for worship before the Ark of the Covenant. The Book of Exodus lays out explicit directives for the sacrifice of the Passover lamb and the eating of the Passover meal. The New Testament also has instructions on worship from the Lord himself. Jesus frequently visited the Temple in Jerusalem for prayer and worship, and he mourned the destruction of the Temple that was to be perpetrated by the Romans within forty years of his return to heaven (cf. Lk 19:41–42). Jesus admired and respected the symbols and rituals of worship that he learned from his childhood, even as he criticized those who worshipped at the Temple with proper outward appearance but with corrupt inner dispositions (cf. Mt 23:13–36).

In fact, it is in the course of a sacred Jewish ritual that Christ instituted the greatest act of worship, the offering of the Holy Sacrifice of the Mass. Jesus chose a Passover meal with his Apostles as the occasion to affirm his love and respect for this particular act of ancient worship while changing the ritual involving bread and wine substantially, saying of the bread, "Take and eat, this is my body" and of the chalice of wine, "Drink from it, all of you, for this is my blood of the covenant, which will be shed on behalf of many for the forgiveness of sins" (Mt 26:26–28), and commanding his followers to do this in his memory until he returns in glory (cf. 1 Cor 11:26).

From the earliest days of the Church the followers of Jesus obeyed his command to offer ritual worship in his name. The early Church established the pattern that would be followed even to this day, and that will be followed until the Lord comes in glory: "They devoted themselves to the teaching of the apostles and to the communal life, to the breaking of the bread and to the prayers" (Acts 2:42). St. Paul instructed early Christians on proper worship (1 Cor 11:23–26) and called for the reform of illicit practices within communal worship (1 Cor 11:27–33). In fact, in the First Letter to the Corinthians, St. Paul introduces two teachings with the solemn phrase, "I received from the Lord what I also handed on to you" (11:23 and with slight variation 15:3), referring to the teaching on the Eucharist and the teaching on the Resurrection. St. Paul's emphasis upon our Lord's institution of the Holy Eucharist is as forceful as his teaching on the truth of Christ's Resurrection.

The early Christians strove to remain faithful to all that had been passed down to them from the Lord through the teaching of the Apostles, even when threatened with the most vile and wicked persecution. The martyrs of the early Church gave their lives attesting to the fact that they would not budge from the teachings and practices that had been handed down to them. Amidst these early Christian communities there existed a strong and robust faith, expressed through faithful worship, sound teaching, and compassionate service to the poor and less fortunate. The rituals celebrated by the early Church were those they had received from the Lord: "The sacraments . . . were . . . all instituted by Jesus Christ, our Lord" (*CCC*, 1114).

82. What did early Christians believe about sacramental worship?

The early Christian beliefs about worship have been passed on to us today. What Christians believed about worship in the catacombs is essentially the same as what Catholics believe today. Worship is not merely the gathering of people of faith for instruction and prayer. Catholic worship is the work of God in which faithful people participate.

83. Why does a Catholic Mass differ from Protestant worship?

This is a very good question, one that perplexes many people. First and foremost, if your experience of Christian worship is mostly in settings that are not Catholic, then your experience is rooted in a different understanding of worship. For example, Jennie Fraser, a moderator on the Coming Home Network forum, recalled the first Mass she attended:

> I crept into the church and the priest was standing there greeting people, so I walked up to him (I now know him as my beloved Monsignor Leo) and asked if I as a Protestant could come and watch what happened at Mass. He said of course, and welcome! So I did. I sat at the very back in a corner feeling very self-conscious indeed. I really didn't like that Mass at all. Two sisters sat in front of me chattering almost the entire time. Nobody sang loudly and lustily like they did in my Protestant churches. It was vaguely Anglican in feeling but without any of the beauty. I walked out thinking to myself, "How on earth could I ever become Catholic and endure *that*." But there was something that kept calling me back because I knew I had found truth there, so I just kept searching and now I am happily Catholic.[1]

Protestant worship is different than a Catholic Mass. This is said not to demean in any way those who worship elsewhere, preaching and learning the Gospel, praising the Lord in word and song. These heartfelt expressions of love and devotion to the Lord can be quite inspiring, and the Church is grateful whenever the Lord is praised "with the lyre and melodious song" (Ps 98:5). Nevertheless, we must distinguish between what is commonly called *worship* today, and the *authentic worship* that has been passed down to us from the time of the Apostles. Many are the number of texts that have survived from the time of the early Church.

With great consistency they tell us of the attitudes and beliefs of early Christians about worship.

One such example of a text that teaches us how the earliest Christians regarded authentic worship comes from St. Ignatius of Antioch, who died a martyr around the year AD 110. In a direct line from Jesus and the Apostles, St. Ignatius was formed in the faith by St. Polycarp of Smyrna, who in turn was a disciple of St. John, the Apostle beloved by the Lord. St. Ignatius spoke of the sacrificial nature of the Holy Eucharist, and it being the singular way to experience the flesh and blood of the Lord. St. Ignatius also highlighted the important role played by the hierarchy of the Church in the celebration of the sacraments: "Be careful to observe [only] one Eucharist; for there is only one Flesh of our Lord Jesus Christ and one cup of union with his Blood, one altar of sacrifice, as [there is] one bishop with the presbyters and my fellow-servants the deacons."[2]

As St. Ignatius was being taken to Rome to be thrown to the lions, he wrote about the Eucharist as the true Body and Precious Blood of the Lord:

> I am God's grain, and I am being ground by the teeth of wild beasts in order that I may be found [to be] pure bread for Christ. My love has been crucified, and there is in me no fire of material love, but rather a living water, speaking in me and saying within me, "Come to the Father." I take no pleasure in corruptible food or in the delights of this life. I want the bread of God, which is the flesh of Jesus Christ, who is the seed of David; and for drink I want his Blood which is incorruptible love.[3]

St. Ignatius of Antioch and the earliest Christians believed whole-heartedly in the real and substantial presence of the Lord in the Holy Eucharist, the importance of offering the Holy Eucharist on Sunday, the "day of the Lord," and being led by the bishop or the priest, using the language and form that had been passed on from the Apostles. As early as the second century, prayers to be said in the Holy Eucharist were carefully written down, providing the Church with the beginning of a stable liturgical tradition that continues to typify Catholic worship to this very day. Catholic worship is a solemn yet joyful experience of a sacred tradition

The Liturgical Year

The worship of the Church progresses through a liturgical year in such a way that we encounter the entirety of the mystery of our Lord's Incarnation, his earthly ministry, his sorrowful Passion, and his glorious Resurrection. The seasons of the liturgical year have particular colors that symbolize different aspects of the life of Christ and the Church (cf. *CCC*, 1169–1171).

Advent is the four weeks leading up to Christmas. Unlike the world around us that carries on Christmas celebrations weeks before the feast, the season of Advent invites us to take to prayer the Scriptures that foretell the birth of Christ and to ready our hearts for his coming into our lives. (The word *advent* means "coming.") The color of the Advent season is violet, the color of the sky before the dawn. A rose-colored vestment may be worn on the Third Sunday of Advent, a glimmer of joy as Christmas draws near.

Christmas is celebrated not only on December 25 but for an octave (eight days) and more. The "twelve days of Christmas" stretch from December 25 to January 6, the day of Epiphany that commemorates the visit of the Magi to the Christ child. White is the color of the season, and the priest often wears gold vestments.

Ordinary Time begins after the Feast of the Baptism of the Lord, usually three weeks after Christmas day. *Ordinary* does not mean plain or blasé; rather, it means "counted." The Sundays of Ordinary Time are counted according to ordinal numbers—for example, the Fifteenth Sunday of Ordinary Time. Vestments are green during the weeks of Ordinary Time.

Lent is the forty-day penitential season by which Christians prepare for the solemn celebration of the Paschal Mystery, the Holy Week and sacred Triduum (three days) in which we remember and participate in our Lord's dying on the Cross and rising from the dead. Violet is the penitential color worn throughout Lent. A rose vestment may be worn on the Fourth Sunday of Lent, a signal of the important liturgical days that are coming soon. Red vestments are worn on Palm Sunday and Good Friday because the account of the Lord's Passion is proclaimed. Red vestments are also worn on the feast days of martyrs, who shed their blood in imitation of Christ.

The *Easter* season extends for fifty days and includes feasts such as Divine Mercy Sunday and the Solemnity of the Ascension of Jesus. White and sometimes gold vestments are worn in the Easter season.

Pentecost Sunday is the feast celebrated fifty days after Easter. Pentecost commemorates the coming of the Holy Spirit upon the Apostles and the Blessed Mother fifty days after the Resurrection (cf. Acts 2:1–13). Red is the color for Pentecost, for the Holy Spirit descended like "tongues as of fire" (Acts 2:3).

After Pentecost the Church enters into a longer series of weeks of Ordinary Time, stretching through the summer months until the end of November. Green is the color of the vestments, symbolizing the virtue of hope. During these weeks we continue to learn from the Lord what it means to follow him for a lifetime. Week by week, we are nourished in the Sacrament of the Eucharist so that we might be sustained and strengthened along the journey, and so grow in fervent hope of the resurrection to the life to come. The celebration of certain feasts interrupts Ordinary Time, such as the Solemnity of the Assumption of the Blessed Virgin Mary, All Saints' Day, and All Souls' Day. The vesture for these feasts is white, although on All Souls' Day the vestments may be violet or black.

The Solemnity of Christ the King of the Universe is the last Sunday of the liturgical year. The vestments are white or gold, for this solemnity celebrates the kingship of our Lord and Savior, Jesus Christ. He rules over heaven and earth, and his Kingdom is without end. Though we struggle in this life against the forces of evil, we know that the Lord will come again in glory, and that he comes to make all things new.

that can be traced all the way back to the nascent Church, which received from the Lord himself the command, "Do this in memory of me."

84.   What is a sacrament?

Catholic children in the United States prior to the Second Vatican Council memorized a simple definition of *sacrament* from the *Baltimore Catechism*: "A sacrament is an outward sign instituted by Christ to give grace." The outward sign of each sacrament corresponds to and effects the inward reality. Each sacrament is instituted by Christ, and each gives the distinctive grace signified by its matter and form. The *Catechism of the Catholic Church* amplifies this definition: "Sacraments are powers that come forth from the Body of Christ, which is ever-living and life-giving. They are actions of the Holy Spirit at work in his Body, the Church. They are the masterworks of God in the new and everlasting covenant" (*CCC*, 1116).

85.   Where does the word *sacrament* come from? Is it in the Bible?

The word *sacrament* is not in the Bible, but the word *mystery* is. St. Paul speaks of Christian marriage as an expression of the love of the Lord and calls it a mystery: "This is a great mystery, but I speak in reference to Christ and the church" (Eph 5:32). The Greek word for *mystery* came to be translated into the Latin language as *sacramentum*, from which we get the word *sacrament*. As we studied in Chapter 6, in ancient Rome, a *sacramentum* was a solemn, sacred oath with binding consequences. The one making the *sacramentum* placed his or her life in the hands of the gods. For example, a soldier in the Roman army would take a solemn oath of allegiance to the emperor. The taking of the oath might be accompanied by the soldier's reception of an indelible mark such as a tattoo or brand on his body. The early Church saw a profound similarity between this secular practice of oath taking and the initiation into the Christian life through Baptism. Both were sacred obligations undertaken, for the word *sacramentum* contains the root word for *sacred*.

Each of the Seven Sacraments is at least alluded to in the Bible, as will be shown as each sacrament is treated individually.

86. Why are the sacraments important today?

The second-century writer Tertullian references Baptism when he writes: "Happy is our sacrament of water, in that, by washing away the sins of our early blindness, we are set free and admitted into eternal life!"[4] In the early twentieth century, St. Pius X said that "Holy Communion is the shortest and safest way to heaven. . . . The surest, easiest, shortest way is the Eucharist."[5]

Sacraments are efficacious, giving the grace that they signify. They bring with them the grace to not only transform us for this world but to bring us to the next. Christ is at work in the sacraments. Of Baptism we can say that it is Christ who baptizes (cf. *CCC*, 1127). In the Holy Eucharist, it is Christ who is the High Priest, and it is the Body and Blood of the Lord that is truly and substantially made present. "From the moment that a sacrament is celebrated in accordance with the intention of the Church, the power of Christ and his Spirit acts in and through it" (*CCC*, 1128). "The sacrament is not wrought by the righteousness of either the celebrant or the recipient, but by the power of God."[6] We can depend upon the sacraments as we make our way through life. The Lord binds himself to the sacraments so that we might have the means necessary for our salvation and so that he might keep his solemn promise, "I am with you always, until the end of the age" (Mt 28:20).

87.   What is the meaning of the word *liturgy*?

Catholic worship is called *liturgy*. The word *liturgy* originally meant "public work" or a "service in the name of or on behalf of the people" (cf. *CCC*,
1069). In the ancient world, the emperor building a bridge, a road, or a
seaport was called a liturgy, for it was a work that benefited greatly the
people of the empire. Zechariah, the priest and father of St. John the Baptist, is described as completing his time of "service " (Lk 1:23); the Greek
word used in this passage is *leitourgia*, from which we get the word *liturgy*.

Today, especially in the Church, *liturgy* has two meanings, both associated with work. *Liturgy* refers to the participation of all Christian faithful in the work of Christ's redemption and Christ's continual work with
and by the Church for our redemption. For example, *liturgy* is the same
word used in the Letter to the Hebrews to describe the saving work or
ministry of Jesus upon the Cross: "Now he has obtained so much more
excellent a ministry as he is mediator of a better covenant, enacted on
better promises" (Heb 8:6).

The action of liturgy as undertaken by the Church in the sacraments
makes the Church present in the world and shows her to be the "visible
sign of the communion between Christ and men" (*CCC*, 1071). At every
Mass, Jesus Christ is the High Priest, the one who "acts through the sacraments he instituted to communicate his grace" (*CCC*, 1084). Catholic
worship involves the participation of the faithful, but at its core it is an
action of Jesus Christ, the High Priest:

> The liturgy then is rightly seen as an exercise of the priestly
> office of Jesus Christ. It involves the presentation of man's sanc-
> tification under the guise of signs perceptible by the senses and
> its accomplishment in ways appropriate to each of these signs.
> In it full public worship is performed by the Mystical Body
> of Jesus Christ, that is, by the Head and his members. From
> this it follows that every liturgical celebration, because it is an
> action of Christ the priest and of his Body which is the Church,
> is a sacred action surpassing all others. No other action of the
> Church can equal its efficacy by the same title and to the same
> degree. (*Sacrosanctum Concilium*, 7)

88. Why are the liturgies of the Church called celebrations?

The liturgy is the formal performance of a solemn ceremony. The liturgies of the Church are solemn actions of the whole Christ, the Body of Christ. When we speak of the Body of Christ, we include not only the members of the Church here on earth but also the Church Triumphant, the saints and angels who forever worship before the throne of God in heaven (cf. *CCC*, 1137–1138). Through the power of the Holy Spirit, when we celebrate the sacraments we participate in the heavenly liturgy (cf. *CCC*, 1139). The earthly liturgy of the Church is a foretaste of the liturgy of heaven. The celebration of the sacraments is where heaven and earth meet, for through the sacraments we are drawn into the mysterious presence of God. The Church will celebrate the sacraments until the Lord returns in glory (cf. *CCC*, 1090).

89. Who celebrates the sacred liturgy?

The liturgy is the celebration of the entire Church, the members united with Christ, the head of the Church. The rites of the Church are public and are open to all who wish to attend. The assembly is the community of the baptized, who share a common priesthood, the priesthood of Christ. By reason of their Baptism and the obligations flowing from it, the People of God are to take part in liturgical celebrations in a full, conscious, and actual way. The People of God are not bystanders but participants in the sacred actions (cf. *CCC*, 1141).

Some of the faithful are called to a vocation of service to the Church. Men consecrated by Holy Orders are given the power "to act in the person of Christ the head, for the service of all the members of the Church" (*CCC*, 1142). The Sacrament of Holy Orders will be discussed in Chapter 12.

90.   Why are there so many symbols at a Catholic Mass, and what is their significance?

We are a people who communicate and interact with one another through symbols and rituals—from a wave or a handshake, to a swearing of an oath in a court of law, to the giving of rings by bride and groom. The rituals that accompany commencement ceremonies, a Fourth of July parade, and the opening and closing of Olympic games become important parts of our corporate memory.

The symbols at Holy Mass fit in beautifully with our human nature. The sacred rituals associated with Mass provide us with a unique entrée into the mystery of our Lord's saving Death and glorious Resurrection. Many of the symbols in the sacred liturgy date back to the observances and worship described in the Old Testament. The assembly that gathers for Holy Mass is itself a symbol of a holy people the Lord gathers to be his own. The word *church* is connected to the Hebrew word *qahal*, which means the assembly or community of the People of God (cf. Ex 16:1–3).

Other symbols are directly associated with the main parts of the Mass, the Liturgy of the Word and the Liturgy of the Eucharist. The Word of God is proclaimed solemnly at every celebration of Holy Mass. Scriptures are read or sung from a pulpit or lectern, properly called the *ambo*, using not a loose sheet of paper but a beautifully bound *lectionary* or *Book of the Gospels*. The deacon, priest, or bishop proclaims the Gospel and elucidates upon the readings in the homily, bringing to the assembly a practical application of God's Word in our own time and place (cf. *CCC*, 1153–1155).

God's People sing at Holy Mass, their voices rising up in prayer and adoration, joining with the hymns of saints and angels in one chorus in praise of God. St. Augustine is attributed with the saying, "He who sings prays twice" (cf. *CCC*, 1156–1158). Incense is used at Holy Mass on the most solemn occasions. Incense burned over hot coals was part of the worship at the Temple in Jerusalem. The psalmist says of the clouds of incense rising in the Temple, "Let my prayer be incense before you" (Ps 141:2).

Within the church or chapel itself, holy images are present, sometimes elaborate and sometimes in the form of a simple crucifix on or near the altar. The images are all related to Christ, especially the images of the Blessed Mother and the various saints, who lived in a way that glorified the person of Jesus Christ and who pray ceaselessly for us poor sinners who are still trying to make our way along the path of life. Christian images (sometimes in the form of icons) express visually the Gospel that is proclaimed in words. "The contemplation of sacred icons, united with meditation on the Word of God and the singing of liturgical hymns, enters into the harmony of the signs of celebration so that the mystery celebrated is imprinted in the heart's memory and is then expressed in the new life of the faithful" (*CCC*, 1162).

Summary and Reflection

Christ instituted the sacraments so that we might encounter him throughout our lives. Just as those who were with Jesus during the time of his earthly ministry received wisdom in his teachings, experienced through his miracles profound healing of body and soul, were nourished with his Body and Blood beginning with his Last Supper, and were brought together in an ordered way into his Church, so too are we instructed, healed, nourished, and formed through the sacraments of the Church. "The mysteries of Christ's life are the foundations of what he would henceforth dispense in the sacraments, through the ministers of his Church, for 'what was visible in our Savior has passed over into his mysteries'" (St. Leo the Great, cited in *CCC*, 1115). To this day, Christ is the High Priest of the sacraments.

⬤ Creation

God said of his creation, "It is good." We cannot fathom how beautiful must have been the Garden of Eden, in which everything was in order, everything worked as it should,

everything was in perfect harmony. How have you experienced goodness and beauty in the Holy Mass?

☉ *Fall*

Sin brings about disorder within the human person and among the members of the human family. Sin keeps us at a distance from God. How does human sinfulness get in the way of closeness with God in worship? How is sinfulness called to mind during Holy Mass?

✝ *Redemption*

An acclamation expressed during the devotion of the Stations of the Cross is, "We adore you, O Christ, and we praise you, for by your Holy Cross you have redeemed the world." How does participation in Mass draw you closer to the Cross of Jesus?

☾ *Restoration*

Sunday is the day of the Lord, the day of the Resurrection, the day of the "new creation." How does participating in the sacred liturgy restore you? How does the Holy Mass give you new life?

CHAPTER 10

The Sacraments of Christian Initiation: Baptism, Confirmation, and the Eucharist

(CCC, 1210–1419)

The most important occasion of the liturgical year is an event called the Easter Vigil, which occurs on the evening before Easter. This is when many adults are baptized or received into the full communion of the Catholic Church. It is a liturgy unlike any other in the church year. Few leave Holy Mass that night with anything less than a heart full of joy for the newly initiated Catholics and their families.

The Easter Vigil is the first celebration of Easter. On Holy Saturday, after sundown, the Paschal or Easter candle is lit from new fire. Scripture accounts following salvation history from the beginning of creation are read. Then the Church welcomes the *elect*, unbaptized persons who have a time of formal study, prayer, and spiritual reflection in preparation for this night, and those who have already been baptized in other Christian communities who are seeking full communion with the Catholic Church. The elect receive three Sacraments of Initiation during the Easter Vigil liturgy: Baptism, Confirmation, and the Eucharist. There is great rejoicing in the central proclamation of the faith: Christ is indeed risen from the dead!

A feature of the Sacraments of Initiation that take place at the Easter Vigil is that they are for adults and those above the age of discretion. The Church has always had two rites of initiation—one for adults and one for children who are baptized as infants and who receive the other two sacraments (Confirmation and the Eucharist) at a later time. Both the infant and adult rites leading to reception of the Sacraments of Initiation continue to have a place in the Church: Christian initiation is for all.

91.   What is the purpose of the Sacraments of Initiation?

Every society has rites of initiation. Those who have spent time in the armed services know all about the process of initiation that includes a haircut, new clothes, and constant but less than gentle reminders about expectations of life in the military. Most jobs come with an onboarding process that includes an introduction to the history and culture of the corporation. With the exception of infants and children, entrance into the Catholic Church usually follows the Order of Christian Initiation for Adults (OCIA) and culminates in the Sacraments of Initiation: Baptism, Confirmation, and the Eucharist.

While the Sacraments of Baptism, Confirmation, and the Eucharist are usually spread out by several years for those who were baptized as infants, those receiving Baptism as adults or children above the age of reason will receive all three sacraments in a single liturgy, often at the Easter Vigil. (Christians who are already baptized are not rebaptized, but instead make a profession of faith and are received into the full communion of the Catholic Church.) The Sacraments of Initiation "lay the foundations of every Christian life. . . . The faithful are born anew by Baptism, strengthened by the sacrament of Confirmation, and receive in the Eucharist the food of eternal life" (*CCC*, 1212).

92.   What does Baptism accomplish?

Jesus gave this command to his Apostles before he ascended into heaven: "Go, therefore, and make disciples of all nations, baptizing them in the name of the Father, and of the Son, and of the holy Spirit, teaching them to observe all that I have commanded you" (Mt 28:19–20). The rite of Baptism accomplishes this. Baptism is the gateway to the other sacraments and to the whole of the Christian life.

Baptism is a sacrament of new life, of being reborn as a child of God. The rite of Baptism is not merely a symbol of what has already happened within the heart of a believer. The pouring of water upon the one being baptized, and the use of the Trinitarian formula of words given by the Lord (cf. Mt 28:19), removes Original Sin and personal sin, remits the punishment for sin, and bestows sanctifying grace.

Jesus said that Baptism is necessary for salvation: "Amen, amen, I say to you, no one can enter the kingdom of God without being born of water and Spirit" (Jn 3:5, cf. *CCC*, 1257). Our Lord himself enters into the waters of the Jordan River for baptism by St. John the Baptist, not because he needed to be baptized, but to make holy the waters of the Sacrament of Baptism (cf. Mt 2:13–17, cf. *CCC*, 1223).

93.   Is faith necessary for Baptism?

Faith is necessary for Baptism, even for infants. Though an infant is not yet capable of personal faith, that child is already benefiting from the faith of the Church. Parents have a duty to be "nurturers of the life that God has entrusted to them" (*CCC*, 1251). Infant baptism has been practiced since the earliest days of the Church, when entire households were baptized (cf. Acts 16:33). There are no recorded objections to infant baptism in the first millennium of Christianity. Rather, the baptism of infants assured parents that their child was free of Original Sin and that nothing stood in the way of that child's eternal life with God in heaven (cf. *CCC*, 1250).

In the case of a child presented for Baptism when faith is not practiced by the parent(s), "there must be a founded hope that the infant will be brought up in the Catholic religion" (*Code of Canon Law*, canon 868). In danger of death, an infant is to be baptized, even by someone who is not a priest or deacon.

Baptism is a sacrament of faith, yet it need not be a mature faith, even for adults. The grace of Baptism and the sacraments that follow will bring about a more deeply rooted faith (cf. *CCC*, 1253). In other words, one does not have to be perfect to be baptized! Baptism is the beginning of the journey, not its end. Whenever possible, those being baptized are instructed in the content of the faith and make a public profession of faith immediately prior to either being immersed or having the water of Baptism poured on their heads.

An adult seeking Baptism does so as a result of an initial conversion to Christ. The Church calls all who are not baptized to turn toward Christ and be baptized, echoing the words of St. Peter: "Repent and be baptized, every one of you, in the name of Jesus Christ for the forgiveness of your sins; and you will receive the gift of the holy Spirit" (Acts 2:38). *Repentance* is a word that translates the Greek word *metanoia*, which means "a change of mind and heart."

94.   What happens after death for those who have not been baptized?

Jesus teaches that Baptism is necessary for salvation (cf. Jn 3:5). The Church does not know of any other way by which a person may get to heaven. Yet the Church recognizes that there are many people on earth who have not heard the message of the Gospel and the call to repentance or who are burdened with obstacles that keep them from understanding and accepting the Gospel. Every person "who is ignorant of the Gospel of Christ and of his Church, but seeks the truth and does the will of God in accordance with his understanding of it, can be saved. It may be supposed that such persons would have desired Baptism explicitly if they had known its necessity" (*CCC*, 1260). Those who are saved seemingly "outside the Church" are saved by the grace that God sends to them mysteriously through the Church.

Regarding children who have died without being baptized, the Church entrusts them to God's mercy. Jesus's tenderness toward children allows us "to hope that there is a way of salvation for children who have died without Baptism" (*CCC*, 1261). "God has bound salvation to the sacrament of Baptism, but he himself is not bound by his sacraments" (*CCC*, 1257). Nevertheless, there is great urgency to evangelize the many people of our age who do not truly know the Lord Jesus and to echo the teaching of the Church from the beginning, that infants should be baptized and that nothing should prevent these little ones from coming to Christ through Baptism even in their earliest days after birth.

95. How is the Sacrament of Confirmation conferred?

Confirmation is the sacrament through which the baptized are strengthened by an increase of the gifts of the Holy Spirit (cf. Is 11:1–3) and are thereby fortified to live out their lives as witnesses of Christ and to share and defend the faith in words and in actions (cf. *CCC*, 1285). The one who is confirmed is anointed on the forehead by the bishop or priest through the laying on of hands with a scented oil known as sacred chrism, a symbol of being more closely configured with Jesus Christ. (*Christ*, recall, is derived from the word meaning "anointed.") The Holy Spirit is invoked upon the ones to be confirmed with a prayer that spells out the seven gifts of the Spirit conferred in the sacrament:

> All-powerful God, Father of our Lord Jesus Christ,
> by water and the Holy Spirit
> you freed your sons and daughters from sin and gave them
>   new life.
> Send your Holy Spirit upon them to be their helper and
>   guide.

The Seven Gifts and Twelve Fruits of the Holy Spirit

The seven gifts of the Holy Spirit perfect the virtues of those who receive them (cf. *CCC*, 1831, cf. Is 11:2). These gifts were perfectly present in the person of Jesus. They work within us and help us to grow in holiness, faith, and union with the Blessed Trinity. They help us to listen more closely to God's Word and to act on that Word in daily life. They are strengthened by the Sacrament of Confirmation so we can better witness to Christ (cf. *CCC*, 1303).

* *Wisdom* is associated with prudence and self-control. It helps us to seek God's Kingdom first and make everything else less important.

- *Understanding* helps us with the larger mysteries of life. We see the spirit behind God's laws and not just the letter of the laws. The gift of understanding is accompanied by empathy and compassion and allows us to view a situation from the perspective of another.

- *Right judgment*, or counsel, relies on the virtue of prudence. This gift helps us to make good decisions based on our desire to do God's will. It encourages us to seek out the wise advice of the Church.

- *Courage*, or fortitude, gives us strength to stand up for our Christian beliefs and remain true to them in the face of hardship.

- *Knowledge* allows us both to know God and to be better known by ourselves and others in the way that God knows us.

- *Reverence*, or piety, helps us to give true worship and praise to God and to show proper respect for everything he has made.

- A *spirit of wonder and awe* makes us receptive to God's loving presence and helps us to never underestimate God or think that we have him figured out.

The Holy Spirit also gives us "fruits" that we enjoy when we practice the virtues. The Latin word for fruit, *frui*, means "to enjoy." These are qualities that blossom and grow to fruition within God's children through the power of the Holy Spirit (cf. *CCC*, 736, 1832, also Gal 5:22–23). They give us satisfaction when we put our natural powers of body and soul into practice. The twelve fruits of the Spirit are: charity (love), joy, peace, patience, kindness, goodness, generosity, gentleness, faithfulness, modesty, self-control, and chastity.

> Give them the spirit of *wisdom* and *understanding,*
> the spirit of *right judgment* and *courage,*
> the spirit of *knowledge* and *reverence.*
> Fill them with the spirit of *wonder and awe* in your presence.
> We ask this through Christ our Lord. (*Rite of Confirmation*)

96.   What is the effect of Confirmation?

Confirmation is a special outpouring of the Holy Spirit as on the day of Pentecost. An indelible character is placed upon the soul, marking the one who is confirmed as a witness to Christ and giving him or her a special strength to carry out that witness. Confirmation brings about growth in the grace of Baptism and brings the one confirmed to a deeper way of being a son or daughter of God. Through Confirmation one is bound closer to Christ and the Church, and the gifts of the Holy Spirit given in Baptism are reinvigorated (cf. *CCC*, 1302–1305).

97.   What is the correct order for the Sacraments of Initiation to be received?

This is a good question, best answered, "It all depends!" The *Catechism of the Catholic Church* lists the Sacraments of Christian Initiation in this traditional order: Baptism, Confirmation, and the Eucharist. However, this is not always the order that they are celebrated, though Baptism *always* comes first.

In the earliest days of the Church, Confirmation by the bishop followed immediately after Baptism. To this very day, in the Eastern Churches, priests have the authority to confirm infants immediately after baptizing them. Immediately after Baptism and Confirmation, the priest places a very small drop of the Precious Blood in the infant's mouth. Therefore we can say that in the Eastern Churches all three Sacraments of Initiation are celebrated on the day of the infant's baptism.

In the Latin Church decisions about the order of the sacraments have changed, and they continue to evolve even in our day. For many centuries infants were baptized shortly after birth and then confirmed when the bishop next visited the parish. First Holy Communion was administered at around the age of twelve. In 1910, Pope Pius X instructed parish priests to administer First Holy Communion to children who had reached the "age of discretion," somewhere around age six or seven. Confirmation was then celebrated sometime afterward, when the bishop next visited the parish.

Today in the United States and elsewhere several dioceses have restored the traditional order of Baptism, Confirmation, Eucharist. Whether this becomes a wider movement is yet to be seen. However, it is the practice of the universal Church to administer all three Sacraments of Initiation in their traditional order to adults and to children who are baptized after reaching the age of discretion.

98.   What is the prominence of the Sacrament of the Eucharist in the Church?

St. Augustine answers this question succinctly but powerfully: "Recognize in this bread what hung on the cross, and in this chalice what flowed from his side. . . . what was in many and varied ways announced beforehand in the sacrifices of the Old Testament pertains to this one sacrifice which is revealed in the New Testament."[1] St. John Vianney puts it even more simply: "There is nothing so great as the Eucharist. If God had something more precious, he would have given it to us."

Reception of the Sacrament of the Eucharist completes Christian initiation and is the beginning of a life lived out in the fullest and deepest communion of the Church. Through the Holy Eucharist, the baptized participate most fully in the Life, Death, and glorious Resurrection of the Lord.

Could God have given us anything more precious than his own life-blood? The Body of Christ in the Eucharist is the very body of Christ that hung upon the Cross. The Precious Blood of Christ in the Eucharist is the very blood that flowed from his side. The Holy Eucharist flows from our Lord's perfect sacrifice upon the Cross, from his very heart.

The Gospel of John reports that after a "soldier thrust his lance into his side . . . immediately blood and water flowed out" (Jn 19:34). This passage affirms the actual death of Jesus, for Roman soldiers were trained on exactly how to thrust a sword or lance into the side of their opponent in order to bring about instant death. For a man who hung upon a cross for three hours, and who died of asphyxiation, blood would certainly have flowed from his heart and water from his pierced chest cavity. Yet this detail is included by St. John to make a much deeper point. The blood and water that flowed from the pierced side of Jesus symbolize the waters of Baptism and the Precious Blood of the Holy Eucharist, the very sacramental life of the Church.

The Church treasures this great gift of Christ's own Body and Blood, so readily available to us in the Sacrament of the Eucharist. The Holy Eucharist is the very heart of the Church, her source and her summit (cf. *CCC*, 1322–1327).

99.   What are the different names of the Sacrament of the Eucharist, and what do they mean?

The Sacrament of the Eucharist is called by various names, each of which points to a certain aspect of the sacrament without excluding other dimensions. In fact, to have a full understanding of the Holy Eucharist one must appreciate the insight in each of these terms:

- *Eucharist,* or *Holy Eucharist.* The Greek word *eucharistein* means "giving thanks," especially for gifts given by God. The Eucharist is the supreme act of thanksgiving for the gift of salvation given through the saving death of the Lord (cf. *CCC*, 1328, 1359–1361).

- *The Lord's Supper.* This term recalls the institution of the Holy Eucharist at the Last Supper, as well as the heavenly and everlasting banquet of the Lamb that awaits those who persevere in faith (cf. Rv 19:6–9, cf. *CCC*, 1329).

- *The breaking of bread.* The disciples who encountered the Risen Lord along the road to Emmaus could not contain their joy upon recognizing Jesus "in the breaking of the bread" (cf. Lk 24:13–35, esp. v. 35, cf. *CCC*, 1329). We meet the Lord in the breaking of the bread that has become his real and substantial presence in the Holy Eucharist.

- *Eucharistic assembly.* The Holy Eucharist is celebrated amidst the assembly of God's People, "the visible expression of the Church" (*CCC*, 1329).

- *Memorial.* When Jesus instituted the Holy Eucharist, he commanded his Apostles to "do this in memory of me" (Lk 19:22). Yet the Eucharist is more than simply recalling the memory of the Last Supper. Through the celebration of the Holy Eucharist, that which is remembered is made present upon the altar (cf. *CCC*, 1330, 1362–1365).

- *The Holy Sacrifice.* "The sacrifice of Christ and the sacrifice of the Eucharist are one single sacrifice" (*CCC*, 1367). The Eucharist is the sacrificial memorial of the perfect sacrifice of Jesus upon the Cross. The body of our Lord that hung upon the Cross and the blood that flowed from his wounds are the same Body and Blood made present and offered upon the altar at Holy Mass, albeit in an unbloody manner (cf. *CCC*, 1365). The Holy Sacrifice of the Mass is the re-presentation of the single sacrifice of our Lord upon the Cross, made for forgiveness of sins (cf. Heb 10:1–14). "The Eucharist is thus a sacrifice because it re-presents (makes present) the sacrifice of the cross, because it is its memorial and because it applies its fruit: [Christ], our Lord and God, was once and for all to offer himself to God the Father by his death on the altar of the Cross, to accomplish there an everlasting redemption" (*CCC*, 1366).

- The *Holy and Divine Liturgy*, or the *Sacred Mysteries*. The celebration of Holy Mass is a unique entrance into the mysteries of our salvation, the great work of our redemption wrought upon the Cross. Through the sacred liturgy we encounter the Lord Jesus, the Suffering Servant prophesied by Isaiah, the one who bore our pain, endured our sufferings, and was pierced for our sins (cf. Is 53). We enter into the mystery of the Lord's saving death at every Mass. We take our place at the foot of the Cross on Calvary every time we participate in the Divine Liturgy (cf. *CCC*, 1330).

- *Most Blessed Sacrament.* This is a fitting term for the sacrament of sacraments. In the other sacraments, we truly encounter Christ, but in this sacrament, we not only encounter Christ but receive him, Body, Blood, Soul, and Divinity. We frequently call the Eucharistic species reserved in the tabernacle by this name (cf. *CCC*, 1330).

- *Holy Communion.* Through this sacrament we are united with Christ in the most profound way. Through this sacrament we are further incorporated into Christ's mystical body. Our communion is holy because we encounter in this sacrament the "holy of holies," the substantial presence of God in our midst, the bread of angels and the medicine of immortality (cf. *CCC*, 1331).

- *Holy Mass.* The word *Mass* comes from the Latin word *missa* for "send," one of the concluding words of the celebration when offered in the Latin language: *Ite missa est* means "Go, the Mass is ended." The encounter with the Lord Jesus in the Eucharistic liturgy ends with a challenge to go forth and to live out the faith in one's daily life, sharing with others in word and deed the great gift that has been received (cf. *CCC*, 1332). The Holy Eucharist must always motivate us to service to the poor and the works of mercy, corporal and spiritual (cf. *CCC*, 1397).

100. What is meant by the Real Presence of Christ in the Eucharist?

We believe that the Lord's presence in the Eucharist is much more profound than his presence in the beauty of nature, or even his presence when experienced in service to the poorest of the poor (cf. Mt 25:31–46, *CCC*, 1373). Since the earliest days, the Church has affirmed the unique mode of Christ's Real Presence in the Eucharist. Catholics not only believe in the Real Presence of Jesus in the Holy Eucharist, but we believe in his *substantial* presence—that is, he is really present in the substance of the consecrated bread and wine.

The Church has used the language of change when teaching about the Holy Eucharist, a change made possible by the power of God's Word and the power of the Holy Spirit: "It is not man that causes the things offered to become the Body and Blood of Christ, but he who was crucified for us, Christ himself. The priest, in the role of Christ, pronounces these words, but their power and grace are God's. This is my body, he says. This word transforms the things offered" (St. John Chrysostom, quoted in *CCC*, 204n). The faith of the ancient Church rests securely in the Lord's own words spoken at the Last Supper, "Take and eat, this is my body" (Mt 26:26) and "Drink from it, all of you, for this is my blood of the covenant, which will be shed on behalf of many for the forgiveness of sins" (Mt 26:27).

Our Lord does not equivocate in his words. He is crystal clear when he says that "unless you eat the flesh of the Son of Man and drink his blood, you do not have life within you. Whoever eats my flesh and drinks my blood has eternal life, and I will raise him on the last day. For my flesh is true food, and my blood is true drink. Whoever eats my flesh and drinks my blood remains in me and I in him" (Jn 6:53–56).

101. What is meant by the term *transubstantiation*?

The term *transubstantiation* refers to the change of the essential nature of the bread and wine into the Body and Blood of Christ during consecration at Mass. The prefix *trans* means "to go across" or "to change," as in the words *transform* and *transport*. *Substance* refers to the very essence of a thing or a person, as opposed to the accidental features such as shape and color. An artist can paint a piece of wood or carve it into a figurine, but its substance remains wood. The artist changes the accidents by carving, but the substance of wood remains unchanged. Or think of this example using a dog. The substance is the dog itself. But a dog may be black or brown, its accidents. Color, weight, and motion are examples of accidents.

In the Holy Eucharist, the opposite occurs. The accidents of the bread and the wine remain, so their weight, color, and shape are unchanged; but by the power of the Holy Spirit and the power of the Word of God spoken over the gifts of bread and wine ("This is my body" and "This is the chalice of my blood"), the substance of the bread and wine is changed. Bread and wine worth in and of themselves but a few pennies are changed into treasures of inestimable value, the very Body and Blood, Soul and Divinity, of the Lord (cf. *CCC*, 1373–1377). Always remember that the *whole Christ* is substantially present in both the Blessed Sacrament and the Precious Blood. In Holy Communion, we receive the whole Christ whether we receive only a fraction of the sacred host or a single drop of the Precious Blood from the chalice.

102. What is the proper way to show respect for the Blessed Sacrament when entering or leaving a church?

When entering or leaving a church in which the Blessed Sacrament is reserved in a tabernacle, or when passing in front of a tabernacle marked with a veil or burning votive candle, it is fitting to genuflect with your right knee or to bow deeply as a sign of adoration. Adoration or worship is due to God alone, Father, Son, and Holy Spirit. In her Eucharistic piety, which includes the reservation of the Blessed Sacrament in the tabernacle and the popular devotions of exposition and Benediction, the Church affirms her belief in the Real Presence (cf. *CCC*, 1379).

Summary and Reflection

Throughout the history of the Church there have always been essential steps to the process of becoming a Christian. These include hearing and accepting the Good News of Christ, making a profession of faith, and, ultimately, receiving the three Sacraments of Initiation. Baptism is "the basis of the whole Christian life, the gateway to the life in the Spirit, and the door which gives access to the other sacraments" (*CCC*, 1213). Confirmation more perfectly binds the person to the Church and enriches him or her with a special strength of the Holy Spirit (cf. *CCC*, 1285). Full welcome into the Church occurs through receiving Holy Communion in the Sacrament of the Eucharist.

◑ Creation

You were made to be in relationship with God. How do the Sacraments of Initiation help you to build a relationship with him? What follow-through is necessary to keep that relationship healthy?

◔ Fall

"For just as through the disobedience of one person the many were made sinners, so through the obedience of one the many will be made righteous" (Rom 5:19). How do the Sacraments of Initiation draw us into the righteousness of Jesus? How does the Holy Eucharist bring us to the Lord's Cross and Resurrection?

✚ Redemption

How is the Holy Eucharist "food for the journey" of life? How is the Bread of Life different from common bread? What sets this sacred meal apart from a common meal?

◕ Restoration

How do the Sacraments of Initiation change us? How does the Sacrament of the Eucharist have an impact on our daily living?

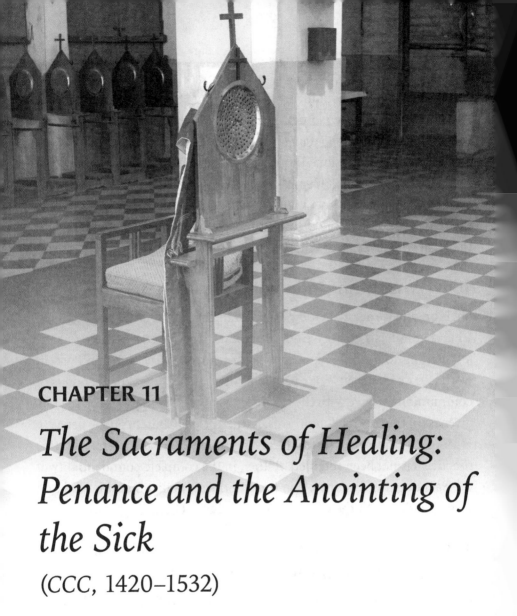

CHAPTER 11

The Sacraments of Healing: Penance and the Anointing of the Sick

(CCC, 1420–1532)

The newly baptized Christian is free of all sin, Original Sin and personal sin. That person's soul is perfectly cleansed and remains perfect—for a very short time! As with our human friendships, our relationship with God is vulnerable to our selfishness, our tendency to rebel, our sinfulness. And as Jesus healed so many people who were broken in body and soul, so does he continue his ministry of healing through the Sacrament of Penance and the Sacrament of the Anointing of the Sick.

For many who are inquiring about entering the Catholic Church, the Sacrament of Penance (sometimes called *Reconciliation* or *Confession*) can seem to be a great challenge. There may be some fear or worry about making a first Confession. Those who were raised Catholic may also feel anxiety about their next Confession, especially if it has been a while since last receiving the sacrament. Yet the less acute these difficulties become, the more we come to see the Sacraments of Healing as encounters with the Lord who loves us dearly.

103. What is sin, and what are its effects?

Sin is an offense against God. Sin also damages our relationship with the Church. Sin has a corrosive effect upon us. It makes us less able to love, less willing to sacrifice, less capable of bearing witness to the Lord in word and deed. Because our personal sin weakens or severs the bonds of communion we have with the Church, it is necessary that we seek the forgiveness of the Church for our sins. In the ancient Church, public penance was done by those who sought forgiveness for mortal sins. Mercifully, this practice has not been retained. Rather, in the complete confidentiality of the Sacrament of Penance, one finds both reconciliation with God and reconciliation with the Church (cf. *CCC*, 1443–1445).

104. Why do I have to think about my sins and express sorrow to God for them?

It is always a good thing to express sorrow for sin to God in your personal prayer. The Church has long recommended an examination of conscience at the end of every day, so that we might tell God in our prayer that we are sorry for what we have done as well as for what we have failed to do. This time-honored practice helps us to make progress in the ongoing conversion of life to which we are called.

Conversion is not just the initial turning away from a sinful past and embracing the Christian life. Conversion is a daily process through which we offer up our lives to God, asking him to refine us according to his will and purpose and expressing our openness to his direction in our lives, so that we might continually choose to turn away from sin and to embrace the Lord, who is the Way, the Truth, and the Life. Other words for conversion are *penance* or *repentance,* derived from the Greek word *metanoia,* which means "a change of mind and heart." "The Lord . . . is patient with you, not wishing that any should perish but that all should come to repentance" (2 Pt 3:9). A sincere examination of conscience at the end of every day is a form of penance, a way of turning back to the Lord.

Within the Christian life there can be moments when we choose to distance ourselves significantly from God's will and God's commandments. "Sin is before all else an offense against God, a rupture of communion with him" (*CCC,* 1440). Mortal sins are the most serious, the gravest, for they are deadly by their very nature (cf. 1 Jn 5:16–17). These are the sins by which baptismal grace is lost and can be restored only by conversion of heart and "a new initiative of God's mercy . . . which is normally accomplished within the setting of the sacrament of reconciliation" (*CCC,* 1856). In Chapter 14 we will learn more about sin, including the difference between mortal sin and venial sin.

105. Why do I have to confess my sins to a priest?

There are two reasons for this. The first has to do with our Lord instituting the Sacrament of Penance. Remember that only God has the power to forgive sins. Our Lord employs this power by saying to others publicly, "Your sins are forgiven" (Mk 2:5). Thus does our Lord exercise his divine prerogative to forgive sins, an authority that he extends to his Apostles on the evening of his Resurrection: "Jesus came and stood in their midst and said to them, 'Peace be with you. . . . As the Father has sent me, so I send you.' And when he had said this, he breathed on them and said to them, 'Receive the holy Spirit. Whose sins you forgive are forgiven them, and whose sins you retain are retained'" (Jn 20:19–23).

Jesus extends this power and authority not to all of his followers, but only to the Apostles, to their successors the bishops, and to the priests who are collaborators with the bishops in the work of reconciliation (cf. *CCC,* 1461). By virtue of the Sacrament of Holy Orders, priests are "configured to Christ the priest in such a way that they are able to act in the person of Christ the head" (*Presbyterorum Ordinis* 2, cf. *CCC*, 1563). We confess to a priest because only a priest (or bishop) has been configured to Christ the Head of the Church and through that configuration has the power to absolve sins. While one might find comfort in disclosing one's sins to a counselor or therapist, one finds absolution only through a priest. This leads into the second reason for confessing to a priest: repairing our relationship with members of the Body of Christ, the Church.

106. To what degree is my confession to a priest held in confidence?

What you say to the priest is held in the strictest confidence. The priest may not reveal to anyone else what he has heard you say in the context of the Sacrament of Penance. This strict confidence is known as the *seal of Confession*; that is, what is disclosed in the confessional is sealed by the sacrament. A priest who is guilty of breaking the seal is subject to the most severe penalties from the Church. Most courts today honor the seal of Penance in criminal and civil cases. In the past, priests have undergone torture and even accepted martyrdom when corrupt regimes have attempted to force them to violate the seal of Confession (cf. *CCC*, 1467). Your priest is absolutely committed to doing nothing less.

107. Why is the Sacrament of Penance called "a second baptism"?

Through the water of the Sacrament of Baptism the soul is cleansed of both Original Sin and personal sin. In the fourth century, St. Ambrose compared the Sacrament of Penance with Baptism, stating that our sins are forgiven first by the water of Baptism, and later by the water of our tears of repentance (cf. *CCC*, 1429). Indeed, compunction (sorrow) for our sins can bring us to tears, especially when we remember that in our sins we not only break God's law but offend against our relationship with him and with our neighbor. Our heart can become hardened and our conscience calloused by giving in to temptation and straying from the path of life. God's grace brings us back, and God gives us the strength to start over again. "It is in discovering the greatness of God's love that our heart is shaken by the horror and weight of sin and begins to fear offending God by sin and being separated from him. The human heart is converted by looking upon him whom our sins have pierced" (*CCC*, 1432, cf. Jn 19:37, Zec 12:10).

When we make a good Confession, we touch the Cross of the Lord and are washed clean by the blood that flows from his wounds. In the Sacrament of Penance we encounter the Lord, who is quick to forgive and incredibly generous in pouring out his grace upon us that we might make progress along the path that leads to heaven. "For God so loved the world that he gave his only Son, so that everyone who believes in him might not perish but might have eternal life. For God did not send his Son into the world to condemn the world, but that the world might be saved through him" (Jn 3:16–17).

108. How is the Sacrament of Penance administered?

The Sacrament of Penance involves the words and actions of both the penitent and the priest. The penitent confesses his or her sins, being sure to state the name and number of mortal sins, expressing sorrow through an Act of Contrition, and making satisfaction by performing the assigned penance (see "How to Go to Confession," page 164). The priest offers a prayer of absolution, which always includes the words, "I absolve you from your sins, in the name of the Father, and of the Son, and of the Holy Spirit."

109. What is an indulgence?

One can be forgiven from sin yet still have a temporal punishment to face. For example, one can be absolved for the sin of verbal abuse but still have to deal with the consequences of that sin.

Indulgence refers to a partial or total wiping away of punishment due for sins that have been forgiven. The Lord gave the keys to St. Peter to bind and loose sin (cf. Mt 16:19) and entrusted the Church with both the ministry of redemption and the inexhaustible treasury of the merits and

How to Go to Confession

Follow these steps for celebrating the Sacrament of Penance:

1. Preparation

Spend some time examining your conscience. Consider your actions and attitudes in each area of your life (for example, faith, family, work, social relationships). Ask yourself: *Is this area of my life pleasing to God? What needs to be reconciled with God? With others? With myself?* How have you—in your thoughts, words, and actions—neglected to live Christ's commands to "love the Lord, your God, with all your heart, with all your soul, and with all your mind" and to "love your neighbor as yourself" (Mt 22:37, 39)? As a help with this examination of conscience, you might review the Ten Commandments or the Beatitudes (Ex 20:2–17; Dt 5:6–21; Mt 5:3–10; or Lk 6:20–26). Sincerely tell God that you are sorry for your sins. Ask God for forgiveness and for the grace you will need to change what needs changing in your life. Promise God that you will try to live according to his will for you.

2. Entering the Confessional

Approach the area for Confession. Wait at an appropriate distance until it is your turn. When you enter, make the Sign of the Cross with the priest. He may say, "May God, who has enlightened every heart, help you to know your sins and trust in his mercy." You reply, "Amen."

3. Confession

Confess your sins to the priest. Simply and directly talk to him about the areas of sin in your life that need God's healing touch. If you are unsure what to say, ask the priest for help. When you are finished, conclude with these or similar words: "I am sorry for these and all my sins."

4. Penance

The priest may talk to you about your life and encourage you to be more faithful to God in the future, and he will impose on you a penance for your sin. The penance corresponds as far as possible with the gravity and nature of the sins committed. It can consist of prayers, offerings, works of mercy, service to neighbor, voluntary self-denial, sacrifices, or patient acceptance of the crosses that you must bear. You should continue in acts of penance, prayer, charity, and bearing sufferings of all kinds for the removal of the remaining temporal punishment for sin.

5. Act of Contrition

The priest will ask you to say an Act of Contrition. You may recite one from memory. A suggested Act of Contrition is:

My God,
I am sorry for my sins with all my heart.
In choosing to do wrong
and failing to do good,

I have sinned against you
whom I should love above all things.
I firmly intend, with your help,
to do penance,
to sin no more,
and to avoid whatever leads me to sin.
Our Savior Jesus Christ
suffered and died for us.
In his name, my God, have mercy.
(*Rite of Penance*, 45)

6. Absolution
The priest will then extend his hands over your head and pray a prayer of absolution for your sins. You respond, "Amen."

7. Praise
The priest may praise the mercy of God and invite you to do the same. For example, the priest may say, "Give thanks to the Lord for he is good." And your response would be, "His mercy endures for ever" (*Rite of Penance*, 47).

8. Dismissal
The priest will wish you peace. Thank him and leave. Go to a quiet place in the church and make your prayer of penance.

satisfactions of Christ and the saints (cf. *CCC* 1476). For this reason, an indulgence is closely related to the Sacrament of Penance. An indulgence depends upon contrition for sins, absolution, and detachment from sin.

110. How frequently must I receive the Sacrament of Penance?

The precepts of the Church dictate that we are to confess our mortal sins at least annually (cf. *CCC*, 1457, 2042). Common sense and the virtue of prudence urge us to receive the Sacrament of Penance as soon as possible after committing a mortal sin, for mortal sin puts one's soul in grave danger of eternal punishment in hell should we die (cf. *CCC*, 1033). One who is guilty of having committed a mortal sin may not receive Holy Communion without having received absolution from the priest in the Sacrament of Penance (cf. *CCC*, 1457). When speaking about the Holy Eucharist, St. Paul warns us of the dangers of partaking of Holy Communion unworthily, that is, in a state of mortal sin (cf. 1 Cor 11:27). Just as we make our house ready to receive a special guest, so too do we make clean our soul of mortal sins before welcoming into our person the Lord of Lords and King of Kings.

Receiving the Sacrament of Penance once every year is a minimum standard that tells us what we must do. The Church also recommends the regular confession of venial sins so that they will not metastasize into patterns that lead us into mortal sin (cf. *CCC*, 1458). It is a healthy practice to confess one's sins monthly whenever possible. When one is careless about small things, that person is likely to be careless about greater things. St. Augustine compares venial sin to a tiny grain of sand, but then directs our attention to a large pile of sand that could not be moved without great difficulty. This image warns us not to be complacent about small sins, for they can quickly add up and become dangerously large.[1]

A multitude of saints have been made holy by drawing near to the Lord in the Sacrament of Penance, encountering him in this sacrament as both a just judge and a skilled physician, whose words and actions heal the soul. When we go to Confession, we place ourselves in the capable hands of the Lord, whom we encounter in a personal way, so that he might say to each of us the words we long to hear, "Your sins are forgiven" (cf. Mk 2:5, *CCC*, 1484). Those who confess their sins may enter the confessional anxious and nervous, but a few minutes later, having received absolution, they leave with a strong sense of the peace that this world cannot give (cf. *CCC*, 1468).

111. What is the purpose of the Sacrament of the Anointing of the Sick?

The sacraments of the Church are celebrated at the most significant moments in a person's life. When a person begins to be in danger of death due to a serious illness, that person is at a significant juncture in life.

Serious illness can bring a person either to self-absorption and rejection of God or toward greater spiritual maturity, leading that person closer to God (cf. *CCC*, 1500–1501). Through the prayers and anointing offered by the priest in the Sacrament of the Anointing of the Sick, the whole Church commends to the Lord the needs of the one whose life is in danger, that the sufferings of the present and the possible sufferings to come might be united with the suffering and Death of the Lord (cf. *CCC*, 1499).

Sometimes physical healing can be traced to the moment the priest anoints a seriously ill person, for miracles continue to happen in our day and age. Yet one might not expect even the most intense prayers to bring about physical healing. Nevertheless, in the long history of the Sacrament of the Anointing of the Sick, its spiritual benefits are undeniable. When anointed through this sacrament, a critically ill person can rightly expect to have a personal experience of Jesus the Healer, be comforted by the prayers of the Church, and receive the grace to unite his or her sufferings with those of the Lord, entrusting the outcome of the illness to fulfill the petition in the Lord's Prayer, "thy will be done."

112. Where can the Sacrament of the Anointing of the Sick be found in the Bible?

Not only did Jesus minister to the sick, but he took on their misery: "He took away our infirmities and bore our diseases" (Mt 7:18, cf. Is 53:4). Yet Jesus did not cure all the sick or set up a hospital. His healing of sick people was a sign of a more radical healing, that which he brought to humanity through his saving Death and Resurrection. By dying on the Cross, Jesus took away sin, "of which illness is only a consequence. By his passion and death on the cross Christ has given a new meaning to suffering: it can henceforth configure us to him and unite us with his redemptive Passion" (*CCC*, 1505).

Along with the many accounts of Jesus and his Apostles healing the blind, the infirm, and the leprous, the Letter of St. James provides a specific instruction to the early Church about taking care of the sick: "Is anyone among you sick? He should summon the presbyters of the church, and they should pray over him and anoint [him] with oil in the name of the Lord, and the prayer of faith will save the sick person, and the Lord will raise him up. If he has committed any sins, he will be forgiven" (Jas 5:14–15, cf. *CCC*, 1510). The Church identifies the *presbyters* spoken of by St. James as the bishops and priests of the Church. Only bishops and priests administer this sacrament. Through the Sacrament of the Anointing of the Sick, a person in danger of death both encounters the Lord and experiences a practice of the Church that goes back to its beginning (cf. *CCC*, 1516).

113. Who may be anointed?

In times past, this sacrament was administered only when a person was in imminent danger of death. The sacrament was formerly called *extreme unction*, or "the last anointing." Today the sacrament is to be offered in broader circumstances and should be given when someone begins to be in danger of death from sickness or old age. The sacrament may be repeated should the person's condition worsen or if he or she should suffer from another grave illness. The sacrament may also be received before surgery performed because of a life-threatening condition. Also, the elderly may receive the sacrament if they become less stable and grow frailer.

It is important that family members call for a priest to administer this sacrament when a sick person *begins* to be in danger of death, so that the graces of the sacrament might be of assistance to the one who is approaching the end of life. Time for Confession should precede the anointing; the priest will invite family members to wait outside the room for a few minutes to ensure privacy for the Sacrament of Penance. Family members *are* invited to be present when the Sacrament of the Anointing of the Sick is celebrated.

Sometimes this sacrament is celebrated in church, even in the context of Holy Mass. The local community and the wider Church, including the saints and angels, are invited to surround those who are ill through prayer and solidarity.

114. How is the Sacrament of the Anointing of the Sick administered, and what are the effects of receiving this sacrament?

The priest administers this sacrament by praying over the sick person for the grace of the Holy Spirit and the forgiveness of sins, and by laying hands and anointing that person with holy oil upon the forehead and, if possible, the hands.

The one who is anointed in this sacrament receives many graces and blessings, including:

- the forgiveness of sins, though the Sacrament of Penance remains the ordinary means by which mortal sins are forgiven (cf. *CCC*, 1520)

- the grace of the Holy Spirit, bestowing peace, acceptance, courage, and physical healing if it is the will of God (cf. *CCC*, 1520)

- union with Christ's Passion, for just as through the first Adam and Original Sin humanity is burdened with suffering, so through the Christ, the New Adam, does suffering acquire a new meaning, a participation in the saving works of the Lord (cf. *CCC*, 1521)

- the grace to assist others through sufferings offered up for the living and the dead (cf. *CCC*, 1522)

- the blessing of being prepared for death, ready to go forth from this life to the next, trusting that God is ever faithful to his promises

A person who is actively dying may also receive the apostolic pardon, granting remission of all temporal punishment due to sin. The priest may also offer the beautiful prayer known as the Commendation of the Dying. If the dying person is capable of receiving Holy Communion, then the Blessed Sacrament is administered as *viaticum*, a word that means "food for the journey" (cf. *CCC*, 1523–24).

Summary and Reflection

The Sacraments of Healing—Penance and the Anointing of the Sick—are available to those who are baptized to provide relief from the burden of sin, the grace of renewal of heart and mind, and preparation for death. The Sacraments of Healing are sacraments of hope, for the Lord is full of mercy and compassion. As St. Paul says so eloquently, "If, then, we have died with Christ, we believe that we shall also live with him. We know that Christ, raised from the dead, dies no more; death no longer has power over him" (Rom 6:8–9).

● *Creation*

God has a plan for your life, a plan that will bring you true happiness in this life and unto eternal life. God is so good and so loving! What motivates you to live a good and holy life? How is the way you live your life pleasing to God?

⊙ *Fall*

Tragically, sin gets in the way of our relationship with God, sometimes in very serious ways. Without revealing the secrets of your heart to your neighbor, what gets you in trouble? What distracts you from the path of life? Why do you seek to find the good life in things that glitter and sparkle, but end up being fool's gold?

✝ *Redemption*

Read Luke 15: 11–32, the parable of the prodigal son. What do you notice about the father in this parable? What is his attitude to the son who returns to him? Why is the reaction of the other son so understandable? What does the father in the parable say and do to each of his sons?

☉ *Restoration*

Many people feel great relief after receiving the Sacrament of Penance and Reconciliation, especially when a heavy burden has been lifted from their hearts. However you might feel after a good Confession, what do you know for sure has happened when you have confessed your sins and received absolution?

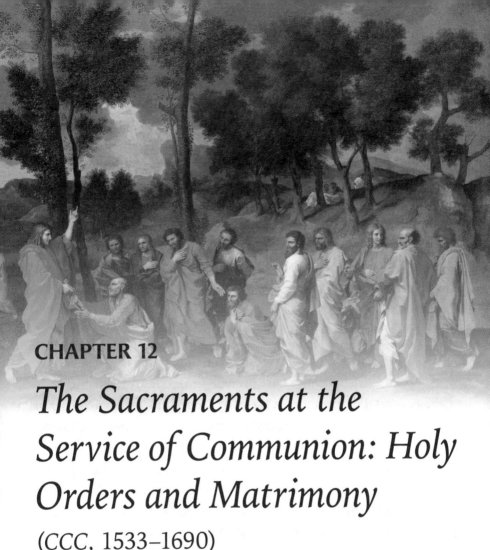

CHAPTER 12

The Sacraments at the Service of Communion: Holy Orders and Matrimony

(CCC, 1533–1690)

It may seem odd to pair the Sacraments of Holy Orders and Matrimony, yet the Church has done just that in calling each a "Sacrament at the Service of Communion." They receive this designation because these sacraments are directed toward the salvation and sanctification of others. Those who are ordained share with the Church God's Word and all of the graces through the sacraments they administer, especially the sacrifice of the Holy Eucharist. Those who are married cooperate as husband and wife to extend the human race through bringing children into the world and work for the salvation of their spouse and children.

Sometimes there is an explicit connection between the two sacraments. In the Eastern Churches, it is not unusual to find married men who have been ordained priests, while in the Latin Church a married priest is a rare exception. Also, many priests participate in the marriage preparation ministry, forming couples called to the vocation of marriage and family life.

This chapter considers Holy Orders and Matrimony as two sacraments through which those who receive them are consecrated to lives of service for the sake of building up the Church in a way proper to each sacrament (cf. *CCC*, 1534–35).

115. What is meant by "order" in Holy Orders?

Going back to the time of the New Testament, the Church has been blessed with groups of Christians who have been organized into established bodies called *orders*. For example, in the early Church there was an *order of widows* who were committed to praying for the needs of others and taking care of the practical needs of other widows with no children to support them. In the ancient Church and even today, there is an *order of catechumens* who are making their way toward the Sacraments of Initiation. (If you are not baptized and sincerely wish to enter the Church through Baptism, you will enter the Order of Catechumens through a sacred ritual as part of your journey to the Sacraments of Initiation.

The orders of bishops, priests, and deacons go back to the earliest days of the Church and are seen as three degrees of the Sacrament of Holy Orders, a sacrament instituted by our Lord at the Last Supper. Members of these three orders have received a sacred ordination through the laying on of hands of a bishop and the invocation of the Holy Spirit. At their ordination, bishops, priests, and deacons receive a gift of the Holy Spirit that permits the exercise of sacred power proper to their order, a power "which can only come from Christ himself through the Church" (*CCC*, 1538).

116. How do Holy Orders relate to the way in which the Church is structured or ordered?

"Christ the Lord set up in his Church a variety of offices which aim at the good of the whole body" (*Lumen Gentium*, 18). These offices are arranged in a *hierarchy*, a word that means the way in which a community is structured or ordered. (Hierarchy even has a meaning in computer programming, related to how memory storage is structured.)

Jesus Christ instituted the Church and is the source of ministry and hierarchy in the Church. Jesus invited all people to follow him, but among his followers were twelve Apostles who were formed by our Lord in a very personal way. The word *apostle* means "one who is sent." Jesus walked with the Apostles, dined with them, and chose them to be with him at his Last Supper. He sent them out to teach in his name, to baptize and to sanctify the Church with the sacraments, and to exercise leadership and governance in the Church. From the Lord, the Apostles received the sacred power to act *in persona Christi Capitis*, meaning "in the person of Christ the Head" of the Church (cf. *CCC*, 875).

The Apostles exercised their ministry in imitation of the way that Jesus ministered to others, always with an eye toward service in word and in deed. Jesus was the Suffering Servant (cf. Is 53) who took upon his own shoulders the sufferings of others. He was the Good Shepherd who freely laid down his life for his flock. In a similar way, the Apostles were no strangers to suffering for the sake of the Gospel. They were willing to face persecution and even martyrdom in witness to the faith. Even to this day, bishops and priests exercise their ministry knowing that authentic service carries with it the duty to give one's all for the sake of the Lord and his flock (cf. *CCC*, 876).

The Apostles, the first bishops of the Church, acted collegially. When a matter of Church practice was disputed, they gathered in Jerusalem to resolve the controversy (cf. Acts 15). Bishops in the Church today exercise their ministry from within the *college of bishops*, in communion with the successor of St. Peter, the bishop of Rome. Likewise do priests exercise ministry under the guidance of their bishop in close collaboration with their brother priests in a fellowship known as the *presbyterium* (cf. *CCC*, 877).

117. How are the bishops of the Church related to the Apostles?

The bishops of the Church are successors of the Apostles, participating in the apostolic succession that traces back to the twelve Apostles. The authority and power given by Jesus to the Twelve has been passed on through the centuries by the laying on of hands (cf. 1 Tm 4:14). The Church is *apostolic* because her bishops are the successors of the Apostles chosen and sent by the Lord to teach, sanctify, and lead the Church (cf. CCC, 861–862, 935).

118. What is the role of the pope, the successor of St. Peter?

Jesus said, "You are Peter, and upon this rock I will build my church, and the gates of the netherworld shall not prevail against it" (Mt 16:18). Jesus chose St. Peter to be the head of the Twelve. St. Peter spoke for the twelve Apostles and was given the keys of the Kingdom of Heaven (cf. CCC, 881).

At the end of his life, St. Peter would find himself in Rome, the capital of the vast and powerful Roman Empire. St. Peter served as the first bishop of the Church in Rome, the city in which he met his death as a martyr at the hands of the Roman emperor Nero. The successive bishops of Rome—and therefore the successors of St. Peter—were looked to by other bishops around the world to mediate conflicts and to settle matters of controversy. The pope, as St. Peter's successor, "is the perpetual and visible source and foundation of the unity both of the bishops and of the whole company of the faithful" (*Lumen Gentium*, 23, cf. CCC, 882). "For the Roman Pontiff, by reason of his office as Vicar of Christ, and as pastor of the entire Church has full, supreme, and universal power over the whole Church, a power which he can always exercise unhindered" (*Lumen Gentium*, 22, cf. CCC, 882).

119. How is the pope infallible?

Bishops of the Church are authentic teachers of the faith handed down by Christ through the Apostles. In teaching the faith, they are "endowed with the authority of Christ" (*Lumen Gentium*, 25). Christ, who is the Truth, willed to confer upon the Church "a share in his own infallibility" (*CCC*, 889). *Infallible* means "incapable of error."

To persevere in the truth, Christ gave to the bishops "the charism of infallibility in matters of faith and morals" (*CCC*, 890). This charism is exercised by the pope *in very specific situations*, not in every word that he speaks or in every opinion he states. "The Roman Pontiff, head of the college of bishops, enjoys this infallibility in virtue of his office, when, as supreme pastor and teacher of all the faithful . . . he proclaims by a definitive act a doctrine pertaining to faith or morals" (*Lumen Gentium*, 25, cf. *CCC*, 891). In other words, the infallibility of the pope pertains to specific teaching moments, and it applies only to matters of faith or morals. Papal infallibility does not mean that the pope cannot make a mistake, only that by virtue of his office, he is protected from error in faith and morals when teaching in clearly defined situations.

120. What are cardinals?

The cardinals are the senior clergy of the Church in Rome. Though the cardinals are from many nations and serve around the world, each cardinal has responsibility for a parish church in Rome.

The cardinals also have a role in electing a new pope. When there is a vacancy in the papacy, cardinals under the age of eighty gather to elect a new pope in an event known as a *conclave*. The word *conclave* means "with a key," for the cardinal electors are locked away from the world in and around the Sistine Chapel in Rome to conduct the election of the new pope. Once the candidate elected by the cardinals accepts, he becomes the visible head of the Church and enjoys "supreme, full, immediate, and universal power in the care of souls" (*CCC*, 937). The new pope customarily takes a new name and is prayed for by name at every celebration of Holy Mass around the world. Upon his election in 2013, Pope Francis became the 265th successor to St. Peter as bishop of Rome.

121. What is the Scriptural foundation for the Sacrament of Holy Orders?

The origins of the sacrament go back to the time of the Old Testament and the offering of sacrifices. In those days, priests taken from the tribe of Levi were consecrated to mediate with God on behalf of the Jewish people, to make offerings of thanksgiving to God and to offer sacrifices for the forgiveness of sins. We can see the priesthood of the Old Covenant, including the priesthood of Aaron, the priesthood of the Levites, and the selection of the seventy elders (Num 11:24–25), as prefiguring the ordained ministry of the New Covenant (cf. *CCC*, 1541).

122. Was Jesus a priest?

Jesus was not of the tribe of Levi, so he did not function as a priest of the Old Covenant. However, everything in the priesthood of the Old Covenant finds its fulfillment in Christ. He is:

- the "one mediator between God and the human race" (1 Tm 2:5)

- "a priest forever according to the order of Melchizedek" (Heb 5:6, cf. Gn 14:18)

- a high priest who is "holy, innocent, undefiled, separated from sinners, higher than the heavens" (Heb 7:26)

Jesus expressed his priesthood most clearly when he went to his Crucifixion as both the spotless lamb of sacrifice and the only high priest who could offer a perfect sacrifice for the forgiveness of sins. By his unique death on the Cross, Jesus offered a single sacrifice that makes perfect for all time those who are sanctified in the Sacrament of Baptism (cf. Heb 10:12, 14, *CCC*, 1544).

In Christian art, Jesus is sometimes depicted upon the Cross clothed in the vestments worn by the priests who offered the sacrifices of lambs, bullocks, and first fruits in the Temple. In so representing Jesus, the artist is communicating the priesthood of Jesus, who alone was capable of offering the perfect sacrifice for the forgiveness of the sins of all human beings. Jesus's sacrifice on the Cross at Calvary is unique, accomplished once for all, yet it is also re-presented upon the altar in the Sacrament of the Eucharist. "The same is true of the one priesthood of Christ; it is made present through the ministerial priesthood without diminishing the uniqueness of Christ's priesthood" (*CCC*, 1545).

123. How does the ministerial priesthood differ from the common priesthood?

The ministerial priesthood is distinguished from but related closely to the priesthood of all believers, called the *common priesthood*. Jesus made his Church "a kingdom, priests for his God and Father" (Rv 1:6, cited in *CCC*, 1546). Each member of the Church, by virtue of the Sacraments of Baptism and Confirmation, is called upon to participate in the mission of Christ as priest (to offer sacrifices pleasing to the Lord), prophet (to spread the Word of God), and king (to build up the Kingdom of God). Regardless of his or her vocation, every baptized person receives "a share in the common priesthood of all believers" (*CCC*, 1268, cf. *CCC*, 1546).

The ministerial priesthood of the bishops, priests, and deacons and the common priesthood of the faithful both share in the one priesthood of Jesus Christ, each in its proper way. While essentially different, the two participations in the priesthood of Jesus Christ are each ordered to the other. The common priesthood is "exercised by the unfolding of baptismal grace, a life of faith, hope and charity, a life according to the Spirit," while "the ministerial priesthood is at the service of the common priesthood" (*CCC*, 1547). Christ builds up and leads the Church through the ministerial priesthood, and for that reason it is conferred by a special sacrament, the Sacrament of Holy Orders (cf. *CCC*, 1547).

124. How does Jesus build up the Church through the three degrees of the ministerial priesthood?

Jesus promises never to leave the Church without his living presence, assuring the Church that he is with us, even to the end of time (cf. Mt 28:20). Jesus keeps this promise through each of the sacraments, and in a particular way through his real and substantial presence in the Holy Eucharist. In the second century, St. Ignatius of Antioch wrote about the three degrees of the Sacrament of Holy Orders—bishops, presbyters (priests), and deacons.[1] Through the Sacrament of Holy Orders, especially through the ministry of bishops, our Lord is present as the Head of the Church. The bishop and the priests and deacons who collaborate with him are called to lives of service for the People of God, in imitation of Jesus, the Suffering Servant of God (cf. *CCC*, 1551).

Those in Holy Orders exercise their service in the person of Christ, the Head of the Church, and in the name of the whole Church. This is not to say that the bishops, priests, and deacons are delegates of the community. Sacred power and an indelible spiritual character are conferred on those who are ordained so they may act and serve as Christ's representative (cf. *CCC*, 1581–82). "It is because the ministerial priesthood represents Christ that it can represent the Church" (*CCC*, 1553).

125. What is the role of the bishop in the life of the Church?

The word *bishop* is associated with the word *episcopal*, a word with deep roots in the New Testament that means "overseer." The important role of bishop is well documented in the New Testament and in the writings of the early post-apostolic era. The bishops are in the unbroken line of apostolic succession. The Holy Spirit, poured out upon the Apostles on the day of Pentecost, has been transmitted to their successors even to this day by the laying on of hands in the episcopal ordination (cf. *CCC*, 1556).

The bishops are chosen from the ranks of the priests (presbyters), and with their episcopal consecration the fullness of the Sacrament of Holy

Orders is conferred upon them. The bishops "in an eminent and visible manner, take the place of Christ himself, teacher, shepherd, and priest, and act as his representative" (*CCC*, 1558). Each bishop is responsible for the pastoral care of the diocese entrusted to him, yet he is also called to participate in the college of bishops so that he might express "solicitude for all the Churches" (*CCC*, 1560). The intervention of the pope, the bishop of Rome, is necessary for the lawful ordination of a new bishop. In fact, the pope's written mandate is shown to all during the rite of ordination of a bishop, demonstrating the soon-to-be ordained bishop's bond with the universal Church through the bishop of Rome (cf. *CCC*, 1559).

The bishop of a diocese (or archbishop of an archdiocese) oversees the life of the local Church, especially in ensuring sound teaching, assigning priests and deacons to parishes, and celebrating the Sacrament of Confirmation. The bishop administers the management of the spiritual and temporal goods of the Church and safeguards the needs of the poor and less fortunate. In liturgical ceremonies in his diocese, the bishop carries a crozier that is shaped like a shepherd's staff, a symbol of his role as chief pastor (shepherd) of the local Church. He often presides at one of the rites of Christian initiation, the Rite of Election and Call to Continuing Conversion.

126. How do priests collaborate with the bishop?

The priests are called "co-workers of the bishops," assisting the bishops in fulfilling their mission as successors of the Apostles (cf. *CCC*, 1562). Priests are ordained for the threefold mission of teaching the faith, celebrating the sacraments, and shepherding God's People. Priests offer Holy Mass and celebrate the other sacraments as "true priests of the New Testament" (*Lumen Gentium*, 28).

On the day of their ordination, diocesan priests promise obedience to their bishop and his successors. This is an outward sign of the solidarity between a bishop and his priests in carrying out their respective duties. Throughout his life, a diocesan priest will be asked to take parochial (parish) assignments for the good of the wider Church. The priest accepts new assignments not out of an obligation of sheer obedience to the bishop but from the desire to serve the particular needs of the Church beyond his present assignment. Wherever he is assigned, the priest has the opportunity to teach, sanctify, and guide the portion of the flock entrusted to his care.

127.   What is the role of deacons?

Deacons are ordained to serve in several ways. In fact, the word *deacon* comes from the Greek word *diakonia*, which means "service." Deacons assist the bishop and the priests in the sacred liturgy by distributing Holy Communion, assisting at weddings and funerals, and proclaiming and preaching the Gospel. The deacon is dedicated to the works of charity, often exercising a leadership role among those who serve the poor, the imprisoned, and those in poor health.

The diaconate was for many years solely a transitional step toward the priesthood. A candidate for Holy Orders was ordained a deacon, and then some months later ordained a priest. While this is still the case, there are other men who are called to serve permanently as deacons, often in parish settings. It is the task of the so-called *permanent deacons* to assist the parish priests and witness in a very positive way to the laity through their stable, public ministry (cf. *CCC*, 1569–1571).

128.   What is the connection between priesthood and celibacy?

The connection between the priesthood and celibacy is rooted in the example of our Lord, who did not marry and was thereby free to offer himself entirely to the mission of proclaiming the Kingdom, even giving his very body upon the Cross for the forgiveness of our sins.

In the Latin Church, those who are ordained priests are normally chosen from men who are living a celibate life and who promise to remain celibate for the sake of the Kingdom for the rest of their lives (cf. *CCC*, 1579). Exceptions are made for a married, male minister of another Christian faith tradition with ordained ministers. In recent years under a provision enacted by Pope John Paul II, several hundred married men have been ordained priests in the Latin Church who had previously served as ministers in Episcopal, Lutheran, Presbyterian, or Methodist communities. Furthermore, Pope Benedict XVI opened the doors for entire Anglican communities to be received into full communion in the Church and to be served by their married, male clergy, who were then ordained Catholic priests.

In the Eastern Churches, a different discipline has been in practice for many centuries, in which bishops are chosen from among the celibate clergy but most priests are ordained from the ranks of married men. The Eastern Churches continue to hold priestly celibacy in high regard. In fact, in the Latin Church and in the Eastern Churches, "a man who has already received the sacrament of Holy Orders can no longer marry" (*CCC*, 1580).

129. Why is the Sacrament of Holy Orders received only by men?

The answer to this question poses a difficulty for many, yet the difficulty is not insurmountable. The Church does not ordain women because it has no authority to do so. The Lord chose twelve males to be his Apostles, and the clear and consistent teaching of the Church from her earliest days is that Holy Orders is reserved for males.

This teaching does not derive from a belief that women are less competent than men or that their human dignity is any less than that of a man. In fact, the Church teaches that "man and woman have been created . . . in perfect equality as human persons" (*CCC*, 369). According to Pope John Paul II, "the fact that the Blessed Virgin Mary, Mother of God and Mother of the Church, received neither the mission proper to the Apostles nor the ministerial priesthood clearly shows that the non-admission of women to priestly ordination cannot mean that women are of lesser dignity, nor can it be construed as a discrimination against them. Rather, it is to be seen as the faithful observance of a plan to be ascribed to the Wisdom of the Lord of the Universe" (*Ordinatio Sacerdotalis*, 3).

The Church Disfigured by Sin

If you were to ask people what good the Catholic Church has done in history and is doing today, how do you think they might respond? Many would likely cite the Church's work with the poor both domestically and internationally through agencies such as Catholic Charities and Catholic Relief Services. Others might mention the Catholic Church's network of hospitals that have been around for hundreds of years or, particularly in the United States, her system of Catholic schools, which have educated many non-Catholics as well as generations of Catholics. Some might mention the Church's unwavering support for life at all stages from conception to natural death.

While these answers about the good the Catholic Church has done and continues to do may vary, if you ask the same people, "What is the worst thing the Catholic Church has done in history?" most would reply, "sexual abuse." The Church's sexual abuse crisis has been at the forefront of the news about the Catholic Church for much of this century, though most of the particular cases of sexual abuse committed by Catholic clergy had been committed decades before, stretching back to the mid twentieth century.

There is no excuse for the heinous sins of priests and bishops, especially the sins that destroy lives and seriously damage the integrity of the Church. Many Catholics have left the Church because of these scandals. Others have become disillusioned about religion in general and Catholicism specifically. The mission of the Church to make disciples of all nations has been critically undermined by the scandals that have been brought to light by the secular press. Yet the Church finds consolation when perpetrators of abuse receive justice for their crimes, when victims are provided with the means by which to rebuild and heal their lives, when the larger problem of abuse in our society is recognized, and when the environments where children and youth gather are increasingly made safer by the diligent application of measures designed to protect the well-being of young people.

The tragedy of sin is no stranger in the life of the Church. The presence of Christ in a priest or bishop does not preserve him from weakness and sin. The sin of the Church's ministers does not impede the effectiveness and grace of the sacraments, but "in many other acts the minister leaves human traces that are not always signs of fidelity to the Gospel and consequently can harm the apostolic fruitfulness of the Church" (*CCC*, 1550). The Church is always in need of purification and reform, and the Church is always deeply wounded by the sins of her clergy, as well as the sins of her other sons and daughters.

Bishop Robert Barron's book *Letter to a Suffering Church: A Bishop Speaks on the Sexual Abuse Crisis* addresses forthrightly the horrible sins committed by priests and bishops, the great harm done to the lives of so many, and the necessity of ongoing vigilance. Bishop Barron also writes of the hope that is more powerful than despair, the light that is stronger than darkness:

In the end, we are not Catholics because our leaders are flaw-less, but because we find the claims of Catholicism both com-pelling and beautiful. We are Catholics because the Church speaks of the Trinitarian God whose very nature is love; of Jesus the Lord, crucified and risen from the dead; of the Holy Spirit, who inspires the followers of Christ up and down the ages; of the sacraments, which convey the Christ-life to us; and of the saints, who are our friends in the spiritual order. This is the treasure; this is why we stay.[2]

Above all, Jesus is the reason we remain Catholic. As some have put it, "Don't leave Jesus because of Judas."

130. When did Jesus institute the Sacrament of Matrimony?

By performing his first miracle at the wedding feast in Cana (Jn 2:1–11), by insisting upon the indissolubility of marriage (cf. Mt 5:31–32, Mt 19:3–9), and by teaching everything that one needs to know about spousal love by his sacrificial death on the Cross, Jesus can be said to have elevated marriage between a baptized man and woman to the level of a sacrament.

In actuality, from the very beginning of creation God established the married state and endowed it with laws. God created the human person out of love, and every human person is called to love. Love is the voca-tion of the human person. The mutual love between husband and wife is not only a good thing, but a "very good thing" (Gn 1:31), "an image of the absolute and unfailing love with which God loves" men and women (*CCC*, 1604). Marriage in God's plan is a "covenant, by which a man and a woman establish between themselves a partnership of the whole of life, [and] is by its nature ordered toward the good of the spouses and the procreation and education of offspring" (*Code of Canon Law*, canon 1055, cf. *CCC*, 1601).

131. What did Jesus's presence at the wedding in Cana indicate about marriage?

Jesus thought so much about the dignity of marriage that he chose a wedding as the location of his first miracle, the changing of water into wine at the wedding feast in Cana (cf. Jn 2:1–11). This setting for such an important event shows our Lord's mind about the goodness of marriage, and it gives an indication that marriage will be regarded as a sacrament, an efficacious sign of the presence of the Lord (cf. *CCC*, 1613).

Note as well that the mother of our Lord was present for this miracle, giving the waiters an instruction that each of us should strive to live by: "Do whatever he tells you" (Jn 2:5). Mary is present at the most significant moments in her Son's life, and she always points to his importance and our call to follow him.

132. What is the marriage bond?

The marriage bond is created through the mutual exchange of consent by the man and woman to the marriage promises. By its nature, the bond is indissoluble and irrevocable once consent is mutually given and consummated. The marriage bond is "an institution, confirmed by the divine law . . . even in the eyes of society" (*Gaudium et Spes*, 48, cf. *CCC*, 1639).

Within the security provided by the marriage bond, Christ "encounters Christian spouses through the sacrament of Matrimony. Christ dwells with them, gives them the strength to take up their crosses and so follow him, to rise again after they have fallen, to forgive one another, to bear one another's burdens, to 'be subject to one another out of reverence for Christ,' and to love one another with supernatural, tender, and fruitful love. In the joys of their love and family life he gives them here on earth a foretaste of the wedding feast of the Lamb" (*CCC*, 1642, cf. Rv 19:5–8).

The grace of the Sacrament of Matrimony builds upon the natural intent of the couple to persevere in their marriage. This grace "is intended to perfect the couple's love and to strengthen their indissoluble unity. By this grace they 'help one another to attain holiness in their married life and in welcoming and educating their children'" (*Code of Canon Law*, canon 1141, cited in *CCC*, 1641). What God has joined, no one may divide: "The Church does not have the power to contravene this disposition of divine wisdom" (*CCC*, 1640).

133. How is the Sacrament of Matrimony celebrated in the Church?

Normally the marriage of two Catholics takes place during Holy Mass, with vows exchanged in the presence of the priest. In the Eastern Churches the bishop or priest receiving the vows places beautiful crowns on the heads of bride and groom as a sign of the marriage covenant (cf. *CCC*, 1623). In having their wedding within a *nuptial* (wedding) *Mass*, the newly married couple is able to have as their first meal together the sharing in the Body and Blood of Christ in the Holy Eucharist (cf. *CCC*, 1621). Because they will be receiving Holy Communion, the Sacrament of Penance is commonly received by the bride and groom within a day of the wedding (cf. *CCC*, 1622).

When a Catholic person marries a non-Catholic Christian, the wedding liturgy takes place within the church sanctuary but is usually outside the context of Holy Mass. Permission from the appropriate authority is required for a marriage to be accomplished according to the laws of the Church. When a Catholic person marries a non-Christian, a dispensation from the bishop is required, and the wedding liturgy is always outside the context of Holy Mass. In both cases, the Catholic party must promise to remain Catholic and to do everything in his or her power to have the children baptized and raised as Catholics (cf. *CCC*, 1634–1636). The non-Catholic partner is fully aware of this promise. While it is important that these couples live in mutual respect for their different faith traditions, it is fitting that the Catholic spouse pray that the non-Catholic spouse be led to a genuine conversion to the Catholic faith (cf. *CCC*, 1636–1637).

134. What did Jesus teach about the indissolubility of marriage?

Our Lord teaches about the divine plan for marriage as being indissoluble, even striking down some of the exceptions that had crept into the religious laws of his day:

> Some Pharisees approached him, and tested him, saying, "Is it lawful for a man to divorce his wife for any cause whatever?" He said in reply, "Have you not read that from the beginning the Creator 'made them male and female' and said, 'For this reason a man shall leave his father and mother and be joined to his wife, and the two shall become one flesh'? So they are no longer two, but one flesh. Therefore, what God has joined together, no human being must separate." They said to him, "Then why did Moses command that the man give the woman a bill of divorce and dismiss [her]?" He said to them, "Because of the hardness of your hearts Moses allowed you to divorce your wives, but from the beginning it was not so. I say to you, whoever divorces his wife (unless the marriage is unlawful) and marries another commits adultery." (Mt 19:3–9, cf. *CCC*, 1614–1615)

Jesus's insistence upon the divine plan for indissolubility of marriage is not meant to impose a burden too heavy to bear. Rather, Jesus inaugurates a new reign of grace, through which couples, by following the Lord wholeheartedly, will receive the Lord's help to overcome the tendency toward selfishness, to accept the daily sacrifices that are an inevitable part of every marriage, and to persevere in hope that God's grace is sufficient to overcome even the most insurmountable difficulties (cf. *CCC*, 1615). Jesus's teaching of the indissolubility of marriage will be treated in greater detail in Chapter 19.

135. What does the Church teach about divorce?

The Church does not recognize the power of civil divorce to end a valid marriage. According to the divine law taught by our Lord, marriage is an unbreakable bond and a lifelong commitment, and no civil law can change this (cf. *CCC*, 1650).

Yet the Church also recognizes that difficulties in marriage do occur. Often these difficulties can be overcome with God's grace. Couples who have troubles but overcome them through prayer, good counsel, and hard work witness to the power of Christ's presence in the Sacrament of Matrimony (cf. *CCC*, 1647). Someone who is experiencing marital troubles should seek the assistance of a trusted priest, especially in the Sacrament of Penance. Often there are paths forward through seemingly insuperable difficulties, for nothing is impossible with God (cf. Lk 1:37).

There are situations, however, when a separation of spouses is prudent, especially in cases of spousal abuse or when other difficulties make remaining together practically impossible. In these cases, the couple remains bound by the bond of marriage and should attempt reconciliation if possible (cf. *CCC*, 1649). (Please see Question 215 for more information on the issue of separation.)

Because the marriage bond persists even with a civil divorce, remarriage is not permitted if the first marriage is valid. "If the divorced are remarried civilly, they find themselves in a situation that objectively contravenes God's law. Consequently, they cannot receive Eucharistic communion as long as this situation persists" (*CCC*, 1650). A person who is divorced but who has not remarried incurs no punishment from the Church, nor is that person deprived of the sacraments (cf. *CCC*, 1651). The Sacrament of Penance and restitution are required of any whose sins have contributed to the divorce.

Few families are spared from suffering and pain when a loved one goes through divorce. Tragically, divorce ruptures not only the bond between husband and wife but also between other family members, and sometimes even with God. At a time when those going through divorce need the Lord and his Church the most, there can be a tendency to distance one's self from the sacraments, often from feelings of guilt or the mistaken notion that a divorced person is no longer able to receive the sacraments. Those who are divorced or who are going through divorce will find in the Church not judgment but solicitude, not isolation but solidarity. God's healing presence has a way of penetrating the heart especially when one needs it the most.

136. How do the blessings of the Sacrament of Matrimony overcome sin in marriage?

Sin corrupts and corrodes things that are intrinsically good. The account of Adam and Eve in the Garden of Eden teaches an all-too-familiar lesson about the consequences of disobedience to God's plan for human happiness. Because Adam and Eve broke their relationship with God by disobeying his commands, their own relationship was broken. It devolved from harmony into discord, from selflessness to self-centeredness, from mutual trust into jealousy and envy (cf. *CCC*, 1607). "The beautiful vocation of man and woman to be fruitful, multiply, and subdue the earth was burdened by the pain of childbirth and the toil of work" (*CCC*, 1607).

Yet the blessings of the Sacrament of Matrimony subsist, though disturbed by sin. God's grace and mercy are never withheld from those who strive to overcome the obstacles and to persist in seeking the good that God intends in marriage. By God's grace, "marriage helps to overcome self-absorption, egoism, pursuit of one's own pleasure, and to open oneself to the other, to mutual aid and to self-giving" (*CCC*, 1609).

137. What is meant by the Theology of the Body and what does it have to do with marriage?

Theology of the Body refers to a series of teachings by Pope John Paul II at the beginning of his pontificate in 1978. Presenting these teachings at his regular Wednesday audiences, the pope took on a subject that was very controversial in secular society and in the Church herself, namely that "each and every marriage act must remain open to the transmission of life" (*Humanae Vitae*, 11, cf. *CCC*, 2366). Many outside the Church claimed that this teaching was behind the times and burdensome to women. Even within the Church there was widespread, public dissent by theologians and parish priests who said that the Church was being insensitive to families with serious reasons to limit the number of their children.

From a deep philosophical and theological background, and with a genuine understanding of the way couples wrestle with questions about the regulation of births, Pope John Paul II presented in a clear, cogent, and compassionate manner how the teaching of the Church could be lived in a manner that would deepen the bonds of love between husband and wife and that would be of benefit to the couple spiritually, emotionally, and physically.

Theology of the Body is well suited for our day and age, in which the sexual revolution holds in esteem and considers normal practices that have been, and continue to be, regarded as grave sins against the Sixth and Ninth Commandments, especially cohabitation before marriage, so-called open marriages, and contraception. Pope John Paul II said so eloquently:

> Conjugal love involves a totality, in which all the elements of the person enter—appeal of the body and instinct, power of feeling and affectivity, aspiration of the spirit and of will. It aims at a deeply personal unity, a unity that, beyond union in one flesh, leads to forming one heart and soul; it demands indissolubility and faithfulness in definitive mutual giving; and it is open to fertility. In a word it is a question of the normal characteristics of all natural conjugal love, but with a new significance which not only purifies and strengthens them, but raises them to the extent of making them the expression of specifically Christian values. (*Familiaris Consortio*, 13)

More information on the Theology of the Body and conjugal love will be presented in Chapter 19.

138. Who are consecrated men and women in the Church who forgo marriage?

Jesus invites some to follow him by renouncing the great good of marriage so as to enter into an intimate union with him alone (cf. Mt 19:12, *CCC*, 1619). St. John Chrysostom compared the vocation of vowed celibacy with marriage:

> Esteem of virginity for the sake of the kingdom and the Christian understanding of marriage are inseparable, and they reinforce each other: "Whoever denigrates marriage also diminishes the glory of virginity. Whoever praises it makes

virginity more admirable and resplendent. What appears good only in comparison with evil would not be truly good. The most excellent good is something even better than what is admitted to be good." (cited in *CCC*, 1620, cf. also 1 Cor 7:33–34)

Examples within the Church include consecrated men and women who are vowed to a life of celibate chastity so as to give themselves to God alone, to pursue a life of service to the Kingdom of God as a public witness to God's goodness, and to proclaim the glory of the world to come (cf. *CCC*, 916). Priests, especially in the Latin Church, are also normally called from the ranks of those who live, and who promise to continue to live, a life of celibate chastity for the sake of the Kingdom (cf. *CCC*, 1618–1620).

Summary and Reflection

All of the sacraments provide a framework for understanding Christian vocations. In Baptism and Confirmation, we receive a share in the common priesthood of Christ, which we live out by participating in his priestly, prophetic, and kingly offices. Two sacraments—Holy Orders and Matrimony—are called Sacraments at the Service of Communion because they are mainly directed to the holiness and salvation of others. The Sacrament of Holy Orders confers a sacred power on priests for the service of the faithful. The ordained man belongs uniquely to the ministerial priesthood. Marriage is a vocation modeled on Christ's union with the Church. The purpose of Christian marriage is to further the human race and to contribute to the eternal destiny of husband, wife, and children.

⊖ *Creation*

Jesus taught about the goodness of marriage, elevating it to a sacrament. From your experience, how is marriage a good? How are married couples called to share their blessings as a couple with others?

◐ *Fall*

In some places, 50 percent of marriages end in divorce. Considering the many things you have learned from the Bible and the teachings of the

Church, what words of encouragement can you offer to couples who are struggling, and what words from the Bible can you offer to those who are striving to recover after a difficult divorce?

✝ Redemption

Jesus expresses perfect love upon the Cross, teaching us that true love is about fidelity, commitment, and sacrifice, even to the point of shedding blood. How do married couples bear witness to the true love that Jesus shows from the Cross? How do bishops, priests, and deacons bear witness to that same love?

Restoration

As you have received and studied the sacraments of the Church, how have you experienced your heart being nudged by God, or what G. K. Chesterton called a "twitch upon the thread"? How do the sacraments call you to ongoing conversion of life?

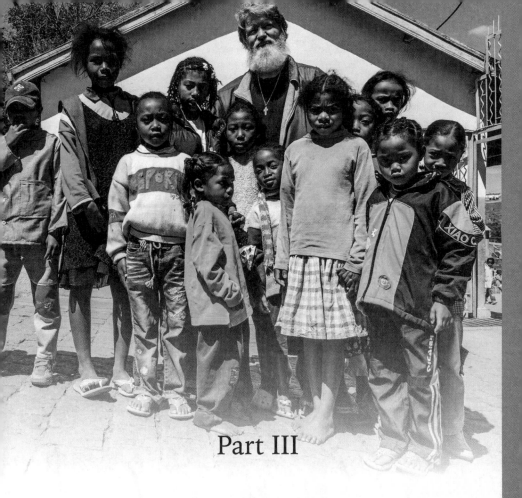

Part III

HOW CATHOLICS LIVE

The goal of the virtuous life is to become like God.

—St. Gregory of Nyssa

CHAPTER 13

The Call to a Good Life
(CCC, 1691–1770)

Within days of his appointment as coadjutor archbishop of Saigon (now known as Ho Chi Minh City) in 1975, François-Xavier Nguyễn Văn Thuận was arrested by the Communist authorities and held in prison for thirteen years. He spent a further three years under house arrest before being exiled from his homeland. Nine of his years in prison were spent in solitary confinement.

As he was being arrested, the first thing the archbishop wondered was if he would ever be able to offer Mass again. Within a few days he would learn the answer to his question. Prisoners were allowed to write home to ask for personal provisions such as toothpaste and medicine. The archbishop asked his family, "Please send me medicine for my stomach-ache." His relatives knew exactly what he meant. Soon a package arrived containing a small bottle of wine marked *Medicine for Stomachaches*. A flashlight was also enclosed in the package, with small, unconsecrated hosts hidden behind the battery.

That night, the archbishop would do what he would repeat every night for the next seventeen years. Lying prone upon his mat, as he was required to do after lights out, with a fraction of a host in one hand, and in the palm of the other hand three drops of wine mixed with one drop of water, the archbishop would recite the prayers of Holy Mass, changing the bread and wine into the Body and Blood of our Lord and then experiencing Holy Communion with Jesus through the gift of the Holy Eucharist.

"Those were the most beautiful Masses of my life," the archbishop later wrote, because "each time I celebrated the Mass, I had the opportunity to extend my hands and nail them to the cross with Jesus, to drink with him the bitter chalice. Each day in reciting the words of consecration, I confirmed with all my heart and soul a new pact, an eternal pact between Jesus and me through his blood mixed with mine."[1]

When word circulated among the prisoners that their new archbishop was with them, they arranged for Catholics to sleep near him. Each night, from underneath the mosquito net that now served as his cathedral, Archbishop Nguyễn Văn Thuận would distribute Holy Communion to the Catholic prisoners. Those with strong faith found their faith growing even stronger. Those who were lukewarm felt an increase in the virtue of faith. Those who were not Catholic soon sought from the archbishop the Sacraments of Baptism and Confirmation so that they, too, could receive Holy Communion. By the power of the Lord Jesus, made possible through what the archbishop would call "the most beautiful Masses of my life," the darkness of that prison gave way to the bright, Paschal light that shone through the great gift of the Holy Eucharist.[2]

In Part III, we will take a deeper look at how Catholics are to live by growing in virtue and holiness, by discerning God's will each and every day, and by keeping the Ten Commandments. Our discussion begins with the nature of human beings and our call to a truly *good life*—our vocation to a happy life here on earth and for all eternity in the glory of heaven. This chapter will explore the true nature of happiness and the desire of all people to be happy. The experiences of the Venerable François-Xavier Nguyễn Văn Thuận and countless saints show us that following Jesus and abiding in the communion of the Church make all the difference.

139. What does following Jesus have to do with living a moral life?

Jesus is the "image of the invisible God" (Col 1:15), the one who comes to rescue from the powers of sin and death all men and women, each of whom is created in the image and likeness of God (cf. Gn 1:27). The image of God in us, disfigured by sin, has been "restored to its original beauty and ennobled by the grace of God" through the saving Death and glorious Resurrection of Jesus (cf. *CCC*, 1708). By the grace of God, what was damaged by the sin of our first parents has been restored by the Lord's saving death on the Cross. We have been delivered from sin and the power of Satan (cf. *CCC*, 1708). Jesus's death merits for us new life in the Holy Spirit, making it possible for us to act rightly and to do good. "In union with his Savior, the disciple attains the perfection of charity which is holiness. Having matured in grace, the moral life blossoms into eternal life in the glory of heaven" (*CCC*, 1709).

140. How does God make us free to choose good over evil?

God creates the human person in his image and likeness, and this distinguishes human beings from the other animals. The human being is "the only creature on earth that God has willed for its own sake" (*Gaudium et Spes*, 24, cited in *CCC*, 1703). Unlike the other marvelous creatures made by God, we possess an immortal soul, which means that we are destined for happiness for all eternity. Also, humans are the only creature with an intellect and will, which gives us freedom to choose God and his goodness:

- Our intellect gives us the gift of reason, through which we can come to know that there is a God (cf. Chapter 1) and to understand the order of God's creation, including God's plan for human happiness.

- Free will gives the human person the capacity to decide in favor of what is truly good. The human person finds perfection "in seeking and loving what is true and good" (*Gaudium et Spes*, 15, cited in *CCC*, 1704).

Our first parents were blessed with an experience of having inner peace, of being in harmony with each other and with nature, and of being in full communion with God. They walked and talked with him "in the cool of the day" (Gn 3:8). Life was very good for our first parents, and they were an "outstanding manifestation of the divine image" (*Gaudium et Spes*, 17, cited in *CCC*, 1705). Our first parents enjoyed true freedom, the freedom to be authentically human, in a beautiful relationship with each other, and to experience a deep and personal relationship with their Creator.

Sadly, the freedom of our first parents was "limited and fallible" (*CCC*, 1739). Led astray by Satan, they fell victim to temptation and chose to do what was evil. The wound of Original Sin (cf. Chapter 2) has left its mark on the human person, who is still desirous of choosing the good but is "inclined to evil and subject to error" (*CCC*, 1707). "Man is divided in himself. As a result, the whole life of men, both individual and social, shows itself to be a struggle, and a dramatic one, between good and evil, between light and darkness" (*Gaudium et Spes*, 13, cited in *CCC*, 1707).

Yet "where sin increased, grace overflowed all the more" (Rom 5:20). Through his saving death upon the Cross, Jesus cancels the debt of sin. "He merited for us the new life in the Holy Spirit. His grace restores what sin had damaged in us" (*CCC*, 1708). The one who believes in and follows Jesus is adopted as a son or daughter of God. This adoption is transformative in nature, giving that person new life in the Holy Spirit. That person matures in grace and is capable of choosing the good and acting in a righteous manner. A child of God possesses the grace to live a good and moral life, a life that "blossoms into eternal life in the glory of heaven" (*CCC*, 1709).

This chapter and the chapters that follow will spell out how we can find happiness by following Jesus along the path of life and will go into specific detail about the meaning of each of the Ten Commandments and the New Commandment given by our Lord: "Love one another as I have loved you" (Jn 13:34).

141. What does Jesus mean by happiness when he delivers the Beatitudes?

For some, happiness connotes a feeling that is both shallow and fleeting, such as the happy feelings during a day at an amusement park or the sincere but quickly passing happiness when one's team wins the big game. However, there is a kind of happiness that is much deeper than a feeling and lasts much longer than even a lifetime. This is the happiness that our Lord wants for us and of which he speaks when he delivers the Beatitudes (cf. Mt 5:1–12), his eight sayings on *blessedness* that form the preamble to his Sermon on the Mount (cf. Mt 5:1–7:29). Some translations of the New Testament have substituted "happiness" for "blessedness." Suffice to say, Jesus wasn't speaking of amusement park or big-game happiness.

The philosophers of ancient Greece wrote about natural happiness several hundred years before Christ. Aristotle spoke of happiness as a state of *eudaimonia*, a word that means "good spirit." Aristotle connected happiness with a life of virtue, ever growing in knowledge and wisdom. Happiness in the natural sense meant living a good and honorable life and contributing according to one's own abilities to the common good, even to the point of sacrifice for the well-being of others. Natural happiness consists not in the attainment of riches, pleasure, and power but in a life of virtue.

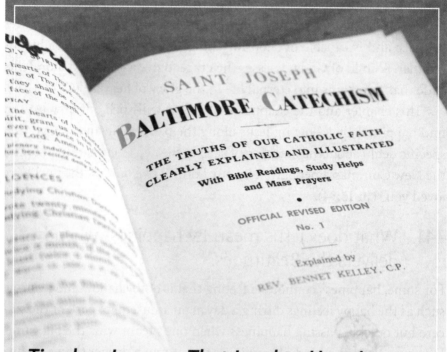

Timeless Lessons That Lead to Happiness

The *Baltimore Catechism* was the standard textbook used in Catholic schools in the United States for generations following its preparation at the Third Plenary Council of Baltimore in 1884 until roughly the 1960s. It listed questions and answers that students—mainly in elementary schools—were expected to memorize. Check out both the simplicity and completeness of some of the answers to questions of faith:

1. **Q. Who made the world?** A. God made the world.

2. **Q. Who is God?** A. God is the Creator of heaven and earth, and of all things.

3. **Q. What is man?** A. Man is a creature composed of body and soul, and made to the image and likeness of God.

4. **Q. Is this likeness in the body or in the soul?** A. This likeness is chiefly in the soul.

5. Q. **How is the soul like God?** A. The soul is like God because it is a spirit that will never die, and has understanding and free will.

6. Q. **Why did God make you?** A. God made me to know him, to love him, and to serve him in this world, and to be happy with him forever in the next.

7. Q. **Of which must we take more care, our soul or our body?** A. We must take more care of our soul than of our body.

8. Q. **Why must we take more care of our soul than of our body?** A. We must take more care of our soul than of our body because in losing our soul we lose God and everlasting happiness.

9. Q. **What must we do to save our souls?** A. To save our souls we must worship God by faith, hope, and charity; that is, we must believe in him, hope in him, and love him with all our heart.

10. Q. **How shall we know the things which we are to believe?** A. We shall know the things which we are to believe from the Catholic Church, through which God speaks to us.

St. Thomas Aquinas (1225–1274) saw much to be admired in Aristotle's teaching on happiness, yet he also saw something missing. He agreed that happiness is living a good life—a life of virtue—but also believed that there is more to life than natural virtue. The supernatural virtues of faith, hope, and charity dispose us to live a life of closeness with God. St. Thomas Aquinas explained that at its very essence, happiness rests in being united to the highest good, which is God himself, and that it is God our Creator who plants in each person the natural desire for happiness. God desires that we be truly happy, and in fact God calls each of us to happiness, a life defined by the Beatitudes. "God alone satisfies," Aquinas summarized (cf. *CCC*, 1718).

142. How, then, do we find happiness?

Every person who has walked this earth has asked this question, but only Jesus has the answer. He is "the way and the truth and the life" (Jn 14:6). Jesus leads us along the path to eternal happiness, a path that is difficult and challenging, a path that requires his divine assistance every step along the way. Jesus calls us to the happiness that surpasses our human desires, a blessedness through which we find the peace that this world cannot give, and the eternal rest promised to the saints.

The Beatitudes confront us with decisive moral choices. They invite us to purify our hearts of bad instincts and to seek the love of God above all else. They teach us that true happiness is not found in riches or well-being, in human fame or power, in any human achievement however beneficial it may be (for example, science, technology, art), or indeed in any creature, but in God alone, the source of every good and of all love (*CCC*, 1723).

143. What is the response to those who say that it is up to each person to determine what is right or wrong, not the Church?

This is a very good question because it points to one of the most serious errors of our day, namely the concept of *relativism*. A *relativist* is convinced that in questions about the morality of an action, there is no right or wrong answer, because it all depends upon a person's point of view. One frequently hears the saying, "I have my truth and you have your truth." This, of course, is a strong contradiction of the words of Jesus, who said, "I am the way and the truth and the life" (Jn 14:6). A person who believes in Jesus cannot at the same time be a relativist. Jesus is the one truth.

144. How does following rules and keeping commandments increase our freedom?

Jesus says, "If you remain in my word, you will truly be my disciples, and you will know the truth, and the truth will set you free" (Jn 8:31–32). True freedom does not mean doing whatever one pleases, whenever and wherever one chooses. This is *licentiousness*, the *license* to choose as we wish, but it is not freedom. In fact, the choice to ignore the truth of God's commandments and to act against them is an abuse of freedom and leads to what St. Paul calls the slavery to sin (cf. Rom 6:17). "By deviating from the moral law man violates his own freedom, becomes imprisoned within himself, disrupts neighborly fellowship, and rebels against divine truth" (CCC, 1740).

There is no freedom without truth—the truth about God, the truth about the human person, the truth about our responsibilities toward others. Rules and commandments do not restrict freedom; rather, they make possible true freedom. "The more one does what is good, the freer one becomes. There is no true freedom except in the service of what is good and just" (CCC, 1733). Nor is there true freedom without Jesus Christ, who redeems us from the bondage of sin and sets us free by his glorious Cross. In him, and in him alone, do we experience "the glorious freedom of the children of God" (Rom 8:21). "The grace of Christ is not in the slightest way a rival of our freedom when this freedom accords with the sense of the true and the good that God has put in the human heart" (CCC, 1742).

145. What are the criteria for judging whether a moral action is good or bad?

We can judge what we can see. We can judge the morality of actions because they can be objectively evaluated as good or bad. We cannot judge what we cannot see. We only know the intentions of the human heart when a person chooses to make them known. Whereas the intentions of the human heart are for God to judge, in cases where the object (the act of what we do) is intrinsically evil, one does not need to know the intention to judge the whole act to be evil.

In order to judge what we can see, we look to three things: the action that is chosen, the intention for which it is chosen, and the circumstances of the action (cf. CCC, 1750).

- The *action* chosen is always perceived as good by the individual who is choosing to act, even though it may not truly conform to the good (cf. *CCC*, 1751). For example, a person who commits the crime of theft might consider the action to be good while ignoring or disregarding how that action has hurt the victim, and how that evil action will eventually be discovered and justly punished. Actions may be judged by the objective standards of morality, as is seen in courtrooms every day.

- The *intention* is the end goal of the one who carries out the action. The thief might steal to provide a better life for his children, but a good end does not justify an intrinsically disordered action such as thievery. The end does not justify the means (cf. *CCC*, 1752–1753).

- The *circumstances* and the consequences of actions are secondary elements. The circumstances do not justify an action that is evil, but they can increase or diminish the moral responsibility of the one who commits the action. The spontaneous theft of a small amount and the carefully executed cracking of a bank safe are both acts of theft, but the second crime is a greater evil than the first. Likewise, stealing five dollars from a beggar's cup and stealing five dollars from a millionaire's wallet are both evil, but the first crime in this case is greater than the second. The judicial system rightly names (and punishes) stealing in different ways according to the value of what was stolen, ranging from petty theft to grand larceny. Circumstances "cannot change the moral quality of acts themselves; they can make neither good nor right an action that is in itself evil" (*CCC*, 1754).

The goodness of a moral action depends upon these three together: a good action chosen, an honorable intention, and the circumstances of the action. An evil intention corrupts the action, such as the case of putting on a display of piety so as to deceive others. Think about a man in the neighborhood who offers to mow the lawn of an elderly woman. The action is good, but if he is only doing it to case the woman's garage and to be able to take some tools, the action becomes evil. Some actions, such as lying, are always wrong because they are in and of themselves morally evil. Other actions are always gravely wrong because of their seriousness, such as blasphemy, perjury, fornication, adultery, and murder (cf. *CCC*, 1756, 2353). It is never permitted to carry out evil for the sake of a good outcome.

146. What are passions?

Passions are feelings or emotions that can prompt us to act or not to act based upon something that is "felt or imagined to be good or evil" (*CCC*, 1763). Our Lord refers to feelings when he speaks about what comes from a person's heart (cf. Mk 7:21). We use the term *heartfelt* to describe the emotions that can move us to speak or to act. Love is the most fundamental passion, since it emerges from an attraction to what is good. Love as a passion "causes a desire for the absent good and the hope of obtaining it; this movement finds completion in the pleasure and joy of the good possessed" (*CCC*, 1765). Be aware, however, that when love is equated with the theological virtue called *charity*, it is *not* a passion. The theological virtues are discussed on page 220.

Passions are neither good nor evil, yet they do affect our opinions and moral decisions. For example, a strong feeling of anger can move a person toward evil, such as striking another person out of cruelty or revenge. On the other hand, a strong feeling of anger can also move a person toward good, such as taking public action to protest or rectify an unjust situation.

Passions are never the decisive element by which the morality of an action is judged, but they do play a part in the moral life. Doing something simply because it feels good leads to moral laxity. Our feelings must be guided by a mind focused on the good and a will motivated by the desire to be close to the Lord and to walk in his way. Passions can be cultivated, either by virtue or by vice. A life of openness to the Holy Spirit and the desire to imitate the lives of the saints will yield feelings that motivate us toward seeking what is good, beautiful, and true.

Summary and Reflection

Our Catholic faith tells us that only in God can we find truth and happiness. God has placed in our hearts a natural desire for happiness in order to draw us to himself, since he alone can fulfill that desire. God reveals himself and gives himself to us most fully in Jesus Christ, who offers us newness of life and eternal happiness. Jesus revealed that God put us in the world to know, love, and serve him; by doing so we enter into the joy of sharing in God's life and love for eternity. Our gift of freedom and reason allows us the opportunity to make our own choice to gravitate to Jesus, who is the Way, the Truth, and the Life. Going even deeper, Jesus presented a formula for deep and abiding happiness in the Beatitudes.

⊖ *Creation*

How do you know that God created you to be truly happy? What brings you happiness that might bring you ridicule from those beholden to a worldly culture?

◐ *Fall*

How do you define relativism? How is God's creation disfigured by the culture of relativism? What do you say to people who speak of their "own truth"?

✝ *Redemption*

How does Jesus call you to happiness? Archbishop Văn Thuận said that he celebrated the most beautiful Masses of his life when he was imprisoned, sharing in the Cross of Jesus in a very personal way. How does Jesus's Death and Resurrection make a difference in how you strive for true and eternal happiness? What does it mean when St. Paul says, "where sin increased, grace overflowed all the more" (Rom 5:20)?

◓ *Restoration*

What is your game plan for happiness? What is the role of the Ten Commandments and the teachings of Jesus as you strive for true freedom and happiness in this life, leading to an eternity of happiness in heaven?

CHAPTER 14

Conscience, the Virtues, and Sin

(CCC, 1776–1876)

If you think of the conscience as an interior voice that informs you of right and wrong, you aren't too far from the truth. The Church defines *conscience* as "the interior voice of a human being, within whose heart the inner law is inscribed" (*CCC*, Glossary). St. Thomas More (1478–1535) is honored as a martyr for his conscience. The Lord High Chancellor of England under King Henry VIII, St. Thomas was executed for his conscientious objection to the legitimacy of the marriage of King Henry to Anne Boleyn. King Henry's divorce and remarriage to his paramour had political motivations; he wanted to ensure a male heir to continue the dynasty.

Thomas refused to do what he clearly knew was wrong. He did not publicly acknowledge King Henry's annulment from his wife Catherine.

Because of this he was arrested and confined in the Tower of London for fifteen months. Several visitors, including fellow lawyer and statesman Thomas Cromwell and Thomas More's own daughter, tried to persuade him to relent and take an oath to King Henry. Thomas continued to reject the oath to Henry, telling the judges that he could not go against his conscience and that he wished they might all meet together in heaven in "everlasting salvation." The jury took only fifteen minutes to find Thomas guilty. To the end, he refused to violate his conscience, though he knew it would mean his execution. He said, "I do nobody any harm, I say none harm, and I think none harm. And if this be not enough to keep a man alive, in good faith I long not to live." For taking this stand, St. Thomas More was led to the scaffold on July 6, 1535, and beheaded at 2:00 a.m. Before the guillotine struck, he called out to a group of gathered spectators that he was dying as "the King's good servant—but God's first."

Today, we witness many examples just the opposite of that of St. Thomas More. In fact, church leaders in the past generations have violated the collective conscience of the Church in case after case splattered across the news of sexual abuse of children, young men, and future priests, damaging the trust Catholics and non-Catholics alike have for the Church. It will take generations to rebuild that trust of conscience. The time to begin is now.

147. What is the purpose of our conscience?

The conscience is our most secret core and sanctuary. "There [the human person] is alone with God whose voice echoes in his depths" (*Gaudium et Spes*, 16, cited in *CCC*, 1776). The moral conscience that rests in the heart of every person moves that person at specific moments to do what is good or to avoid doing evil. The conscience judges the morality of choices made, affirming good choices and denouncing evil choices. The conscience speaks to the truth that comes from God and the eternal good to which every person is called. The conscience must always be obeyed, and this is why it is incredibly important to educate and to form our conscience. A necessary part of this is studying God's law, his commandments. Through the conscience, we hear the voice of God (cf. *CCC*, 1777).

148. How do we know if our conscience is working?

The conscience works best in a person who has cultivated an appreciation for quiet and who is disciplined in prayer. In the busy world in which many of us live, we are never far from the ringing of a cell phone or the streaming of news, music, and entertainment. Living a good life means taking time to form one's conscience and to allow it to be formed, especially by listening to the still, small voice of God that speaks to our heart (cf. 1 Kgs 19:9–12). We don't expect to hear the conscience with our ears but rather in the depths of our heart. An inner life of reflection and self-examination is needed for the conscience to work.

149. How do we form our conscience?

The formation of conscience is a life-long task, beginning in childhood. Parents help their children with this task. The conscience of a child is formed by learning right from wrong, appreciating how the feelings of others can be hurt by careless words, and having empathy for the suffering of those who experience loss and pain. A child who learns the virtues of courage, generosity, humility, and the zeal for doing good is on the right path to true freedom and peace of heart (cf. *CCC*, 1783–1784). There is no substitute for frequent reading of the Holy Bible and the lives of the saints, and regular participation in the sacramental life of the Church even at a young age.

The role of parents, teachers, and other role models in the moral formation of children is indispensable. Children learn from praise and correction, and they have a clear sense of good and bad based upon the amount of guidance and direction in their lives. This guidance is mostly external to them. But the formation of conscience does not end in childhood.

In adolescence, life becomes more difficult. There are more choices to be made, many of which involve delayed gratification and choosing between two goods. Adolescence is a time of rebellion and reaction; it is also a time of opportunity. Adulthood is a time of acquiring moral maturity. We live our lives not in mere conformity to external standards but having interiorized the values of those standards. We are moved not by external coercion, but by an interior desire for good.

At every moment in life's journey, "we are assisted by the gifts of the Holy Spirit, aided by the witness or advice of others and guided by the authoritative teaching of the Church" (*CCC*, 1785). Chapters 21–24 offer specific guidance about the life of prayer that is necessary for the formation of conscience.

150. How specifically is my conscience formed through the teaching of the Church?

The Church is both Mother and Teacher. Through her motherly care, we receive the Word of God and all the moral instruction it contains. We receive the sacraments that nourish and sustain us on the path of righteousness. We learn the example of the holiness of the Blessed Virgin Mary and all the saints (cf. *CCC*, 2030). Through the Holy Eucharist, we participate in the perfect sacrifice offered by Jesus upon the Cross, so that we might offer our own bodies as a living sacrifice, holy and acceptable to God (cf. Rom 12:1). "As does the whole of the Christian life, the moral life finds its source and summit in the Eucharistic sacrifice" (*CCC*, 2031).

Through the Church's role as Teacher, we receive from the Magisterium, the teaching office of the Church, truths taught by Christ that bring salvation. The pope and bishops of the Church are "authentic teachers, that is, teachers endowed with the authority of Christ, who preach the faith to the people entrusted to them, the faith to be believed and put into practice" (*Lumen Gentium*, 25, cited in *CCC*, 2034).

The truths taught by the Magisterium include moral principles and judgments about human affairs to the extent that they apply to the fundamental rights of human beings or the salvation of souls (cf. *CCC*, 2032). The basis of the moral teaching of the Church has been, and always will be, the *Decalogue*, also known as the Ten Commandments. The Magisterium passes on to us what has been handed down through the centuries of Christian life, a "body of rules, commandments, and virtues proceeding from faith in Christ and animated by charity" (*CCC*, 2032) so that we might know clearly the truth about the human person and how we should strive to stand with a clear conscience before God (cf. *CCC*, 2036).

Ever merciful, Holy Mother Church always stands ready to embrace her children when they fall and to extend the forgiveness of sins that awaits a contrite sinner in the Sacrament of Penance and Reconciliation (cf. *CCC*, 2040).

151. What are virtues?

A virtue is "a habitual and firm disposition to do the good" (*CCC*, 1803). A virtue gives a person the ability to keep the commandments, to resist temptations, to follow the will of the Lord, and to live a good life. A virtuous person does not struggle to do what is right. The virtuous person enjoys the inner freedom and practical wisdom to consistently choose and do the good. *Virtue* is related to the term *virtuoso*, which refers to someone so skilled in a particular talent that they make doing the difficult look easy. World-class athletes, first-chair violinists, and gifted artists perform at the highest levels and do incredible things. These *virtuosi* have attained greatness because of their determination and hard work in building upon their natural, God-given abilities.

There are two kinds of virtues: the moral virtues, often called the cardinal virtues, and the theological virtues.

152. What is the purpose of cardinal virtues in the moral life?

The cardinal virtues dispose us to live good lives. The cardinal virtues make possible the living out of a moral life with ease, self-mastery, and joy (cf. *CCC*, 1804). They receive their name from the Latin word *cardo*, meaning "hinge." The cardinal virtues are acquired by human effort: education, repeated good acts, and perseverance in the good. Even non-Christian people recognize these virtues, which is why they are sometimes called "human virtues." All other virtues "hinge" on or are grouped around

An Old Irish Prayer and Your Conscience

A portion of a prayer attributed to St. Patrick and dated based on its linguistic style to the eighth century provides a simple formula for forming and following your conscience. It is a prayer of protection known as the "Lorica of St. Patrick." *Lorica* is an old Irish word for "armor." You might have heard it called "St. Patrick's Breastplate." It is believed that St. Patrick used this prayer in battle, particularly when facing ambush by an enemy.

Though the prayer is divided into eleven sections, it is the following section that captures its essence and is best known. It also captures the best practice for forming and following your conscience: make Christ a part of every decision and engrained in your very life:

> Christ with me, Christ before me, Christ
>   behind me,
> Christ in me, Christ beneath me, Christ
>   above me,
> Christ on my right, Christ on my left,
> Christ when I lie down, Christ when I sit
>   down,
> Christ in the heart of every man who
>   thinks of me,
> Christ in the mouth of every man who
>   speaks of me,
> Christ in the eye that sees me,
> Christ in the ear that hears me.

Our task in forming our conscience is to be conformed with Christ. We are meant to be an *alter Christus*, another Christ.

the cardinal virtues, which are "purified and elevated by divine grace" (*CCC*, 1810).

Four cardinal virtues play a "pivotal role" (*CCC*, 1805) in the moral life:

Prudence

The virtue that disposes us to choose wisely, always looking ahead to the consequences of an action (cf. *CCC*, 1806). The word *prudence* is related to the word *providence*, which means "to look ahead."

Justice

The virtue that disposes us to give to every person his or her due. A just person shows great respect for the possessions of others, including the goods and the good name of every person (*CCC*, 1807).

Fortitude

The virtue that disposes us to do what is right regardless of the circumstance or difficulty. Fortitude gives us strength to resist temptation, to overcome obstacles, and to conquer fear, even to the point of giving one's life for the sake of a higher good (cf. *CCC*, 1808).

Temperance

The virtue that disposes us to control our desires and to set honorable limits in our use of created goods that are pleasurable, such as food and drink. A temperate person exercises restraint and moderation for the sake of a higher good (cf. *CCC*, 1809).

"To live well is nothing other than to love God with all one's heart, with all one's soul, and with all one's efforts; from this it comes about that love is kept whole and uncorrupted (through temperance). No misfortune can disturb it (and this is fortitude). It obeys only [God] (and this is justice), and is careful in discerning things, so as not to be surprised by deceit or trickery (and this is prudence)" (St. Augustine, *De moribus eccl.* 1, 25, 46: PL 32, 1330–1331, cited in *CCC*, 1809).

153. What are the theological virtues, and what is their purpose in the moral life?

The theological virtues dispose us to live in right relationship with God. "We cannot gain these virtues by human efforts. Rather, they are infused into our souls by God to make us capable of choosing goodness over sin, right over wrong, and eternal life over death. The theological virtues are the foundation of Christian moral activity; they animate it and give it its special character" (*CCC*, 1813). These three virtues enable us to live in relation to the Holy Trinity:

Faith

The virtue by which we believe divinely revealed truths, based upon the credibility of God, who reveals them, and the Church, who teaches them. By faith, the believer seeks to live according to the truth and to conform his or her life to the will of God, no matter the cost (cf. *CCC*, 1814–1816).

Hope

The virtue by which we trust in the promises of God and in his mercy, through which he has in store for us eternal happiness and the means by which to attain it. Hope orders our lives toward heaven, keeps us from becoming discouraged along the way, and opens our hearts to live in joyful expectation of the good things to come in heaven (cf. *CCC*, 1817–1818).

Charity

Charity, or love, is the virtue by which we love God above all things for his own sake and our neighbor as ourselves for the love of God. Charity is known as the queen of virtues, for it "upholds and purifies our human ability to love, and raises it to the supernatural perfection of divine love" (*CCC*, 1827).

The theological virtues of faith, hope, and charity distinguish a virtuous Christian from an ethical pagan. They help explain how an atheist can live a decent life, being a good neighbor and a good citizen, while still needing a relationship with God and participation in the sacramental life of the Church so as to have eternal life (cf. *CCC*, 1813). For example, in moments of pain and suffering, a virtuous Christian will exemplify an extraordinary patience that goes far above what would be expected of an ethical pagan.

154. How does sin impact living a moral life?

Sin is defined as an offense against God and the Church. Sin offends against truth and God's commandments. Sin not only hurts our relationship with God and neighbor but corrupts us within. Sin corrodes, disfigures, and disintegrates that which is truly good within us. Sin gets in the way of our own well-being in this life and can keep us from life in heaven with God for all eternity (cf. *CCC*, 1849–1850). Sin offends against Jesus, who went to the Cross to save us from the power of sin. In fact, every sin is a mockery of the tremendous love our Savior shows us through his sorrowful Passion. St. Francis of Assisi said so hauntingly, "Nor did demons crucify him; it is you who have crucified him and crucify him still, when you delight in your vices and sins" (*Admonitio* 5, 3, cited in *CCC*, 598).

The hour of darkness, when Jesus died upon the Cross and when the powers of sin and death seemed to have triumphed, became the hour of Divine Mercy. Sin does not have the final word, for the Eternal Word of Life has conquered its power to deliver us unto the eternal fires of hell. "At the very hour of darkness, the hour of the prince of this world, the sacrifice of Christ secretly becomes the source from which the forgiveness of our sins will pour forth inexhaustibly" (*CCC*, 1851). Jesus's blood is "shed on behalf of many for the forgiveness of sins" (Mt 26:28).

The very name *Jesus* means "God saves." Jesus calls us to conversion of heart, to turn away from sin and to accept his forgiveness and healing mercy through Baptism and the Sacrament of Penance and Reconciliation.

155. What is mortal sin?

Mortal sin is a sin unto eternal death. The word *mortal* means "being subject to death." For a sin to be mortal, it must be seriously wrong, committed with full knowledge of its gravity, and committed with the full consent of one's will. All three of these conditions must be true:

- *The sin must be serious or, as it is sometimes called, grave.* The gravity of a mortal sin turns a person away from God and destroys charity within that person's heart. Sins that are considered serious include blasphemy, perjury, homicide, fornication, and adultery (cf. *CCC*, 1856, 2353). Some sins are serious because of the harm they bring into the lives of others. For example, a stockbroker who takes home an inexpensive pencil from the office is not guilty of committing a grave sin. That same stockbroker who knowingly defrauds senior citizens out of their life savings certainly commits a grave sin.

- *One must have full knowledge that the sin is wrong in the eyes of God.* Some sins are known to be wrong by every person, regardless of their culture or religion, for there is a *natural law* written upon the conscience of every human being (cf. *CCC*, 1860). (Natural law will be discussed in Chapter 15.) However, there are certain actions that are wrong that not everyone is aware of, especially those who live in a culture of promiscuity and licentiousness with little or no awareness of God's commandments. Unintentional ignorance can reduce or even remove the guilt of sin, as can the pathological inability to understand the difference between right and wrong. However, every human being has the personal responsibility to learn the difference between right and wrong. A person is culpable for sinful actions if that person "takes little trouble to find out what is true and good, or when conscience is by degrees almost blinded through the habit of committing sin" (*Gaudium et Spes*, 16, cited in *CCC*, 1791).

- *One must sin with the full consent of the will.* The person who acts because of undue force or pressure does not have full consent of the will, for that person is not deliberately making a personal choice but is being used as the instrument of another or is the victim of circumstance (cf. *CCC*, 1859). A person whose freedom to consent fully to an action is impaired because of a previous, willful choice to anesthetize temporarily through alcohol or drugs his or her capacity to consent freely is nonetheless culpable for any ensuing immoral actions.

Mortal sins make us susceptible to eternal death because they deprive us of sanctifying grace. This is a matter of life and death for the soul. If a person is unrepentant of a mortal sin and does not receive the Lord's forgiveness, the mortal sin "causes exclusion from Christ's kingdom and the eternal death of hell, for our freedom has the power to make choices for ever, with no turning back" (*CCC*, 1861). The Sacrament of Penance and Reconciliation is the normal setting for obtaining forgiveness for mortal sins (cf. *CCC*, 1856). The Church knows no other way for a person to obtain forgiveness for a mortal sin, save only through the mercy of God.

156. What is venial sin?

A lesser sin or a sin that is not mortal is called *venial sin*. A venial sin is the failure to observe the standard of the moral law in a less serious matter. St. John tells us, "There is such a thing as deadly sin. . . . All wrongdoing is sin, but there is sin that is not deadly" (1 Jn 5:16–17). A venial sin could involve grave matter, but the sin would be venial if committed without full knowledge or full consent of the will (cf. *CCC*, 1862).

The word *venial* comes from a word that means "excusable." While mortal sin destroys charity in the heart of the sinner and deprives us of sanctifying grace, venial sin merely wounds charity and allows the sinner to remain in the state of grace (cf. *CCC*, 1852). Venial sin is an offense against God, but it does not sever our relationship with God or put us in danger of losing out on eternal happiness with God in heaven (cf. *CCC*, 1863).

Nevertheless, one must not underestimate the dangers of venial sin. Venial sins committed habitually can numb the conscience and get in the way of our making progress in the virtues. Venial sin without repentance has a dangerous, cumulative effect that can lead to more serious sin. St. Augustine wisely comments, "While he is in the flesh, man cannot help but have at least some light sins. But do not despise these sins which we call 'light': if you take them for light when you weigh them, tremble when you count them. A number of light objects makes a great mass; a number of drops fills a river; a number of grains makes a heap. What then is our hope? Above all, confession" (*In ep. Jo.* 1, 6: PL 35, 1982, cited in *CCC*, 1863).

157. Is there an unforgivable sin?

Jesus says, "whoever blasphemes against the holy Spirit will never have forgiveness, but is guilty of an everlasting sin" (Mk 3:29). Blasphemy against the Spirit is to be deliberate in refusing to be repentant for sins and to reject obstinately the forgiveness of sins and the gift of new and eternal life offered by the Holy Spirit. The Scriptures use the term *hardness of heart* to describe a person who is seemingly impenetrably stubborn in regard to God's grace. Sadly, this can lead to final impenitence and the loss of heaven (cf. *CCC*, 1864), not because of God's unwillingness to forgive, but because of the sinner's unwillingness to repent. God's mercy knows no limits, but God always respects human freedom.

158. Can a person be guilty of a sin committed by others?

Just as in criminal law a person can be found guilty of a crime for being an accomplice, there are ways in which we can incur guilt for the immoral actions of others. In fact, there are nine ways in which we might be guilty of the sin of another person:

1. By counsel (urging or encouraging someone to sin)
2. By command (forcing someone to sin)
3. By consent (giving permission for another person to sin or telling that person that it is okay)
4. By provocation (goading someone into sin)
5. By praise or flattery (building up the sinner's ego through compliments)
6. By concealment (covering up the sin of another)
7. By partaking (sharing in the spoils of another's sin)

8. By silence (failing to rebuke or warn the sinner)
9. By defense of the sin (offering excuses for the evil behavior of another)

Sin is not just a personal matter. Sin affects others profoundly and can even impact negatively the common good (cf. *CCC*, 1868–1869). More will be said about social sin in the next chapter.

Summary and Reflection

The *Catechism of the Catholic Church* defines *conscience* as "a judgment of reason whereby the human person recognizes the moral quality of a concrete act that he is going to perform, in the process of performing, or has already completed" (*CCC*, 1778). Our conscience must be formed. Many of our moral decisions come automatically, born out of vice or virtue. We are asked to increase the practice of our virtues and overcome our vices in order to make good decisions. When our conscience is formed and informed, when we have paid attention to church teaching concerning morality, we are obliged to follow it. The practice of virtues and avoidance of vices helps us to refrain from sin. There are two types of sin. Mortal sin is grave sin that left unrepented can cause the loss of eternal life. Venial sin is less serious and does not deprive the soul of sanctifying grace; however, it is habit-forming and can lead to mortal sin.

⬤ *Creation*

God created you for happiness. Your conscience is a gift from God so that you might find true happiness in this life and in the next. When has your conscience kept you from falling into sin in a way similar to St. Thomas More?

⬤ *Fall*

Sin is destructive. Sin offends against Jesus, who went to the Cross to save us from its power. Sin brings discord, disappointment, and unhappiness into our lives. How have you experienced Jesus as the Good Shepherd, the one who brings back to the fold the lost sheep, the one who is willing to lay down his life for the sake of his sheep?

✚ *Redemption*

What does it mean to you when it is said, "Sin does not get the final word"? How is the death of the Lord a triumph of Divine Mercy?

⬤ *Restoration*

God never stops inviting you to conversion of heart and a new and abundant life. How have you experienced growth in one or more of the virtues? How is God glorified when you pay attention to the cardinal virtues of prudence, temperance, fortitude, and justice?

CHAPTER 15

Justice and the Human Community
(CCC, 1877–1948)

The previous two chapters focused on the way we are all called to a life of happiness, setting our sights on the greatest possible good, namely eternal happiness in heaven. There is great freedom found in following the Lord, even when that means taking up our cross daily and choosing not the easy path but the often arduous, sacrificial path of virtue and holiness.

In this chapter we focus upon how we live out our call to happiness amidst the human community. "No man is an island," says John Donne. Every person on earth shares the same call to live in the freedom of a child of God. In fact, it is within the human community that one makes progress in the life of holiness and virtue, and in turn, by participation in the affairs of society, each disciple of Jesus can help to build up a human community that promotes the exercise of the virtues (cf. *CCC*, 1878–1880).

159. What is social justice?

Giving another person his or her due is part of how an *individual* exercises the virtue of justice. Social justice has to do with the right order within a *society* through which individuals and groups can obtain what is their due (cf. *CCC*, 1807, 1928). Respect for the God-given dignity of the human person and the rights that flow from that dignity are fundamental to social justice: "What is at stake is the dignity of the human person, whose defense and promotion have been entrusted to us by the Creator, and to whom the men and women at every moment of history are strictly and responsibly in debt" (Pope John Paul II, *Sollicitudo Rei Socialis*, 47, cited in *CCC*, 1929).

The dignity and rights of human beings "are prior to society and must be recognized by it. They are the basis of the moral legitimacy of every authority" (*CCC*, 1930). To show respect for the human person is to follow the commandment "You shall love your neighbor as yourself" (Mk 12:31). "Everyone should look upon his neighbor (without any exception) as 'another self,' above all bearing in mind his life and the means necessary for living it with dignity" (*Gaudium et Spes*, 37, cited in *CCC*, 1931).

160. "And who is my neighbor?"

This question posed by a legal scholar prompted Jesus to tell the parable of the good Samaritan, the man who treated with mercy one who had been brutally attacked by thieves (cf. Lk 10:25–37). This parable reminds us of the importance of looking out for the well-being of *every* human person, especially those who look, think, or act differently from us. Jesus teaches us to love our enemies even if we despise their evil actions (cf. Mt 25:40, *CCC*, 1931–1933). Furthermore, "every form of social or cultural discrimination in fundamental personal rights on the grounds of sex, race, color, social conditions, language, or religion must be curbed and eradicated as incompatible with God's design" (*Gaudium et Spes*, 29, cited in *CCC*, 1935).

There exists a fundamental equality between all human persons, even though every person has a unique set of talents, with some people being more gifted than others. Those who are blessed with particular talents are obliged to use them for the benefit of the poor and less fortunate, for "much will be required of the person entrusted with much, and still more will be demanded of the person entrusted with more" (Lk 12:48, cf. *CCC*, 1936–1937).

As good neighbors, we may not ignore the sinful inequalities affecting so many people who live in the scourge of generational poverty:

> Their equal dignity as persons demands that we strive for fairer and more humane conditions. Excessive economic and social disparity between individuals and peoples of the one human race is a source of scandal and militates against social justice, equity, human dignity, as well as social and international peace. (*Gaudium et Spes*, 29, cited in *CCC*, 1938)

161. What is meant by solidarity in relation to social justice?

Solidarity is the virtue through which we take personal responsibility for easing the burdens of our neighbor. Social justice hinges upon human solidarity, working with great diligence to reform those social conditions that are "in open contradiction to the Gospel" (*CCC*, 1938).

In the light of faith, solidarity seeks to go beyond itself, to take on the specifically Christian dimension of total gratuity, forgiveness and reconciliation. Our neighbor is then not only a human being with rights and a fundamental equality with everyone else but also the living image of God the Father, redeemed by the blood of Jesus Christ and placed under the permanent action of the Holy Spirit. Our neighbor must therefore be loved, even if an enemy, with the same love with which the Lord loves him or her; and for that person's sake one must be ready for sacrifice, even the ultimate one: to lay down one's life for the brethren.[1]

162. What does the Church teach about the dignity of the human person in society?

"The human person is and ought to be the principle, the subject, and the end of all social institutions" (*Gaudium et Spes*, 25, cited in *CCC*, 1881). When the human person is regarded as a mere means to an end, society is disordered. Institutions such as slavery, human trafficking, apartheid, state-directed communism, and laissez-faire capitalism reflect this disorder. The first and foremost theme of Catholic social teaching is the dignity of the human person, created in the image and likeness of God.

163. What does the Church teach about the importance of the family?

The family is the fundamental cell, the primordial society that "must be helped and defended by appropriate social measures" (*CCC*, 2209). God's plan for the family is articulated in the Church's teaching on the Fourth Commandment (which is covered in Chapter 18).

164. How does the Church safeguard the rights of the family?

In the same way that the Church supports and defends the dignity of individual human persons, she also holds to the critical importance of safeguarding the family. To do this the Church encourages the virtue of subsidiarity, allowing important decisions to be made at the lowest appropriate level. The principle of subsidiarity says that no community of a higher order (such as a national or state government) should do what can be done equally well or better by a community of a lower order (such as a local community or especially a family). The Church is opposed to all forms of collectivism, attaching restrictions to the power and authority of the state.

Under the principle of subsidiarity, the role of the state is limited to coordinating the activities of a society with a view to the common good and working toward goodwill and peace among nations (cf. *CCC*, 1883, 1885).

World Events and the Social Encyclicals

With the Industrial Revolution in the eighteenth and nineteenth centuries, new challenges arose as the "Gospel encountered modern industrial society with its new structures for the production of consumer goods, its new concept of society, the state of authority, and its new forms of labor and ownership" (*CCC*, 2421). Pope Leo XIII and succeeding popes understood the Church's role in shaping justice and fairness in the new society. A need for systematic teachings that would help governments, families, and individuals apply the principles of the Gospel to changing social situations was evident. Key world events—including those in literature, politics, and economics—accompanied these church documents on social justice.

1760s
Industrial Revolution begins. Large cities quickly become more populous because of the need for factory workers.

1831
Death of Georg Hegel, a German philosopher who greatly influenced Karl Marx.

1834
Death of Thomas Malthus, an advocate of population control.

1839
Charles Dickens writes *Oliver Twist*, the first of his novels that decry the poor conditions of factory workers and the conditions of large cities.

1848
Karl Marx publishes his *Communist Manifesto*.

1862
Victor Hugo writes *Les Misérables*, another novel that describes in great detail the cruelty of the Industrial Revolution.

1867
Karl Marx publishes *Das Kapital*, emphasizing the importance of the state in the production of goods.

1891 | Church Teaching
   Pope Leo XIII promulgates his encyclical *Rerum Novarum* (*Of New Things*) on the conditions of the working class, speaking out against inhumane and unhealthy working conditions and their deleterious effect upon family life.

1902
Upton Sinclair writes *The Jungle*, a novel about poor working conditions in the Chicago meatpacking industry.

1917
The Communist Revolution takes place in Russia. Vladimir Lenin is the first head of the Soviet Union.

1926
Adolf Hitler writes *Mein Kampf*, sowing the seeds for Fascism and Nazism that will bring the nations of the world to war.

1931 | Church Teaching
   Pope Pius XI issues *Quadragesimo Anno* on the fortieth anniversary of *Rerum Novarum* and against the backdrop of a worldwide depression. Pope Pius vigorously condemns communism.

1945
Chairman Mao imposes communism upon China.

1961 | Church Teaching
   Pope John XXIII writes *Mater et Magistra* (*Mother and Teacher*), teaching about Christianity in a time of social change.

1963 | Church Teaching

Pope John XXIII writes *Pacem in Terra* (*Peace on Earth*), an encyclical about the growing interdependence among nations and the need to work for social and economic rights of workers.

1964

Mao's *Little Red Book* is published.

1965 | Church Teaching

The Second Vatican Council and Pope Paul VI issue *Gaudium et Spes* (*Joy and Hope*), a pastoral constitution on the Church in the modern world.

1980

The Communist government of Poland recognizes the legitimacy of the Solidarity union of workers at the shipyard in Gdansk. Solidarity leader Lech Walesa received guidance from recently elected Pope John Paul II, the first pope from Poland. This important event would become known as the beginning of the peaceful overthrow of the Communist stronghold in Eastern Europe.

1981 | Church Teaching

Pope John Paul II *writes Laborem Excercens* (*Through Work*), extolling the great dignity of human labor, as opposed to a Communist understanding of human labor being at the service of the state.

1987 | Church Teaching

Pope John Paul II writes *Sollicitudo Rei Socialis*, eloquently expressing the legacy of the social teachings of the Church.

1989

The fall of the Berlin Wall, which leads to the rapid disintegration of Communist rule throughout Eastern Europe and the Soviet Union over the next few years.

1991 | Church Teaching

Pope John Paul II writes *Centesimus Annus* on the one hundredth anniversary of *Rerum Novarum*. The pope wrote and spoke extensively on the Church's social teaching, stressing the preferential option for the poor and warning against the dangers of both liberal capitalism and collective socialism.

2009 | Church Teaching
In the midst of a worldwide financial crisis, Pope Benedict XVI writes a social encyclical entitled *Caritas in Veritate (Charity in Truth)*. Pope Benedict reminds us, "Charity is at the heart of the Church's social doctrine."

2020 | Church Teaching
Pope Francis writes *Fratelli Tutti (All Brothers)* in the wake of the COVID-19 pandemic, calling for greater cooperation among nations, more human fraternity, and an end to wars.

The *Compendium of the Social Doctrine of the Church* is an excellent summary of the many facets of Catholic social teaching. This document is published by the Pontifical Council for Justice and Peace and is available online.

Reform is necessary when the state either usurps its legitimate authority to the detriment of human dignity or abdicates its responsibility to uphold the societal order in which virtue and goodness can thrive (cf. *CCC*, 1886–1888).

165. Why does the Church speak out on matters that seem to be secular in nature?

Pope Leo XIII (1810–1903) began his 1891 encyclical *Rerum Novarum* by calling out "the misery and wretchedness pressing so unjustly on the majority of the working class" and the conditions of poverty and injustice brought about "by covetous and grasping men." With no other institution giving voice to these troubles, the pope considered it to be the Church's urgent duty to speak out with clarity. Pope Leo XIII began what is known as Catholic social teaching, carried out to this very day especially on behalf of those whose human rights are being violated and who have an insufficient voice with which to speak for themselves.

166. What is the proper exercise of authority by those who have power over others?

Even when Christians were being unfairly and brutally persecuted by the Roman government in the first century, St. Paul spoke of the importance of obedience to higher authorities: "Let every person be subordinate to the higher authorities, for there is no authority except from God, and those that exist have been established by God. Therefore, whoever resists authority opposes what God has appointed, and those who oppose it will bring judgment upon themselves" (Rom 13:1–2). Pope John XXIII echoed St. Paul's words: "Human society can be neither well-ordered nor prosperous unless it has some people invested with legitimate authority to preserve its institutions and to devote themselves as far as is necessary to work and care for the good of all" (*Pacem in Terris*, 46, cited in *CCC*, 1897).

Authority over others derives from God's plan for human happiness and well-being; therefore, it must be exercised according to the principles of morality and seek the common good. Although obedience to higher authorities is part of the moral law, if "rulers were to enact unjust laws or take measures contrary to the moral order, such arrangements would not be binding in conscience" (*CCC*, 1903). Furthermore, there should be a system of checks and balances to prevent an abuse of authority: "It is preferable that each power be balanced by other powers and by other spheres of responsibility which keep it within proper bounds. This is the principle of the 'rule of law,' in which the law is sovereign and not the arbitrary will of men" (Pope John Paul II, *Centesimus Annus*, 44, cited in *CCC*, 1904).

167. What is meant by "the common good"?

The common good is defined as "the sum total of social conditions which allow people, either as groups or as individuals, to reach their fulfillment more fully and more easily" (*Gaudium et Spes*, 26, cited in *CCC*, 1906). There is a strong relationship between the dignity of the human person and the common good: "The good of each individual is necessarily related to the common good, which in turn can be defined only in reference to the human person" (*CCC*, 1905).

168. What does the common good depend on?

The common good depends upon three things:

1. Respect for the inalienable rights of every human person, especially in regard to the exercise of religious freedom (cf. *CCC*, 1907).
2. Attentiveness to the well-being of the group, including making sure that every person has access to what is needed for survival and development, such as "food, clothing, health, work, education and culture, suitable information, the right to establish a family, and so on" (*CCC*, 1908).
3. Peace with other communities and a stable and secure civil order. The state has a duty to protect and defend its citizens and to ensure their ability to contribute to the common good (cf. *CCC*, 1909). A *universal common good* is a noble and important goal in a time of increasing global interdependence (cf. *CCC*, 1911).

The exercise of personal responsibility in one's own life and in the life of the family is indispensable to the common good. The dignity of the human person is affirmed when the state permits and encourages every person to participate in public life as fully as possible.

Summary and Reflection

The Church has the duty to apply the gospel message of peace, justice, and love to the lives of both individuals and societies. With deep roots in the ordering of the People of God as related in the Old Testament, and with an understanding of a just social order that can be traced back to Plato, the Church most clearly articulated her social teaching in the wake of widespread social change occasioned by both the brutal conditions facing workers from the beginning of the Industrial Revolution and the misguided teachings of the highly influential Karl Marx, who proposed solutions contrary to the truth about the dignity of the human person. Especially since the Industrial Revolution, the Church has developed, with the guidance of the Holy Spirit, a body of social justice doctrine based first and foremost on the dignity of the human person, who has been created in the image and likeness of God.

◗ Creation

God has a plan for your life. How does God's plan for your life involve the virtue of justice, especially justice in the society in which we live?

◖ Fall

There were many injustices in the eighteenth and nineteenth centuries that offended against human dignity, such as slavery, child labor, and unsafe working conditions. When have you experienced social conditions that were in open contradiction to the Gospel? What gives you hope for those who struggle with injustice in our world?

✝ Redemption

"Greater love hath no one than to lay down his life for a friend." How is the Cross of Jesus a source of hope in your life? When have you witnessed someone imitating the transformative love of Jesus by bringing light into darkness, joy into sadness, hope into despair?

◕ Restoration

Marriage and family are fundamental to a just society. How do you see your commitment to your family as changing the world?

CHAPTER 16

God's Salvation: Law and Grace

(CCC, 1949–2082)

Though we are called to beatitude (happiness), we are wounded by sin. God sends us help "in Christ and through the law that guides him and the grace that sustains him" (*CCC*, 1949). This chapter focuses on the various types of laws God provides us to aid us on the path to happiness in this life and even greater happiness in the life to come. Through the gift of law God shows his divine wisdom. The moral law is God's pedagogy, his fatherly instruction. God's law teaches us the path that leads to beatitude, and it denounces the sins that leads us away from God's love. God's law is firm both in its precepts and in its abundant promises (cf. *CCC*, 1950).

Nevertheless, God's law itself is not an antidote for sin and the cause of our salvation. For that we need the grace of the Holy Spirit, who has the power to justify us. It is only through faith in Jesus Christ and Baptism that we can share in the justice or holiness of God. We have to be open to the gift of faith in order to receive it and to find a way out of our sinfulness. St. Augustine described the anguish of sinfulness and his despair in looking for a way out in *Confessions*, his autobiography (see page 113):

> To find my delight in your law as far as my inmost self was concerned was of no profit to me when a different law in my bodily members was warring against the law of my mind, imprisoning me under the law of sin which held sway in my lower self. For the law of sin is that brute force of habit whereby the mind is dragged along and held fast against its will, and deservedly so because it slipped into the habit willingly. In my wretched state, who was there to free me from this death-doomed body, save your grace through Jesus Christ our Lord?[1]

St. Augustine realized that his only hope was in the Lord Jesus, but he did not know how to find him. He lamented: "'O Lord, how long? How long? Will you be angry forever? Do not remember our age-old sins.' For by these I was conscious of being held prisoner. I uttered cries of misery: 'Why must I go on saying, "Tomorrow . . . tomorrow"? Why not now? Why not put an end to my depravity this very hour?'"[2]

In a well-told story of his conversion, Augustine heard the voice of a neighboring child singing "*Tolle lege, Tolle lege*" over and over: "Take up and read. Take up and read." When Augustine opened a nearby Bible to a random page in the Letter to the Romans, a passage on the page changed his life: "Let us conduct ourselves properly as in the day, not in orgies and drunkenness, not in promiscuity and licentiousness, not in rivalry and jealousy. But put on the Lord Jesus Christ, and make no provision for the desires of the flesh" (Rom 13:13–14). Recalled St. Augustine, "No sooner had I reached the end of the verse than the light of certainty flooded my heart and all dark shades of doubt fled away."[3]

St. Augustine is not alone in his experiences and in his anguish. Few are the individuals who have *not* been troubled with deep questions about the meaning of life, and who have *not* been burdened by either a life of sin or persistent sins seemingly resistant to prayer or mortification. A previous chapter discussed the tragedy of sin. St. Augustine is called the "Doctor of Grace." This chapter treats the salvation from the power of sin that God provides us in Christ through his law and his amazing grace (cf. *CCC*, 1949).

169. What is God's law, and how do we know it?

Psalm 119 is a veritable thesaurus of the word *law*. Every one of its 176 verses contains a synonym for *law*. *Testimonies, ways, command, statutes, commandments*, and *righteous judgments* are but a few of the words used by the psalmist to describe God's law.

God's law is differentiated and known in three ways: first, through the *natural law*, which is written upon the human heart; second, through the *Old Law*, the law given by God to the people of Israel; third, through the *New Law*, or the law of the Gospel of Jesus Christ (cf. *CCC*, 1951–1953). A different psalm shares the abundance and perfection of God's law:

> The law of the LORD is perfect, refreshing the soul.
> The decree of the LORD is trustworthy, giving wisdom to
>   the simple.
> The precepts of the LORD are right, rejoicing the heart.
> The command of the LORD is clear, enlightening the eye.
> The fear of the LORD is pure, enduring forever.
> The statutes of the LORD are true, all of them just. (Ps
>   19:7–9)

170. What is natural law?

Natural law (also called moral law) is that which is accessible through the use of reason and is therefore available to every person. Natural law is *not* what might occur in nature, such as in the animal kingdom, but what occurs in accordance with human nature, which is oriented to union with God. The natural law tells us from within that certain actions are contrary to the aim of human nature: "The natural law is nothing other than the light of understanding placed in us by God; through it we know what we must do and what we must avoid. God has given this light or law at the creation" (St. Thomas Aquinas, *Dec. praec. I*, cited in *CCC*, 1955).

The pagan world before the time of Christ had an understanding that natural law was common to human beings of all places and ages. Cicero (106–43 BC) writes: "For there is a true law: right reason. It is in conformity with nature, is diffused among all men, and is immutable and eternal; its orders summon to duty; its prohibitions turn away from offense. ... To replace it with a contrary law is a sacrilege; failure to apply even one of its provisions is forbidden; no one can abrogate it entirely" (*Rep. III*, 22, 33, cited in *CCC*, 1956).

Although the principles of natural law are written in the heart, their application can vary according to the circumstances of time and place. Natural law can also be misunderstood. God must reveal his law so that the truth about the dignity of the human person and our vocation to happiness may be known by all people "with facility, with firm certainty and with no admixture of error" (Pope Pius XII, *Humani Generis*, cited in *CCC*, 1960).

Natural law must be understood as the *foundation* of the law given by God through Divine Revelation, the law that is accessible to us through Sacred Scripture and the teachings of the Church (cf. *CCC*, 2032).

171. What is the Old Law?

The Old Law is called *old* not because it has been discarded but because it prepares God's People for the coming of Christ and his New Law. The Old Law expresses many of the truths that are part of the natural moral law accessible to human reason. The Ten Commandments (sometimes called the *Decalogue*, or *Ten Words*) provide a summary of the Old Law by succinctly expressing those things that lead human beings to God and those things that offend against God's will for the human person. St. Augustine says, "God wrote on the tables of the Law what men did not read in their hearts" (*En. in Ps.* 57, 1, cited in *CCC*, 1962).

The Old Law, as its name implies, is not the final word from God about his will for human beings. St. Paul calls the Old Law a "tutor" or "disciplinarian" (Gal 3:24), for its role is temporary. A student does not have permanent need of a tutor. The grace of Jesus Christ replaces the tutor. The Old Law teaches "what must be done, but does not of itself give the strength, the grace of the Spirit, to fulfill it" (*CCC*, 1963). The Old Law teaches us what sin is and denounces it, but does not have the power to help us rise above sin (cf. Rom 7:7–25).

The Old Law is the Old Covenant that prepares us for the Gospel, the New Law in Christ, "'a pedagogy and a prophecy of things to come.' It prophesies and presages the work of liberation from sin which will be fulfilled in Christ: it provides the New Testament with images, 'types,' and symbols for expressing the life according to the Spirit" (*CCC*, 1964).

172. What is the New Law?

The New Law is the fulfillment of the prophecy of Jeremiah, that God would give to his people a law not written on stone tablets, but upon their hearts: "This is the covenant I will make with the house of Israel.... I will place my law within them, and write it upon their hearts; I will be their God, and they shall be my people" (Jer 31:33). This prophecy is fulfilled and the law of God made perfect through the preaching of our Lord and his sacrificial death upon the Cross. Jesus gives the precepts of the New Law through the Beatitudes and the Sermon on the Mount (cf. Mt 5:1–7:28). The Sermon on the Mount gives us "all the precepts needed to shape one's life" (St. Augustine, *De serm. Dom.* 1, 1, cited in *CCC*, 1966).

"The New Law is the *grace of the Holy Spirit*, given to the faithful through faith in Christ" (*CCC*, 1966). It is a law of charity, teaching us how we must live, and giving us the grace we need to keep the New Commandment: "I give you a new commandment: love one another. As I have loved you, so you also should love one another" (Jn 13:34). The sacraments that flow forth from our Lord's great gift of charity, his sacrificial death upon the Cross, give us the grace to rise above sin and to keep the commandments, especially the New Commandment (cf. *CCC*, 1966). Jesus communicates the New Law in word and in the great deed of his Cross. We live the New Law through our words and through our actions: "Do to others whatever you would have them do to you" (Mt 7:12).

173. Does the New Law do away with the Old Law?

Jesus says, "Do not think that I have come to abolish the law or the prophets. I have come not to abolish but to fulfill" (Mt 5:17). The New Law *fulfills* the Old Law; it does not abolish the prescriptions of the Old Law but instead releases their potential.

Do not think that the New Law is less demanding than the Old Law. The New Law shows that in the light of the Lord's saving Death and glorious Resurrection, there are demands placed upon us far more significant than the requirements of the Old Law. The New Law is written on the heart and transforms the heart, the place from which human choices are made and where the virtues are formed. "The Gospel . . . brings the Law to its fullness through imitation of the perfection of the heavenly Father, through forgiveness of enemies and prayer for persecutors, in emulation of the divine generosity" (*CCC*, 1968).

174. As Christians, why aren't we bound to follow the many laws of the Old Testament such as those about diet, circumcision, and worship?

The New Law is a law of freedom. The Lord revealed to St. Peter that the Jewish laws regarding diet are no longer binding upon Christians (cf. Acts 10), nor are the laws about circumcision (cf. Acts 15). Laws pertaining to the Jewish Temple are likewise no longer binding. The Jewish Temple was destroyed by the Romans in AD 70 and was never rebuilt. God has a greater plan, a New Law, a *"law of freedom*, because it sets us free from the ritual and juridical observances of the Old Law, inclines us to act spontaneously by the prompting of charity and, finally, lets us pass from the condition of a servant who 'does not know what his master is doing' to that of a friend of Christ" (*CCC*, 1972), even to the status of a son or daughter of God, an heir to the Kingdom. This is truly the Good News!

175. What does it mean to be justified?

In common usage, *justify* can mean "to make straight, or to align." For example, the text on this page is *justified*, meaning that it is aligned on both the left and right margins. *To justify* can also mean to explain that one's actions or behavior is acceptable morally or legally.

St. Paul uses the word *justification* to refer to the grace of the Holy Spirit that cleanses us from sin and makes us right again in the sight of God: "For if, by the transgression of one person, death came to reign through that one, how much more will those who receive the abundance of grace and of the gift of justification come to reign in life through the one person Jesus Christ" (Rom 5:17).

"The grace of the Holy Spirit has the power to justify us, that is, to cleanse us from our sins and to communicate to us 'the righteousness of God through faith in Jesus Christ' (Rom 3:22) and through Baptism" (*CCC*, 1987).

176. What does justification mean for the Christian?

"Justification is the *most excellent work of God's love* made manifest in Christ Jesus and granted by the Holy Spirit" (*CCC*, 1994). Justification heals what was wounded in the hearts of human beings through the Fall of our first parents. Justification sanctifies the whole person, even unto everlasting life (cf. *CCC*, 1995).

By the power of the Holy Spirit, the one who is justified by faith and by Baptism participates in the Death and Resurrection of Jesus, dying to sin and rising to new life in the Body of Christ that is the Church (cf. *CCC*, 1988). St. Paul says, "We were indeed buried with him through baptism into death, so that, just as Christ was raised from the dead by the glory of the Father, we too might live in newness of life" (Rom 6:4).

177. How is justification accomplished, and what does it merit?

Justification is accomplished by God's amazing grace, which brings sinners to accept God's forgiveness and to enter into conversion of life, an interior renewal of one's heart (cf. *CCC*, 1989). "Justification is conferred in Baptism, the sacrament of faith" (*CCC*, 1992). Justification frees one from enslavement to sin, and it purifies and heals the heart (cf. *CCC*, 1990). Virtue is poured into the heart of the one who is justified, that is, *made right with God* through faith in Jesus and Baptism (cf. *CCC*, 1991).

"Justification has been merited for us by the Passion of Christ" (*CCC*, 1992). By the Precious Blood of the Lamb of God we are saved. Just as the people of the Exodus were saved from death by the blood of the Passover lamb, we are justified by the Blood of Jesus, the Lamb of God (cf. Ex 12:7, Rom 5:9, Rv 12:11).

"Justification establishes cooperation between God's grace and man's freedom" (*CCC*, 1993). The encounter with God's Word invites conversion of heart. The Holy Spirit prompts our cooperation and sustains our free assent to God's initiative (cf. *CCC*, 1993). Responding to the sixteenth-century objections of those who separated themselves from full communion with the Church, the Council of Trent states succinctly:

> When God touches man's heart through the illumination of the Holy Spirit, man himself is not inactive while receiving that inspiration, since he could reject it; and yet, without God's grace, he cannot by his own free will move himself toward justice in God's sight. (*Denzinger-Schönmetzer* 1525, cited in *CCC*, 1993)

Faith, Good Works, or Both?

How are we saved? Through faith, good works, or both? This question demands an in-depth answer, for it was one of the main questions that led to the so-called Protestant Reformation and has persisted in differences between Catholics and Protestants to this day.

With the nailing of his Ninety-Five Theses on the door of the Church of All Saints in Wittenberg, Germany, on October 31, 1517, Martin Luther launched the great tragedy that would separate millions from full communion with the Catholic Church and that continues to splinter and divide Christian communities of these traditions. The theological roots of the Protestant Reformation involve an unfortunate misunderstanding of the Church's teaching on justification, grace, and Sacred Scripture.

In very general terms, Protestant theology can be said to rest upon several *solas*. The Latin word *sola* means "alone." Classic Protestant theology teaches that justification comes through faith *alone*, that salvation is won by grace *alone*, and that Christian teaching and practice rest upon the authority of Sacred Scripture *alone* (and that every person should interpret Scripture according to his or her own mind). The misunderstandings of Protestant theologians were rebutted by the teachings of the Council of Trent, a gathering of Catholic bishops held over the course of eighteen years in the northern Italian city of Trento (1545–1563). The Council of Trent rejected and condemned the erroneous teaching of the Protestant *solas* about justification and grace by expressing them in a positive way. These teachings remain articulated in the *Catechism of the Catholic Church*. Listed here are some of the main points:

> **"Justification has been merited for us by the Passion of Christ who offered himself on the cross as a living victim, holy and pleasing to God, and whose blood has become the instrument of atonement for the sins of all men" (CCC, 1992).**
>
> Full stop. Catholics do not believe, as some detractors say, that we can be saved by our own efforts, by our own good works. We are justified by the merits of the suffering and Death of our Lord Jesus Christ.

> **"Our justification comes from the grace of God" (CCC, 1996) and "is conferred in Baptism, the sacrament of faith" (CCC, 1992).**
>
> Note that the Church *agrees* with Luther that justification comes from faith, but the Church *disagrees* that justification comes from faith alone. The Sacrament of Baptism, a sacrament instituted by Christ and conferred through the Church, is necessary for justification.

> **"Grace is favor, the free and undeserved help that God gives us to respond to his call to become children of God" (CCC, 1996).**
>
> Luther would agree with this statement, but his assertion that salvation comes from grace alone is not in keeping with the teaching of the Church that a human response to

God's initiative of grace is also required. "God's free initiative demands man's free response" (*CCC*, 2002), and that response is ongoing. It is not true, as many Protestants assert, that "once saved, always saved." Rather, as St. Paul encourages us, "work out your salvation with fear and trembling. For God is the one who, for his good purpose, works in you both to desire and to work" (Phil 2:12–13). "See, then, the kindness and severity of God: severity toward those who fell, but God's kindness to you, provided you remain in his kindness; otherwise you too will be cut off" (Rom 11:22).

Grace is known only through faith, for as God's free and unmerited gift, it is of the supernatural order. "We cannot therefore rely on our feelings or our works to conclude that we are justified and saved" (CCC, 2005).

Feelings are ephemeral, changing sometimes like the wind. The sacraments are instituted so we might know clearly that God's grace is at work in us. God binds himself to the sacraments. Sacramental graces, proper to each sacrament, are given to us so that our faith might be strengthened and that we might contribute to the building up of the Church (cf. *CCC*, 2003).

We are justified by faith, but not by faith alone.

Nothing could be clearer from the testimony of Sacred Scripture: "What good is it, my brothers, if someone says he has faith but does not have works? Can that faith save him?" (Jas 2:14). Also, "Faith of itself, if it does not have works, is dead" (Jas 2:17). And, "See how a person is justified by works and not by faith alone. . . . For just as a body without a spirit is dead, so also faith without works is dead" (Jas 2:24–26).

We do not believe that we are saved by our own merit, as say some detractors of Catholic teaching and practice.

"With regard to God, there is no strict right to any merit on the part of man. Between God and us there is an immeasurable inequality, for we have received everything from him, our Creator" (*CCC*, 2007). Nevertheless, the virtue of justice is still relevant to how we will be judged according to our deeds. St. Paul tells us that God "will repay everyone according to his works: eternal life to those who seek glory, honor, and immortality through perseverance in good works, but wrath and fury to those who selfishly disobey the truth and obey wickedness" (Rom 2:6–8).

God takes the initiative in our salvation, freely choosing to associate us with his grace (cf. CCC, 2008); "no one can merit the initial grace of forgiveness and justification, at the beginning of conversion" (CCC, 2010).

What good we do in this life that will merit for us the eternal reward of heaven is all due to the grace of God, which moves, encourages, and sustains us in our good works. In the words of St. Augustine, "Grace has gone before us; now we are given what is due. . . . Our merits are God's gifts" (*Sermon* 298, 4–5, cited in *CCC*, 2009).

You might be challenged on some or all of these points by Christians who hold other views. The quotes here and throughout this book from the *Catechism of the Catholic Church* can help you to discuss these important distinctions with others. The *Catechism of the Catholic Church* is chock-full of footnotes that will help you to show that Catholic teaching comes from Sacred Scripture and from the verifiably consistent, two thousand years of teaching that faithfully presents us with the authentic faith that comes from the Apostles.

The Catholic Church is the "pillar and foundation of truth" (1 Tm 3:15). The Church is our Mother and our Teacher, guaranteeing the faithful "the objective possibility of professing the true faith without error" (*CCC*, 890). Truth cannot change; the constantly changing teachings of non-Catholic communities cannot be true (cf. *CCC*, 2030–2040).

Summary and Reflection

Divine law is truly a work of God's providence—that is, God's wisdom, power, and goodness by which he guides his creation toward its perfection. Law also serves as an objective standard outside of yourself to measure our desired actions against. Good law can warn you of harmful consequences of poor decisions. St. Thomas Aquinas defined law as "an ordinance for reason for the common good, promulgated by the one who is in charge of the community" (*CCC*, 1796). Laws help to regulate our freedom toward what is true and good and, therefore, toward God.

● *Creation*

St. Augustine's conversion is counted as one of the most significant conversions in the history of the Church, yet it is no more important than the way in which you are walking more closely with Jesus day by day. The twentieth-century poet Eleanor Farjeon compared conversion to a "new day," and a "new creation":

Mine is the sunlight!
Mine is the morning
born of the one light
Eden saw play!
Praise with elation,
praise every morning,
God's recreation
of the new day!

How have you seen your own ongoing conversion as the dawn of a new day?

🌑 Fall

The word *justification* means "setting things aright." St. Paul speaks of justification being accomplished by God's grace, for which we are ever grateful. St. Paul also says that you must "work out your salvation with fear and trembling" (Phil 2:12). How do you see your salvation as being brought about both by God's amazing grace and by your cooperating with that same grace?

✝ Redemption

Read Psalm 119:1–16, noting that every verse has two synonyms for the Law of the Lord. Which synonym resonates with you most clearly? How would you describe to someone the importance in your own life of the Law or will of God?

🌓 Restoration

St. Augustine says that in his conversion moment, "the light of certainty flooded my heart and all dark shades of doubt fled away." How would you describe your experience of conversion, either an initial conversion like St. Augustine's or an ongoing experience of conversion?

CHAPTER 17

Love of God: The First Three Commandments

(CCC, 2083–2195)

Monuments or tapestries of the Ten Commandments are not an uncommon sight in the United States. Though a disputed matter in the courts, the Ten Commandments are sometimes displayed in front of courthouses because they represent one of the foundations of the legal tradition.

Sometimes the artist will place five commandments on one tablet and five on another. The older tradition is to place the first three commandments on one tablet and the remaining seven on the other. This is the case because the first three commandments have to do with the love of God, and the remaining seven concern love of neighbor. This arrangement corresponds with Jesus's answer to the question raised by a lawyer about which commandment is the greatest. Jesus responded, "The first is this. . . . You shall love the Lord your God with all your heart, with all your soul, with all your mind, and with all your strength. The second is this: 'You shall love your neighbor as yourself'" (Mk 12:29–31).

Although men and women could arrive at the precepts of the Decalogue (the Ten Commandments) through the use of reason alone, God chose to reveal them. "From the beginning, God had implanted in the heart of man the precepts of the natural law. Then he was content to remind him of them. This was the Decalogue" (St. Irenaeus, cited in *CCC*, 2070).

God engraves the Ten Commandments upon the human heart. And when we follow Jesus and abide in his love, Jesus's New Commandment becomes the rule and law of our own heart: "This is my commandment, that you love one another as I have loved you" (Jn 15:12, cf. *CCC*, 2074).

The two tablets of the Decalogue shed light on each other, for one honors God by respecting and honoring one's neighbor, and one makes a very good neighbor by adoring and worshipping God. The Decalogue brings together a person's religious and social life (cf. *CCC*, 2069).

This chapter provides more details on the first three commandments.

178. Why are the Ten Commandments sometimes numbered differently?

The numbering of the Ten Commandments is based on either Exodus 20:1–17 or Deuteronomy 5:6–21. Depending on which source is used, you may notice slight differences. A traditional catechetical formulation from Deuteronomy 5 and the *Catechism of the Catholic Church* is listed as follows:

1. I am the LORD, your God: you shall not have strange gods before me.
2. You shall not take the name of the LORD, your God, in vain.
3. Remember to keep holy the LORD's Day.
4. Honor your father and your mother.

5. You shall not kill.
6. You shall not commit adultery.
7. You shall not steal.
8. You shall not bear false witness against your neighbor.
9. You shall not covet your neighbor's wife.
10. You shall not covet your neighbor's goods.

For those who learned the Ten Commandments in a non-Catholic setting, it might seem strange that Catholics sometimes number the commandments differently. In fact, that is the only difference. All Christians are exhorted to live according to the Ten Commandments as they appear without worrying about the numbers! People of goodwill can disagree about the numbering of the Ten Commandments while being in complete agreement about their content and their importance.

179. What is required by the First Commandment?

The First Commandment is about worship of the one true God, who brought his beloved people out of Egypt and rescued them from slavery: "You shall not have other gods beside me. You shall not make for yourself an idol or a likeness of anything in the heavens above or on the earth below or in the waters beneath the earth; you shall not bow down before them or serve them" (Ex 20:3–5). We are created in the image and likeness of God, and one way we live out the First Commandment is by showing great respect for the image and likeness of God within every human being. Worship is due to God alone, Father, Son, and Holy Spirit.

180. What are the sins against the First Commandment?

The First Commandment requires that we nourish and protect our faith in God with vigilance and that we reject all that is opposed to it. Specific ways of violating this commandment include:

- *Voluntary doubt of God's law.* Disregarding or refusing "to hold as true what God has revealed and the Church proposes for belief" (*CCC*, 2088).

- *Involuntary doubt of matters of faith.* Hesitating to believe or being reluctant to accept the wisdom that leads one out of doubts about the faith. While doubt is not sinful in itself, one can become spiritually blind by cultivating doubt (cf. *CCC*, 2088). It is always proper to ask questions about the faith, for often we find great and even life-changing wisdom in the truth within the answers to our questions.

- *Heresy.* The post-baptismal denial of some truth that must be believed or an obstinate doubt about the same.

- *Apostasy.* "The total rejection of the Catholic faith" (*CCC*, 2089).

- *Schism.* "The refusal of submission to the Roman Pontiff or of communion with the members of the Church subject to him" (*CCC*, 2089).

- *Despair.* The absence of hope in one's salvation or in the forgiveness of one's sins.

- *Giving up on God* by completely ignoring God's merciful nature (cf. *CCC*, 2091).

- *Presumption.* Either to believe in one's own capacity to save oneself without God's help or to presume upon God's mercy by hoping for his forgiveness without the requisite conversion of heart (cf. *CCC*, 2092).

- *Indifference.* Neglecting or refusing to reflect upon the goodness and power of God's love.

- *Ingratitude.* Failing or refusing to acknowledge and respond with love to God's love.

- *Lukewarmness.* Hesitating or neglecting to respond to God's love.

- *Acedia, or spiritual sloth.* Refusing the joy that comes from God and being repelled by God's goodness. This is sometimes called the noonday devil, as it implies giving in to weariness and failing to pray and live as we ought.

- *Hatred of God.* Pride is the deadliest sin; hatred of God comes from the pride that would have us deny God's goodness or curse God for forbidding sin and inflicting punishment for our sins.

- *Active membership in Freemasonry.* This secular, secretive group that has existed since the eighteenth century holds up arcane rituals and symbols that are opposed to Christianity. Freemasonry promotes religious indifferentism, claiming that all religions are equal. Catholics who belong to Masonic organizations are in a state of grave sin and may not receive Holy Communion.

Worship of any strange gods, be they pagan deities or the false gods of riches, fame, popularity, or worldly success, leads us away from the closeness to God that is our calling (cf. *CCC*, 2085) and is opposed to the First Commandment.

181. How do we keep the First Commandment positively?

The virtue of justice is called the virtue of religion when it disposes us to give God what is God's due. We keep the First Commandment when we serve God alone in thought, word, and deed and through adoration, prayer, and sacrifice.

Adoration is due to God alone, Father, Son, and Holy Spirit. Adoration gives glory and honor to God "as the Creator and Savior, the Lord and Master of everything that exists, and as infinite and merciful Love" (*CCC*, 2096). Adoration brings out the best in us as well, for humble adoration of our God is the antidote to destructive self-centeredness, slavery to sin, and the worship of worldly idols (cf. *CCC*, 2096).

Prayer, as the lifting up of one's mind to God in adoration, contrition, thanksgiving, and supplication, is absolutely necessary in order to keep God's commandments (cf. *CCC*, 2098). (Much more will be said about prayer in Chapters 21–24.)

Sacrifice means that "every action [is] done so as to cling to God in communion of holiness, and thus achieve blessedness" (St. Augustine, cited in *CCC*, 2099). The sacrifices of the Old Covenant were pleasing to God only when they were outward expressions of inner devotion. One cannot purchase God's favor with a visible sacrifice that lacks a spiritual dimension. God is honored and adored by the daily sacrifices of showing responsibility for the care and well-being of others, following the sometimes arduous path of virtue, and suffering for doing what is right and good. We offer a living sacrifice to God when we unite ourselves to the perfect sacrifice offered by our Lord upon the Cross (cf. *CCC*, 2100).

182. What are some of the false gods referred to in the First Commandment?

False gods are associated with the principal sins against the First Commandment. These include:

- *Superstition* is a "perverse excess of religion" (*CCC*, 2110). Superstition attributes or hopes for good to be accomplished or evil to be avoided by performing actions or saying prayers without the inner disposition that they require and that God desires.

- *Idolatry* is worshipping or placing one's trust in false divinities or honoring another creature in place of God. Money, power, prestige, popularity, and even the state can become idols for some. "An idolater is someone who transfers his indestructible notion of God to anything other than God" (*CCC*, 2114).

- *Divination* is an unhealthy curiosity about the future rather than trusting in God's providence. Examples of divination include horoscopes, clairvoyance, the use of mediums, palm reading, and the like. Divination sometimes uses means such as conjuring the dead and invoking the help of Satan or other demons. Grave spiritual harm can come about when children or adults play with Ouija boards and related items (cf. *CCC*, 2115–16).

- *Magic* or *sorcery* attempts to "tame occult powers, so as to place them at one's service and have supernatural power over others" (*CCC*, 2117).

Even when the goal is one's own or another person's good, it is always a sin against the First Commandment to call upon false gods, to wear charms, and to invoke evil powers. The Lord our God is the source of all that is good, and he alone should be called upon when we or our loved ones need help. Forbidden by the First Commandment are practices such as yoga, Reiki, transcendental meditation, centering prayer, and the use or display of devices such as crystals, dream catchers, and other items that are part of the New Age movement.

- *Tempting God* or *putting God to the test* so as to prove his presence, existence, or mercy is exactly how Satan tried to tempt our Lord in the desert (cf. Lk 4:9). Tempting God violates the First Commandment as it expresses profound doubt about God (cf. *CCC*, 2119).

- *Sacrilege* is any action that profanes what is holy, including persons, places, and things consecrated to God, such as priests, religious men and women, church buildings, and objects reserved for use in the celebration of the sacraments. Sacrilege is a grave sin when it involves the Holy Eucharist, especially receiving Holy Communion when not in the state of grace (cf. *CCC*, 2120).

- *Simony* is the "buying or selling of spiritual things" (*CCC*, 2121), including blessed medals or religious relics. Spiritual goods have their source in God, and one receives them only from him, without cost. If a blessed item is indeed sold, only the object is sold, not the blessing. Once it is sold, it is no longer considered blessed. Offerings made for the support of the Church or those who minister in the Church is not considered simony (cf. *CCC*, 2122).

- *Atheism* is a rapidly expanding phenomenon in our world and a most serious problem of our day. Atheism is a rejection of God and religion. Atheism can take several forms, including practical materialism, in which one sees value only in that which can be measured in time and space, and atheistic humanism, in which the existence of God is denied and the human person is seen as "an end to himself, and the sole maker, with supreme control of his own history" (*Gaudium et*

Spes, 20, cited in *CCC*, 2124). The evil legacy of communism is deeply rooted in atheism. Karl Marx held that religion is "the opiate of the masses," falsely asserting that belief in God and the practice of religion deceive the human person by the promise of heavenly rewards and prevent individuals from striving for that which would build up a better life in the here and now (cf. *CCC*, 2124).

Catholics Venerate Sacred Images and Do Not Worship Them

The Old Law—particularly the First Commandment of the Decalogue—from the Hebrew Bible prohibited Jewish people from making "graven" images, that is, "carvings" of God, because of the tendency of the Chosen People to worship states and objects in their history, like their pagan neighbors. God was understood to be completely transcendent; the almighty, one true God can never be contained in a mere statue.

But this Old Testament prohibition was not absolute. The First Commandment did allow for images that would facilitate worship of God, such as the gold angels on top of the Ark of the Covenant and the decorations of trees, fruits, and animals on the Temple.

Many of the earliest Christians came from a Jewish milieu and were well aware of the prohibition against artwork that was representative of God. Yet when we visit the catacombs in Rome and other places where the first Christians worshipped, we find that they are decorated with images of our Lord as the Good Shepherd, our Lord offering the Last Supper, and many others that depict Jesus, the Son of God.

The early Christians did not break the First Commandment by making an image of the Second Person of the Holy Trinity, Jesus Christ, truly God and truly man. Rather, early Christians recognized that "by becoming incarnate, the Son of God introduced a new 'economy' of images" (*CCC*, 2131). In other words, because Jesus made the face of God known in his earthly ministry, so now can those who worship him as Lord and God make use of his image to remind them that the Eternal Word, transcendent from all ages, has become flesh and dwelt among us (cf. Jn 1:14, cf. *CCC*, 2131).

The artistic sensibilities of the early Church have been passed on to successive generations of Christians, who have generated many beautiful images of our Lord, our Lady, the saints, and the angels. The statues and images in Catholic homes and church buildings are not placed there to be worshipped, for that would be giving to a created object the worship due to God alone. Rather, Catholics show respect for those images, because they are visible reminders of the invisible God, who once took flesh and dwelt among us. Catholics can often be found praying on their knees in front of works of art that depict our Lord, not worshipping the artwork, but the one who is represented in it. "The movement [in prayer] toward the image does not terminate in it as an image, but tends toward that whose image it is" (St. Thomas Aquinas, cited in *CCC*, 2132).

- *Agnosticism* is not the denial of the existence of God but the belief that God's existence cannot be proven or known. Most agnostics are in reality practical atheists, acting as if God does not exist or his existence does not matter.

183. What is required by the Second Commandment?

The Second Commandment governs our speech in sacred matters (cf. *CCC*, 2142): "You shall not invoke the name of the LORD, your God, in vain" (Ex 20:7). The name of God is so sacred that it was revealed to Moses only upon the holy ground of Mount Sinai. The name revealed to Moses was YHWH, meaning "I Am Who Am." However, the name was and is so revered by Jewish people that it was only spoken once every year, by the high priest in the Holy of Holies of the Temple in Jerusalem. When Jesus read aloud from the Scriptures, he followed what remains the practice of Jews to this day to not pronounce the name out loud.

Instead, the holy name of God (YHWH) is pronounced as if it were a different word, *Adonai*, which means "Lord." In many translations of the Old Testament the name of God (YHWH) is similarly translated as LORD, all in capital letters, to remind us that the name of God is so holy that we ought not to utter it irreverently. These are the sensibilities to this day of our Jewish brothers and sisters, and we must respect them. There is never an occasion in Catholic worship for the speaking of the holy name YHWH, nor should we speak of God by that holy name. Like the Jewish people, we say instead the word *Lord*.

We must not speak the name of God except when doing so will render it glory and honor. The name of God is unique, it must not be abused; instead, it must be kept in mind in "silent, loving adoration" (*CCC*, 2143). Thus do we exercise the virtue of justice, rendering to God what is his due, especially respect for his holy name. Catholic custom directs us to offer a bow of our head whenever we say the holy name of Jesus, and likewise the holy name of Mary. In this way, we show respect for the holy name of the one who is truly God and who extends his name to us so that we might enter into a deep, personal relationship with him.

184. What are the offenses against the Second Commandment?

The Second Commandment forbids the abuse of God's name, as well as the improper use of the names of Jesus, Mary, and the saints whose names the Lord has sanctified (cf. *CCC*, 2146). Other specific sins against the Second Commandment revolve around the following:

- *Promises* made in God's name are to be kept dutifully, lest God's holy name be misused and God be made out to be a liar (cf. *CCC*, 2147).

- *Blasphemy* is the most serious abuse of God's name, misusing our outward or inward speech to direct to God words of hatred or to speak poorly of God, our Lord Jesus, the Church, or holy things (cf. *CCC*, 2148). Blasphemy is a grave sin because of the greatness of the holy name that is taken in vain.

- *Oaths* that mock God's name or use his name lightly offend against God's name and violate the Second Commandment (cf. *CCC*, 2194). We are to take oaths in God's name only for the most serious of reasons, such as when testifying in a court of law, when taking a high office, or entering into the service of one's country (cf. *CCC*, 2153–2155).

- *Perjury* is making a promise without the intent to keep it or not keeping a promise made under oath. Perjury shows a grave lack of respect for the one in whose holy name we have pledged truthfulness and can also have deleterious effects in the lives of others and in the life of our society (cf. *CCC*, 2152).

185. How do we keep the Second Commandment positively?

We keep the Second Commandment not only by avoiding speech that offends against the holiness of the names of God and others but also by remembering to use the holy name of God prayerfully throughout the day. We are baptized *in the name of the Father, and of the Son, and of the Holy Spirit.* We take at Baptism or Confirmation the holy name of a patron saint who intercedes for us and whose example of holiness we can follow reliably. We make the Sign of the Cross in our prayers using these holy names of Father, Son, and Holy Spirit (cf. *CCC*, 2157).

We are to surround ourselves every day with words and things that are holy as a reminder of our vocation to serve the Lord, the one who calls each of us by name to come and follow him so that one day our name might be written in the Book of Life (cf. Rv 21:27). Each person's name is an icon, demanding respect from others as a sign of its dignity and as an acknowledgment that God calls every person by name (cf. *CCC*, 2158). The Second Commandment is lived out positively when we show respect for the name of God, our own name, and the names of others.

186. What is required by the Third Commandment?

The Third Commandment directs us to follow God's example in resting on the Sabbath, the seventh day. God rested on the seventh day of creation, thereby making the Sabbath holy (cf. Gn 2:2). The Sabbath recalls the liberation of the people of Israel from slavery to the Egyptians (cf. Dt 5:15). God commands us, "Remember the sabbath day—keep it holy" (Ex 20:8).

Christians have always placed great importance upon gathering for the Holy Eucharist on the first day of the week (Sunday) and not the seventh day (Saturday). The first day of the week is interpreted by Christians in the light of the Resurrection, the beginning of the new creation (cf. *CCC*, 2174). Although Scripture is silent in regard to the specific day on which Christians worshipped, in the first and second centuries St. Justin Martyr (cf. *CCC*, 2174) and St. Ignatius of Antioch spoke of the importance of the first day of the week for Christians: "Those who lived according to the old order of things have come to a new hope, no longer keeping the sabbath, but the Lord's Day, in which our life is blessed by him and by his death" (St. Ignatius, cited in *CCC*, 2175).

The observance of Sunday as the Lord's Day replaces the observance of the Sabbath, just as the Holy Sacrifice of the Mass replaces the observances of the Temple, and as the Old Testament laws about diet and the practice of circumcision have been replaced by laws that open the doors of the Church to those not from the Jewish world (cf. Acts 10, 15). Jesus says, "The sabbath was made for man, not man for the sabbath. That is why the Son of Man is lord even of the sabbath" (Mk 2:27–28, cf. *CCC*, 2176).

187. How do we keep the Third Commandment positively?

"The Sunday Eucharist is the foundation and confirmation of all Christian practice" (*CCC*, 2181). We observe the Third Commandment by participating in the Holy Eucharist on Sundays and holy days of obligation. This is a binding obligation for Catholics, an obligation that may be fulfilled by participating in the sacred liturgy in any Catholic Mass on the day of obligation or the evening before (cf. *CCC*, 2180). It is not enough to keep the obligation, for example, by praying at home.

Another requirement of the Third Commandment is to make Sunday a day of rest and freedom from work. Rest enables us to enjoy the leisure we need "to cultivate familial, cultural, social and religious lives" (*CCC*, 2184). We are to avoid the kind of work that hinders us from participating in the Holy Eucharist or gets in the way of the time we need for family, rest, and recreation.

Also, we keep the Third Commandment by being attentive to the needs of others, especially by not making unnecessary demands that would prevent them from keeping holy the Lord's Day themselves. Something we can and should do on Sunday is to perform works of mercy and charity by visiting the sick, elderly, or lonely.

188. What are holy days of obligation?

Holy days of obligation are feast days so important to Catholics that participation in Holy Mass is required, either on the day itself or on the evening before. Even when these holy days fall on workdays, Catholics are to arrange a time and place to participate in Holy Mass. Some holy days of obligation are for the universal Church, while others are left to the discretion of the local conference of bishops with the approval of Rome.

In addition to every Sunday, these days oblige participation in Holy Mass (cf. *CCC*, 2177):

- The Solemnity of Mary, Mother of God (January 1)

- Epiphany (a holy day that is moved to the Sunday nearest to January 6)

- The Feast of St. Joseph (March 19; not obligatory in the United States)

- The Ascension of the Lord (forty days after Easter or moved to the nearest Sunday in most of the United States)

- Corpus Christi, the Feast of the Body and Blood of Christ (moved to the nearest Sunday after the second Thursday after Pentecost)

- The Solemnity of Sts. Peter and Paul (June 29; not obligatory in the United States)

- The Solemnity of the Assumption of the Blessed Virgin Mary (August 15)

- All Saints' Day (November 1)

- The Solemnity of the Immaculate Conception (December 8)

- Christmas, the Solemnity of the Nativity (December 25)

189. Are there any exceptions to missing Mass on a Sunday or holy day of obligation?

The Third Commandment obliges us to remember the Lord in prayer and in good works, and specifically by attending Mass, but there are circumstances that interrupt or prevent us from keeping the Lord's Day as we would prefer.

When one is too ill or infirm to attend Mass on Sunday or a holy day, or when the illness of a loved one requires one to attend to that person's needs, there is no obligation to attend Mass. Likewise, when weather conditions make travel to church for Sunday or a holy day Mass difficult without risking one's own life or the time and attention of first responders, then there is no obligation to do so. When important travel plans make it impossible or unlikely to fulfill the Sunday or holy day obligation, then one may obtain a dispensation from one's parish priest.

When legitimately excused from an obligation to attend Holy Mass, one should spend time in prayer, especially by making use of Scripture and the Holy Rosary. Many who are infirm or homebound find great consolation in viewing or listening to the Mass on television or online. While participation in the Holy Mass in this way can be of great spiritual benefit, it never replaces the obligation to attend Holy Mass when one is able to do so (cf. *CCC*, 2183).

Responsibility for the needs of others can make attending Holy Mass impossible, especially for those who are first responders and those engaged in the work of health care, transportation, hospitality, and public service. Family needs and social services can excuse one from the obligations of Sunday rest, but one should avoid allowing excuses to turn into habits that would diminish one's health or one's religious or family life (cf. *CCC*, 2185).

Summary and Reflection

God's commandments remind us of the importance of loving God and neighbor. The first three commandments of the Decalogue concern worship and love of God. The First Commandment embraces faith, hope, and charity. The Second Commandment requires respect for God's holy name through blessing, praise, and adoration. Catholics observe the Third Commandment by celebrating the Eucharist every Sunday and holy day of obligation.

The first three commandments concern the love of God. Love of God is the foundation for love of our neighbor. And in a similar way, love of neighbor is necessary for loving God, "for whoever does not love a brother whom he has seen cannot love God whom he has not seen" (1 Jn 4:20).

⊖ Creation

How do the first three commandments help you to stay focused on your call to be a disciple of Jesus? How is keeping the Sabbath rest an experience of renewal, an experience of the new creation? When have you experienced the blessings of a Sabbath rest?

☾ Fall

The abuse of God's name and other foul language have become commonplace in our contemporary culture. How are you affected by the decline in the standards of public discourse? How have you challenged another person to show respect for God's name and the standards of decency?

✚ Redemption

False gods lead us away from God and into a life of sin. An undue attachment to the fleeting and false gods of fame, popularity, and material possessions is a recipe for sadness in this life and the life to come. Which teachings of Jesus help you to store up for yourself "treasures in heaven"? How does remembering his sacrifice on the Cross keep you from self-centeredness and stinginess?

⟳ Restoration

Prayer is the lifting up of one's soul to the Lord. How is prayer a foretaste of the new creation? When have you been touched by beauty, truth, and goodness at church or in personal prayer?

CHAPTER 18

Love of Neighbor through Respect for Human Life: Commandments Four and Five

(CCC, 2196–2327)

The life of St. Teresa of Kolkata—better known as "Mother Teresa"—is a testament to both the dignity of the human person and the importance of the family, two prominent themes that run through our discussion of the Fourth and Fifth Commandments.

When thinking of Mother Teresa, it is difficult to name a person from the twentieth century more widely known and acknowledged as someone who exemplified love of neighbor. During her tenure as the principal of a school for young ladies who came from families of wealth, Sr. Teresa received a special calling from God, an experience that she would describe as a "call within a call." She left the school's comfortable campus and went into the areas of Kolkata afflicted with poverty of the direst sort. There she made a difference, one person at a time. She and the sisters who gathered around her fed the hungry by hand, washed the sores of lepers, tended to the needs of the dying, and rocked babies born of drug-addicted mothers.

During her lifetime, Mother Teresa was recognized for her service to the poor through medals given by governments around the globe and honorary degrees bestowed by prestigious universities. She was even awarded the Nobel Peace Prize in 1979. The Missionaries of Charity, the religious community founded by Mother Teresa, has grown to more than five thousand sisters serving the poorest of the poor in over 135 countries.

St. Teresa of Kolkata is remembered as a woman of small stature and wrinkled face who never stopped looking for opportunities to uphold the dignity of the poor and less fortunate, or to speak out strongly about the evils of contraception and abortion. Often these two issues collided as she would plea for the life of children born and unborn: Please don't kill a child! I am willing to accept any child who would be aborted, and to give that child to a married couple who will love the child, and be loved by the child."

The sanctity and care of all life is vital; the Fourth and Fifth Commandments speak to the importance of giving all people a chance to live and grow and be loved while supported by a mother, father, and other family members.

190. What are the requirements of the Fourth Commandment?

"Honor your father and your mother" (Ex 20:12) is the Fourth Commandment. Although the Fourth Commandment is addressed primarily to children in relation to their parents, obedience to this commandment requires right relationship between all family members and the fulfillment of duties of subordinates to those who rightly exercise authority over them. The Fourth Commandment also requires the proper exercise of the authority of parents, teachers, and all those who are in positions of authority (cf. *CCC*, 2199).

191. What is unique about the Fourth Commandment among the other commandments?

The Fourth Commandment is the first of the final seven commandments that concern love of neighbor. It sets the tone for the commandments that follow. St. Paul teaches, "the one who loves another has fulfilled the law. The commandments . . . are summed up in this saying, [namely] 'You shall love your neighbor as yourself.' Love does no evil to the neighbor; hence, love is the fulfillment of the law" (Rom 13:8–10).

The Fourth Commandment is the only one of the ten that carries with it the promise of the reward of a "long life in the land the LORD your God is giving you" (Ex 20:12). This reward speaks to the profound connection between responsibility to one's family and the preservation of the common good of society. "Respecting this commandment provides, along with spiritual fruits, temporal fruits of peace and prosperity. Conversely, failure to observe it brings great harm to communities and individuals" (*CCC*, 2200).

192. What is God's plan for the family?

God is the author of marriage between a man and a woman, and therefore the author of the human family in total. As such, God has a plan and a vision for the family. "Marriage and the family are ordered to the good of the spouses and to the procreation and education of children" (*CCC*, 2201). The members of the family are equal in dignity and share responsibility for the good of the family (cf. *CCC*, 2203).

According to God's plan, every family is a "privileged community" (*CCC*, 2206) with an inherent right to be recognized by the state. Every Christian family may be called a *domestic church*, for it is the place where children first learn about the communion of Father, Son, and Holy Spirit. The Christian family grows through prayer, formation in the faith, and the encounter with Jesus in the Holy Sacrifice of the Mass. This domestic church—this privileged community—has great importance within the Church and is vital to the task of evangelization (cf. *CCC*, 2204–2206).

193. How is the family connected with and protected by the state?

Within the family, children experience the order and stability upon which the wider society is founded. Within the family, children learn morality and grow strong in the virtues that make possible the living of a truly good life in society (cf. *CCC*, 2207). Family members learn to care for one another and for the elderly and infirm in the extended family and beyond. Family members learn about the importance of sacrifice for the sake of the common good and the blessings that come from selfless generosity. These are the qualities that build up a wider society that is stable, respectful of the dignity of every human person, and ever seeking the common good (cf. *CCC*, 2208). The state has a responsibility to protect and defend the institution of the family, this "original cell of social life" (*CCC*, 2207).

194. What are ways the state must uphold God's plan for marriage and family life?

The state is called to uphold God's plan for marriage and family life in the following ways:

- The state must acknowledge the truth about marriage between a man and a woman, and safeguard the unique role of the family (cf. *CCC*, 2210).

- The state must protect the freedom of a man and a woman to enter into marriage and to establish a family, to have children, and to bring them up according to their own religious and moral convictions.

- The state must protect the institutions of marriage and family within the structure of the wider community and ensure that families have access to the means by which they can thrive, such as work, housing, food, education, health care, and civil rights.

- The state must protect families from threats to their stability, such as civil unrest and the dangers of pornography and drugs (cf. *CCC*, 2211).

195. What are the duties of children toward their parents?

Children are obliged to show honor and respect for their parents, as well as docility and obedience (cf. *CCC*, 2216). Children living at home should obey their parents for the sake of their own good and the good of the family. Obedience is not required of the child when to obey would violate conscience. Children are not obliged to assist their parents in immoral conduct (cf. *CCC*, 2217).

After they cease living at home, adult children are still obliged to show respect to their parents and assist them materially when needed and to the extent that they are able. Obedience to parents is not required of adult children who have left home (cf. *CCC*, 2217–2218).

Children are also obliged by the Fourth Commandment to treat their siblings with kindness and understanding. All are called to show great respect for their grandparents and those who are *spiritual parents*, such as pastors, teachers and mentors in the faith (cf. *CCC*, 2120).

196. What are the responsibilities of parents?

A major gift of marriage is fecundity, that is, the ability to produce off-spring. However, fecundity means more than procreation; it extends to the moral education and spiritual formation of children. Nothing can substitute for the role of parents in education: "The right and the duty of parents to educate their children are primordial and inalienable" (*CCC*, 2221). Parents are the primary educators of their children, and they do this by:

- creating a home life that is characterized by tenderness, compassion, and forgiveness

- forming their children in the cardinal virtues and helping them make progress toward self-mastery

- setting a good example, especially by evangelizing their children—teaching them about Jesus even in their most tender years and cultivating within them a spiritual life of prayer, devotion, and the sacramental life of the Church (cf. *CCC*, 2223–2226)

- safeguarding their home and family from the negative influences of the world (cf. *CCC*, 2224)

Practically, parents must provide for the physical needs of their children as well as the spiritual, helping them to grow in the ability to make good decisions and life choices (cf. *CCC*, 2228). This often means choosing the educational path that is in the best interest of their children. "Parents have the right to choose a school for [their children] which corresponds to their own convictions. This right is fundamental" (*CCC*, 2229). This right also protects the choice to homeschool.

197. How should parents encourage and respect the vocational choices of their children?

"Family ties are important but not absolute" (*CCC*, 2232). Jesus calls some to a vocation that involves leaving family and homeland behind for the sake of following him (cf. Mt 10:37–38). Parents should respect and encourage a child's vocation from God: "They must be convinced that the first vocation of the Christian is to follow Jesus" (*CCC*, 2232). A vocation to consecrated life or the priesthood should be welcomed by parents with joy and thanksgiving (cf. *CCC*, 2233).

198. How do the obligations of the Fourth Commandment go beyond the family?

We are obliged by the Fourth Commandment to honor those who "have received authority in society from God" (*CCC*, 2234). The Fourth Commandment also requires those in authority to exercise their leadership in a spirit of service and never to command or compel any action that offends the dignity of the human person (cf. *CCC*, 2235).

In fact, the dignity of the human person is always to be upheld in the exercise of authority, especially in matters of distributive justice and human rights (cf. *CCC*, 2236). Because the Church recognizes the rights of individuals and families to emigrate (cf. *CCC*, 2211), it is the duty of those in authority in more prosperous nations to welcome those who come seeking a better life, though immigration may be regulated by public authorities for the sake of the common good. "Immigrants are obliged to respect with gratitude the material and spiritual heritage of the country that receives them, to obey its laws, and to assist in carrying civic burdens" (*CCC*, 2241).

199. What are the duties of citizens that apply to following the Fourth Commandment?

Respect must be shown to those in authority over us. St. Paul teaches, "Let every person be subordinate to the higher authorities, for there is no authority except from God, and those that exist have been established by God" (Rom 13:1). Loyalty to those in authority includes the right and duty to offer just criticism and to contribute to the building up of the community (cf. *CCC*, 2238–2239). Paying taxes, voting, and defending one's country are moral obligations that derive from submitting to authority and are a way of taking responsibility for the common good (cf. *CCC*, 2240).

Citizens have an obligation in conscience not to obey the directives of civil authorities if they go against the moral order, the dignity of the human person, or the teachings of the Gospel. Situations do arise when the just person stands with St. Peter in saying, "We must obey God rather than men" (Acts 5:29, cf. *CCC*, 2242). Armed resistance to civil authority is a last resort, permitted only under strict conditions (cf. *CCC*, 2243, where those conditions are outlined).

God gives us the Fourth Commandment to remind us of our duty and responsibility to love our neighbor, beginning within the family, the fundamental cell of our society. We are commanded to extend broadly the love that we learn and experience in the home, treating every person not only as neighbor, but as brother or sister. Even while enduring the persecution ordered by the Roman emperor (the king), St. Peter exhorts, "Give honor to all, love the community, fear God, honor the king" (1 Pt 2:17).

200. What is the teaching of the Fifth Commandment?

The Fifth Commandment is expressed as an unambiguous prohibition against the most heinous offense against love of neighbor: "You shall not kill" (Ex 20:13). "Human life is sacred because from its beginning it involves the creative action of God and it remains forever in a special relationship with the Creator, who is its sole end. God alone is the Lord of life from its beginning until its end: no one can under any circumstance claim for himself the right directly to destroy an innocent human being" (*Donum Vitae*, intro 5, cited in *CCC*, 2258). Jesus even broadens the Fifth Commandment to include nonlethal offenses against the dignity of the human person, such as anger, hatred, and violence (cf. Mt 5:21–22).

201. What is the prohibition stated in the Fifth Commandment?

Since their fall from paradise, and precisely because of the effects of Original Sin, human beings have shown a tendency to violence, beginning with Cain shedding the blood and taking the life of his brother Abel, an action immediately condemned by God (cf. Gn 4:8–12, *CCC*, 2259). The prohibition against the taking of human life is made specific when God says, "The innocent and the just you shall not put to death" (Ex 23:7). "The deliberate murder of an innocent person is gravely contrary to the dignity of the human being, to the golden rule, and to the holiness of the Creator. The law forbidding it is universally valid: it obliges each and everyone, always and everywhere" (*CCC*, 2261).

202. Are there occasions when the taking of human life does not violate the Fifth Commandment?

When exercised in a manner proportionate to the threat, legitimate, lethal defense of oneself, one's family, or one's neighbor does not break the Fifth Commandment, for such defense does not take the life of an innocent (cf. *CCC*, 2263). In fact, legitimate defense can be a duty for those who have responsibility for the lives of others. Those in the military and those in law enforcement are duty-bound to protect and defend those under their care (cf. *CCC*, 2265).

203. Is capital punishment permissible?

Some who support capital punishment quote the Bible saying, "an eye for an eye, a tooth for a tooth" (Ex 21:24). To this Mahatma Gandhi reportedly said, "An eye for an eye will leave everyone blind." When an innocent life is taken in violence, a natural reaction is to seek justice by taking the life of the murderer. Experience has shown the dangers of both vigilantism and precipitous judgment. In recent years, more than a few death-row inmates have been released from prison on the basis of irrefutable DNA evidence that was unavailable at the time of their sentencing. "Better that ten guilty persons escape than that an innocent suffer" has long been a legal maxim in many countries. Nevertheless, the question of capital punishment is perennially controversial.

The Church teaches that to safeguard the common good, the state "has the right and duty to inflict penalties commensurate with the gravity of the crime" (*CCC*, 2266). Punishment is always first aimed at redressing the offense, and when accepted by the one convicted of a crime, it can be expiatory of the offense, medicinal for society, and a means of correcting the behavior of the offender (cf. *CCC*, 2266). The death penalty has long been considered appropriate in proportion to the gravity of certain crimes when carried out after a fair trial by the legitimate authority. There is today a growing sense that even after commission of a grievous crime, the dignity of the criminal is not lost, and that there is still an opportunity for redemption. Advances in engineering and technology have made prisons better able to protect the public from criminals likely to reoffend, in countries with such resources.

Pope John Paul II acknowledged that in the past the execution of those guilty of the most serious crimes was necessary to protect society, but "today however, as a result of steady improvements in the organization of the penal system, such cases are very rare, if not practically non-existent" (*Evangelium Vitae*, 56). Pope Francis has added to this teaching, saying

The Just War Doctrine

Jesus calls us to peace and denounces hatred as evil (cf. Mt 5:22, 44–45). The Church prays that war and the evils that accompany it be avoided (cf. *CCC*, 2307). Sadly, wars exist. The right to self-defense cannot be denied once peace efforts have failed (cf. *CCC*, 2308). Aggression brings nations to defend their borders and their interests.

The Church has a well-developed teaching that is known as the "just war doctrine," which it employs to maintain some human justice amidst violence and killing. In recent years the doctrine has stressed the *avoidance* of war due to the threat of weapons of mass destruction. This doctrine has its roots in pre-Christian sources such as the Roman lawyer Cicero and has been refined by such great teachers as St. Augustine and St. Thomas Aquinas. The doctrine covers both "justice leading up to war" (*jus ad bellum*) and "justice within war" (*jus in bello*).

Leading up to war (*jus ad bellum*), and after the peace process has been thoroughly tried and exhausted and there are no other practical or effective means to stop the aggressor, these criteria apply:

- The damage caused by the aggressor must be "lasting, grave, and certain" (*CCC*, 2309).

- There must be a serious chance of success.

- "The use of arms must not produce evils and disorders graver than the evil to be eliminated" (*CCC*, 2309).

- Those responsible for the common good must evaluate these conditions and act accordingly (cf. *CCC*, 2309); they have "the right and duty to impose on citizens the obligations necessary for national defense" (*CCC*, 2310).

- "Those who are sworn to serve their country in the armed forces are servants of the security and freedom of nations. If they carry out their duty honorably, they truly contribute to the common good of the nation and the maintenance of peace" (*CCC*, 2310).

Once war has begun, for the war to be carried out justly (*jus in bello*) it must follow these criteria:

- "Non-combatants, wounded soldiers, and prisoners must be respected and treated humanely" (*CCC*, 2313).

- "Actions deliberately contrary to the law of nations and to its universal principles are crimes, as are the orders that command such actions" (*CCC*, 2313). Blind obedience to such orders is not an excuse.

- Genocide is a mortal sin that cries out to heaven for vengeance and must be universally condemned (cf. *CCC*, 2314, Gn 4:10).

The dangers of war in our present day frighten even the bravest among us. We pray for peace and for the coming of the Lord, when peace will reign for all eternity. On that day, "they shall beat their swords into plowshares and their spears into pruning hooks; One nation shall not raise the sword against another, nor shall they train for war again" (Is 2:4).

that the death penalty is *inadmissible* particularly in modern societies and that the Church works with determination for its worldwide abolition: "It must be clearly stated that the death penalty is an inhumane measure that, regardless of how it is carried out, abases human dignity" (Pope Francis, Address to Participants in the Meeting Organized by the Pontifical Council for the Promotion of the New Evangelization, October 11, 2017, cited in *CCC*, 2267).

204. What are the offenses against the Fifth Commandment?

"Thou shall not kill" is a clear command. It forbids murder of all types and advocates for the protection of human life from the time of conception to natural death. The offenses against the Fifth Commandment are delineated in these categories:

- *Intentional homicide* is the direct and intentional killing of human life and is gravely sinful. Guilty are both the murderer and those who cooperated voluntarily in the murder. Especially grievous are infanticide or the murder of a relative because of the offense against natural and familial bonds. Murder cannot be justified under any circumstance, not even concern for the public well-being (cf. *CCC*, 2268).

- *Indirect killing* also offends against the Fifth Commandment. One may not expose another to mortal danger without grave reason, nor may one refuse assistance to one whose life is in danger. One is guilty of a serious offense if he acted without proportionate reason so as to bring about a person's death, even without the intention of doing so (cf. *CCC*, 2269). An example would be a reckless, intoxicated driver causing another person to die in an automobile accident.

- *Abortion*, the deliberate killing of unborn life by means of medical or surgical intervention, is a grave and unjustified attack on human life and "contrary to the moral law" (*CCC*, 2271). A human being has rights from the moment of conception, especially the right to life itself: "Human life must be respected and protected absolutely from the moment of conception" (*CCC*, 2270). Such has been the unchanging and unchangeable teaching of the Church since the first century.

The Church imposes the penalty of excommunication upon one who obtains an abortion or formally cooperates in one. This penalty makes clear the gravity of this offense. Excommunication is not intended to last forever, but rather to encourage contrition and the reception of the Sacrament of Penance and Reconciliation. The Lord is always full of understanding and generous with the forgiveness and grace that he provides through that sacrament, and the Church always stands ready to lift the excommunication and to reconnect the penitent to the sacraments.

- *Embryonic exploitation* is a grave offense against the dignity of the human person. The embryo must always be cared for and protected. Prenatal diagnosis is permitted provided it is directed toward the benefit of the child in the womb, but not if it is done with the possibility of inducing abortion based upon its results. It is not permitted to produce or use an embryo for scientific research that would exploit and later discard the embryo as biological waste. Nontherapeutic, genetic manipulation of the embryo is immoral (cf. *CCC*, 2274–2275). Chapter 19 will treat the subject of in vitro fertilization, also known as IVF.

- *Euthanasia* is the direct taking of the life of someone whose life is diminished by sickness or disability, and is always a grave offense against the Fifth Commandment (cf. *CCC*, 2277). Discontinuing overly zealous treatment of a patient is permissible, provided those decisions are made by the patient or in the patient's best interest by those who are entitled to act on behalf of the patient (cf. *CCC*, 2278).

  Ordinary care including hydration and nutrition is due to all patients, including the dying, unless the body is unable to assimilate water or food. Painkillers that risk shortening the life of a dying patient can be morally acceptable "if death is not willed as either an end or a means, but only foreseen and tolerated as inevitable" (*CCC*, 2279). Palliative care for the dying is always encouraged (cf. *CCC*, 2299).

- *Suicide* is contrary to the love of self and a grave sin against one's
  neighbor because it breaks the bonds of solidarity with one's family,
  friends, and wider community. We are but stewards of our lives who
  must give account to God at the end of our days. Suicide is scandalous
  when committed to give a bad example (cf. *CCC*, 2281). Cooperating
  with suicide is also a serious sin.

    "Grave psychological disturbances, anguish, or grave fear of hard-
  ship, suffering, or torture can diminish the responsibility of the one
  committing suicide" (*CCC*, 2282). We should pray for the one who
  commits suicide, commending that troubled person's soul to the loving and tender mercy of the Lord. We do not despair, for "the LORD is
  close to the brokenhearted, saves those whose spirit is crushed. Many
  are the troubles of the righteous, but the LORD delivers him from them
  all" (Ps 34:19–20, cf. *CCC*, 2283).

Other grave sins against the Fifth Commandment are kidnapping, the
taking of hostages, terrorism, and torture.

205. What is scandal, and how does it violate the Fifth Commandment?

The word *scandal* comes from a Greek word that means "stumbling block."
A scandalous action tempts another and could lead that person into sin.
Scandal is a grave sin when, by omission or commission, one is deliberately led to sin (cf. *CCC*, 2284). Examples include soliciting a person to tell
a lie, sexual sins, drunkenness, and drug use. Scandal is especially grave
when given by persons of authority or by teachers, or when those scandal-
ized are particularly weak (cf. *CCC*, 2285). Jesus says, "Temptations to sin
are sure to come; but woe to him by whom they come!" (Lk 17:1 NRSV).

206. Does the Fifth Commandment apply to actions that harm but do not kill?

Many people are surprised to learn that the Fifth Commandment can
be broken even when a life is not taken. In fact, it is a grave sin to *intend*

to murder another human being (cf. *CCC*, 2269). Furthermore, our Lord extends the application of the Fifth Commandment even to matters of the heart: "You have heard that it was said to your ancestors, 'You shall not kill; and whoever kills will be liable to judgment.' But I say to you, whoever is angry with his brother will be liable to judgment" (Mt 5:21–22). Remember this poetic phrase from the word **WATCH**:

> We Watch our Thoughts, for Thoughts lead to Words, and Words lead to Actions, and Actions lead to Habits, and Habits form our Character.

The Fifth Commandment also applies to the stewardship of our bodily, mental, and emotional health, as well as the health of those entrusted to our care (cf. *CCC*, 2288). The virtue of temperance is important to develop, so that we might be moderate in what we consume, especially in matters of food, alcohol, and tobacco, as well as in what we read and watch and the time we spend on the internet (cf. *CCC*, 2290).

Taking drugs, except when for strictly therapeutic purposes, gravely damages health and life and is a sin against the Fifth Commandment (cf. *CCC*, 2291). Given its mind-inhibiting effects, addictive properties, and long-term dangers, many bishops in the United States have concluded that the use of cannabis for the purpose of getting high is a grave violation of the Fifth Commandment, despite its legalization in many states. "I would like to say with great clarity: One does not conquer drug abuse with a drug! Drug abuse is an evil, and with evil there can be no concessions or compromises."[1]

207. Can the human body be studied as part of scientific research?

Scientific research on human beings that leads to advances in medicine and public health is acceptable unless the research involves actions that are contrary to human dignity or against the moral law, even with the consent of the patient. Research must never place in undue jeopardy the subject's life or physical or psychological integrity. Research on a human being without consent offends against human dignity (cf. *CCC*, 2292–95).

208. What does the Church teach about surgeries for "gender transition"?

Amputations, mutilations, and the sterilization of the innocent are forbidden except when performed for strictly therapeutic purposes, that is, when they repair a defect or when it is necessary to sacrifice one part of the body for the welfare of the whole body (cf. *CCC*, 2297). Regarding hormonal or surgical interventions for so-called gender transitioning, these are not morally permissible: "These technological interventions are not morally justified either as attempts to repair a defect in the body or as attempts to sacrifice a part of the body for the sake of the whole."[2]

209. Can Catholics participate in organ transplants?

Organ transplants are acceptable when the risks to the donor are proportionate to the benefit sought by the recipient. Donation after natural death is morally permissible and should be encouraged as a way to sustain or save the life of another human being. However, it is a grave offense against the Fifth Commandment "to bring about the disabling mutilation or death of a human being, even in order to delay the death of other persons" (*CCC*, 2296).

Summary and Reflection

The Fourth Commandment underscores the importance of the family as society's foundational unit. The Fourth Commandment also promotes a moral relationship between citizens and civil authorities. The Fifth Commandment forbids murder and the anger, envy, and hate that cause it. It is morally permissible to take another's life if it is absolutely necessary in order to defend one's own life or the life of an innocent person. War should always be the last resort in solving conflict. Nations do have the right to self-defense, following the just war doctrine. The moral law continues to hold during time of war. Church teaching opposes the use of capital punishment.

◒ *Creation*

The Fourth Commandment is about the relationships between children and parents, children and their siblings, and with those who exercise legitimate authority over us. What are the blessings you experience through the keeping of the Fourth Commandment?

◔ *Fall*

The family is the fundamental cell in our society. There are movements and forces in our world that are at odds with God's plan for family life. What offenses against the Fourth and Fifth Commandments do you find most troublesome? How are you called to stand up for families as you participate in the life of our society?

✝ *Redemption*

Even from the Cross Jesus was thinking about family, calling St. John to regard the Blessed Mother as his mother and calling his Blessed Mother to be like a mother to St. John (cf. Jn 19:25–27). How do you experience God's care for the family?

◕ *Restoration*

What are the good habits that you are called to develop so as to bring healing or strength to your own family? How do the Fourth and Fifth Commandments call you to ongoing conversion of life?

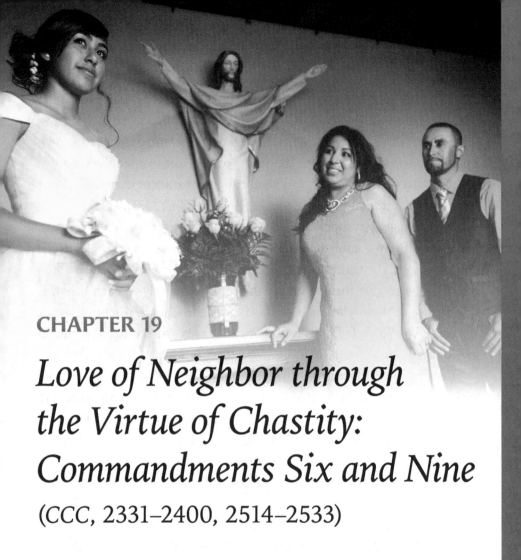

CHAPTER 19

Love of Neighbor through the Virtue of Chastity: Commandments Six and Nine

(CCC, 2331–2400, 2514–2533)

When hearing Confessions, priests frequently hear penitents say they have sinned against the Sixth and Ninth Commandments. What they are referring to are sins against the virtue of chastity, sometimes called "sins of the flesh." The Sixth Commandment—"You shall not commit adultery"—and the Ninth Commandment—"You shall not covet your neighbor's wife"—both address the proper use of sexuality.

Sometimes the Sixth and Ninth Commandments are thought of only as prohibitions against certain actions, an assertion that is only partially true. The Sixth and Ninth Commandments are all about God's plan for human happiness, the good life of virtue, the joy that comes from experiencing true love, the love that fulfills the deepest and most pure desires of the human heart. "God is love and in himself he lives a mystery of personal loving communion. Creating the human race in his own image.... God inscribed in the humanity of man and woman the *vocation*, and thus the capacity and responsibility, *of love* and communion" (Pope John Paul II, *Familiaris Consortio*, 11, cited in *CCC*, 2331).

In marriage, a husband and wife make a total gift of self to each other. Since the human person is both body and soul, this self-gift involves the entire person. The intimate act of sexual intercourse, in which the husband and wife give themselves totally and exclusively to each other, is the essence of their relationship. This is why the Church teaches that sex is reserved exclusively for marriage: "Sexuality is ordered to the conjugal love of man and woman" (*CCC*, 2360).

Keeping the Sixth and Ninth Commandments helps to make us more authentic people in the eyes of God and closer to experiencing true and lasting happiness. Chastity is a virtue that helps all people—husbands and wives, couples engaged to be married, priests and consecrated religious, and single people—to keep these commandments. Chastity is a hard-won virtue that requires a lifelong commitment to self-control. The rewards for doing so are great.

210. What does the Sixth Commandment prohibit?

The Sixth Commandment prohibits *adultery*, which is sexual intercourse between a man and woman who are married to other people or intercourse between an unmarried person and a married person (cf. *CCC*, 2380). Adultery is a grave offense against the marriage bond. Adultery undermines the stable bond between husband and wife, to which children have great need. Jesus not only condemned adultery absolutely, but he also condemned adultery by desire (cf. Mt 5:27–28, *CCC*, 2380–2381).

Yet, the commandment is also meant to "encompass the whole of human sexuality" (*CCC*, 2336). Sexuality affects deeply a person's capacity to experience fully what it means to be created in the image and likeness of God (cf. Gn 1:27). Other offenses against the Sixth Commandment are named on page 297.

211. What is meant by the "whole of human sexuality"?

Sexuality affects every aspect of the human person, especially a person's capacity to love another person and to bring new life into the world. To love another person means to will the good of that person (cf. *CCC*, 1766). Sexuality concerns "the capacity to love and to procreate" and the aptitude to experience the blessing of true communion with others (*CCC*, 2332). God's plan for human happiness depends upon the physical differences and the spiritual and moral complementarity of the sexes. "Male and female he created them" (Gn 1:27), thus ordering the human race toward "the goods of marriage and the flourishing of family life. The harmony of the couple and of society depends in part on the way in which the complementarity, needs, and mutual support between the sexes are lived out" (*CCC*, 2333).

Sin distorts God's plan for human happiness, hence the need for the Sixth Commandment. Jesus comes to restore what is broken by sin and "to restore creation to the purity of its origins" (*CCC*, 2336). The rich legacy of Catholic teaching on human sexuality gives us great insight into the true meaning of the Sixth Commandment and God's wise plan and great desire for human happiness.

212. What is the virtue of chastity?

Chastity is part of the cardinal virtue of temperance, the virtue by which the passions and appetites within the human person are guided by reason (cf. *CCC*, 2341). Virtue is a power, a strength. Just as through rigorous training an athlete builds up strength, speed, quickness, endurance, and agility, so through dedication to the practice of good actions does a person grow stronger in virtue: the ability to do what is right and good and to do it with ease. Openness to God's grace given through the sacraments allows those particular graces to build upon nature.

Chastity involves the whole person, the unity of body and soul, the integration of the power to love and to beget new life. It also involves the integrity of the gift of oneself in relating with others, especially within the context of Holy Matrimony (cf. *CCC*, 2337). Chastity is about commitment, and it leaves no room for a double life (cf. *CCC*, 2338).

Like other virtues, chastity makes possible the ease of a joy-filled life in accord with God's will and plan for human happiness (cf. *CCC*, 1804). Practicing this virtue means self-mastery of one's sexuality, attained through a sustained and sometimes arduous effort (cf. *CCC*, 2342). Either one masters the passions or is dominated by them. Either one is moved by conscious and free choice, or one is moved by blind impulses or external constraints. One gains great dignity when he or she moves away from slavery to the passions and presses forward toward the goal of self-mastery by consistently and freely making sound, moral choices. Through perseverance, a person gains the inclination and strength to live a life of integrity and virtue (cf. *CCC*, 2339).

"to thine own self be true"

Keys to Chastity

Virtue is both acquired by human effort and a gift from God. Acquiring the virtue of chastity therefore requires sustained awareness, effort, and openness to God's grace, without which one will never succeed. Here are six keys for perfecting the virtue of chastity:

1. *Know yourself.* "Know thyself" and "to thine own self be true" are phrases that do not appear in the Bible but are nonetheless important for growth in the virtue of chastity. Knowledge of one's capabilities and weaknesses helps a person to choose more consistently to stay on the path of virtue and not depart from it. Catholic chastity educator Jason Evert said, "Chastity isn't about following a bunch of rules so you don't go to hell. It's about wanting heaven for the person you love."

2. *Be disciplined.* Self-discipline, accompanied by self-denial, helps to build up the virtues, especially the virtue of chastity. "Lust indulged became habit, and habit unresisted became necessity."[1]

3. *Keep the commandments, especially the Sixth and Ninth Commandments.* Chastity means living a pure life, abstaining from all voluntary sensual pleasure before and outside of marriage. St. Alphonsus Liguori taught: "In temptations against chastity, the spiritual masters advise us, not so much to contend with the bad thought, as to turn the mind to some spiritual, or, at least, indifferent object. It is useful to combat other bad thoughts face to face, but not thoughts of impurity."

4. *Exercise the virtues.* Progress in one virtue brings about progress in the others. The good habit of embracing difficult tasks and activities gives a person confidence to persevere in the exacting work needed to acquire the virtue of chastity. "To be pure, to remain pure, can only come at a price, the price of knowing God and loving him enough to do his will. He will always give us the strength we need to keep purity as something as beautiful for him," said St. Teresa of Kolkata.

5. *Be faithful in prayer.* Pray humbly, in contrition for sins committed and in thanksgiving for being rescued from the emptiness of a life of sin. "Holy Purity is granted by God when it is asked for with humility."[2] Make frequent use of the Sacrament of Penance, through which we encounter the Divine Physician who binds up our wounds, the Just Judge who delivers a sentence of mercy, the Lord Jesus by whose Blood we are made clean.

6. *Cultivate good friendships.* Look for those who will support you and walk with you along the path of virtue. "The virtue of chastity blossoms in friendship" (*CCC*, 2347). "Blessed is the man who does not walk in the counsel of the wicked. . . . Rather, the law of the LORD is his joy; and on his law he meditates day and night" (Ps 1:1–2).

213. Who is called to live out the virtue of chastity?

Every person is called to the virtue of chastity, according to his or her state in life.

The person who is single is called to live a chaste life, living in complete continence, refraining from all sexual activity. The word *continence* derives from a Latin word that means "holding back."

Those who are courting or engaged are also called to live in chaste continence, holding back until marriage those actions that are appropriate only when the couple has made the commitment to Holy Matrimony in the sight of God and the Church. The time before marriage should be a time to grow in the virtue of chastity, for that virtue is very important for the sake of the marriage.

Those who are married are called to *conjugal chastity*, as described on page 300.

Some in the Church are called to profess virginity or consecrated celibacy so they might give themselves wholly to God. Chastity in this case is a solemn vow before God to be sexually pure. Celibacy is a public promise made before God to remain unmarried and continent for the sake of the Kingdom.

214. What are sins against the Sixth Commandment?

As any sin corrupts and corrodes the soul of the sinner, sins against the Sixth Commandment disfigure what is truly beautiful and good in God's gift of human sexuality as expressed in Holy Matrimony, "the complete and lifelong mutual gift of a man and a woman" (*CCC*, 2337). Besides the offense of one or both married people having violating the command to "not commit adultery" (Ex 20:14), other sins that offend against the gift of sexuality include:

- *Lust* is the "disordered desire for or inordinate enjoyment of sexual pleasure" (*CCC*, 2351). Sexual pleasure is disordered when it is not both open to procreation and directed toward the unity between husband and wife.

- *Masturbation* is "the deliberate stimulation of the genital organs in order to derive sexual pleasure" (*CCC*, 2352). Masturbation is a sin against the Sixth Commandment because sexual pleasure is obtained selfishly and outside "the sexual relationship which is demanded by the moral order and in which the total meaning of mutual self-giving and human procreation in the context of true love is achieved" (Congregation for the Doctrine of the Faith, *Persona Humana*, 9, cited in *CCC*, 2352).

- *Fornication* is sexual intercourse and other sexual sins between an unmarried man and an unmarried woman. Fornication is a sin against the Sixth Commandment because it is contrary to human dignity and human sexuality, which is ordered toward procreation and the union between husband and wife (cf. *CCC*, 2353).

- *Pornography* is a grave offense against the dignity of the human person because it puts on display that which should remain intimate and radically distorts the conjugal act, the mutual giving of self between husband and wife. Pornography harms all who participate in its production and all who consume it. "It immerses all who are involved in the illusion of a fantasy world" (*CCC*, 2354).

- *Prostitution* is a grave offense because it reduces the other to a mere instrument of pleasure. Prostitution is degrading to both parties and is a scourge in our society. Many prostitutes are victims who have been exploited through the serious sin of human trafficking and therefore have diminished culpability for their actions (cf. *CCC*, 2355).

- *Rape* is always an intrinsically grave offense against the Sixth Commandment. It so violates human dignity that victims can suffer damage that endures for a lifetime.

Also forbidden by the Sixth Commandment are polygamy, incest, and "any sexual abuse perpetrated by adults on children or adolescents entrusted to their care" (*CCC*, 2389, cf. *CCC*, 2387–2389). This prohibition also extends to the sexual abuse of vulnerable adults.

215. What does divorce have to do with the Sixth Commandment?

Divorce claims to break the unbreakable covenant to which husband and wife consented "until death do we part." Contracting a new union with another compounds the offense and constitutes an entry into permanent adultery (cf. *CCC*, 2384). Nevertheless, church law recognizes that there are some situations in which the separation of spouses or civil divorce may be necessary to protect certain rights, including those of the children (cf. *CCC*, 2383). Church law also recognizes that there are tragic cases when what purports to be a valid marriage is lacking in something essential to the marriage. An ecclesiastical court called a tribunal can conduct an objective investigation of a so-called marriage that has ended in divorce and can, with sufficient evidence, decide with moral certitude that the union lacked a constitutive element, such as the ability to consent freely to the marriage. In such a case, the tribunal would issue a declaration of nullity, thereby making it possible for both parties to marry within the Church. If you have experienced the tragedy of divorce and have questions about how church law applies, please discuss your particular situation with your parish priest or deacon.

216. What do studies reveal about cohabitation before marriage?

Trial marriages, or cohabitation, and *free unions*, or common-law marriages, are also sins against the Sixth Commandment. Many people insist that it is better for a couple to live together before entering into marriage so as to test the waters. Conventional wisdom might support such a proposition, but scientific studies have shown that cohabitation before marriage increases the risk of divorce. The most recent data indicate that little has changed over the decades. An Institute for Family Studies survey found that cohabitation before marriage was associated with a lower risk of divorce in the first year of marriage but a higher risk thereafter. The institute interpreted this finding in light of experience theories, noting that living together before marriage could give couples a leg up at the very start of marriage because there is less of an adjustment to being married and specifically to living together. But they found this advantage to be short-lived because other factors related to experience may take over from there, such as how cohabitation can increase acceptance of divorce.[3]

Trial marriages "can scarcely ensure mutual sincerity and fidelity in a relationship between a man and a woman, nor, especially, can they protect it from inconstancy of desires or whim" (CDF, *Persona Humana*, 7).

217. How does the Sixth Commandment serve and protect those in Holy Matrimony?

Aside from the clear boundaries that it establishes, the Sixth Commandment serves to safeguard God's plan for marriage and family life. God is the author of marriage, establishing it as the means by which a man and a woman establish a lifelong partnership of commitment and sacrificial self-giving for the sake of the other and the glory of God (cf. *CCC*, 1601). The chaste love of husband and wife involves an intimacy that is noble and honorable, one that is the source of pleasure of body and spirit (cf. *CCC*, 2362).

218. What is the purpose of the sexual union between a husband and wife in marriage?

The sexual union of husband and wife achieves the two ends of marriage:

- the unity of the spouses (fidelity)
- the transmission of life (fecundity)

"These two meanings or values of marriage cannot be separated without altering the couple's spiritual life and compromising the goods of marriage and the future of the family" (*CCC*, 2363).

Fidelity means keeping one's word, just as God himself is faithful to his word. By keeping the Sixth Commandment and persevering in marital chastity, the couple bears public witness to the mystery of the love and fidelity of Christ for his Body, the Church (cf. Eph 5:21–33, *CCC*, 2365). *Fecundity* is a blessing, a gift from God to the couple and from the couple to the Church and the world. Fidelity and fecundity are the two ends of marriage, each one witnessing to Christ's love. On the Cross, Jesus teaches us everything that we need to know about marital love. Love is about fidelity, love is about commitment, and love is about sacrificial self-giving. "No one has greater love than this, to lay down one's life for one's friends" (Jn 15:13, cf. *CCC*, 2366).

Love is also about *fruitfulness*, another lesson that Jesus teaches from the Cross. Just as from the side of the first Adam did God fashion Eve both to be Adam's helpmate and so that they could be fruitful and multiply, so from the wounded side of the second Adam (Jesus, cf. Rom 5:14, 1 Cor 15:21–23, 45) is born the sacramental life of the Church. St. John tells us that when the soldier thrust a lance into the side of Christ crucified, "immediately blood and water flowed out" (Jn 19:34). While this verse speaks of a phenomenon that would be true physiologically, there is also a deeply spiritual meaning. The Church has consistently taught that the water from the side of Christ is a sign of the Sacrament of Baptism through which are born new sons and daughters of God. The blood that flows out is both a symbol and the reality of the Blood of Christ offered in the Sacrament of the Eucharist, that great gift that nourishes and strengthens the sons and daughters of God (cf. *CCC*, 766).

Just as the great love that Jesus shows upon the Cross is the epitome of both fidelity and fecundity, so also is the chaste love of husband and wife ordered to fidelity and fecundity. In fact, these two ends of marriage may not be separated without doing great damage to the marriage itself. The Church, always standing up for life, teaches that "each and every marriage act must remain open 'per se' to the transmission of life" (*Familiaris Consortio*, 30, cited in *CCC*, 2366). This consistent teaching of the Magisterium is based upon God's plan for marriage and the inseparable connection of fidelity and fecundity, the connection of marital love and new life, "which man on his own initiative may not break, between the unitive significance and the procreative significance which are both inherent to the marriage act" (*Humanae Vitae*, 12, cited in *CCC*, 2366).

219. What does the Church teach about procreation and family planning?

Large families are traditionally seen as a blessing from God and a sign of the generosity of the parents (cf. *CCC*, 2373). In bringing new life into the world, parents share in the creative power of God, hence the term *procreation* (cf. *CCC*, 2367). Married couples should always act in accord with objective standards of morality by respecting the unitive and procreative dimensions of the marriage act (cf. *CCC*, 2369). Although not every marriage act necessarily brings new life into the world, the couple must not introduce anything into the marriage act that would make procreation impossible, such as contraceptive devices or drugs. Such interference with the procreative dimension of the marriage act is intrinsically evil (cf. *CCC*, 2370).

There are other moral difficulties with many means of contraception. Contraceptive drugs can act both to hinder ovulation and to cause a spontaneous abortion should ovulation occur. The use of contraceptive drugs can have long-term, serious effects upon the health of the woman, for while medicines are intended to improve bodily functions, contraceptive drugs are intended to do the opposite, that is, to render infertile one who is naturally fertile. Intrauterine contraceptive devices (IUDs) can also be abortifacients, as they irritate the lining of the uterus, making it inhospitable for the newly fertilized ovum.

Nevertheless, some couples have serious and just reasons for spacing the births of their children. In so doing, they should not be motivated by selfishness, but by the generosity appropriate to parenthood (cf. *CCC*, 2368). To achieve the goal of spacing the births of children, the couple must not use immoral means. The couple may make use of periodic abstinence during the fertile time of the cycle, provided that the motivation for doing so is not purely selfish and that they have a grave reason for doing so.

Periodic abstinence is no longer equated with the so-called rhythm method, which aimed to predict the fertile and infertile times of the cycle. Today's various methods are known collectively as Natural Family Planning (NFP) and have a high degree of success. In fact, couples struggling with infertility are encouraged to learn about and follow these same methods to identify more precisely the fertile times of the cycle. Natural Family Planning methods "respect the bodies of the spouses, encourage tenderness between them, and favor the education of an authentic freedom" (*CCC*, 2370).

220. How is the Sixth Commandment relevant to couples that struggle with infertility?

The suffering of a couple that struggles with infertility can be profound. As a community, we are to walk with them carefully as they bear this cross. Research and medical procedures aimed at finding a remedy for sterility are praiseworthy only if they are in keeping with the dignity of the human person (cf. *CCC*, 2374–2375).

The Church leaves open the possibility of scientific or medical techniques that assist the couple to achieve a pregnancy while respecting the integrity of the conjugal act. At present, most moral theologians view as legitimate the low tubal ovum transfer (LTOT), which involves "transferring the wife's egg beyond a blockage in the fallopian tube so that marital relations can result in pregnancy."[4] Couples facing difficulty in conceiving a child should consult a physician knowledgeable and supportive of Catholic teaching, and consult with their parish priest as they discern the way forward.

On the other hand, techniques that dissociate the sexual union of a husband and wife are gravely immoral. These include sperm or ovum donation from outside the marriage, and also the use of a surrogate uterus. These techniques infringe upon the right of the child to be born of his or her own mother and father, bound to one another in Matrimony. They also offend against the right of each spouse "to become a father and a mother only through each other" (CDF, *Donum Vitae* II, 1, cited in *CCC*, 2376).

While there are some medical techniques that do involve the sperm of the husband and the egg of the wife, they nevertheless dissociate the procreative action from the marriage act. A child should not be deprived of the right to be conceived through an act of self-giving between mother and father. Instead, the origin of that child's life is dominated by technology and the power of scientists. Techniques such as these include artificial insemination and in vitro fertilization.

The child possesses the right "to be the fruit of the specific act of the conjugal love of his parents, [and] the right to be respected as a person from the moment of his conception" (CDF, *Donum Vitae* II, 4, cited in *CCC*, 2378). "Only respect for the link between the meanings of the conjugal act and respect for the unity of the human being make possible procreation in conformity with the dignity of the person" (CDF, *Donum Vitae* II, 5, cited in *CCC*, 2377).

Sterility is not a curse, nor is it a sign of disfavor from God. Couples that have exhausted morally licit means to conceive a child can pray to find solace in the Cross and unite their sufferings with those of the Lord. Many couples find a beautiful expression for their desire to be fertile by adopting children and raising them in a loving home. Such generosity is indeed praiseworthy (cf. *CCC*, 2379).

221. How does the Sixth Commandment address homosexuality?

The number of people who identify as lesbian, gay, bisexual, or transgender has increased dramatically in the last decade. In a 2022 Gallup survey, 7.2 percent of adults polled in the United States identified as LGBT, double the number in 2012. Among those born from 1997 to 2004 (sometimes called Generation Z, aged eighteen to twenty-five at the time), 19.7 percent identified in the poll as LGBT.[5]

These numbers are not negligible, yet morality is not determined by polling data. Those who experience "an exclusive or predominant sexual attraction toward persons of the same sex" (*CCC*, 2357) are nonetheless called to the virtue of chastity and not to act upon those attractions. Scripture and Tradition teach that "homosexual acts are intrinsically disordered" (CDF, *Persona Humana*, 8) because they violate natural law, they are closed to the gift of life, and "they do not proceed from a genuine affective and sexual complementarity. Under no circumstances can they be approved" (*CCC*, 2357). To keep the Sixth Commandment, "homosexual persons are called to chastity" (*CCC*, 2359).

Like all Christians, homosexual persons are called to follow the path of virtue and self-mastery and to find the true freedom that brings genuine happiness. With prayer, the grace of the sacraments, and friends who are looking out for their spiritual good, homosexual persons can and should make great progress in the virtue of chastity (cf. *CCC*, 2359).

Dealing with same-sex attraction and remaining chaste can be difficult. Every cross is to be borne with courage, but not necessarily alone. Courage International is a support network for those who experience same-sex attraction and who strive to follow the path of chastity. Courage International is also a tremendous resource for the family and friends of homosexual persons.

Of homosexual people, Pope Francis wrote: "I am glad that we are talking about 'homosexual people' because before all else comes the individual person, in his wholeness and dignity. And people should not be defined only by their sexual tendencies: let us not forget that God loves all his creatures, and we are destined to receive his infinite love" (*The Name of God is Mercy*).

222. What is required by the Ninth Commandment?

In the Catholic moral tradition, the Ninth Commandment—"You shall not covet your neighbor's wife" (Ex 20:17)—forbids carnal concupiscence, that is to say, lust of the flesh or lust of the eyes (cf. *CCC*, 2514). Jesus expanded the Ninth Commandment by teaching that "everyone who looks at a woman with lust has already committed adultery with her in his heart" (Mt 5:28).

Concupiscence refers to disordered human desires that are a consequence of Original Sin. Concupiscence produces in us an inclination to sin, also expressed as "the rebellion of the 'flesh' against the 'spirit'" (*CCC*, 2515). St. Paul speaks for himself and for all of humanity when he confesses, "The willing is ready at hand, but doing the good is not. For I do not do the good I want, but I do the evil I do not want. Now if I do what I do not want, it is no longer I who do it, but sin that dwells in me. So, then, I discover the principle that when I want to do right, evil is at hand" (Rom 7:18–21).

Yet St. Paul does not leave us without hope amidst this sometimes daily battle between the spirit and the flesh: "All of us once lived among them in the desires of our flesh, following the wishes of the flesh and the impulses, and we were by nature children of wrath, like the rest. But God, who is rich in mercy, because of the great love he had for us, even when we were dead in our transgressions, brought us to life with Christ" (Eph 2:3–5). Pope John Paul II explains that for St. Paul,

it is not a matter of despising and condemning the body which
with the spiritual soul constitutes man's nature and personal
subjectivity. Rather, he is concerned with the morally good or
bad works, or better, the permanent dispositions—virtues and
vices— which are the fruit of submission (in the first case) or of
resistance (in the second case) to the saving action of the Holy
Spirit. For this reason [St. Paul] writes: "If we live by the Spirit,
let us also walk by the Spirit." (Gal 5:25, cited in *Dominum et
Vivificantem*, 55, and in *CCC*, 2516)

223. How do we keep the Ninth Commandment positively?

The Ninth Commandment is kept through ongoing purification of the
heart and living out the virtue of temperance. Our Lord assures us,
"Blessed are the clean of heart, for they will see God" (Mt 5:8). Keeping
the Ninth Commandment well is a good way to avoid disobeying the
Sixth Commandment. Purity of heart enables us to regard as a temple of
the Holy Spirit the human body, our own and the body of our neighbor
(cf. *CCC*, 2519). Some practical ways to cultivate pureness of heart are:

- Be vigilant about the call to chastity as expressed in the Sixth
  Commandment.

- Fill your mind with the lessons Jesus teaches us about the dignity of
  every human being and pray for the grace to treat your neighbor as
  yourself.

- Guard your eyes by developing the discipline to avert your gaze when
  encountering scenes, images, or situations that may get you in trouble.

- Refuse to go along with the crowd; stay away from places that are
  occasions of sin.

- Pray daily for the grace to remain pure, especially invoking the intercession of the Blessed Virgin Mary (cf. *CCC*, 2520).

- Maintain modesty in dress, words, actions, and feelings, especially
  by keeping in mind that the standards of decency presented in

contemporary culture rarely conform fully to the objective standards of morality that we learn from Christ and the Church.

"Purity of heart brings freedom from widespread eroticism and avoids entertainment inclined to voyeurism and illusion" (*CCC*, 2521–2525).

Summary and Reflection

Keeping the Sixth and Ninth Commandments helps to make us more authentic people in the eyes of God and closer to experiencing true and lasting happiness. St. Augustine is a good mentor for those who seek true happiness, especially in the midst of a world that is anything but chaste and pure: "The faithful must believe the articles of the Creed 'so that by believing they may obey God, by obeying may live well, by living well may purify their hearts, and with pure hearts may understand what they believe'" (*De Fide et Symbolo*, 10, cited in *CCC*, 2518). The world around us is hellbent on promoting a moral permissiveness based upon a distorted understanding of human freedom. True freedom does not mean doing whatever one pleases. True freedom consists in possessing the virtue needed to do consistently what is right, noble, honorable, holy, and true. True happiness comes from accepting the truth about the dignity of the human person and acting accordingly (cf. *CCC*, 2526). All that glitters and sparkles is not gold, nor is everything that catches one's eyes truly beautiful. We must work to educate our senses to appreciate that which is genuinely good, true, and beautiful.

◔ *Creation*

From the beginning, God had a plan for marriage and family life. God is the author of marriage. How have the Sixth and Ninth Commandments provided for you a path of goodness and happiness?

◐ *Fall*

Sin distorts God's plan for human happiness. Sin sometimes masquerades as goodness, like a wolf in sheep's clothing. What is God's response to those who fall into sins against the Sixth and Ninth Commandments?

✟ *Redemption*

"Greater love has no one than to lay down his life for a friend." Jesus's life is one of total dedication to the will of his heavenly Father. How is Jesus's life a model for both those called to the married state and those who consecrate their lives to celibate chastity for the sake of the Kingdom?

◑ *Restoration*

How does purity of heart help us to see the human body, our own and that of our neighbor, as a temple of the Holy Spirit, an expression of divine beauty (cf. *CCC*, 2519) and a participation in the new creation?

CHAPTER 20

Love of Neighbor through Justice and Truth: Commandments Seven, Eight, and Ten

(CCC, 2401–2463, 2464–2513, 2534–2557)

From an early age, we learn not only the difference between right and wrong but also how to break the rules and get away with it! Fortunately, we learn about the importance of personal integrity through the moral guidance we receive in the Ten Commandments, the teachings of Jesus, and from parents, teachers, and mentors. We learn that integrity is about doing the right thing, especially when nobody is looking.

The word *integrity* is related to the mathematical word *integer*. An integer is a whole number, as opposed to a fractional number. Similarly, integrity is about wholeness in our approach to life, as opposed to being divided and compartmentalized. A person with integrity does not have a secret life of cheating and stealing. A person with integrity returns at once the extra dollar in change mistakenly given by the store cashier. A person with integrity tells the truth even at great personal expense. A person with integrity does not get carried away with "get rich quick" schemes, nor does he get hopelessly immersed in debt by living beyond his means.

The Seventh, Eighth, and Tenth Commandments point the way not only to personal integrity but also to the well-being of society. Sadly, the lessons of history teach us what happens to societies that lose their moral integrity, accepting as normal wanton burglary and theft, a press that lies, and a government that lives beyond its means.

224. What is required by the Seventh Commandment?

The Seventh Commandment is clear and direct: "You shall not steal" (Ex 20:15). This commandment is about justice, which is the virtue of giving to the other that which is due and to not take from another unjustly. The Seventh Commandment also requires that we exercise charity with the goods that we possess, remembering that we are but stewards of the gifts with which we are blessed and that we are called to share those gifts with others out of responsibility and charity. The Seventh Commandment requires a balance between the right to private property and profound respect for what is known as the "universal destination of goods" (cf. CCC, 2401).

225. What is included under the Seventh Commandment?

The Seventh Commandment prohibits the unjust taking of a variety of things that rightfully belong to others. This is known as theft and most commonly means taking another's physical possessions. The commandment prohibits several other versions of theft, including:

- "business fraud; paying unjust wages; forcing up prices by taking advantage of the ignorance or hardship of another" (*CCC*, 2409)

- price manipulation

- bribery of a public official

- irresponsibility or neglect of one's fiduciary responsibilities in a company

- deliberately not giving one's best effort on the job

- knowingly writing checks that will not clear the bank

- damaging public or private property

- forgery for the sake of gain

- excessive or wasteful spending at work

- the deliberate breaking of a promise or a contract entered into in good faith

Criminal penalties apply in many of these cases; each offense requires restitution (cf. *CCC*, 2409), including when contracts are broken to the detriment of others (cf. *CCC*, 2410–2412).

While gambling is not in itself a sin against the Seventh Commandment, it becomes sinful when the needs of others are compromised by gambling losses. It is immoral to take risks with the lives and well-being of others, and all too frequently a gambler does not know when to quit (cf. *CCC*, 2413).

A grave offense against the Seventh Commandment (and sometimes the Fifth and Sixth Commandments) is the enslavement of others, also known as human trafficking, which is a serious violation of human dignity (*CCC*, 2414).

226. What is the "universal destination of goods"?

Stewardship of God's creation is best exercised when individuals justly take ownership of certain goods, oftentimes through the sweat of their brow, the work of their hands, and the fruit of their ingenuity and imagination.

It is refreshing to see a young person with his or her first car, purchased with funds earned mowing many lawns or babysitting for many long hours. The car is washed, waxed, and maintained with great attention and devotion, quite unlike the way one would treat a rental car or the drive-on-demand vehicles available in major cities. Homeowners have this same kind of pride of ownership, as do those who operate their own small businesses. The right to private property is essential to the common good and the proper stewardship of God's creation, which includes the work of human hands (cf. *CCC*, 2402–2403).

At the same time, the right to private property is not absolute, especially when some people are denied the necessities of life (food, water, clean air, etc.). The universal destination of goods teaches that the goods of the earth should be divided to ensure freedom and dignity of the human person, so that all might meet basic needs. "Goods" means more than just food and other natural resources. Although these types of property will always be of value, especially in the modern world the idea of "property" takes on a new dimension and includes "knowledge, technology, and know-how." In all of these areas, "the universal destination of goods remains primordial" (*CCC*, 2403).

All who own property are obliged to be good stewards and to exercise both responsibility in the use of those goods and generosity in sharing them. Generosity does not necessarily mean giving one's goods away, but using them in ways that benefit other people. There is a difference between the miser who hoards millions of dollars for his own purposes and one who uses millions of dollars to build factories and enterprises that create jobs, allowing many families to rise out of poverty.

The state has a legitimate interest in regulating the exercise of private property for the sake of the common good and to protect the dignity of the human person. The state's interest does not extend to denying a person's right to private property or unreasonably requiring that his goods to be transferred unwillingly (cf. *CCC*, 2404–2406). Also, one may presume permission to take from another what is necessary in the event of an emergency or in the urgent need for what is essential for life (cf. *CCC*, 2408).

227. How does the Seventh Commandment affect broader social concerns?

The Seventh Commandment is about the justice that is due to other human beings. Justice always depends upon personal integrity, such as doing an honest day's work for a fair wage or not manipulating a bill to extract more from the customer than what is fair. Sometimes justice depends upon the right ordering of society, such as we have witnessed in the reforms to the practice of child labor, apartheid, and laws that mandated racial segregation. The Church has a responsibility to speak out against grave and persistent offenses to human dignity and to offer a vision of the way society should be ordered. The social doctrine of the Church that emerged amidst the Industrial Revolution "proposes principles for reflection; it provides criteria for judgment; it gives guidelines for action" (*CCC*, 2423, cf. *CCC*, 2419–2425). A brief summation never does justice to the rich legacy of Catholic social teaching. Each bullet point below represents a major theme developed by the Pontifical Council for Justice and Peace in its *Compendium of the Social Doctrine of the Church*:

- *The dignity of the human person* is the fundamental principle in Catholic social teaching and is always to be respected and defended. The human person is created in the image and likeness of God (cf. *CCC*, 2424).

- *The common good* must never be used as an excuse to degrade human dignity; specifically, the systems of socialism and communism are to be rejected. Likewise, laissez-faire or free-market capitalism without government intervention has been tried and found wanting. "Reasonable regulation of the marketplace and economic initiatives, in keeping with a just hierarchy of values and a view to the common good, is to be commended" (*CCC*, 2425).

- *The universal destination of goods* is in keeping with God's plan for the human race (see *CCC*, 2402–2406).

- *Subsidiarity* is one of the most constant aspects of Catholic social teaching. Decisions are to be made at the lowest appropriate level in society (cf. *CCC*, 1885).

- *Participation* in economic initiatives and contributing to the common good is a right and responsibility enjoyed by every human person (cf. *CCC*, 2426–2429).

- *Solidarity* is a virtue and is key to building up human interdependence and a just social order (cf. *CCC*, 1939–1942, 2437–2442).

- *Truth, freedom, and justice are fundamental values of social life* that must never be neglected in the social order (cf. *CCC*, 2426–2436).

- *The family is the vital cell of society* and must always be protected and sustained by the laws of society (cf. *CCC*, 2207).

- *Marriage is the foundation of the family,* and God is the author of marriage. He has a specific plan for its place in the social order. Public authorities have an obligation to protect marriage and family for the sake of a just society (cf. *CCC*, 2202).

- *Human labor* has great dignity, and workers have rights: the right to work, the right to a just wage, the right to have recourse to a strike when necessary to preserve or achieve those rights (cf. *CCC*, 2427, 2433–2436).

- *The state, the political community, and those responsible for business enterprises* have a responsibility to work together to ensure the rights of the individual and to secure the common good (cf. *CCC*, 2430–2432).

- *The international community* forms a broader network of nations that must work together in peace and in justice to secure the dignity of every human person and to build up the global common good. Wealthy nations have a responsibility to be good neighbors to developing nations, to avoid exploitation of any kind (cf. *CCC*, 2437–2440).

- *Care for God's creation* must never be neglected (cf. *CCC*, 2415–2418). The earth's resources must be used wisely, not depleting them or depriving future generations of their use. Animals are to be treated

Coming to the Aid of the Poor

God blesses those who love the poor. Jesus himself teaches us that we will be judged on the basis of how we took care of the least of our brothers and sisters (cf. Mt 25:31–46). Love for the poor is more than a feeling. Love for the poor is made manifest in concrete actions. Being poor does not necessarily mean having material needs. Even those who are wealthy beyond the dreams of King Midas can experience a great emptiness of heart.

Hence, the Church names two kinds of works of mercy. One is the corporal works of mercy. The word *corporal* comes from the Latin word *corpus*, which means "body." The corporal works of mercy address practical needs. Addressing physical necessities should be more than just well-wishing that a person's needs will someday be met; instead, it includes active involvement in providing for them. "If a brother or sister has nothing to wear and has no food for the day, and one of you says to them, 'Go in peace, keep warm, and eat well,' but you do not give them the necessities of the body, what good is it?" (Jas 2:15–16). The corporal works of mercy remind us to put our words into action and to practice what we preach. The corporal works of mercy are:

1. Feed the hungry.
2. Give drink to the thirsty.
3. Clothe the naked.
4. Shelter the homeless.
5. Visit the sick.
6. Visit the imprisoned.
7. Bury the dead.

The spiritual works of mercy address the needs of those who have significant inner poverty. A person may be materially satisfied and yet may be enduring a certain poverty of the spirit, such as loneliness, ignorance, or distance from God. You are called to reach out to those experiencing these types of poverty by doing the following:

1. Counsel the doubtful.
2. Instruct the ignorant.
3. Admonish sinners.
4. Comfort the afflicted.
5. Forgive offenses.
6. Bear wrongs patiently.
7. Pray for the living and the dead.

The Lord directs us to keep an eye out for the poor and less fortunate and to reach out to them as a good neighbor, in the spirit of the Good Samaritan (cf. Lk 10:25–37, *CCC*, 2443–2449). St. Vincent de Paul encourages us, "Do the good you can do, and do it today." "Love for the poor is incompatible with immoderate love of riches or their selfish use" (*CCC*, 2445).

gently and kindly, although the Seventh Commandment does not prohibit their use for food and clothing. Medical experimentation on animals is legitimate if kept within reasonable limits and if it will save the lives or improve the health of human beings. Pope Francis says, "Our insistence that each human being is an image of God should not make us overlook the fact that each creature has its own purpose. None is superfluous. The entire material universe speaks of God's love, his boundless affection for us. Soil, water, mountains: everything is, as it were, a caress of God" (*Laudato Si'*, 84).

- *Peace among nations* is considered a universal duty. "All citizens and all governments are obliged to work for the avoidance of war" (*CCC*, 2308). The principles of a just war must always be observed when war is inevitable (cf. *CCC*, 2307–2317).

Catholic social teaching relates not only to the Seventh Commandment but also to the other nine commandments. It is a holistic vision by which the Church expresses her earnest concern for the dignity of the human person, the just production and exchange of goods, and right relations among nations. The Church has long been, and always will be, at the ready to help negotiate a peaceful resolution of conflicts between nations, especially for the sake of the poor and less fortunate.

228. What is required by the Eighth Commandment?

The Eighth Commandment instructs, "You shall not bear false witness against your neighbor" (Ex 20:16). Because telling the truth is vitally important in personal and societal relationships, misrepresenting the truth offends against God's plan for human happiness. It also offends against the Lord Jesus, who is "the way and the truth and the life" (Jn 14:6). Telling the truth is at the heart of human integrity. A follower of Jesus is called to be a person of integrity, to abide in him who is the Truth: "If we say, 'We have fellowship with him,' while we continue to walk in darkness, we lie and do not act in truth" (1 Jn 1:6, cf. *CCC*, 2470).

One who lies is said to be *duplicitous*, a word that means "divided." A liar is also a *hypocrite*, a word that comes from the Greek word for "actor," that is, one who takes the stage pretending to be another person (cf. *CCC*, 2468). Truth is a matter of justice, for we owe it to others to be truthful in our words and actions (cf. *CCC*, 2469). Telling the truth is important for our own happiness and well-being, for the one who tells a lie soon discovers that maintaining that lie is much like pushing around a snowball—it just gets bigger and bigger, and more difficult to manage. The great heroes of the Catholic faith who shed their blood for the sake of the Gospel are known as *martyrs*, a word that means "witnesses." A martyr is a witness to the Truth. We are called to imitate the martyrs in life and, if necessary, in death (*CCC*, 2471–2474).

229. What are the offenses against the Eighth Commandment?

The main offense against the Eighth Commandment is lying. A lie is a falsehood uttered intentionally to deceive, thereby leading another person into error. However, "no one is bound to reveal the truth to someone who does not have a right to know it" (*CCC*, 2489). Lying does great damage to the fabric of our society, for human relationships rely upon truthful words. Reparation for damage done is always required of one who lies (cf. *CCC*, 2482–2487). Lying takes several forms that become occasions of sin, including:

- *False witness and perjury*, which rank as the most serious violations of the Eighth Commandment, for they can contribute to a miscarriage of justice and an unjust judgment in a court of law. Perjury is especially serious because it involves breaking an oath, which also violates the Second Commandment (cf. *CCC*, 2152, 2476).

- *Disrespect for the reputation of others*, through rash judgment, detraction, or calumny. A judgment is rash when it is without sufficient foundation. Calumny is falsely attributing faults to another person. Detraction is disclosing truthfully the faults of others to those who have no business knowing about them (cf. *CCC*, 2477–2479).

- *Encouraging another person to commit a sin* through flattery, adulation, or encouragement (cf. *CCC*, 2480).

- *Boasting and bragging*. Using words maliciously to disparage another is also a sin (cf. *CCC*, 2481).

Even true words can cause harm, and one should always exercise great reserve in disclosing the private lives of others (cf. *CCC*, 2490–2491). Professional secrets are to be kept strictly except in cases when grave harm can be avoided only by breaking confidentiality.

Breaking the seal of Confession is the most serious of all sins against the Eighth Commandment, for the seal is absolutely inviolable and the keeping of the seal admits no exceptions. The strictest ecclesiastical penalties are levied against any priest who breaks the seal of the Sacrament of Penance and Reconciliation.

230. How do we keep the Eighth Commandment positively?

Practice of the virtue of truthfulness helps us to avoid sins against the Eighth Commandment. Scripture reminds us that:

> Whoever walks without blame, doing what is right, speaking truth from the heart; Who does not slander with his tongue, does no harm to a friend, never defames a neighbor; Who disdains the wicked, but honors those who fear the LORD. . . . Whoever acts like this shall never be shaken. (Ps 15:2–5)

> Therefore, putting away falsehood, speak the truth, each one to his neighbor, for we are members one of another. (Eph 4:25)

Truthfulness involves both honesty in revealing what should be known and discretion in not expressing what justice requires should not be revealed. Truthfulness is related to the virtue of justice by which we give others their just due—in this case, truth.

231. What is required by the Tenth Commandment?

The Tenth Commandment teaches, "You shall not covet your neighbor's house . . . or anything that belongs to your neighbor" (Ex 20:17). The Tenth Commandment demands integrity of one's heart, one's inner desires, for as the Lord teaches, "where your treasure is, there also will your heart be"

(Mt 6:21, cf. *CCC*, 2534). Greed, covetousness, and envy distract our hearts from seeking the Lord and storing up for ourselves treasures in heaven.

232. What are the offenses against the Tenth Commandment?

The Tenth Commandment forbids *greed*, which is the desire for earthly riches without limit. A greedy person does not know how or when to stop the accumulation of material goods and allows desire for riches to dominate his life. "He who loves money never has money enough" (*Roman Catechism*, cited in *CCC*, 2536).

Covetousness is a disordered desire for another person's goods and another offense against the Tenth Commandment. Striving to obtain what one's neighbor has is not a sin, provided it is accomplished using just means. Sadly, the desire for more and more can consume one's heart, even unto plotting to take what is not rightly one's own.

Envy is a sin so grave that it is numbered among the capital sins. The word *envy* comes from the Latin word *invidia*, which means "looking inappropriately at the affairs of another." Envy is the sin of allowing oneself to be dominated and saddened by the fantasy of owning something well beyond one's means. Envy can also be the sin of wishing that a wealthier neighbor will be stricken with a misfortune that would cause his wealth to fail (cf. *CCC*, 2538–2539). When envy leads to acquiring something through immoral means, it is stealing.

233. How do we keep the Tenth Commandment positively?

In the Lord alone do we find our true and lasting happiness. Striving for detachment from material riches is a time-tested way of following the path of holiness. Detachment does not mean living in the squalor of poverty, but it does mean embracing our call to be stewards of the blessings God has bestowed. We do this by:

- *thanking God every day for our blessings*, especially the blessings of family, friends, and faith.

- *being responsible in the use of our material blessings*, taking care of them, and not falling into the bad habits encouraged by a throwaway culture. Clean your closets regularly and give unused clothing and household items to a secondhand store that services the poor. Resist the temptation to upgrade your electronic devices too frequently, but rather be content with what you have.

- *sharing generously with others*, beginning with our own family, and extending out into our local area and beyond. Support financially and prayerfully those who go on mission trips, and consider going along to help if you can. Tithe 10 percent of your income in support of your parish, your (arch)diocese, and other worthwhile charities. The practice of tithing is a great way to learn detachment from material possessions, for when we tithe the first 10 percent, we find that we are always left with exactly what we need.

Make a return to the Lord with increase. When we stand before the judgment seat, the Lord will ask each of us, "What did you do with your life? What did you do with all the time I gave you? What did you do with all the material blessings that came to you through my providence? What did you do with all of the wonderful people I put in your life? What did you do with your life?" Please God that we will be able to answer honestly, "Lord, every day I thanked you for your great mercy and kindness. And every day I did my best to take care of what you gave me. I always tried to be generous in sharing with others the good things with which you blessed me. Lord, I entrust my soul to your mercy." If we can say that honestly, surely the Lord in his great mercy will say in return, "Well done, my good and faithful servant. . . . Come, share your master's joy" (Mt 25:21, cf. *CCC*, 2544–2550).

Summary and Reflection

Commandments Seven, Eight, and Ten have much to do with personal integrity. It is far too easy to steal, lie, and allow our desires for finer things to get the better of us. The Seventh Commandment—"You shall not steal"—requires us to respect the property of others. The Tenth Commandment—"You shall not covet your neighbor's goods"—is often paired with the Seventh Commandment. It requires that we refrain from desiring the material goods of others, which is the root of theft, robbery, and fraud. Integrity is also a central value taught by the Eighth Commandment—"You shall not bear false witness against your neighbor." This commandment supports our natural inclination to truthfulness; by nature, all humans are inclined to truth.

⬤ *Creation*

God creates you to be a person of integrity, and he gives you his Word and the sacraments to guide and strengthen you along the right path. What does integrity mean to you? Who among your circle of friends, acquaintances, and relatives do you regard as a person of great integrity, and why?

☉ *Fall*

Sin is a breakdown in integrity, a failure to be true to one's self and one's relationship with God. Our first parents were misled by a lie told by the great deceiver. How does the evil one continue to lie to us about what is in our best interest and how to find happiness?

✟ *Redemption*

Jesus gave up everything for our salvation. He who was rich became poor so that we might become wealthy (cf. 2 Cor 8:9). How is your relationship with Jesus and his Church a treasure worth far more than silver or gold? How do prayers of thanksgiving for the many blessings God has given you keep you from falling into the sins of envy, jealousy, and covetousness?

☯ *Restoration*

How is the rich legacy of Catholic social teaching and the call to practice the works of mercy a participation in the new creation?

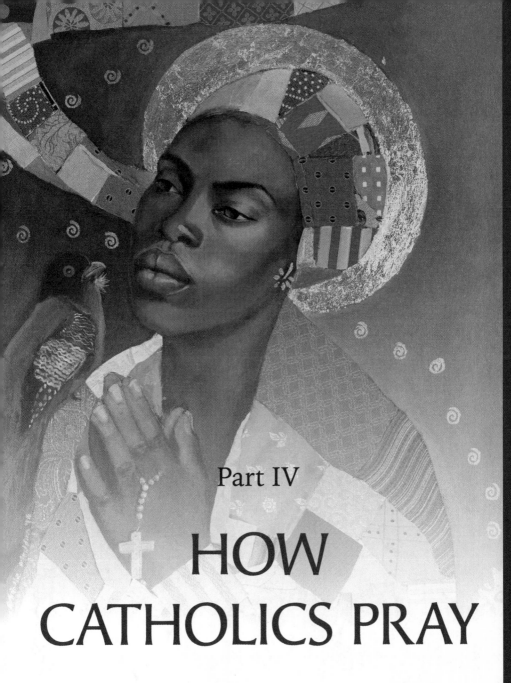

Part IV

HOW CATHOLICS PRAY

The Christian prays in every situation, in his walks for recreation, in his dealings with others, in silence, in reading, in all rational pursuits.

—St. Gregory of Nyssa

CHAPTER 21

Your Call to Holiness
(CCC, 2558–2649)

Every Christian is called to holiness. This means that *you* are called to holiness. Yes, you! And if that sounds beyond your reach, there is something else you should know: You are called to be a saint! There is no discernible difference between the word *holy* and the word *saint*. In Romance languages such as Spanish, Italian, and French, the two words are identical. To be holy means to be a saint. St. Paul begins his Letter to the Romans with the salutation, "to all the beloved of God in Rome, called to be holy" (Rom 1:7). To the Corinthians, St. Paul addresses his first letter "to the church of God that is in Corinth, to you who have been sanctified in Christ Jesus, called to be holy, with all those everywhere who call upon the name of our Lord Jesus Christ, their Lord and ours" (1 Cor 1:2).

St. Paul writes his letters not only to the first-century Christians of Rome, Corinth, and other places but to the whole Church of every age and every place. His words are meant for you. And you are called to be holy, you are called to be a saint!

The remaining chapters cover the concluding part of the *Catechism of the Catholic Church*, entitled "Christian Prayer." In these chapters we will discuss what it means to pray, how to be a person of prayer, and how prayer makes all the difference in the challenging life of a follower of Jesus. The focus of these chapters is not so much about what prayer is as about how to pray, and how to remain faithful in prayer. If you are new to the Church or recently getting back into the practice of the faith, you might find in these chapters some new ways of praying that help you stay on the path of life. Faithful prayer is essential to being holy, to being a saint.

234. What is a definition of prayer?

St. John Damascene defined prayer as "the raising of one's mind and heart to God or the requesting of good things from God" (cited in *CCC*, 2558). St. Thérèse of Lisieux, one of the most popular saints of the modern era who lived only to the age of twenty-four, left behind a rich treasury of wisdom about the path of holiness for which she was named a Doctor of the Church in 1997. About prayer, St. Thérèse wrote, "For me, prayer is a surge of the heart; it is a simple look turned toward heaven, it is a cry of recognition and of love, embracing both trial and joy" (*Manuscrits Auto-biographiques*, C 25r, cited in *CCC*, 2558).

The *Catechism* defines prayer in several ways. Whenever you raise your mind or heart to God, whenever your heart surges to God with expressions of joy or sorrow, you are praying in a manner pleasing to God. In fact, prayer is a gift, for God places in your heart the desire to pray (cf. *CCC*, 2559). Additionally:

- Prayer is Jesus meeting us at the well and asking us for a drink (cf. Jn 4:7).

- Prayer is the encounter of God's thirst with our own (cf. *CCC*, 2560).

- Prayer is a response to God's thirst for us and the means by which we partake of the living water that only he can give (cf. *CCC*, 2561).

- Prayer comes from the heart, the very center of our being, the place of encounter with God (cf. *CCC*, 2562–2563).

- Prayer is a relationship with God, an action of both God and the human person, an action that comes from both the Holy Spirit and ourselves (cf. *CCC*, 2564).

- Prayer is the habit of being in God's presence and in communion with him. This communion is always possible because in Baptism we have been united with Christ.

- Prayer is never private, though it is often personal. When we pray, we pray in communion with Christ and his Body, the Church (cf. *CCC*, 2565).

We learn many prayers as a child. The prayers you have been praying are dear to God, and you are blessed for having been taught your prayers and how to pray them. The simple prayers a person learned as a child are often the words that come to mind upon that person's deathbed. It is not unusual for someone with profound or terminal dementia to be able to make the Sign of the Cross and to pray along with the Lord's Prayer (Our Father) or the Hail Mary.

As we continue to grow through adulthood and deepen our faith, we want an even deeper connection with God through prayer. As St. John Vianney expressed: "The more we pray, the more we wish to pray. Like a fish which at first swims on the surface of the water, and afterwards plunges down, and is always going deeper; the soul plunges, dives, and loses itself in the sweetness of conversing with God."

235. Why is the Book of Psalms a source of prayer?

A psalm is a sacred poem or song used in worship. In fact, the word *psalm* comes from a Greek word that means "to pluck," as in the strings of a lyre. Each of the psalms was written to be sung, which made it easy for those who prayed the psalms to memorize them and pray them by heart. (Some people are not good at memorizing lines of text, but they can sing dozens of songs from memory.)

The Book of Psalms contains 150 chapters, each of which is a separate psalm. The psalms were the public and personal prayers of the Jewish people, and they were the prayers of Jesus, Mary, and Joseph. The psalms were the prayers known by the Apostles and other Jewish disciples of Jesus and quickly became the prayers of the nascent Church after our Lord's Ascension into heaven. To this day, the psalms are a cherished part of the worship of the Church. They speak of the many emotions and feelings we bring to prayer.

There are many different kinds of psalms with several different themes. There are psalms that ring out joyful praise of God for the many blessings we have received, such as Psalms 4, 66, and 97. There are psalms that lament utter disappointment at the circumstances of our lives, such as Psalms 6, 22, and 44. There are psalms of sorrow for sins, such as Psalm 79 and Psalm 51, also known as the Miserere, the Latin word that begins the psalm: "Have mercy on me, God, in accord with your merciful love; in your abundant compassion blot out my transgressions. Thoroughly wash away my guilt; and from my sin . . . cleanse me" (vv. 3–4). There are psalms that beseech the Lord for his help, such as Psalms 16, 86, and 130. Psalm 130 is known as the De Profundis, from its haunting opening words, "Out of the depths I call to you, LORD; LORD, hear my cry! May your ears be attentive to my cry for mercy" (vv. 1–2).

Perhaps the most familiar psalm is Psalm 23, a beautiful hymn praising God for taking care of us, protecting us, feeding us, and leading us to heaven, just as a good shepherd never stops caring in a particular way for each sheep of the flock (cf. CCC, 2585–2589).

236. How do the psalms connect with the life of Christ?

The psalms are cherished prayers of the Church because in addition to being beautiful and inspiring of their own accord, each of the 150 psalms has a specific connection to Jesus, who fulfills their meaning through his Life, Death, and Resurrection. For example:

- Psalm 16 is recited by Sts. Peter and Paul about the Death and Resurrection of Jesus (cf. Acts 2:25–32, 13:35).

- Psalm 23 was referenced by our Lord when he said, "I am the Good Shepherd" (Jn 10:11).

- Psalm 110 is the most quoted psalm in the New Testament, whose meaning is fulfilled in the perfect sacrifice on Calvary in which Jesus is both victim and priest, a victim without spot or blemish (1 Pt 1:19) and a priest according to the order of Melchizedek (v. 4, cf. Heb 7:17).

One-Hour ACTS

Traditional forms of prayer are sometimes summarized by the acronym ACTS, which stands for **A**doration (cf. *CCC*, 2626–2628, 2639), **C**ontrition (sorrow for sins, cf. *CCC*, 2613), **T**hanksgiving (cf. *CCC*, 2637–2638), and **S**upplication (a humble request, cf. *CCC*, 2634–2636). You can practice all forms of prayer in a one-hour exercise. If possible, do this exercise before the Blessed Sacrament. If not, have a crucifix visible. Follow these steps:

First Five Minutes

Find a suitable place and time to pray. Settle into prayer by offering some of the prayers that you can say by heart, perhaps those you learned as a child. Find peace knowing that you are in the presence of the Lord. "Be still, and know that I am God" (Ps 46:11).

Next Ten Minutes

Pray prayers of adoration and praise. Read Psalm 66 slowly, considering carefully all of the ways in which God is praised in that psalm. Read it again slowly, adding to it your own expressions of awe and wonder of God's love for you and your family. If you are in the presence of the Blessed Sacrament, be sure to speak to the Lord, being mindful that he is substantially in your midst. Reserve the last five minutes of this period for quiet prayer, gazing upon the tabernacle, monstrance, or crucifix.

Next Fifteen Minutes

Pray prayers of contrition. You are in the presence of the Lord, yet you know that you are a poor sinner in need of his great mercy. Slowly read Psalm 51, the psalm composed by King David when he recognized his great sin against the Lord. Read it again slowly, pausing when you remember particular sins for which you are sorry. Perhaps these are sins from your past that still weigh heavily upon your heart. Perhaps these are sins that you will be bringing to your next experience of the Sacrament of Penance and Reconciliation. After every sin that you recall, say the ancient prayer "Kyrie eleison" (Lord have mercy"). Reserve the final five minutes of this segment for quiet prayer, gazing upon the tabernacle, monstrance, or crucifix, expressing gratitude for the Lord's tender mercies and asking him to keep you away from anything that might lead you back into sin. Express your resolution to receive the Sacrament of Penance regularly.

Next Fifteen Minutes

Pray prayers of thanksgiving. "Merciful and gracious is the LORD, slow to anger, abounding in mercy" (Ps 103:8). You have so much for which to give thanks to God. Read Psalm 103 slowly. When a phrase in that psalm reminds you of a blessing you have received from God, say quietly, "Thank you, dear Lord." Remember the ways in which God has blessed you, giving you the gift of life, giving you talents and abilities, blessing you with your family, bringing friends into your life, answering your prayers in times of need. Be specific in identifying the blessings God has bestowed upon you, and with each one say quietly, "Thank you, dear Lord." Reserve the final five minutes of the segment for quiet prayer, gazing upon the tabernacle, monstrance, or crucifix, thanking God especially for the gift of faith and the ability to experience his real and substantial presence in the Holy Eucharist, the gift worth far more than silver or gold.

Next Ten Minutes

Pray prayers of supplication, asking the Lord to take care of the needs of others. Pray Psalm 16 slowly. Think about the world in which we live, and offer prayers for the poor and less fortunate. Call to mind the needs of our Church locally and universally. Be mindful of friends, family, and neighbors who are struggling. Consider those who are trying to find their way to God, those who are discerning the best way to serve the Lord, and those who have fallen away from the faith. After each intention say, "Lord, hear our prayer," for you are praying with the Church. Reserve the final five minutes of the segment for quiet prayer, gazing upon the tabernacle, monstrance, or crucifix. Remember one person for whom you prayed, and if possible, send a short note telling that person when you prayed for him or her and where you offered that prayer.

Final Five Minutes

Thank the Lord for this opportunity for prayer. Ask the Lord to keep you close to him. Pray once again those prayers that have been dear to you from your childhood, making them the bookends of your prayer time and the foundation upon which you build an ever stronger relationship with the Lord, day by day. Go in peace, renewed in mind, heart, and soul by the opportunity you had to draw near in prayer to the Lord of Lords and the King of Kings!

If you wish, dedicate a corner of a quiet room for prayer so that you can pray exercises like this often. Decorate the walls with holy images, and arrange the space so the whole family may gather there together in prayer (cf. *CCC*, 2691). You may ask your parish priest or deacon to bless your prayer corner when he comes to bless your home.

237. How can we pray with the Book of Psalms?

From his childhood, our Lord himself committed to memory the Book of Psalms, the prayer book of the People of God. Jesus prayed the psalms by heart throughout his life, especially at the most significant moments. From the Cross Jesus prayed Psalm 22, which begins with the words, "My God, my God, why have you abandoned me?" (Ps 22:2; Mt 27:46; Mk 15:34). We hear a reading from the Book of Psalms after the first reading at every Mass. These psalm responses become familiar to us, and we can likewise commit them to memory and make them a mantra for our own prayer.

238. How does Jesus teach us to pray?

Jesus teaches his disciples a prayer that you probably know by heart, the Our Father, sometimes called the Lord's Prayer. A meditation using the Our Father is found in Chapter 23. Jesus also teaches lessons about how and when to pray with several examples recorded in the Gospels.

For example, Jesus goes up to the Temple in Jerusalem for the major feasts of Judaism, praying the psalms and being present with his people at the place of sacrifice. Jesus frequently finds time to pray in solitude, sometimes going out into the desert or climbing atop a high place (cf. Mk 1:35, 6:46). These examples teach us to discipline ourselves to find a suitable place to pray—a place of quiet, a place that is holy—and to set aside time for prayer when we are alert and able to engage in prayer without the inclination to fall asleep (cf. *CCC*, 2601).

Jesus teaches us to persevere and to ask boldly in our prayer, trusting that God always hears us (cf. *CCC*, 2609–2610). Discipline and fidelity in prayer forms us to accept God's will with a childlike spirit, just as a child learns that parents do not always give them everything they want, but what they need and what is in their best interest (cf. *CCC*, 2611, 2614).

Prayer was part of the Last Supper, when Jesus prayerfully entered into the new and perfect sacrifice of his Body and Blood upon Calvary, re-presented in an unbloody manner in the Holy Eucharist (cf. *CCC*, 2599). In spite of the terrible suffering that he was about to endure, Jesus thought not of himself but of others; he thought of you and me as he offered the perfect sacrifice for the forgiveness of our sins (cf. *CCC*, 2605–2606). At the Last Supper he fully exercised his priestly mediation for us poor sinners.

Jesus teaches us that our prayer is not about self-help or inwardly focused meditation. Prayer is about going to the Cross with Jesus, opening ourselves up to God and bringing before him the needs of others, the needs of the world, the needs of the Church. In this context do we dare to ask for our own needs—the need for our daily bread, for forgiveness, for guidance through the thicket of temptations, and for deliverance from evil. We will speak of these petitions in Chapter 23.

Summary and Reflection

Because we were created by God and for God, only in him will we ever be completely satisfied. Having union with God is the state of being sanctified or made holy. Related to our desire for lasting holiness is our call to be a saint. Only by God's grace can we reach this perfection. Along the way we keep our intimate connection with God through prayer. We pray in many forms, including prayers of praise and thanksgiving. We pray as Jesus taught us to pray. Through prayer we witness our growth in holiness.

⬤ Creation

God has a special plan for your life. God is calling you to be a saint! Maybe not the kind of saint whose face is depicted on a stained-glass window, but a saint nonetheless. What does this mean to you? How do you feel about this? What is keeping you from being holy, being a saint?

◐ Fall

Read Psalm 130, which begins, "Out of the depths I call to you, LORD. . . ." This is the psalm of a person in the depths of sin, crying out for God's mercy. Sin gets in the way of our relationship with the Lord. In his goodness, God desires from us a contrite heart and is quick to forgive. How do you feel about approaching the Sacrament of Penance and Reconciliation? If you are nervous or apprehensive, how can you keep those feelings from getting in the way of making a good Confession and receiving the forgiveness and grace that come through the Sacrament of Penance?

✝ *Redemption*

Pray for at least thirty minutes following the method of the ACTS prayer exercise on page 333. Which part of the prayer was easiest for you to pray? Which part was most difficult?

☯ *Restoration*

"I Thirst" is the phrase that the Missionaries of Charity see every time they pray in their chapels. *Tengo Sed* means "I Thirst" in Spanish (see page 333). The Lord thirsts for you to be holy. As you gaze upon the crucifix in church, for what virtue or spiritual gift do you pray?

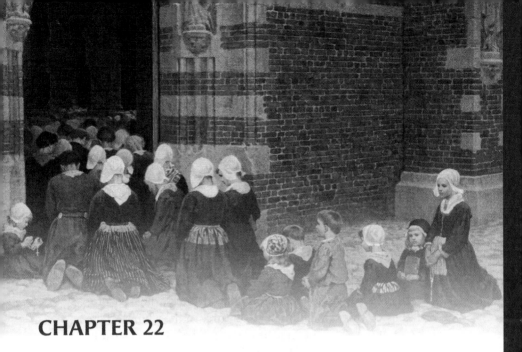

CHAPTER 22

Praying with the Communion of Saints

(CCC, 2650–2778)

Pope Francis said, "When we pray, we never do so alone: even if we do not think about it, we are immersed in a majestic river of invocations that precedes us and proceeds after us." The Catholic teaching on the Communion of Saints echoes the pope's comments that the Church is a community of faith united by the Holy Spirit. By the power of the Spirit, the Risen Lord, the source of all holiness, binds us into a communion of faithful.

All members of the Church—those alive today and those who have died—make up one big family united in the Spirit of Christ Jesus. Family members depend on one another. Such is the case of God's family bound together in love. Family members must communicate to grow and thrive. In God's family, prayer is the supreme way to keep alive a relationship with all the members of the Church:

- the pilgrim Church (those living on earth today, also known as the Church militant)

- the Church suffering (those undergoing purification in Purgatory)

- the Church triumphant (the blessed in heaven)

Pope Francis also said:

> Prayer is always born again: each time we join our hands and open our hearts to God, we find ourselves in the company of anonymous saints and recognized saints who pray with us and who intercede for us as older brothers and sisters who have preceded us on this same human adventure. In the Church there is no grief that is borne in solitude, there are no tears shed in oblivion, because everyone breathes and participates in one common grace. It is no coincidence that in the ancient church people were buried in gardens surrounding a sacred building, as if to say that, in some way, the multitude who preceded us participate in every Eucharist. Our parents and grandparents are there, our godfathers and godmothers are there, our catechists and other teachers are there. . . . That faith that was passed on, transmitted, that we received. Along with faith, the way of praying and prayer were also transmitted. . . . Saints are still here, not far away from us; and their representations in churches evoke that "cloud of witnesses" that always surrounds us (cf. Heb 12:51).[1]

Prayer is personal, to be sure. But prayer is never private. Even when praying in the silence of our hearts, we never pray alone.

239. Why do Catholics make the Sign of the Cross at the beginning and end of their prayer?

At the beginning and end of our prayers we make the Sign of the Cross, thereby offering them in the name of the Father, and of the Son, and of the Holy Spirit. This act of piety is more than a formality; it is a reminder of our Baptism, through which we have been incorporated into the Church, the Body of Christ, and drawn into the life of the Holy Trinity (cf. *CCC*,

1267). Through Baptism we receive an indelible spiritual mark, a character imprinted upon our souls that consecrates us for worship of God the Father, God the Son, and God the Holy Spirit (cf. *CCC*, 1272–1273).

240. How do we pray to each of the Divine Persons of the Holy Trinity?

Just as we are not alone when engaged in conversation with a dear friend on the phone, we are not alone when we offer our prayer in the name of the Father, and of the Son, and of the Holy Spirit:

- *We pray to God the Father through the Son, as the Holy Spirit teaches us to pray.* Our prayer "has access to the Father only if we pray 'in the name' of Jesus. The sacred humanity of Jesus is therefore the way by which the Holy Spirit teaches us to pray to God our Father" (*CCC*, 2664).

- *We pray to God the Son even just by invoking the holy name of Jesus.* Jesus is "the name that is above every name" (Phil 2:9), the only name "that contains the presence it signifies" (*CCC*, 2666). We can certainly use more words in our prayers to Jesus than his divine name, but what consolation we have and what solace it brings to know that through the twists and turns of life, Jesus is but a single word away. The very name of Jesus is itself a prayer, perhaps the simplest of all prayers, but one that has the power to chase away temptations and to restore our focus on the Way of Life (cf. *CCC*, 2666–2669).

- *We pray to God the Holy Spirit, often using the familiar "Come, Holy Spirit" invocation.* In times of doubt or frustration, and in times when we are searching for guidance or patience, we can do no better than to pray to the Holy Spirit, the one who teaches us and guides us in our prayer. In fact, we should always pray to the Holy Spirit when starting or completing an important endeavor.

241. Who are the saints who join us in prayer and pray for us?

Some saints have been canonized by the Church. *Canon* in Latin can mean "list," so the canonized saints are those who have been recognized and listed publicly by the Church as having lived lives of heroic virtue and holiness, and whose lives are reliable guides to follow (cf. *CCC*, 828). Not all the saints in heaven are canonized, for the virtue and fidelity of some are known to God alone.

Many consider some of their deceased relatives and friends to be saints for having lived lives of remarkable faith, hope, and charity. Pope Francis reminds us, "there are saints, everyday saints, hidden saints, or as I like to say, the 'saints next door,' those who share their lives with us, who work with us and live a life of holiness." While our deceased relatives might well be in heaven, the Church permits public veneration or honor of only those saints whose names have been added to the list, a process known as *canonization*.

In addition to being great models for us to follow, the saints are powerful intercessors. Just as we would not hesitate to ask a "saint next door" to pray for us or for a loved one in need, nor should we hesitate to ask a saint in heaven to do the same. "We can and should ask them to intercede for us and for the whole world" (*CCC*, 2683). We are never alone with the saints praying with us and for us.

242. What is the Blessed Virgin Mary's role in our prayer?

Of the great cloud of witnesses in heaven, we have no more powerful or loving saint praying with and for us than the Blessed Virgin Mary. She is our mother, according to the order of grace (cf. *CCC*, 501). From the Cross, Jesus looked upon his mother and his beloved disciple, St. John: "When Jesus saw his mother and the disciple there whom he loved, he said to his mother, 'Woman, behold, your son.' Then he said to the disciple, 'Behold, your mother.' And from that hour the disciple took her into his home" (Jn 19:26–27).

"Like the beloved disciple we welcome Jesus' mother into our homes, for she has become the mother of all the living. We can pray with and to her. The prayer of the Church is sustained by the prayer of Mary and united with it in hope" (*CCC*, 2679). We never pray alone, especially because of the maternal care of the Blessed Mother for her spiritual daughters and sons.

243. What is the meaning of the Hail Mary prayer?

The Hail Mary (*Ave Maria*) is a prayer whose words echo verses from Sacred Scripture and give voice to those who strive to live holy lives and eventually be numbered among the saints in heaven. Each part of the prayer has special meaning worthy of reflection.

- *Hail* is the greeting of the archangel Gabriel (cf. Lk 1:48). *Hail* can also mean "rejoice." When we honor Mary with the salutation "Hail," we imitate God, who first honored her by choosing the ever-humble Mary to be the mother of his Son.

- *Full of grace, the Lord is with thee* are also words first spoken to Mary by the archangel Gabriel (Lk 1:28, 30). Mary is "full of grace" precisely because the Lord has looked upon her lowliness and chosen her to be the dwelling place of the glory of the Lord, the new ark of the covenant. "Full of grace" is the translation of the Greek word *kecharitomene*, a word found nowhere else in the Bible or in Greek literature. It is a unique word for a unique Lady, pointing to the singular grace bestowed upon Mary in being conceived without sin, the Immaculate Conception (cf. *CCC*, 491).

- *Blessed art thou among women, and blessed is the fruit of thy womb, Jesus* is a phrase spoken by Elizabeth, the mother of St. John the Baptist and a kinswoman of the Blessed Virgin Mary (cf. Lk 1:42). We are told that Elizabeth was "filled with the Holy Spirit" when she uttered this greeting. Mary, ever virgin, is made fruitful through the power of the Holy Spirit. Mary is blessed because she believed, and she is fruitful beyond measure as the mother of all who believe in Jesus (cf. *CCC*, 2676).

Prayer Time with Our Lady

The Blessed Mother is your mother according to the order of grace, and she is your friend. For this prayer time, you might need the help of a Catholic partner if you are not familiar with the Holy Rosary and other prayers to Our Lady. Find a suitable place to pray. The place should be calm and peaceful. Hopefully your parish church has a place for quiet prayer, ideally in the presence of the Blessed Sacrament and before an image of the Blessed Mother. There is a long and steady tradition of using an image (icon) of the Blessed Mother as a help to prayer. Follow each of the steps below. The time durations are only recommendations. You may pray longer (especially) or shorter (possibly) for each of the segments.

First Five Minutes

Settle into the quiet, putting aside distractions from a busy day and a noisy world. Enter into your time of prayer with gratitude to God for calling you near. Offer a prayer to the Holy Spirit, asking for inspiration and direction: *Come, Holy Spirit, open my mind and my heart to the power of the Word.*

Next Ten Minutes

Read slowly the account of the Annunciation (cf. Lk 1:26–38). Pause and gaze upon the image of Our Lady. Read the account of the Annunciation again, slowly and prayerfully. Take note of any word or phrase that strikes you in a particular way. Repeat that word or phrase several times until you have memorized it and taken it to heart. (Note that this form of prayer is known as *lectio divina*, referenced in *CCC*, 2708).

Next Ten Minutes

Offer prayer to the Lord from your heart, as you are inspired to do so by the Holy Spirit, the same Holy Spirit who came upon the Blessed Mother and filled her with the only begotten Son of God. Allow the Holy Spirit to guide your words and to teach you to pray. Continue to gaze upon the image of the loving, tender Blessed Mother.

Next Ten Minutes

Rest in the presence of the Lord. Experience the peace that comes from being with the Lord in prayer. Just as you can enjoy being in the presence of a good friend without necessarily being chatty, so you can enjoy the presence of the Lord without saying a single word. Allow the Lord to lead you along this step.

Remaining Time You Have Set Aside for Prayer

Offer thanksgiving to God for the great gift of his presence in your life and for giving you the gift of himself through the Blessed Mother. Alone or with a friend, pray the Holy Rosary, meditating upon the joyful mysteries using these directions:

- Make the Sign of the Cross.

- Pray the Apostles' Creed.

- Pray an Our Father.

- Pray three Hail Marys, asking for an increase in the gifts of faith, hope, and love.

- Pray the Glory Be.

- Meditate for a moment on the first joyful mystery: The Annunciation.

- Pray an Our Father, ten Hail Marys, a Glory Be, and the Fatima Prayer.

- Meditate for a moment on the second joyful mystery: The Visitation.

- Pray an Our Father, ten Hail Marys, a Glory Be, and the Fatima Prayer.

- Meditate for a moment on the third joyful mystery: The Nativity of Our Lord.

- Pray an Our Father, ten Hail Marys, a Glory Be, and the Fatima Prayer.

- Meditate for a moment on the fourth joyful mystery: The Presentation in the Temple.

- Pray an Our Father, ten Hail Marys, a Glory Be, and the Fatima Prayer.

- Meditate for a moment on the fifth joyful mystery: The Finding in the Temple.

- Pray an Our Father, ten Hail Marys, a Glory Be, and the Fatima Prayer.

- Conclude with the Hail, Holy Queen.

- Make the Sign of the Cross.

If this is your first time with the Holy Rosary, don't worry about saying all the prayers correctly and in the right order. Hopefully your partner will do the "driving," and you can simply ride along, enjoying in every Hail Mary the recitation of the words of the archangel, the words of Elizabeth, and the words of countless souls who have turned to the Blessed Mother as a friend along the way. As you pray these familiar prayers, ask the Lord for whatever help you need to say with Mary, "May it be done to me according to your word" (Lk 1:38).

- *Holy Mary, Mother of God* begins the final sentence of the prayer. While the title "Mother of God" is not found directly in Scripture, neither does it contradict Scripture. Elizabeth asks, "And how does this happen to me, that the mother of my Lord should come to me?" (Lk 1:43). "Lord" becomes the title used by the earliest Christians to express their deep faith in the divinity of Jesus (cf. *CCC*, 446–451). In Elizabeth's choice of words, we can see the inspiration of the Holy Spirit with which she was filled, a proclamation of the biblical truth that Mary is indeed the Mother of God, according to his human nature (cf. *CCC*, 495, 2667).

- *Pray for us sinners, now and at the hour of our death* is an acknowledgment of both our own sinfulness and our trust in the Divine Mercy, who is our Lord and Savior, Jesus Christ.

In the Hail Mary we ask for the powerful intercession of the Blessed Virgin Mary, who presents to the world through her Son the superabundant mercy of God. Mary is our mother, a task entrusted to her at the hour of the death of her Son, Jesus (cf. Jn 19:26–27). We entrust the fate of our souls to Mary's maternal care. Jesus, the Lord of Mercy, entered our world through her, and we pray that she will lead us into the world of her Son through her maternal love, her example of faith, and her hope-filled prayers for our happiness in this world and the next (cf. *CCC*, 2677). Amen!

Summary and Reflection

Once we get to heaven, we will be amazed at how much others have done for us through their prayers, love, and good works. The Catholic doctrine of the Communion of Saints stresses that we are all members of God's family. Together with Jesus, we are never alone. This is the essence of the message from Pope Francis at the beginning of this chapter. Through the Letter to the Hebrews we are urged to persevere in prayer and in Christian living, mindful that we never follow Jesus alone: "Therefore, since we are surrounded by so great a cloud of witnesses, let us rid ourselves of every burden and sin that clings to us and persevere in running the race that lies before us while keeping our eyes fixed on Jesus, the leader and perfecter of faith" (Heb 12:1–2). The phrase "great cloud of witnesses" refers to the saints in heaven.

⬤ Creation

God created you to be a saint, perhaps a kind of "saint next door" described by Pope Francis. God gives you the Blessed Virgin Mary and a "great cloud of witnesses" to pray with you and for you. How do you find that to be a source of encouragement to persevere in the discipline of prayer?

☾ *Fall*

The Blessed Mother prays for every poor sinner, now and at the hour of death. The Blessed Mother prays always that we will be faithful disciples of her Son, our Lord Jesus Christ. Why does the tradition of the Church bestow upon the Blessed Mother the title "Refuge of Sinners," and what does this title mean to you?

✝ *Redemption*

Pray the joyful mysteries of the Holy Rosary as found on page 109. How does praying the joyful mysteries help you to enter more fully into the mystery of Mary's yes to God's will? How does praying the Holy Rosary help you to stay closer to Jesus?

� *Restoration*

We invoke the Holy Trinity with the Sign of the Cross at the beginning and end of our prayers. How is the Holy Spirit a help to you as you enter into prayer? As the Holy Spirit was part of the creation of heaven and earth, how is the Holy Spirit a key part of the new creation taking place within you?

CHAPTER 23

Encouragement to Pray

(CCC, 2697–2758)

We know that we should pray every day. St. Paul encourages us to "pray without ceasing" (1 Thes 5:17). One's entire life should be a prayer, dedicated and consecrated to doing the will of the Lord. Yet the saints remind us that if we desire to pray *always*, we have to pray *sometimes*! The discipline of regular, faithful prayer is the hallmark of a saint and those who desire to be saints (cf. *CCC*, 2697).

Here are words of encouragement from a few saints in heaven:

St. Augustine

"Pray always, and do not lose heart."

St. Teresa of Avila

"Prayer is being on terms of friendship with God, frequently conversing in secret with him who, we know, loves us."

St. Teresa Benedicta of the Cross

"Let go of your plans. The first hour of your morning belongs to God."

St. Pio of Pietrelcina

"Pray, hope, and don't worry."

St. Josemaría Escrivá

"Turn your eyes to the Passion of Jesus Christ, our Redeemer. Be convinced that he is asking each one of us, as he asked those three intimate Apostles of his in the Garden of Olives, to 'watch and pray.'"

St. Teresa of Kolkata

"Love to pray. Prayer enlarges the heart until it is capable of containing God's gift of himself."

Bl. Carlo Acutis

"To always be close to Jesus, that's my life plan."

May being close to Jesus always be your life plan. Faithfulness to prayer, the wisdom of the Sacred Scripture, and the sacramental life of the Church will bring to completion the great desire for holiness that God has placed within you (cf. Phil 1:6).

244. What are some different ways to pray?

Every person is led by the Lord in prayer, and each responds in a unique, personal way. There are three major expressions of prayer in the tradition of the Church: vocal prayer, meditation, and contemplation. Each one involves composure of heart, and each one can have a place in your rhythm of prayer (cf. *CCC*, 2699).

245. What is vocal prayer?

Vocal prayer is the most frequent practice of prayer for many people. As the term implies, vocal prayer gives expression to our prayer in the words that we direct to God, whether spoken aloud or expressed only in our minds. Jesus prayed the psalms and taught us to pray using the specific words known as the Lord's Prayer (cf. *CCC*, 2701). Jesus even prayed in ways that are repetitive, for example Psalm 136, in which the phrase "for his mercy endures forever" is repeated twenty-six times in as many verses.

Vocal prayer is essential and is pleasing to God. Vocal prayer allows groups to pray and worship together. Vocal prayer gives honor and glory to God when it "rises from the depths of the soul" (*CCC*, 2703), whether the prayer be memorized or spontaneous, formal or informal.

Yet the mere repetition of words is insufficient to establish a relationship with anyone, let alone our God: "Whether or not our prayer is heard depends not on the number of words, but on the fervor of our souls" (St. John Chrysostom, cited in *CCC*, 2700).

246. What is meditation?

Meditation is another expression of prayer. Meditation is a venerable practice in the Christian life with roots deep within the Old Testament: "This book of the law shall not depart out of your mouth; you shall meditate on it day and night, so that you may be careful to act in accordance with all that is written in it" (Jos 1:8 NRSV).

Meditation is sometimes called *mental prayer*, for meditation engages one's mind to seek the meaning of the Christian experience. "Meditation is above all a quest. The mind seeks to understand the why and how of the Christian life, in order to adhere and respond to what the Lord is asking" (*CCC*, 2705). *Lectio divina* (divine reading) is the way to meditate on Scripture, as we meditated on the Annunciation in Chapter 22. Indeed, the Holy Rosary is principally a way of meditating upon the mysteries of our Lord's Life, Death, and Resurrection (cf. *CCC*, 2708).

We must distinguish between the beautiful practice of meditation that has been practiced by the saints down through the ages and other forms of meditation that characterize religious traditions far removed from Christianity. One should never dabble in transcendental meditation, yoga, centering prayer, or any other so-called New Age practice with deep roots in Buddhism, Hinduism, and other religions and philosophies. These forms of meditation are the polar opposite of the venerable tradition of Christian meditation and are very dangerous waters in which to swim.

Whereas Christian meditation mobilizes our mental faculties so as "to deepen our convictions of faith, prompt the conversion of our heart, and strengthen our will to follow Christ" (*CCC*, 2708), Buddhist meditation encourages the emptying of one's mind. When one attempts to empty one's mind, the door is wide open to those "evil spirits who prowl about the world seeking the ruin of souls" (Prayer to St. Michael the Archangel). We are not to empty our minds, but rather fill them with the things that are good, noble, holy, and true (cf. Phil 4:8). There is no better way to do this than to meditate upon the life of Christ.

247. What is contemplation?

It might be difficult to imagine prayer without words, yet the third expression of prayer is just that. *Contemplation* or "contemplative prayer" is described by St. Teresa of Avila as "nothing else than a close sharing between friends; it means taking time frequently to be alone with him who we know loves us" (cited in *CCC*, 2709). Just as enjoying time with a good friend often means not having to do or say anything, and not experiencing any awkward silence, so is contemplative prayer. The anxious feeling of wondering what to say during an uncomfortable pause in a conversation is perfectly natural in many social situations, but not when you are with a good friend. In fact, the silence can be golden. Such is spending time with the Lord in contemplative prayer.

Contemplative prayer is a grace, a gift from God, meant to be enjoyed and accepted in humility (cf. *CCC*, 2713). Like a true friendship, contemplative prayer cannot be forced. "Contemplation is a gaze of faith, fixed on Jesus" (*CCC*, 2713). Nor is contemplation just for those who might be called "experts" in prayer, those who live in cloistered monasteries. Rather, contemplative prayer is about:

- attentiveness to God's Word, and responding to it with the yes of Jesus and the "Let it be" of the Blessed Virgin (cf. *CCC*, 2716)

- silence, allowing the Lord to speak to you in the depth of your heart (cf. *CCC*, 2717)

- union with the prayer of Jesus, being drawn into a deeper and fuller participation in the mystery of the Holy Eucharist so as to better manifest that mystery in your daily living (cf. *CCC*, 2718)

- friendship with Jesus, not keeping your distance but being close to him and even being willing to endure difficulties in prayer, such as those endured by Jesus in the Garden of Gethsemane

In the nineteenth century, in the small, backwater, French village of Ars served a holy priest who is now called St. John Vianney. St. John Vianney noticed that a man from the village would come to the church every day to spend time before the Blessed Sacrament. The man carried no prayerbook, for he was illiterate, yet he remained still and calm for his hour of prayer. The man always had a smile on his face when he was in the church. One day, St. John Vianney asked the man, "What do you do when you look at the tabernacle every day?" The man replied, "I look at him and he looks at me" (*CCC*, 2715).

Contemplation is the fruit of perseverance in prayer, preferring nothing than to be with Jesus when he invites you to abide with him, to stay with him, to rest in him, and to watch one hour with him (cf. *CCC*, 2719).

248. What are difficulties to be expected in prayer?

A life of prayer is a battle. Sometimes the battle is from within, much like the battle to persevere in a program of physical wellness. The battle is also waged from outside, as the evil one will always do his best to impede our progress along the path of life. Awareness of potential difficulties and challenges is necessary to form the discipline that leads to perseverance in prayer (cf. *CCC*, 2725). Unrealistic expectations can be the undoing of any relationship, including one's relationship with the Lord in prayer.

For example, it is unrealistic to expect instant results; prayer requires patience and dedication. The farmer who plants does not expect to harvest the next day. Prayer takes time. It is also unrealistic to anticipate that every time of prayer will bring feelings of elation. Relationships are not grounded in pleasant feelings but in the decision to love. God has already

Prayer in the Presence of the Blessed Sacrament

The moment of the elevation of the sacred host during the Eucharistic Prayer is a moment so filled with awe and wonder that many wish it would last longer than it does. If it did, surely the poor priest's arms would grow weary! Upon receiving Holy Communion one is touched by heaven, receiving in our person the very Body and Blood, Soul and Divinity of the Lord, the Bread of Angels and the Medicine of Immortality. Yet that experience likewise is brief, followed by only a few minutes of prayers of gratitude. Fortunately, when the Blessed Sacrament is exposed, our Holy Communion with the Lord is extended not through the sense of taste but through the sense of sight, as we gaze upon the beauty of the Lord (cf. Ps 27:4).

After Holy Communion the priest reserves the unconsumed consecrated hosts in the tabernacle. A red sanctuary lamp indicates that the tabernacle contains sacred elements and that Jesus is present. At certain times the consecrated host is removed from the tabernacle and exposed in a *monstrance*. The word *monstrance* comes from a Latin verb that means "to show or to uncover." The Blessed Sacrament is shown or uncovered when it is exposed to make possible the extension of that moment of awe and wonder before the Lord.

When we are dismissed from Holy Mass, we are challenged to live out our faith with great conviction. Having encountered the Lord in the Holy Eucharist, we must strive to become what we have celebrated, making the Lord's living presence known to others through our corporal and spiritual works of mercy. We need to be reminded frequently of our call to be in solidarity with the materially and spiritually poor. Prayer before the exposed Blessed Sacrament is a contemplative extension of the Holy Mass, a spiritual communion that strengthens us for the task of putting our faith into action.

Many Catholics speak of their closeness to Jesus when they pray before the exposed Blessed Sacrament. Many parishes designate certain times when the Blessed Sacrament will be exposed for the adoration of the faithful. This practice can take place throughout various intervals of time, such as a holy hour of prayer, nocturnal adoration from dusk to dawn, and the devotion of forty hours. Some parishes practice perpetual adoration, in which the Blessed Sacrament is exposed for adoration twenty-four hours a day, seven days a week. The Blessed Sacrament is never to be exposed without at least one person present, requiring a parish with perpetual adoration to enlist hundreds of parishioners in this ministry, each committing to at least one hour per week in adoration. Many parishioners who make a commitment to rise in the wee hours to adore the Lord consider that time to be their favorite hour of the week.

Please take time to become familiar with this devotion, and build into your schedule regular opportunities to pray before the exposed Blessed Sacrament however that is possible in your parish or your local area. Just as one cannot step out into the sun without being affected by its rays, nor can one be in the presence of the Son of God without experiencing his transforming power.

chosen to love you. God has planted in your heart the desire to love him in return. You must choose to pray every single day.

On your end, don't expect that your schedule will miraculously open to allow you a convenient time to pray. Life doesn't work that way! Perseverance in prayer comes from the discipline to put first things first in one's life. God must always come first. Your time for prayer must always be the first thing placed in your daily schedule (cf. *CCC*, 2726–2728).

249. What should I do when I get distracted in prayer?

Distractions are to be expected in prayer. Whether the distraction is an unexpected noise or a wandering mind, the holy name of Jesus is the remedy. Simply say the name "Jesus" quietly, and he will bring you back. A wandering mind can reveal that to which we are attached, be it a worry about a problem at work or something more mundane such as trying to remember what you need at the grocery store. These are not bad things to think about, but they pale in comparison to the opportunity to be attentive and alert before the Lord in prayer. Humbly and resolutely, we choose again to open our hearts to the Lord in prayer, placing our cares and concerns before him, trusting that he alone will provide (cf. *CCC*, 2729). "Pray, hope, and don't worry."

250. What is meant by dryness in prayer, and how can it be overcome?

Dryness in prayer refers to not sensing God's presence as much as we think we should or wish we could. Even the great saints experience dryness in prayer. It can be caused by one of three things: mortal sin, our own lack of discipline, or something quite the opposite.

"Mortal sin destroys charity in the heart" (*CCC*, 1855) and turns a person away from God. If you are in mortal sin, your prayer will be dry. Examine your conscience and bring your mortal sins to the Lord in the

Sacrament of Penance and Reconciliation. You will be brought back to the state of grace and the dryness will disappear.

Dryness could be the result of a lack of discipline in setting proper time aside for prayer, not giving God our best in prayer, or choosing not to deal with distractions in a positive manner. Pay close attention to what is going on in your prayer time, and the consolations you once felt in prayer will return.

There is another cause of dryness, very different from mortal sin or a lack of discipline. The hand of God could be at work. God could be calling you to deeper prayer, in which you desire not God's consolations but God himself. God could be using the dryness to expand the capacity of your heart to receive an even greater outpouring of his love.

It is not uncommon for a faithful, devoted, well-disciplined person of prayer who is in the state of grace to experience aridity in prayer. This is understandably puzzling and disconcerting (cf. *CCC*, 2731). Fortunately, many great saints wrote about this kind of dryness from their own personal experience. St. Alphonsus Liguori spoke of the experience of the dryness of the soul in feminine terms, also explaining its purpose:

> The time of spiritual desolation is also a time for being resigned. When a soul begins to cultivate the spiritual life, God usually showers his consolations upon her to wean her away from the world; but when he sees her making solid progress, he withdraws his hand to test her and to see if she will love and serve him without the reward of sensible consolations.[1]

God calls us to holiness. If you are experiencing dryness in prayer, be not afraid.

251. Does God hear and answer all our prayers?

There is a certain irony in the fact that we are rarely concerned about whether our prayers of praise and thanks are heard, yet we want instant, tangible results from our petitions. If God does not answer a prayer, it is not because he has not heard you. Perhaps what you are asking for is not in your best interest, or it is not the right time, or God desires something even greater for you (cf. *CCC*, 2737).

God loves you more than you can imagine, and he always provides the very best for you, even permitting suffering to be the crucible through which your soul is refined. "For a little while you may have to suffer through various trials, so that the genuineness of your faith, more precious than gold that is perishable even though tested by fire, may prove to be for praise, glory, and honor at the revelation of Jesus Christ" (1 Pt 1:6–7).

Someone who is mature in faith readily understands the dynamic of God providing for our greater good by not granting our every prayer. Yet great is the mystery of why God sometimes does not answer our prayers for the well-being of others. A grieving parent once asked, "Why did my little child succumb to cancer, even though everyone at church was storming heaven with their prayers?" There are no human words that can adequately console such profound grief, for no parent should ever have to bury a child. Yet the one to whom we address our prayers is the God and Father of our Lord and Savior Jesus Christ. God did not spare the life of his only begotten Son; he permitted Jesus to die so that we might be saved. Without the Cross there could be no Resurrection. "Christ, raised from the dead, dies no more; death no longer has power over him" (Rom 6:9).

Summary and Reflection

Christian prayer comes from the heart and is expressed in different ways. Vocal prayers can be said mentally and out loud. These include prayers that we have memorized. In meditation, we actively use our thoughts, emotions, imaginations, and desires to think about God and his presence. Mental prayer typically focuses on Jesus and can sometimes lead to contemplation. Eucharistic Adoration is centered on mental prayer. Dryness in prayer is something to be expected; it too can be a sign of God's grace and an appreciation of our reliance on him.

◑ *Creation*

"To always be close to Jesus, that's my life plan." These words of Bl. Carlo Acutis should be ours as well. We are especially close to Jesus when we are at prayer, our hearts open to his presence. Reread the sayings from the saints about prayer on page 353. To which saying can you relate most closely?

☯ *Fall*

Why is it important to you to stay close to the Sacrament of Penance and Reconciliation as you seek to make progress in the spiritual life, the life of prayer?

✝ *Redemption*

We are never alone in our prayer. Nor does the Lord ignore our prayer, even when we might think otherwise. How is the Cross of Jesus a consolation for you when you are having difficulty praying or when prayers have seemingly gone unanswered?

☘ *Restoration*

Experience for yourself prayer before the exposed Blessed Sacrament. Some describe exposition as praying before the King of Kings upon his glorious throne. What was your experience of this form of prayer? For you, how is praying before the Blessed Sacrament a glimpse of God's glory in heaven, the new creation?

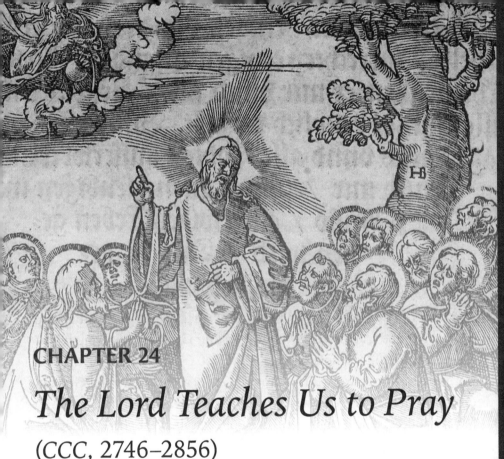

CHAPTER 24

The Lord Teaches Us to Pray
(CCC, 2746–2856)

Those who heard Jesus with their own ears recognized him as a gifted teacher, one who "taught them as one having authority, and not as their scribes" (Mt 7:29). Those in the crowds affectionately addressed Jesus with the title *rabbi*, a word meaning "teacher." Jesus was an exceptional teacher, holding large crowds spellbound and asking his listeners significant questions that penetrated the depths of their hearts. News about him spread quickly and widely, "and great crowds assembled to listen to him" (Lk 5:15). Like every rabbi, Jesus knew the proverb, "Train the young in the way they should go; even when old, they will not swerve from it" (Prv 22:6). When Jesus's students, his disciples, asked him, "Lord, teach us to pray" (Lk 11:1), he was quick to oblige.

Two versions of the Lord's Prayer appear in the Gospels. St. Matthew tells us that Jesus taught the multitudes how to pray during his Sermon on the Mount, giving us the traditional version that is prayed universally (cf. Mt 6:14–19). St. Luke's Gospel speaks of Jesus offering a slightly different version of the prayer (cf. Lk 11:2–4) when he was asked to do so by one of his disciples. There is nothing contradictory between the two versions; good teachers are well known for repeating lessons frequently and in a variety of ways. Jesus gives us in the Lord's Prayer both a beloved vocal prayer formula and a pattern for Christian living, for "prayer and Christian life are inseparable" (*CCC*, 2745).

252. What makes the Lord's Prayer unique?

The Lord's Prayer comes from the words given to Jesus by the Father, and it speaks to the true needs of the restless human heart, showing us the way to find rest in the house of the Father (cf. *CCC*, 2765). From the first words of the prayer, we are dared to call God "Father," a term for God not unknown in the Old Testament and in Jewish life, but hardly a common form of address in Jewish prayer. The Book of Psalms, the cherished prayer book of the Jews, never addresses God as "Father."

Because he is God the Son, Jesus can draw those whom he loves into the life of God the Father, inviting them to tread upon holy ground by addressing God with a familial term that was theretofore unthinkable. Only Jesus's invitation gave his first disciples and therefore us the confidence to call God Father: "When would a mortal dare call God 'Father,' if man's innermost being were not animated by power from on high?" (St. Peter Chrysologus, *Sermo* 71, 3: PL 52, 401 CD, cited in *CCC*, 2777).

253. What can we learn about God from addressing him as *Father*?

Calling God Father requires great humility, for it is a privilege and an honor to be adopted as a beloved son or daughter (cf. *CCC*, 2782). "No one knows the Son except the Father, and no one knows the Father except the Son and anyone to whom the Son wishes to reveal him" (Mt 11:27, cf. *CCC*, 2779). We participate in an unfathomable mystery by sharing in the relationship between the Son and the Father. Every time we pray the Lord's Prayer, every time we dare to say "Our Father," we do so with great humility and with the ardent desire to live our lives accordingly. "You cannot call the God of all kindness your Father if you preserve a cruel and inhuman heart; for in this case you no longer have in you the marks of the heavenly Father's kindness" (St. John Chrysostom, *De orat Dom.* 3: PG 51, 44, cited in *CCC*, 2784).

Addressing God as Father day after day is a steady reminder that we can be confident in placing childlike trust in God, who will never leave his children disappointed. "Our Father: at this name love is aroused in us . . . and the confidence of obtaining what we are about to ask. . . . What would he not give to his children who ask, since he has already granted them the gift of being his children?" (St. Augustine, *De serm. Dom. in monte* 2, 4, 16: PL 34, 1276, cited in *CCC*, 2785).

254. What if calling God "Father" is difficult for someone whose father was abusive, neglectful, or absent?

Our earthly fathers can influence our relationship with God in ways both positive and negative. Those for whom a paternal figure does not engender a sense of affection or trust can have difficulty calling God "Father." For some, this is an impetus to getting to know the goodness of God the Father. For others, this is a very difficult cross to carry. Sadly, such is the tragedy of sin that not all fathers provide adequately for the material, psychological, and spiritual needs of their children. Yet God is the source of fatherhood, and the model for all fathers to follow. God our Father transcends this world and its categories. We pray to the Father not as we perceive him but as he is, the merciful and loving Father that the Son has revealed him to be (cf. *CCC*, 2779).

255. What does it mean to call God *our* Father?

Because Jesus is the one teaching us this prayer, the "our" includes Jesus and all with whom he is in relationship, first and foremost the Father and the Holy Spirit. The Lord's Prayer expresses a new way of relating to God, Father, Son, and Holy Spirit. "When we pray to the Father, we adore and glorify him together with the Son and the Holy Spirit" (*CCC*, 2789).

In addition to expressing our communion with the Holy Trinity, praying with the word *our* before "Father" implies a relationship with all who address God as Father (cf. *CCC*, 2790). The prayer common to all Christians summons each follower of Jesus to pray to the Father with him, "that they may be one" (Jn 17:22, cf. *CCC*, 2791).

Praying the Our Father reminds us that God's fatherly love extends to all, including those who worship him differently and those who have yet to come to belief in him. We are called to be in solidarity with all people and to extend Christian charity without regard to creed or lack thereof—to draw all people into Christ that they too may call upon God as our Father with us (cf. *CCC*, 2793).

256. Does "who art in heaven" refer to the place where God is apart from us?

No it doesn't, even though a song popular a few decades ago made the charts by describing God watching over us "from a distance." God being in heaven does not limit his transcendence. Yes, God dwells in heaven, and God also plants within every human heart a deep longing for his presence (cf. *CCC*, 27, 1718, 2563, 2794), a longing that is fulfilled only in our Lord Jesus, who promises solemnly, "I am with you always, until the end of the age" (Mt 28:20).

Through the Lord Jesus we already partake of the good things of heaven, especially when we draw near to his real and substantial presence in the Holy Sacrifice of the Mass. God is neither distant nor aloof, for God makes his dwelling in our world (cf. Jn 1:14) so that one day we might live forever with him and the saints in heaven (cf. Phil 3:20).

257. What does it mean to say that God's name is *hallowed*?

"Hallowed be thy name" is the first of seven petitions in the Lord's Prayer. This petition gives glory to God's holy name: the ineffable name of God given to Moses upon Mount Sinai and the powerful, holy name of Jesus (cf. Phil 2:9–11, *CCC*, 2810–2812). The language of the Lord's Prayer in English includes a few words and expressions that are not part of our everyday speech. Although it is not used frequently outside of the Lord's Prayer, the word *hallowed* means "holy."

When prayed in the Lord's Prayer, *hallowed* has two senses. First, "hallowed be thy name" is a declaration of the holiness of the name of God and the resolution to always treat God's name with the highest degree of respect as prescribed in the Second Commandment (cf. *CCC*, 2142–2155, 2807). We enter into the holiness of God in a substantial way when we receive Holy Communion, as we are preparing to do when we pray the Lord's Prayer at Holy Mass.

Second, "hallowed be thy name" expresses our fervent hope that God's name may be made more holy in our own hearts and within the hearts of those who do not yet believe. We pray for nonbelievers, and we pray that we will be open to the promptings of the Holy Spirit when we have the opportunity to share the Good News of the Gospel with them. Every day our paths cross with those who are indifferent or hostile to the Gospel. We pray "hallowed be thy name" in anticipation of the opportunity to share the precious gift of faith with others. As St. Peter urges each of us, "Always be ready to give an explanation to anyone who asks you for a reason for your hope" (1 Pt 3:15). "For 'everyone who calls on the name of the Lord will be saved.' But how can they call on him in whom they have not believed? And how can they believe in him of whom they have not heard? And how can they hear without someone to preach? And how can people preach unless they are sent? As it is written, 'How beautiful are the feet of those who bring [the] good news!'" (Rom 10:13–15, cf. *CCC*, 2814).

258. What does it mean to pray the second petition, "thy kingdom come"?

Jesus spoke frequently about the Kingdom, likening it to things such as a mustard seed (cf. Mt 13:31–32), a treasure buried in a field (cf. Mt 13:44), and a net cast into the sea (cf. Mt 13:47–50). The Kingdom of God proclaimed by Jesus is still to come, yet it is also in our midst. Christians have been praying for the coming of the Kingdom since the earliest days of the Church, when some who were alive remembered firsthand the Lord's promise that he would soon return. *Marana tha* has always been the prayer of Christians: "Come, Lord Jesus." "Thy kingdom come" implies the ardent hope for the return of the Lord in glory, when the Lord Jesus will make all things new (cf. Rv 21:5), establishing the Kingdom once and for all (cf. *CCC*, 2817).

Although "thy kingdom come" refers to the final coming of Christ in glory, the Church is conscious of not being distracted from her mission here and now. In fact, the desire for the coming of the Kingdom commits the Church to her work more strongly, being ever committed to the works of mercy, justice, peace, and evangelization. Longing for the coming of the Kingdom at the end of time does not distract a follower of Jesus but instead reinforces within that person the desire to put faith into practice in daily living (cf. *CCC*, 2820).

The Lord's Prayer has long been prayed at Holy Mass just prior to receiving Holy Communion. The Kingdom of God is present in every offering of the Holy Sacrifice of the Mass, with heaven and earth touching through the Sacrament of the Eucharist. "The Kingdom of God has been coming since the Last Supper and, in the Eucharist, it is in our midst. The kingdom will come in glory when Christ hands it over to his Father" (*CCC*, 2816).

259. What does it mean to pray the third petition, "Thy will be done, on earth as it is in heaven"?

The will of the Father is that the whole human race be saved. God sent his only begotten Son into this world "so that everyone who believes in him might not perish but might have eternal life" (Jn 3:16, cf. *CCC*, 2822). The Father's will is revealed in Christ Jesus, through whom we have salvation and from whom we receive the New Commandment to "love one another" (Jn 13:34). The Father's will is already fully realized in heaven. We pray in the Lord's Prayer that his will might be accomplished here on earth as well (cf. *CCC*, 2823). This happens only to the extent that we learn to conform our wills to God's, learning obedience to God's will by being more closely united to Christ, surrendering our will to his, striving to live our lives in a manner that is pleasing to the Father (cf. *CCC*, 2825).

It is fitting that we pray "thy will be done" in the context of the Holy Sacrifice of the Mass, and in anticipation of soon receiving Holy Communion. Jesus surrenders his will to his Father by stretching out his arms on the Cross. Through the Holy Eucharist we are united with the Lord's act of self-giving even to the point of great sacrifice. By drawing near to the Lord in the Holy Eucharist we renew our commitment to following him, and we allow the Lord to draw us into the great prayer he offered at Gethsemane in anticipation of his perfect sacrifice on the Cross: "Father, if you are willing, take this cup away from me; still, not my will but yours be done" (Lk 22:42, cf. *CCC*, 2825–2827).

260. What does it mean to pray the fourth petition, "Give us this day our daily bread"?

Much is packed into these seven words of the Lord's Prayer:

- *Give us* expresses childlike trust in the Father, who always provides for his children. Our request gives glory and honor to the Father, for in doing so we acknowledge his unfailing goodness (cf. *CCC*, 2828). *Us* reminds us of our solidarity with all of God's People. We ask God to take care of the needs of the hungry and poor (cf. *CCC*, 2829).

- In praying for *bread*, we ask the Father for everything we need, materially and spiritually. We place our trust in the Lord, who promises his care and concern for us (cf. Mt 6:25–31, *CCC*, 2830). We recall how Jesus multiplied five loaves of bread to feed the multitude, the only miracle that appears in all four Gospels (cf. Mt 14:13–21 and parallels). We place our trust in God's providential care for our material as well as our spiritual needs. "Bread" refers not just to food for the body but also to the life-giving Word of God that fills the deepest longings of our mind and heart. "One does not live by bread alone, but by every word that comes forth from the mouth of God" (Mt 4:4). In a particular way, "bread" refers to the Bread of Life, the great gift of the Holy Eucharist, through which we draw near to our Lord, Body and Blood, Soul and Divinity (cf. *CCC*, 2835).

- In praying for "*our* bread," we are reminded once again of our solidarity with the poor, both the materially poor and the spiritually deprived. As a family partakes of one loaf, sharing that loaf among the many who are gathered at the table, so we are called to share our material and spiritual gifts with the many, trusting that the Lord will multiply our gifts as he miraculously fed the multitude in abundance, even with twelve baskets of food left over (cf. *CCC*, 2833). When we pray for "*our* bread," we pray "that the abundance of some may remedy the needs of others" (*CCC*, 2833).

- In praying for bread "this day," we express urgency in our childlike trust in God. "'This day' is also an expression of trust taught us by the Lord, which we would never have presumed to invent. Since it refers above all to his Word and to the Body of his Son, this 'today' is not only that of our mortal time, but also the 'today' of God" (*CCC*, 2836). "This day" expresses not only urgency but also our connection with the day of the Lord, the day of the Resurrection of Jesus from the dead: "If you receive the bread each day, each day is today for you. If Christ is yours today, he rises for you every day. How can this be? 'You are my Son, today I have begotten you.' Therefore, 'today' is when Christ rises" (St. Ambrose, *De Sacr.* 5, 4, 26: PL 16, 453A, cf. Ps 2:7, cited in *CCC*, 2836).

- We pray not just for bread, but for our "daily" bread, a distinction of great importance. The word *daily* in the original Greek is *epiousios*, a word that appears nowhere else in the Bible except in the accounts of the giving of the Lord's Prayer in the Gospels of Matthew and Luke. Nor does this word appear in ancient Greek literature. The word seems to have been coined by the Lord himself. *Epiousios* (daily) does not mean simply occurring every day. *Epiousios* means quite literally "superessential." "Taken literally . . . it refers directly to the Bread of Life, the Body of Christ, the 'medicine of immortality,' without which we have no life within us" (*CCC*, 2837). When we pray the Lord's Prayer at Mass, immediately before the time for Holy Communion, we are praying for the Bread of Life that we will soon receive into our persons. When we pray the Lord's Prayer at other times, we express our yearning to be united with the Lord in the closest manner possible this side of heaven: "The Father in heaven urges us, as children of heaven, to ask for the bread of heaven. [Christ] himself is the bread who, sown in the Virgin, raised up in the flesh, kneaded in the Passion, baked in the oven of the tomb, reserved in churches, brought to altars, furnishes the faithful each day with food from heaven" (St. Peter Chrysologus, *Sermo 67* PL 52, 392, cf. Jn 6:51, cited in *CCC*, 2837).

261. What does it mean to pray the fifth petition, "Forgive us our trespasses, as we forgive those who have trespassed against us"?

Jesus dies upon the Cross so that sins may be forgiven. The virtue of justice obliges us to extend forgiveness to others (cf. *CCC*, 1933). Jesus teaches the parable about a man who was forgiven a huge debt, only to throw into prison someone who was unable to repay a much lesser debt (cf. Mt 18:23–35). Jesus taught this parable to illustrate to St. Peter that he must forgive the one who has sinned against him not just seven times, but seventy times seven times (cf. Mt 18:21–22).

In the fifth petition of the Lord's Prayer, we pray that we will conform ourselves more and more to the Lord's will, first by the awareness of our own sinfulness and our own need for the Lord's mercy. We pray that the Lord's mercy will flow through us in forgiving others, even our enemies. From the Cross Jesus prays for those who have crucified him: "Father, forgive them, they know not what they do" (Lk 23:34, cf. *CCC*, 2844). We pray that we will be quick to forgive others, for in doing so we imitate the Lord, who has first forgiven us. Reconciliation requires the cooperation of two or more people; forgiveness takes only one.

St. Luke's Gospel records Jesus teaching us to ask our heavenly Father to "forgive us our sins for we ourselves forgive everyone in debt to us" (Lk 11:4). In St. Matthew's Gospel, Jesus uses the phrase "forgive us our debts, as we forgive our debtors" (Mt 6:12). The difference in phrasing is not contradictory. In fact, the difference highlights the crippling nature of sin. It is not unusual for a person to feel burdened by debt, longing one day to be debt free. In the same way, sin burdens the sinner. Sin impedes or blocks a person from being truly free and truly happy. "For freedom Christ set us free; so stand firm and do not submit again to the yoke of slavery" (Gal 5:1). "So if the Son makes you free, you will be free indeed" (Jn 8:36 NRSV, cf. *CCC*, 2844).

One more point about this petition: remember that we pray the Lord's Prayer at Holy Mass just before the Holy Sacrifice has been completed by the priest's reception of Holy Communion. Jesus said in regard to the offering of sacrifice in the Temple, "if you bring your gift to the altar, and there recall that your brother has anything against you, leave your gift there at the altar, go first and be reconciled with your brother, and then come and offer your gift" (Mt 5:23–24). Through the Lord's Prayer, Jesus teaches us that prayer is not a flight from reality but instead is deeply connected to the way in which we love one another. The fifth petition reminds us not to allow disputes and grudges to fester, but to be quick to forgive and to reconcile.

The Chaplet of Divine Mercy

From one of the darkest chapters of the twentieth century originated a new appreciation of and devotion to Divine Mercy. Because everything about our lives is a gift from God, we only live, move, and have our very being due to his mercy. For that reason, we express our devotion to the great gift of Divine Mercy, which is rooted deeply in the Gospels and has long been a part of Catholic prayer.

St. Maria Faustina Kowalska (1905–1938) was a Polish nun from a poor family with only a rudimentary education. St. Faustina received extraordinary revelations from the Lord, which she recorded in her diary. Her diary has since become one of the most popular Catholic spiritual works and the source of a daily devotion known as the Chaplet of Divine Mercy. Most Catholics know of the chaplet through an accompanying image based on St. Faustina's vision of the Risen Lord that an artist later painted under her guidance. Under the image one finds the consoling prayer, "Jesus, I Trust in You."

St. Faustina was canonized on April 30, 2000, as the first saint of the new millennium by her fellow countryman St. John Paul II. The pope also instituted the Feast of Divine Mercy to be observed universally on the first Sunday after Easter. He would die on the evening of that feast five years later.

The Chaplet of Divine Mercy is prayed regularly in many parishes and by individuals, usually at 3:00 p.m., the hour our Lord expired on the Cross, and is a source of grace to those who pray it with devotion. The one praying the chaplet makes use of a rosary to keep count of the prayers. The directions for praying the Chaplet of Divine Mercy follow. If you would like a further demonstration, search the internet under its title and you will find many Catholics leading this devotion online.

Make the Sign of the Cross.
Recite the opening prayer:
You expired, Jesus, but the source of life gushed forth for
     souls, and the ocean of mercy opened up for the
     whole world. O Fount of Life, unfathomable Divine
     Mercy, envelop the whole world and empty Yourself
     out upon us.

(Repeat three times.)

Blood and Water, which gushed forth from the Heart of Jesus
     as a fount of mercy for us, I trust in You!
On the first three beads pray one of each:
Our Father
Hail Mary
The Apostles' Creed
To begin each decade, pray:
Eternal Father, I offer you the Body and Blood, Soul and Divin-
     ity, of your dearly beloved Son, our Lord, Jesus Christ,
     in atonement for our sins and those of the whole
     world.
On the ten small beads for each decade, pray:
For the sake of his sorrowful Passion, have mercy on us and on
     the whole world.
After five decades, pray:

Holy God, Holy Mighty One, Holy Immortal One, have mercy on us and on the whole world.

(Repeat three times.)

Recite the closing prayer:
Eternal God, in whom mercy is endless and the treasury of compassion inexhaustible, look kindly upon us and increase Your mercy in us, that in difficult moments we might not despair nor become despondent, but with great confidence submit ourselves to Your holy will, which is Love and Mercy itself.

262. What does it mean to pray the sixth petition, "Lead us not into temptation"?

The Lord proves himself to be the Good Shepherd, who would never lead us into temptation. Why do we pray this sixth petition? In fact, the original Greek of this petition is better understood to mean "do not allow us to enter into temptation" or "do not let us yield to temptation" (*CCC*, 2846). The present translation remains, both for the unity of those who pray in English and for the sake of continuity with centuries of prayer in the English language. Questions arise from time to time about this petition, so it is good for us to remember that "God . . . tempts no one" (Jas 1:13) and that we are asking in this petition always for the wisdom and strength to reject sin absolutely.

The sixth petition is a prayer for perseverance in the daily battle against sin. The psalmist urges us to raise our voices in prayer three times a day, morning, noon, and evening (cf. Ps 55:18). The tradition of the Church sustains the devotion of praying the Lord's Prayer at those times as well, so that we might remain vigilant and alert in the battle against sin and ultimately be caught up in Christ's definitive victory over the evil one, who prowls about seeking only "to steal and slaughter and destroy" (Jn

10:10, cf. *CCC*, 2853). We pray the sixth petition as we prepare to receive Holy Communion, for the Holy Eucharist protects and preserves us from sin (cf. *CCC*, 1393).

263. What does it mean to pray the seventh petition, "Deliver us from evil"?

The seventh petition follows naturally from the sixth. We pray that we will be delivered from the power of the evil one, who seeks always to distract us, to deceive us, and to lead us far away from the path of life. "In this petition, evil is not an abstraction, but refers to a person, Satan, the Evil One, the angel who opposes God. The devil (*dia-bolos*) is the one who 'throws himself across' God's plan and his work of salvation accomplished in Christ" (*CCC*, 2851).

In this petition we pray not only for ourselves but for the whole world. We pray for the salvation of the souls of those who have become ensnared in sin, imprisoned by finding comfort in the things that wither and fade, rather than seeking the indestructible treasures of the Kingdom of God.

Christ's victory over the evil one was accomplished once and for all upon the Cross. The war has been won, but battles continue. The Book of Revelation offers a vivid image of Satan, portrayed as the dragon who has been cast out, the one who seeks to destroy the offspring of "a woman clothed with the sun, with the moon under her feet" (Rv 12:1), a reference strikingly similar to the image of Our Lady of Guadalupe found on the tilma of St. Juan Diego (cf. page 104). Although the plans of the dragon were frustrated, the dragon continued to pursue the woman but could not harm her. "Then the dragon . . . went off to wage war against the rest of her offspring, those who keep God's commandments and bear witness to Jesus" (Rv 12:17).

The Church continues to pray for the definitive defeat of the evil one that will transpire in the Second Coming of the Lord in glory (cf. *CCC*, 1042–1050, 2853). We pray as well for "the precious gift of peace and the grace of perseverance in expectation of Christ's return" (*CCC*, 2854). As we prepare for Holy Communion, we rightly pray "deliver us from evil," for the Blessed Sacrament that we are about to receive is a foretaste of the everlasting banquet, the heavenly celebration of having been forever delivered from the powers of sin and death.

During troubled times Christians have taken refuge in the prayer that Jesus taught us. May we continue to do the same, by daring to pray in the words our Savior taught us.

264. Why don't Catholics pray the doxology of the Lord's Prayer that is prayed by other Christians?

When Catholics pray the Lord's Prayer, the final phrase is simply, "Amen." Christians of other traditions add a *doxology*, an expression of praise to God: "For thine is the kingdom, and the power, and the glory, forever. Amen." In Holy Mass, a form of these beautiful words is prayed moments after the completion of the Lord's Prayer: "For the kingdom, the power, and the glory are yours, now and forever."

The doxology is believed to have originated in the decades that followed the apostolic era. The doxology is found in an early second-century Christian work known as the *Didache* ("Teaching"). These words are found in some Protestant and Orthodox Bibles, but they do not appear in Catholic Bibles. Other similar doxologies are part of the New Testament read by all Christians (cf. Rom 6:25–27, 1 Tm 1:17). Nevertheless, the Church accepts this doxology as rightly appended to the Lord's Prayer in the earliest liturgical practices (cf. *CCC*, 2760).

These beautiful words should not divide Christians either by their inclusion or exclusion from the praying of the Lord's Prayer. They are words offered in praise of God the Father, who sends his Son and the Holy Spirit to teach us to pray.

Summary and Reflection

The Lord's Prayer is rightly called "the summary of the whole gospel" (Tertullian, *De orat.* 1: PL 1, 1155, cited in *CCC*, 2761). St. Augustine teaches that all the prayers recorded in the Bible can be summed up by the Lord's Prayer: "Run through all the words of the holy prayers [in Scripture], and I do not think that you will find anything in them that is not contained and included in the Lord's Prayer" (Ep. 130, 12, 22: PL 33, 503, cited in *CCC*, 2762). The Lord's Prayer has always been regarded as a great gift from the Lord to his Church and to all believers. It is even a prayer in which some non-Christians will join. It comes from the words the Father gave Jesus, and it speaks to the true needs of the human heart (cf. *CCC*, 2765). May you pray it often and well.

⊖ *Creation*

Our lives are generated by a loving God who we are privileged to call "our Father." What are elements of loving fatherhood you have witnessed personally or in the world at large that give a glimpse of God as Father? How do you imagine God surpassing human fatherhood?

◐ *Fall*

How is God's Kingdom at once present yet to come? In what parts of your life do you feel threatened by the evil one? Make this part of the Lord's Prayer a mantra in those situations: "Deliver me from evil."

✝ *Redemption*

"Give us this day our daily bread" means praying for physical sustenance that only the Bread of Life can give, friendship, companionship, and acceptance by all of the Word of God. Write a short prayer addressing one of these areas of this petition.

◑ *Restoration*

The Lord's Prayer is a prayer of unity, not division. Meditate on the words of the doxology. What do you find meaningful about them?

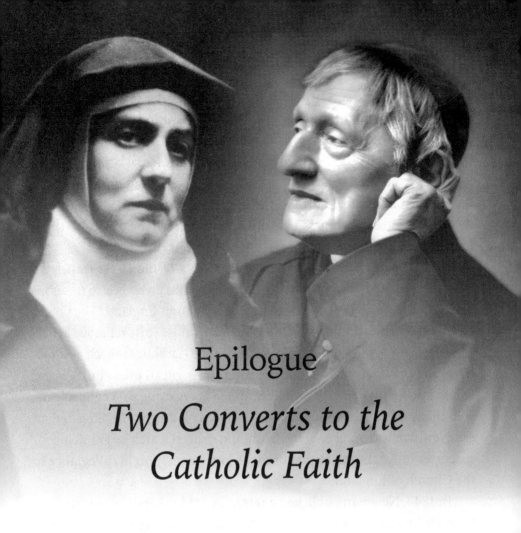

Epilogue
Two Converts to the Catholic Faith

Edith Stein (1891–1942) had once been an observant Jew, but she fell into agnosticism as a teenager. The experience of seeing a woman at prayer in the Frankfurt Cathedral touched Edith deeply and led her to be baptized Catholic in 1922. Already a decorated professor (a rarity for a woman of the time) at the University of Freiburg in Germany, Edith wrote extensively, enjoying great acclaim within the academic community in Europe and beyond after her Baptism. But the work in academia lessened in meaning for Edith as time when on. Influenced by the writings of St. Teresa of Avila, Edith was drawn to the religious life.

As Adolf Hitler rose to power in 1933, Edith joined the Carmelite religious community, taking the name Sr. Teresa Benedicta of the Cross. She continued to publish works of philosophy from within the walls of the cloister. Sr. Teresa's Catholic faith did not keep her safe from the Nazi persecution of Jews; she was deported to Auschwitz in 1942 and executed in the gas chamber two days later, "faithful to the crucified Lord Jesus Christ and, as a Jew, to her people in loving faithfulness."[1] In 1998 Edith Stein was canonized by Pope St. John Paul II and was later named one of the six patron saints of Europe. The life and writings of St. Teresa Benedicta of the Cross continue to inspire those who seek the truth and strive to live a life of holiness.

In her academic work, St. Teresa Benedicta of the Cross translated many essays and books of another Catholic convert who is also a canonized saint, St. John Henry Newman (1801–1890) of England. The young Newman was a distinguished Oxford scholar whose early religious beliefs were decidedly anti-Catholic; he described the Catholic Church as idolatrous and polytheistic. Newman became an Anglican priest in 1825 and would lead an influential movement aimed at restoring to Anglican worship many of the Catholic elements abandoned during the Elizabethan era. Newman was a seeker of the truth, and in his research he found inconsistencies in Anglicanism that brought him to question his allegiance to the Church of England.

In 1843, Newman published a retraction of his harsh criticism of the Catholic Church and preached his last sermon as an Anglican priest. Newman was received into the Catholic Church in 1845, ordained a Catholic priest in 1847, and within a few decades would come to be regarded as one of the greatest and most articulate proponents of the Catholic faith. Pope Leo XIII honored Fr. Newman's work by creating him a cardinal of the Church in 1879. Beloved by his Catholic countrymen and admired from afar, Cardinal Newman died in 1890. In 2019, in St. Peter's Square and in the presence of the future King Charles III, Pope Francis canonized John Henry Newman, a saint whose writings continue to bear great fruit theologically and whose story of conversion remains compelling.

St. Teresa Benedicta of the Cross was greatly inspired by St. John Henry Newman, a fellow seeker of truth. She stated, "His entire life was a search for religious truth and led him, inevitably, to the Catholic Church."[2]

Newman found the truth exactly where he hoped to find it when, as a young man, he wrote the now-cherished hymn "Lead, Kindly Light." May the lyrics of this hymn inspire you to continue your search for truth. When one seeks the truth with a sincere heart, one finds it. And upon finding the truth, one finds Jesus, the Way, the Truth, and the Life. And upon finding Jesus, one finds his Bride, the Church. And finding the Church, one finds the sacraments of the Church, through which one is nourished with the Bread of Life and the Medicine of Immortality that is the Most Holy Eucharist.

> Lead, kindly Light, amid the encircling gloom.
> Lead thou me on!
> The night is dark, and I am far from home,
> Lead thou me on.
> Keep thou my feet; I do not ask to see
> The distant scene—One step enough for me.
>
> I was not ever thus, nor pray'd that thou
> Shouldst lead me on.
> I loved to choose and see my path; but now,
> lead thou me on.
> I loved the garish day, and, spite of fears,
> Pride ruled my will: Remember not past years.
>
> So long thy power hath blest me, sure it still
> will lead me on
> O'er moor and fen, O'er crag and torrent, till
> the night is gone.
> And with the morn those angel faces smile,
> Which I have loved long since, and lost awhile!

APPENDIX

Beliefs

Apostles' Creed

I believe in God,
the Father almighty,
Creator of heaven and earth,
and in Jesus Christ, his only Son, our Lord,
who was conceived by the Holy Spirit,
born of the Virgin Mary,
suffered under Pontius Pilate,
was crucified, died, and was buried;
he descended into hell;
on the third day he rose again from the dead;
he ascended into heaven,
and is seated at the right hand of God the Father almighty;
from there he will come to judge the living and the dead.
I believe in the Holy Spirit,
the holy catholic Church,
the communion of saints,
the forgiveness of sins,
the resurrection of the body,
and life everlasting. Amen.

Nicene Creed

I believe in one God,
the Father almighty,
maker of heaven and earth,
of all things visible and invisible.
I believe in one Lord Jesus Christ,
the only begotten Son of God,
born of the Father before all ages.

God from God, Light from Light,
true God from true God,
begotten, not made, consubstantial with the Father;
through him all things were made.
For us men and for our salvation
he came down from heaven,
and by the Holy Spirit was incarnate of the Virgin Mary,
and became man.
For our sake he was crucified under Pontius Pilate,
he suffered death and was buried,
and rose again on the third day
in accordance with the Scriptures.
He ascended into heaven
and is seated at the right hand of the Father.
He will come again in glory
to judge the living and the dead
and his kingdom will have no end.
I believe in the Holy Spirit, the Lord, the giver of life,
who proceeds from the Father and the Son,
who with the Father and the Son is adored and glorified,
who has spoken through the prophets.
I believe in one, holy, catholic and apostolic Church.
I confess one Baptism for the forgiveness of sins
and I look forward to the resurrection of the dead
and the life of the world to come. Amen.

Precepts of the Church

1. To attend Mass on Sundays and holy days of obligation
2. To confess your sins at least once a year
3. To receive Holy Communion at least once a year during the Easter Season
4. To observe the days of fast and abstinence
5. To contribute to the support of the Church

Traditional Prayers and Devotions

Sign of the Cross

In the name of the Father,
and of the Son,
and of the Holy Spirit. Amen.

Our Father

Our Father
who art in heaven,
hallowed be thy name;
thy kingdom come,
thy will be done on earth as it is in heaven.
Give us this day our daily bread,
and forgive us our trespasses,
as we forgive those who trespass against us;
And lead us not into temptation,
but deliver us from evil.
Amen.

Glory Be

Glory be to the Father,
and to the Son,
and to the Holy Spirit;
as it was in the beginning,
is now,
and ever shall be,
world without end. Amen.

Hail Mary

Hail Mary, full of grace,
the Lord is with thee.
Blessed art thou among women,
and blessed is the fruit of thy womb, Jesus.
Holy Mary, Mother of God,
pray for us sinners
now and at the hour of our death.
Amen.

The Fatima Prayer

O my Jesus, forgive us our sins, save us from the fires of hell, lead
all souls to heaven, especially those in most need of thy mercy.

The Memorare

Remember, O most gracious Virgin Mary,
that never was it known
that anyone who fled to thy protection,
implored thy help,
or sought thy intercession was left unaided.
Inspired by this confidence, I fly unto thee,
O Virgin of virgins, my mother.
To thee I come, before thee I stand,
sinful and sorrowful.
O Mother of the Word Incarnate,
despise not my petitions,
but in thy mercy hear and answer me.
Amen.

Hail, Holy Queen

Hail, holy Queen, Mother of Mercy,
our life, our sweetness, and our hope.

To thee do we cry,
poor banished children of Eve.
To thee do we send up our sighs,
mourning and weeping in this valley of tears.
Turn then, most gracious advocate,
thine eyes of mercy toward us,
and after this exile,
show unto us the blessed fruit of thy womb, Jesus.
O clement, O loving,
O sweet Virgin Mary.

The Angelus

V. The angel of the Lord declared unto Mary.
R. And she conceived of the Holy Spirit.
Hail Mary . . .
V. Behold the handmaid of the Lord.
R. Be it done unto me according to your word.
Hail Mary . . .
V. And the Word was made flesh.
R. And dwelt among us.
Hail Mary . . .
V. Pray for us, O holy Mother of God.
R. That we may be made worthy of the promises of Christ. Let us pray: Pour forth, we beseech thee, O Lord, thy grace into our hearts; that we, to whom the Incarnation of Christ, thy Son, was made known by the message of an angel, may by his Passion and Cross be brought to the glory of his Resurrection, through the same Christ our Lord.
Amen.

Morning Offering

O Jesus, through the Immaculate Heart of Mary,
I offer you my prayers, works, joys, and sufferings of this day

in union with the holy sacrifice of the Mass throughout the world.
I offer them for all the intentions of your Sacred Heart:
the salvation of souls, reparation for sins, and the reunion of all
    Christians.
I offer them for the intentions of our bishops and all members of the
    apostleship of prayer and in particular for those recommended by
    our Holy Father this month. Amen.

Act of Faith

O my God, I firmly believe that you are one God in three Divine
Persons, Father, Son, and Holy Spirit. I believe that your divine Son
became man and died for our sins and that he will come to judge
the living and the dead. I believe these and all the truths which
the Holy Catholic Church teaches because you have revealed them
who are eternal truth and wisdom, who can neither deceive nor be
deceived. In this faith I intend to live and die. Amen.

Act of Hope

O Lord God, I hope by your grace for the pardon of all my sins and
after life here to gain eternal happiness because you have promised
it who are infinitely powerful, faithful, kind, and merciful. In this
hope I intend to live and die. Amen.

Act of Love

O Lord God, I love you above all things and I love my neighbor for
your sake because you are the highest, infinite and perfect good,
worthy of all my love. In this love I intend to live and die. Amen.

Act of Contrition

O my God, I am heartily sorry for having offended thee, and I detest
all my sins because of thy just punishment, but most of all because
they offend thee, my God, who art all good and deserving of all my

love. I firmly resolve with the help of thy grace to sin no more and
to avoid the near occasion of sin. Amen.

Grace before Meals

Bless us, O Lord,
and these your gifts,
which we are about to receive from your bounty,
through Christ our Lord.
Amen.

Grace after Meals

We give you thanks, almighty God,
for these and all the gifts
which we have received
from your goodness
through Christ our Lord.
Amen.

Angel of God

Angel of God, my guardian dear,
to whom God's love commits me here,
ever this day be at my side,
to light and guard, to rule and guide.
Amen.

Prayer for the Faithful Departed

Eternal rest grant unto them, O Lord,
and let perpetual light shine upon them.
May they rest in peace. Amen.

The Jesus Prayer

Lord Jesus Christ, Son of God, have mercy on me, a sinner.

Suscipe

Take, Lord, and receive all my liberty, my memory, my understanding, my entire will—all that I have and call my own. You have given it all to me. To you, Lord, I return it. Everything is yours: do with it what you will. Give me only your love and your grace. That is enough for me.

Mary Undoer of Knots

O Mary, you who know how to untangle the knots of our existence and know the desires of our heart, come to our help. We trust that you will provide for those needs so that, as at Cana of Galilee, joy and celebration may return to our homes after this moment of trial. Help us, Mother of Divine Love, to conform ourselves to the will of the Father and to do what Jesus tells us, who took our suffering upon himself to lead us through the Cross to the joy of the Resurrection. Amen.

The Divine Praises

These praises are traditionally recited after the Benediction of the Blessed Sacrament.

Blessed be God.
Blessed be his Holy Name.
Blessed be Jesus Christ, true God and true man.
Blessed be the Name of Jesus.
Blessed be his Most Sacred Heart.
Blessed be his Most Precious Blood.
Blessed be Jesus in the Most Holy Sacrament of the Altar.
Blessed be the Holy Spirit, the Paraclete.
Blessed be the great Mother of God, Mary most holy.
Blessed be her holy and Immaculate Conception.
Blessed be her glorious Assumption.
Blessed be the name of Mary, Virgin and Mother.
Blessed be St. Joseph, her most chaste spouse.
Blessed be God in his angels and in his saints.

Prayer for Peace (attributed to St. Francis of Assisi)

Lord, make me an instrument of your peace.
Where there is hatred, let me sow love;
where there is injury, pardon;
where there is doubt, faith;
where there is despair, hope;
where there is darkness, light;
where there is sadness, joy.
O Divine Master,
grant that I may not so much seek
to be consoled as to console,
to be understood, as to understand,
to be loved, as to love.
For it is in giving that we receive,
it is in pardoning that we are pardoned,
and it is in dying that we are born to eternal life.

Stations of the Cross

The Stations of the Cross is a meditative prayer based on the Passion of Christ. This devotion developed in the Middle Ages as a way to allow the faithful to retrace the last steps of Jesus to Calvary without making the journey to the Holy Land. Most Catholic churches have images or symbols of the Stations depicted on side walls to help Catholics imagine the sufferings of Jesus and focus on the meaning of the Paschal Mystery. Praying the Stations means meditating on each of the following scenes:

1. Jesus is condemned to death.
2. Jesus takes up his Cross.
3. Jesus falls the first time.
4. Jesus meets his Mother.
5. Simon of Cyrene helps Jesus carry his Cross.
6. Veronica wipes the face of Jesus.
7. Jesus falls the second time.

8. Jesus consoles the women of Jerusalem.
9. Jesus falls the third time.
10. Jesus is stripped of his garments.
11. Jesus is nailed to the Cross.
12. Jesus dies on the Cross.
13. Jesus is taken down from the Cross.
14. Jesus is laid in the tomb.

Some churches also include a fifteenth station, the Resurrection of the Lord.

Canon of the Bible

There are seventy-three books in the canon of the Bible, that is, the official list of books the Church accepts as divinely inspired: forty-six Old Testament books and twenty-seven New Testament books.

THE OLD TESTAMENT			
THE PENTATEUCH		**THE WISDOM BOOKS**	
Genesis	Gn	Job	Jb
Exodus	Ex	Psalms	Ps(s)
Leviticus	Lv	Proverbs	Prv
Numbers	Nm	Ecclesiastes	Eccl
Deuteronomy	Dt	Song of Songs	Sg
THE HISTORICAL BOOKS		Wisdom	Ws
Joshua	Jos	Sirach	Sir
Judges	Jgs	**THE PROPHETIC BOOKS**	
Ruth	Ru	Isaiah	Is
1 Samuel	1 Sm	Jeremiah	Jer
2 Samuel	2 Sm	Lamentations	Lam
1 Kings	1 Kgs	Baruch	Bar
2 Kings	2 Kgs	Ezekiel	Ez
1 Chronicles	1 Chr	Daniel	Dn
2 Chronicles	2 Chr	Hosea	Hos
Ezra	Ezr	Joel	Jl
Nehemiah	Neh	Amos	Am
Tobit	Tb	Obadiah	Ob
Judith	Jdt	Jonah	Jon
Esther	Est	Micah	Mi
1 Maccabees	1 Mc	Nahum	Na
2 Maccabees	2 Mc	Habakkuk	Hb
		Zephaniah	Zep
		Haggai	Hg
		Zechariah	Zec
		Malachi	Mal

THE NEW TESTAMENT			
THE GOSPELS		**THE CATHOLIC LETTERS**	
Matthew	Mt	James	Jas
Mark	Mk	1 Peter	1 Pt
Luke	Lk	2 Peter	2 Pt
John	Jn	1 John	1 Jn
		2 John	2 Jn
Acts of the Apostles	Acts	3 John	3 Jn
THE NEW TESTAMENT LETTERS		Jude	Jude
Romans	Rom	Revelation	Rv
1 Corinthians	1 Cor		
2 Corinthians	2 Cor		
Galatians	Gal		
Ephesians	Eph		
Philippians	Phil		
Colossians	Col		
1 Thessalonians	1 Thes		
2 Thessalonians	2 Thes		
1 Timothy	1 Tm		
2 Timothy	2 Tm		
Titus	Ti		
Philemon	Phlm		
Hebrews	Heb		

Glossary

abortifacient A drug that causes an abortion.

absolution The statement by which a priest, speaking as the official minister of Christ's Church, declares forgiveness of sins to a repentant sinner in the Sacrament of Penance. The formula of absolution reads: "I absolve you from your sins in the name of the Father, and of the Son, and of the Holy Spirit. May our same merciful and loving God pardon your every transgression. Amen."

adult stem cell research A scientific procedure that involves the collection, manipulation, and study of adult human stem cells, as opposed to embryonic stem cell research, which leads to the unnecessary destruction of innocent human life. Adult stem cell research is approved by the Church and has a positive success rate for finding solutions to illness and disease.

adultery Sexual intercourse between two people, at least one of whom is married to another person" (cf. *CCC* 2380).

Advent The four-week season in the liturgical year that prepares for the Nativity of Jesus Christ, our Savior.

Advocate A name for the Holy Spirit, who lives in us by faith and baptism, making them members of Christ's Body, the Church, sanctifies them, and guides them into all truth

Amen A Hebrew word for "truly" or "it is so," thus signifying agreement with what has been said. New Testament and liturgical prayers, creeds, and other Christian prayers end with Amen to show belief in what has just been said.

angels Spiritual creatures, created by God with intelligence and will, who surpass humans in perfection. They are personal and immortal creatures.

annulment An official declaration by a tribunal (Church court) that what appeared to be a Christian marriage never existed in the first place.

Annunciation The visit by the angel Gabriel to the Virgin Mary to announce that she would be the Mother of the Savior. After giving her consent, Mary became Mother of Jesus by the power of the Holy Spirit. The Feast of the Annunciation is on March 25.

Anointing of the Sick A sacrament of healing, administered by a priest to a baptized person, in which the Lord extends his loving, healing touch through the Church to those who are seriously ill or dying. God gives the sick person grace to strengthen them to bear their illness well, offer it up, and if needed, a holy death. Also, on occasion, God grants physical healing.

Apostle "One sent" to be Christ's ambassador, to continue his work. In its widest sense, the term refers to all of Christ's disciples whose mission is to preach his Gospel in word and deed. Originally, it referred to the Twelve whom Jesus chose to help him in his earthly ministry and to govern the Church. The successors of the Twelve Apostles are the bishops of the Catholic Church.

apostolic succession The handing on of the teaching, preaching, and sanctifying office of the Apostles to their successors, the bishops, through the laying on of hands.

apostolic One of the marks of the Church describing her continuity through all ages with the Apostles chosen by Christ.

apparition A supernatural appearance. A Marian apparition is an appearance of the Blessed Virgin Mary to a person, typically to deliver an important message. In order for an apparition to be considered authentic, it must first be verified by the Vatican.

Arianism A heresy of the fourth century that took its name from Arius, a priest from Alexandria. The heresy denied the divinity of Jesus, claiming that he was like the Father except that he was created by the Father.

Ark of the Covenant The most important symbol of the Jewish faith. It served as a portable shrine in which the tablets of the Torah were carried. The Ark was built while the Israelites wandered in the desert and was used in the First Temple and contained there until the Temple was destroyed.

Ascension The event that "marks the definitive entrance of Jesus' humanity into God's heavenly domain" (CCC, 665). It is from heaven that Christ will come again.

Assumption of the Blessed Virgin Mary The Church dogma formalized by Pope Pius XII in 1950 that teaches that the Blessed Mother was taken body and soul into heaven when her earthly life was over. The Solemnity of the Assumption is on August 15 and is a holy day of obligation.

Baptism of blood The belief that martyrs people who die for their faith in Jesus who had not yet been baptized by water may receive forgiveness for their sins and experience God's saving mercy.

Baptism of desire The grace of salvation that may be given to those who have at least an implicit desire for Baptism but who die without receiving the Sacrament of Baptism.

beatific vision The contemplation of God in his full glory, the sight of which perfectly fulfills us and makes us happy for all eternity beatific vision The ability to contemplate God in his full glory when we are in heaven. Beatific vision is a gift from God that is essential to our eternal happiness.

Beatitudes *Beatitude* means "supreme happiness," especially our desire for eternal happiness of heaven. The Beatitudes are the heart of the New law, the fulfillment of the Torah, the Ten Commandments.

begotten A term that means "to bring about; this refers symbolically to the Son of God, who comes from God the Father from all eternity. This is not to be understood in any biological sense, but it is meant to convey the truth that, as in the case of human parents and their children, the Son of God shares the same nature as God the Father.

Bible The inspired Word of God; the written record of Revelation.

bishop A successor to the Apostles who governs the local Church in a given diocese and governs the worldwide Church in union with the pope and the rest of the College of Bishops. A bishop receives the fullness of the Sacrament of Holy Orders.

blasphemy According to Mosaic Law, blasphemy was hateful, defiant, or disrespectful actions or words against God. The punishment under Mosaic Law for blasphemy was death.

Blessed Sacrament "A name given to the Holy Eucharist, especially the consecrated elements reserved in the tabernacle for adoration, or for the sick" (*CCC*, Glossary).

Blessed Trinity The central mystery of the Christian Faith. It teaches that there are Three Divine Persons in one God: Father, Son, and Holy Spirit.

calumny Slander, that is, lies told about another person in order to harm his or her reputation and lead others to make false judgments about the person.

capital punishment The infliction of the death penalty on persons convicted of serious crimes. There are few contemporary conditions that warrant the death penalty due to the state's effectiveness at keeping criminals inoffensive through keeping criminals securely imprisoned.

cardinal virtues The four pivotal virtues that support moral living: prudence (right reason in action), justice (giving God and each person his or her due by right), fortitude (courage to persist in pursuing the good despite difficulties), and temperance (moderation in controlling desires for pleasures).

catechesis A process of education in the faith for young people and adults with the goal of making them mature disciples of Christ.

catechists Ordained ministers and laypeople who instruct others in Christian doctrine and for entry into the Church.

catechumen An unbaptized person who is preparing to receive all of the sacraments of Christian initiation.

catechumenate From a Greek word that means "study or instruction." In the early Church, the catechumenate was a two- to three-year period of study about Jesus and the Christian faith. Celebration of the Sacraments of Christian Initiation did not occur until after the catechumenate.

Catholic From a Greek word meaning "universal" or "general." The Catholic Church is the Christian community that is one, holy, apostolic, and catholic that is, open to all people everywhere at all times and that preaches the fullness of God's Revelation in Jesus Christ.

celibacy The renunciation of marriage for more perfect observance of chastity made by those who receive the Sacrament of Holy Orders. Celibacy also extends to consecrated life and to those who forgo marriage for some honorable end.

charism A special gift or grace of the Holy Spirit that directly or indirectly builds up the Church, helps a person live a Christian life, or serves the common good.

chastity The moral virtue that enables persons to integrate their sexuality into their stations in life.

Chrismation The name in the Eastern rites for the Sacrament of Confirmation. It comes from the chrism used as part of the sacrament.

Chrism Blessed by the bishop, this perfumed oil is used for anointing in the Sacraments of Baptism, Confirmation, and Holy Orders. Chrism is an essential part of the sacrament of Confirmation and is the vehicle by which the Holy Spirit descends on the one being confirmed Christ A title for Jesus meaning "the anointed one." In Greek, the word *Christos* translated the Hebrew *Messiah*.

Christ A title for Jesus meaning "the anointed one." In Greek, the word *Christos* translated the Hebrew *Messiah*.

Church The Body of Christ, that is, the community of those joined to Christ and so animated by the Holy Spirit to live in union under the pope and the bishops through the profession of faith, the sacred liturgies, and the life of Christian love and prayer. The Roman Catholic Church is guided by the pope and his bishops.

common good The collective well-being of society as a whole, particularly in matters of spiritual conditions and those related to material and social needs.

common priesthood of the faithful The priesthood of all the baptized in which we share in Christ's work of salvation.

Communion of Saints The unity in Christ of all those he has redeemed: the Church on earth, in heaven, and in Purgatory.

concupiscence "Human appetites or desires which remain disordered due to the temporal consequences of Original Sin, which remain even after Baptism, and which produce an inclination to sin" (*CCC*, Glossary).

conscience The name for a person's "most secret core and sanctuary" (*CCC*, 1776), which helps him or her to discern between good and evil.

consubstantial A term that means "of the same substance." Jesus is consubstantial with God the Father; he is God from God, light from light, true God from true God.

contemplation Wordless prayer whereby a person's mind and heart rest in God's.

contraception Any artificial means (e.g., pills, condoms, diaphragms, surgeries) that deliberately and directly has an outcome of closing off the chief aim of sexual intercourse the openness to life. Contraception also opposes the unitive aspect of the conjugal act by not allowing for the total self-giving of the couple to one another.

covenant The partnership between God and humanity that God has established out of his love. The New Covenant is offered through Christ; the blood that Christ shed on the Cross is a sign of the New Covenant.

creation The action of God by which he gave a beginning to all that exists outside of himself.

declaration of nullity The Church's declaration that a particular marriage whether presumed as a sacramental bond or simply a natural bond was never valid.

Deposit of Faith "The heritage of faith contained in Sacred Scripture and Sacred Tradition, handed down in the Church from the time of the Apostles, from which the Magisterium draws all that it proposes for belief as being divinely revealed" (*CCC*, Glossary).

disciples Followers of Christ. A disciple is someone who learns from and follows Jesus in obedience. Animated by his grace, disciples have a share of the Trinitarian life of God and take part in his mission in the world

discipleship The mandate of all baptized Christians to follow Jesus and participate in his role as priest, prophet, and king.

Docetism An early heresy associated with Gnosticism that taught that Jesus had no human body and only appeared to die on the Cross. The word *Docetism* has Greek origins and literally means "illusion."

Doctor of the Church A title conferred by the pope or by a general council declaring a saint to be holy, wise, learned, and therefore a source of sound theological teaching for the Church.

dogma Central truths of Divine Revelation that the Magisterium has infallibly defined.

Eastern Catholic Churches The twenty-three Churches of the East that are in union with the Roman Catholic Church and the bishop of Rome, the pope. The Eastern Catholic Churches have developed their own liturgical and administrative traditions.

ecumenical council An assembly of all (or most) bishops from throughout the world in union with the pope. Such a council is the highest authority in the universal Church when it is conducted in unison with the pope.

ecumenism The movement, inspired and led by the Holy Spirit, that seeks the union of all Christian churches and ecclesial communities and eventually the unity of all peoples throughout the world within the Catholic Church.

eschatological Related to the "last things" (death, judgment, heaven, hell, Purgatory, the second coming of Christ, and the resurrection of the body).

Eternal Word A name for Jesus who is God's knowledge of himself and the one who brings God's Word into the world.

Eucharistic Prayer The Church's great prayer of sacrifice and thanksgiving to God in the Liturgy that makes present the Passion, Death, and Resurrection of Christ to us. During this prayer, Jesus becomes present under the likeness of bread and wine. There are many different Eucharistic Prayers in the Eastern and Western Catholic churches. All Eucharistic Prayers include a memorial of the Last Supper and an invocation of God's Spirit.

Eucharistic species The Real Presence of Jesus' Precious Body (under the mere appearance of the bread) and Jesus' Precious Blood (under the mere appearance of grape wine), accompanied by the fullness of his soul and divinity, after the bread and wine have been consecrated by the priest at Mass.

euthanasia Any "action or omission which of itself and by intention causes death, with the purpose of eliminating all suffering" (*Evangelium Vitae*, 65).

evangelical counsels Christ's teachings of the New Law that lead to perfection. The public profession of the evangelical counsels of poverty, chastity, and obedience are made when a man or woman enters the consecrated (religious) life.

evangelist The one who proclaims in word and deed the Good News of Jesus Christ. The "four evangelists" refers to the authors of the four Gospels: Matthew, Mark, Luke, and John.

evangelization The bringing of the Good News of Jesus Christ to others through words and actions.

examination of conscience An honest self-assessment of how well you have lived God's covenant of love, leading you to accept responsibility for your sins and to realize God's merciful forgiveness.

Extreme Unction A term from the Latin for "last anointing." It is an older term referring to the reception of the Sacrament of the Anointing of the Sick just before death. It is accompanied by Viaticum.

faith The theological virtue of the intellect assenting to God's grace. Though only possible by grace and the interior helps of the Holy Spirit, faith is truly a human action. "Trusting in God and cleaving to the truths he has revealed are contrary neither to human freedom nor to human reason" (*CCC*, 154).

Fall The revelation in the Book of Genesis about how sin entered human history. The Bible begins with the story of the original sin committed by the first humans. The fall also refers to the fall of the angels and the emergence of Satan before the world began.

Fathers of the Church Those men from the first through eighth centuries AD who were given this title based on their monumental contributions to the Church, especially their extensive teaching and writing about the faith in order to help it grow, expand, and develop.

First Council of Nicaea The first ecumenical council; a meeting of bishops in the city of Nicea near Constantinople. The Council dogmatized that Jesus God from God, equal in nature to the Father and condemned the Egyptian priest, Arius, who claimed that the Son of God was not eternal.

fortitude The courage that Christians are called to embrace and rely on in order to evangelize and live their faith openly; also, one of the four cardinal virtues (along with temperance, justice, and prudence).

Fraction Rite The time during the Communion Rite when the priest breaks the host. He puts a piece of the consecrated host into the chalice containing the Blood of Christ to signify the unity of the Body and Blood of Christ.

free will "The power, rooted in reason and will, to act or not to act, to do this or that, and so to perform deliberate actions on one's own responsibility" (*CCC*, 1731).

fruits of the Holy Spirit Perfections the Holy Spirit forms in you as the first fruits of eternal glory. The twelve fruits are charity, joy, peace, patience, kindness, goodness, generosity, gentleness, faithfulness, modesty, self-control, and chastity.

gifts of the Holy Spirit An outpouring of God's gifts to help you live a Christian life. The traditional seven gifts of the Holy Spirit are wisdom, understanding, counsel (right judgment), fortitude (courage), knowledge, piety (reverence), and fear of the Lord (wonder and awe).

Gospel A term meaning "Good News." The term refers to (1) Jesus' own preaching, (2) the preaching about Jesus the Savior (Jesus Christ is the Good News proclaimed by the Church), and (3) the four Spirit-inspired written versions of the Good News the Gospels of Matthew, Mark, Luke, and John.

grace The free and undeserved help that God gives you to respond to his supernatural call to become his adoptive sons and daughters, partakers of the divine nature and of eternal life. Grace is a participation in the intimacy of God's own Trinitarian life, offered *from* the Father, *through* the Son, and *in* the Holy Spirit.

Guardian Angel An angel that stands by each person from infancy to death to protect us and guide us to eternal life.

heresy An obstinate denial after Baptism to believe a truth that must be believed with divine and Catholic faith, or an obstinate doubt about such truth.

holy days of obligation Special days (other than Sundays) in the Church year when all Catholics are obliged to participate at Mass. See page 268 for a list of holy days of obligation in the United States.

idolatry The worship of something or someone other than the true God.

Immaculate Conception The belief that Mary was conceived without Original Sin. The Feast of the Immaculate Conception is on December 8 and is a Holy Day of Obligation.

Incarnation The act by which the Father sent his Son into the world by the power of the Holy Spirit came to exist as a man within the womb of Mary. The Son of God assumed human nature and became man in order to accomplish salvation for humanity in that same nature. Jesus Christ, the Son of God, the Second Person of the Trinity, is both true God and true man, not part God and part man.

indulgences The remission before God of the temporal punishment still due to forgiven sins. Indulgences are, as the *Catechism of the Catholic Church* teaches, "closely linked to the effects of the sacrament of Penance" (*CCC*, 1471).

infallibility A gift of the Holy Spirit whereby "the pope and bishops in union with him can definitively proclaim a doctrine of faith or morals for the belief of the faithful" (*CCC*, Glossary). The word itself refers to "something that is preserved without error."

intercession A prayer of petition for the sake of others.

justification The grace of the Holy Spirit to justify you that is, to renew your being through faith in Jesus Christ and through Baptism.

kerygma A Greek word that means proclamation, announcement, or preaching. It is the message of the Gospel.

Kingdom of God Refers to God's reconciling and renewing all things through his Son and to his will being done on earth as it is in heaven. The process has begun with Jesus and will be perfectly completed at the end of time. The Kingdom of God proclaimed by Jesus and inaugurated in his life, Death, and Resurrection is one of peace, justice, and love.

liturgical year Also known as the Church Year, it organizes the seasons of Advent, Christmas, Lent, the Triduum,, Easter, and Ordinary Time around major events of Jesus's life.

liturgy The official public worship of the Church. The sacraments and the Divine Office constitute the Church's liturgy. Mass is the most important liturgical celebration.

Liturgy of the Word The part of the Mass that includes the Old Testament reading and psalm, the New Testament epistles and the Gospel, the homily, the Profession of Faith, and the intercessions for the world.

Magisterium The bishops, in union with the pope, the successor of St. Peter, who are the living teaching office of the Church. The Magisterium is entrusted with guarding and handing on the Deposit of Faith and with authentically interpreting God's Revelation, in the forms of both Sacred Scripture and Sacred Tradition.

marks of the Church Four essential signs or characteristics of Christ's Church that mark her as his true Church. The Church is one, holy, catholic, and apostolic.

marriage vows The promises made by the bride and groom to honor one another and to be faithful in good times and in bad, in sickness and in health, throughout their lives. By their consent to one another, the couple establishes a permanent covenant in love.

martyr A word that means "witness." A martyr is someone who has suffered and died for the truth of the faith and of Christian doctrine; martyrdom is the ultimate act of fortitude.

meditation A form of prayer where the mind and imagination focus on Christ or some truth of Divine Revelation with the purpose of applying the lessons we learn to our lives.

Messiah From the Hebrew for "the Chosen One" or "the Anointed One"; the role that Jesus filled.

ministerial priesthood The priesthood of Christ, consisting of priests and bishops, received in the Sacrament of Holy Orders. Its purpose is to serve the common priesthood by building up and guiding the Church in the name of Christ.

modesty The virtue associated with temperance that applies to how a person speaks, dresses, and conducts himself or herself. Related to the virtue of purity, modesty protects the intimate center of a person by refusing to unveil what should remain hidden.

Monophysitism The heresy taught in the fifth century that asserted that there is only one nature in the Person of Christ his divine nature.

monotheistic Religions that believe that there is only one God. Christianity, Judaism, and Islam are the three great monotheistic world religions.

Monothelitism The heresy taught in the seventh century that claimed that Jesus has two natures but only one will his divine will.

mortal sin A grave infraction of the law of God. Mortal sin is personal sin that involves serious matter, sufficient reflection, and full consent of the will. It results in total rejection of God and alienation from him.

mystagogia A Greek term that means "leading into the mystery"; the period following the Baptism of adults. During this time, the newly baptized are to open themselves more fully to the graces received in Baptism.

mystery A reality filled with God's invisible presence. This term applies to the Blessed Trinity's plan of Salvation in Jesus Christ, the Church that is his body, and the sacraments.

Natural Family Planning (NFP) A Church-approved method for regulating births within marriage; it is in accord with God's will because it is pursued by spouses without external pressure or motives of selfishness and is practiced through natural means of periodic continence and use of infertile periods.

natural law Moral knowledge written in every human heart and that every human person innately possesses. It is universal, permanent, and unchanging.

neophytes Those newly received into the Church through the Sacraments of Christian Initiation at the Easter Vigil.

Nestorianism The heresy spread by Nestorius, a fifth-century patriarch of Constantinople, that denied the union of the human and divine natures of Christ, said there was instead a union of two persons, and denied that Mary is the Mother of God. New Adam The Protoevangelium is an announcement of the New Adam, who is Jesus Christ. "For since death came through a human being, the resurrection of the dead came also through a human being. For just as in Adam all die, so too in Christ shall all be brought to life" (1 Cor 15:20–21).

New Age A range of spiritual practices that revolve around the mind and body. It is a term difficult to define as New Age encompasses an eclectic set of beliefs and practices. It became popular in the West during the 1970s.

New Covenant The covenant established by God in Jesus Christ to fulfill and perfect the covenants of the Old Testament. The New Covenant, also called the Law of the Gospel, is the perfection here on earth of the natural law and the Law of Moses. The New Covenant is the law of love, grace, and freedom. The New Covenant, made in the Blood of Jesus, is the climax of salvation history and is God's eternal covenant with human beings.

New Eve By her complete obedience to God's will, Mary is the New Eve. As announced in the Protoevangelium, Mary is clearly the New Eve who, unlike the original Eve, will avoid temptation and sin and remain always pure.

Nicene Creed The formal Profession of Faith usually recited at Mass. It came from the first two ecumenical councils, at Nicaea in 325 and Constantinople in 381.

nuptial blessing A blessing intended for the bride and groom and the marriage covenant that takes place after the couple gives their consent during a wedding. The word *nuptial* comes from a Latin word that means "wedding."

oil of catechumens Olive oil that is blessed by a bishop at the Chrism Mass on or around Holy Thursday and used to anoint those preparing for Baptism.

oil of the sick Olive or another plant oil that is blessed by a bishop at a Chrism Mass or, in case of necessity, by any priest at the time of anointing. Anointing with the oil of the sick is an efficacious sign of healing and strength that is part of the Sacrament of the Anointing of the Sick.

Order of Christian Initiation of Adults (OCIA) The process by which an unbaptized adult or an adult baptized in another ecclesial community prepares for full initiation into the Catholic Church.

original holiness and original justice The original state of human beings in their relationship with God before sin entered the world. Original holiness was the state of Adam and Eve in which they shared in the divine life. Original justice was their state of inner harmony, harmony between man and woman, and harmony between the first couple and all creation.

original sin "The sin by which the first human beings disobeyed the commandment of God, choosing to follow their own will rather than

God's will. As a consequence they lost the grace of original holiness, and became subject to the law of death; sin became universally present in world. Besides the personal sin of Adam and Eve, Original Sin describes the fallen state of human nature which affects every person born into the world, and from which Christ, the 'New Adam' came to redeem us" (*CCC*, Glossary).

Paraclete A name for the Holy Spirit that means "Advocate." In John 14:26, Jesus promised to send the Holy Spirit as the Advocate who would continue to guide, lead, and strengthen the disciples.

particular judgment The individual judgment of every person right after death, when Christ will rule on his or her eternal destiny in heaven (after purification in Purgatory, if needed) or in hell.

Paschal Mystery Christ's work of redemption, accomplished principally by his Passion, Death, Resurrection, and glorious Ascension. The mystery is commemorated and made present through the sacraments, especially the Eucharist.

Passion of Christ The suffering of Jesus leading to his death.

Pelagianism A heretical view from the fifth century holding that Adam's sin did not affect future generations and that man can save himself by his own works unaided by grace. Under this heresy, humans did not a savior from sin except perhaps as an example of how to save themselves.

penitent A person who admits his or her sins, is truly sorry for having sinned, and wishes to be restored to relationship with God and the Church.

Pentateuch In Greek it means "five books." The term refers to the first five books of the Bible: Genesis, Exodus, Leviticus, Numbers, and Deuteronomy.

Pentecost From a Greek word meaning "fiftieth day," the day on which the Church celebrates the descent of the Holy Spirit upon Mary and the Apostles.

predestination A belief that one's actions are not only preknown by God, but also predetermined. The Catholic position is that God does have knowledge of who will be saved and who will be lost, yet it is God's desire that all will be saved. To this end, he provides graces and helps, which people are free to accept or reject. This means that while God knows certain people will be lost, this is not the choice of God, but of those individuals.

presbyters A term to refer to priests to distinguish them from bishops. Priests are co-workers with the bishop and servant to God's people, especially in celebrating the Eucharist.

prophet In the Old Testament, a person sent by God to form the people in the Old Covenant thereby preparing them for the hope of salvation.

Protestant Reformation An erroneous effort to reform the Catholic Church in the sixteenth century which led to the separation of large numbers of Christians from communion with Rome and with each other.

Protoevangelium A Greek term meaning "first gospel" that is the initial sign from Genesis 3:15 of the Good News that God did not abandon humanity's first parents or their descendants after they committed sin. Eve's offspring (Jesus) would someday destroy the snake (sin and death).

prudence The moral virtue that inclines you to discern a good, ethical, and moral life and to choose the means to accomplish it.

Purgatory The final purification of all who die in God's grace and friendship but remain imperfectly purified. Purgatory is the final cleansing away of all sin and of all punishments of sin.

Real Presence The doctrine that Jesus Christ is truly present in his Body and Blood under the appearance of bread and wine in the Eucharist.

Redemption The restoration of humankind from the bondage of sin to freedom as children of God through the satisfaction and merits of Jesus Christ.

religion The relationship between God and humans that results in a body of beliefs and a set of practices: creed, cult, and code. Religion expresses itself in worship and service to God and by extension to all people and all creation.

resurrection of the body The Christian belief that when Christ comes again he will reunite the bodies of every human with their souls.

Revelation God's communication of himself by which he makes known the mystery of his plan.

Rosary A prayer in honor of the Blessed Virgin Mary which repeats Hail Mary's over five decades of prayers separated by the Our Father. Each decade meditates on a mystery in the life of Jesus.

sacrament An outward (visible) sign of an invisible grace. An "efficacious" symbol that brings about the spiritual reality to which it points. This term applies to Christ Jesus, the great sign of God's love for us; to the Church, his continuing presence in our world; and to the Seven Sacraments.

Sacrament of Christian Initiation One of the three sacraments Baptism, Confirmation, and Eucharist through which a person enters into full membership in the Church.

Sacrament of Holy Orders The sacrament of apostolic ministry at the service of communion whereby Christ, though the Church, ordains men through the laying on of hands. It includes three degrees: episcopate, presbyterate, and diaconate. Those who exercise these orders are bishops, priests, and deacons.

Sacrament of Matrimony A Sacrament at the Service of Communion in which Christ binds a man and woman into a permanent covenant of love and life and bestows his graces on them to help them live as a community and as a loving family, if he blesses them with children.

Sacrament of Penance A Sacrament of Healing, also known as reconciliation or confession, through which Christ extends his forgiveness to sinners, bringing about reconciliation with God and the Church. Its essential elements consist of the acts of the penitent (contrition, confession of sins, and satisfaction) and the prayer of absolution of the priest.

Sacrament of the Holy Eucharist The liturgical action known as the Holy Sacrifice of the Mass. It "constitutes the principal liturgical celebration of the Paschal Mystery of Christ" (*CCC*, glossary).

sacramental A sacred sign (e.g., an object, a place, or an action) that resembles the sacraments. Through the prayers of the Church, graces are signified and obtained through them.

sacramental character An indelible spiritual mark that configures a person to Christ and is the permanent effect of the Sacraments of Baptism, Confirmation, and Holy Orders.

sacramental seal The secrecy priests are bound to keep regarding any sins confessed to them.

Sacred Scripture The *written* transmission of the Divine. It is faithfully preserved, handed down, and interpreted by the Church's Magisterium.

Sacred Tradition The *living* transmission of the Church's Gospel message found in the Church's teaching, life, and worship. It is faithfully preserved, handed down, and interpreted by the Church's Magisterium.

saint A "holy one" of God who lives in union with God through the grace of Jesus Christ and the power of the Holy Spirit and whom God rewards with eternal life in Heaven.

salvation God's forgiveness of sins, accomplished through the mercy of Jesus Christ, resulting in the restoration of friendship with God.

salvation history The story of God's action in human history. Salvation history refers to the events through which God makes humanity aware of and brings humanity into the Kingdom of God. It began with the creation of the world and will end with the second coming of Christ.

second coming of Christ Also known as the Parousia; the time when Jesus will return to earth, the Kingdom of God will be fully established, and victory over evil will be complete.

Second Vatican Council The twenty-third and most recent ecumenical council of the Church which was announced by Pope St. John XXIII in 1959 and opened in 1962. An intent of the council was to discuss ways in which the Church should direct her efforts to spread the Gospel in a modern world.

sensus fidei A Latin term for "sense of the faith"; it refers to the supernatural appreciation of the faith by all Catholics.

sin "An offense against God as well as a fault against reason, truth, and right conscience" (*CCC*, Glossary). The basic cause of sin is love for self over love for God. Sin wounds both human nature and the solidarity of the human race. Sin was most intense at Christ's Passion, as witnessed by the hatred of Jesus' enemies for the Son of God. However, Christ's sacrifice on the Cross opened the way for God's forgiveness and mercy.

social justice The form of justice that applies the Gospel message of Jesus Christ to the structures, systems, and laws of society in order to protect the dignity of persons and guarantee the rights of individuals.

soul "The spiritual principle of human beings" (*CCC* Glossary). The soul and body together form one human nature. The soul does not die with the body. Once created, it is eternal and will be reunited with the body in the final resurrection.

subsidiarity The principle of Catholic social doctrine that says that no community of higher order (such as a national or state government) should do what can be done equally well or better by a community of lower order (such as a family or local community).

synod of bishops A group of bishops, usually chosen from throughout the world, who come together to advise the pope on certain issues.

theological virtues Three important virtues bestowed at Baptism that bind a person to God: *faith* (belief in and personal knowledge of God), *hope* (trust in God's salvation and in his gift of the graces needed to attain it), and *charity* (love of God and love of neighbor).

Theology of the Body Pope John Paul II's integrated vision of the human person body and soul which he expressed in a series of 129 Wednesday audiences from 1979 to 1984. Drawing mostly from Scripture, Pope John Paul II taught that the body is a true gift from God. The talks highlight how sexuality is a beautiful gift from God intended to be a means for self-giving love.

transubstantiation Church teaching which holds that the substance of the bread and wine is changed into the substance of the Body and Blood of Christ at the consecration at Mass.

Triduum The three-day-long liturgy that is the Church's most solemn celebration of the Paschal Mystery. It begins with the Mass of the Lord's Supper on Holy Thursday, continues through the Good Friday service, and ends on Holy Saturday with the conclusion of the Easter vigil. Although it takes place over three days, the Triduum is considered one single liturgy.

venial sin A sin that weakens and wounds your relationship with God, but does not causes the loss of grace in your soul.

Virgin Birth A Church dogma that teaches that Jesus was conceived through the Virgin Mary by the power of the Holy Spirit without the cooperation of a human father.

Words of Institution The words said by Jesus over the bread and wine at the Last Supper. The priest repeats these words over the bread and wine at Mass as they are changed into the Body and Blood of Christ.

YHWH The sacred Hebrew name for God that means "I am who am," I am," or "I am who I am." This name reveals God as noncontingent existence the one on whose existence all creatures depend for their existence.

Notes

Introduction: The Heart of Our Faith

1. Wayne Coffey, *The Boys of Winter: The Untold Story of a Coach, a Dream, and the 1980 U.S. Olympic Hockey Team* (New York: Crown Publishers, 2005).

2. G. K. Chesterton, *The Annotated Innocence of Father Brown*, ed. Martin Gardner (New York: Dover Publications, 1998), 78–79.

2. God, Creation, and the Fall

1. Irenaeus (ca. AD 180), *Against Heresies*, III.22.4.

2. *Against Heresies*, V.17.3.

8. Life Everlasting

1. *Saint Augustine: Confessions*, translated by R. S. Pine-Coffin (London: Penguin Books, 1961), 198–99.

9. The Sacred Liturgy

1. Jennie Fraser, "What Do You Remember about Your First Mass?" Catholic Home Network International, January 9, 2017.

2. Ignatius, *Letter to the Philadelphians*, 4.

3. Ignatius, *Letter to the Romans*, 7.

4. Tertullian, *On Baptism*, 1.

5. Pius X, Presentation to Confraternity of the Blessed Sacrament.

6. Thomas Aquinas, *Summa Theologica* III, 68, 8.

10. The Sacraments of Christian Initiation

1. Augustine, *Sermon*, 228.

11. The Sacraments of Healing

1. Cf. *Sermon* 6, paragraph 12.

12. The Sacraments at the Service of Communion

1. Cf. *To the Trallians*, 3.

2. Robert Barron, *Letter to a Suffering Church: A Bishop Speaks on the Sexual Abuse Crisis* (Park Ridge, IL: Word on Fire, 2019), 78.

13. The Call to a Good Life

1. François-Xavier Nguyễn Văn Thuận, *Testimony of Hope: The Spiritual Exercises of Pope John Paul II* (Boston: Pauline Press, 2000), 131.

2. *Testimony of Hope*, 132–33.

14. Conscience, the Virtues, and Sin

1. Pope John Paul II, *Sollicitudo Rei Socialis*, 40.

16. God's Salvation: Law and Grace

1. *The Confessions of St. Augustine*, translated by Anthony Esolen (TAN Books, 2023), Book VIII, 5, 12.

2. *Confessions*, Book VIII, 12, 28.

3. *Confessions*, Book VIII, 12, 29.

18. Love of Neighbor through Respect for Human Life

1. Pope Francis, address to the participants in the International Drug Enforcement Conference, Rome, June 20, 2014.

2. *Doctrinal Note on the Moral Limits to Technological Manipulation of the Human Body, Committee on Doctrine*, United States Conference of Catholic Bishops, March 20, 2023, no. 15.

19. Love of Neighbor through the Virtue of Chastity

1. *Confessions*, Book VIII, 5, 10.

2. Josemaría Escrivá, *The Way* (Chicago: Scepter, 1954), 41, no. 118.

3. Scott Stanley, Institute for Family Studies, writing about the Michael Rosenfeld and Katharina Roesler study of 2018.

4. John M. Haas, *Begotten Not Made: A Catholic View of Reproductive Technology*, USCCB website, https://www.usccb.org/

issues-and-action/human-life-and-dignity/reproductive-technology/begotten-not-made-a-catholic-view-of-reproductive-technology.

5. Jeffrey M. Jones, "U.S. LGBT Identification Steady at 7.2%," Gallup News, February 22, 2023, https://news.gallup.com/poll/470708/lgbt-identification-steady.aspx.

22. Praying with the Communion of Saints

1. Pope Francis, General Audience Talk, April 7, 2021.

23. Encouragement to Pray

1. Alphonsus Liguori, *Uniformity with God's Will*, trans. Thomas W. Tobin (1755; Charlotte, NC: TAN Books, 2013), 23.

Epilogue: Two Converts to the Catholic Faith

1. John Paul II, Mass of Beatification, May 1, 1987.

2. *The Collected Works of Edith Stein*, vol. 12, *Letters to Roman Ingarden*, ed. Maria Amata Neyers, trans. Hugh Candler Hunt (Washington, DC: ICS Publications, 2014), 208.

Index of Questions

Photo Credits

Alamy pages xxiii, xxv, 19, 41, 84, 101, 204, 226, 311, 375

Associated Press pages 199, 289

Bridgeman Images page 327

Getty Images pages xiii, xix, xxix, 1, 8, 16, 43, 47, 57, 59, 64, 70, 73, 80, 87, 92, 98, 104, 111, 113, 118, 122, 125, 127, 140, 143, 148, 157, 159, 164, 171, 173, 184, 194, 197, 210, 213, 218, 229, 233, 239, 241, 249, 253, 255, 262, 270, 273, 282, 291, 294, 308, 317, 324, 329, 333, 338, 341, 346, 347, 350, 353, 358, 363, 365, 380, 383

Saint Meinrad Archabbey page 30

University of Notre Dame Photography page xvii

Subject Index

abortion, 284–285
Abraham, 5–6, 20, 22, 77
absolution, 166
acedia, 258
Act of Contrition, 163, 165–166, 394–395
Act of Faith, 394
Act of Hope, 394
Act of Love, 394
ACTS acronym, 333–336
Adam, 30, 36, 38, 67, 191, 300
Adonai (Lord), 51, 264
adoration, 259
adultery, 292–293
Advent, 132
agnosticism, 264
All Saints' Day, 133
All Souls' Day, 133
Alphonsus Liguori, St., 361
ambo, 138
Ambrose, St., 162
Amos, 6
Angel of God, 395
angels, 34
Angelus, 393
anointing, 74–75, 147
Anointing of the Sick, 75, 118, 167–170
Apollinarism, 54
apostasy, 258
Apostles, 10, 11, 76, 81–82, 84–85, 96–97, 129, 175–176
Apostles' Creed, 8, 21, 67, 389
apostolic, Church as, 96–97
apostolic pardon, 170
apostolic succession, 176
Archabbey Church of Our Lady of Einsiedeln, 30
Arianism, 53
Aristotle, 203
artistic images, 138–139, 262–263

Ascension into heaven, 69, 79
Assumption of Mary, 108
atheism, 261–262
Augustine, St., 94, 113–114, 138, 167, 242–243, 244, 282, 308, 353
authority, 237

Baltimore Catechism, xv, 134, 204–205
Baptism, 39, 75, 91, 93, 98, 135, 145–147, 150–151, 157, 162, 301, 342–343
Barron, Robert, 185–186
Beatitudes, 203, 206, 210, 245
belief
    creeds as summaries of, 21, 41
    in God, 3–4, 24
    Sign of the Cross as statement of, 25
Benedict XVI, Pope, 64–66, 183, 236
Bernadette, St., 7
Bible
    canon of, 399–400
    Catholic vs. Protestant, 14–15
    Church teaching on, 13–14
    navigating, xxiii
    teaching about the Church in, 84–85
    types of, xxiv
bishops, 175–176, 180–182, 216
blasphemy, 265
Blessed Sacrament, 154, 156, 358–359
Blessed Virgin Mary
    apparitions of, 7, 104–105
    Assumption into heaven, 108
    devotion to, 101–102
    divine motherhood, 103, 106
    essential teachings about, 111
    faith of, 20
    honor for, 102
    Immaculate Conception, 103
    Mother of God, 53–54
    as the New Eve, 40

Healing, Sacraments of, 159–160, 171
heaven, 115–116, 117, 368
hell, 117, 120
heresies, 52–55, 258
hierarchy, 175
holiness, 329–330, 338
holy, Church as, 95–96
Holy Communion, 154
holy days of obligation, 268–269
Holy Mass, 154
Holy Orders, 63, 75, 91, 137, 161–162,
    174–175, 178, 183, 194
Holy Sacrifice, 153
Holy Saturday, 143–144
Holy Spirit
    anointing and, 74–75
    descriptions of, 76
    fruits of, 149
    gifts of, 147–150, 216
    God as, 26
    grace of, 242, 245, 247
    knowledge of, 74
    Paraclete (Advocate), 75
    present in the life of Christ, 78–79
    in the Resurrection, 79
    sin against, 224
    spoken through the prophets,
        77–78
    titles for, 76
Holy Week, 61, 133
homicide, 284
homosexuality, 304–305
hope, 205, 220
Hosea, 6
human beings
    created in image and likeness of
        God, 34–35, 201–202, 257
    dignity of, 230, 232, 237–238,
        278–279, 315
    equality between, 230–231
    God's plan for, 35–36
    scientific research on, 287–288
human trafficking, 313
hypostasis, 53–54

iconoclasts, 55
icons, 139
idolatry, 260
Ignatius of Antioch, St., 87, 131, 180,
    266–267
Immaculate Conception, 103
immigration, 279
in persona Christi Capitis, 175
Incarnation, 51–52
incense, 138
indirect killing, 284
indulgences, 163, 166
infallibility, 176–177
infant baptism, 145–146
infertility, 302–304
Initiation, Sacraments of, 144–145,
    150–151
Innocent III, Pope, 93
integrity, 311–312, 324
intentions, 208
Irenaeus, St., 30, 87
Isaac, 22
Isaiah, 6, 77

Jacob, 22
James, St., 168–169
Jeremiah, 77
Jesus Christ
    Ascension into heaven, 69, 79
    baptism of, 145
    betrayal of, 61
    condemnation to death, 62
    control over Passion, Death, and
        Resurrection, 60
    Crucifixion, 59–60, 62–63
    death of, 63, 152
    descent into hell, 67
    Divine Person, 106
    divinity of, 52–55
    entry into Jerusalem, 61
    events in the life of, 47–51, 55–56
    Holy Spirit present in life of, 78–79
    Incarnation, 51–52
    as Lord, 46, 51

Fr. Daniel J. Mahan, a priest of the Archdiocese of Indianapolis, is the first director of the USCCB's Institute on the Catechism.

Mahan earned a bachelor of arts degree from St. Meinrad Seminary, a bachelor of sacred theology degree from Pontifical University of St. Thomas Aquinas in Rome, and a licentiate in sacred theology degree from the Pontifical Athenaeum of St. Anselm.

In collaboration with the Franciscans of the Immaculate, Mahan produced *A Tour of the Catechism of the Catholic Church*, a seventy-two-part video presentation in which he teaches the Catechism from cover to cover in ten-minute segments.

He resides in Washington, DC.

FREE Companion Resources for
A Journey through the Catechism

Enhance your Catechism study
with these **FREE** resources.
Perfect for individuals, parishes, small groups,
and classrooms, they include:

- highlight videos with Fr. Daniel J. Mahan
- downloadable study guide for RCIA/OCIA